POULTRY PRODUCTS TECHNOLOGY

SECOND EDITION

some other AVI books

POULTRY PRODUCTS TECHNOLOGY

SECOND EDITION

by GEORGE J. MOUNTNEY, Ph.D.

Research Management Specialist (Food Science),
Cooperative State Research Service,
United States Department of Agriculture,
Washington, D.C.

Formerly Professor, Department of Poultry
Science, Ohio State University,
Columbus, Ohio

Formerly Professor, Department of Poultry
Science, Food and Nutrition Division,
School of Home Economics,
Columbus, Ohio

WESTPORT, CONNECTICUT

THE AVI PUBLISHING COMPANY, INC.

1976

Preface to the Second Edition

An attempt has been made in the Second Edition to bring the original book up to date, especially by adding new material. A new section on eggs was added because in many colleges and universities both poultry and egg products technology are taught in the same course. The laboratory methods used by the U.S. Department of Agriculture for evaluation of eggs and egg products have also been added. Directions are complete enough so that some of the tests can be used for actual laboratory exercises.

I wish to think Dr. Glen Froning, University of Nebraska; Dr. Morris Mast, Pennsylvania State University; and Dr. William Shakelee, Cooperative State Research Service of the United States Department of Agriculture for reviewing portions of the revised manuscript and for many helpful suggestions.

Special acknowledgment is due Dr. R. G. Garner, Cooperative State Research Service, United States Department of Agriculture, for the gift of his library of reprints in the area of poultry technology.

July, 1975   George J. Mountney

Preface to the First Edition

Since World War II, much knowledge has accumulated in the area of poultry products technology. This book was written for the purpose of organizing and classifying the areas which deal with the processing, handling, marketing, and preparation of poultry meat products and by-products. It is hoped that the information contained herein will help to point out areas where more research is needed, define the breadth and scope of the over-all problems in the industry as they exist at the time of this writing, and characterize the science and technology of the industry as it exists at present.

When one attempts to write a book for the first time, it is often with a firm resolve to give a detailed and complete review of all the current literature and to include some of the older papers which are classics in the field because they were the first to demonstrate new and basic principles. It soon becomes evident that such an approach is not only unrealistic but impossible. In some areas, there are numerous papers covering only a very small area of the field in great detail; in other areas there are very few, if any, technical papers on the subject. In those areas where few technical papers are available, an author must write from his own limited personal experiences, rely on personal communications, trade journal articles and whatever other sources of information he can obtain. Unfortunately, many of the articles from such sources, although quite valuable, are based on field observations rather than on experimental data.

This book was written so that it could be used as a text for those just becoming acquainted with the field, for individuals who wish to start work or learn about the over-all status of work in a particular area before starting on an extensive review of literature, and for those in industry who quite often need specific bits of information for making decisions and projecting plans for the future.

Because there are an increasing number of good books becoming available on many food processing methods which go into detail on the principles of the various methods of preservation without regard for commodities, only enough background on the various methods of preservation required to introduce the subject have been included. One of the criteria used to determine whether certain material should be included or eliminated was whether it was directly related to poultry products.

In some cases attempts were made to compile, edit, and classify the results of work carried out by a number of different scientists, each of whom used his own methods. In a few cases, it was impossible to obtain comparative data; in other cases, because much data on poultry carcasses have the same large degree of variability well known to other biological work, ranges as well as averages were included.

It is hoped that this, the first book in the field, will serve as an outline for future books in the area and possibly for revision in a few years of this current volume.

I wish to thank the following who reviewed and criticized one or more of the several chapters:

Dr. Robert Baker, Cornell University; Mr. Jules Bauermann, Pennsylvania State University; Dr. Owen Cotterill, University of Missouri; Dr. Larry Dawson, Michigan State University; Dr. E. O. Essary, Virginia Polytechnic Institute; Dr. James Gwin, St. Louis, Missouri; Mr. John Hammond, Transportation and Facilities Branch, U.S. Dept. Agr.; Mr. H. C. Kennett, Jr., Standardization and Marketing Practices Branch, U.S. Dept Agr.; Mr. Lester Kilpatrick, Standardization and Marketing Practices Branch, U.S. Dept. Agr.; Dr. Kenneth May, University of Georgia; Mr. Henry Orr, Ontario Agricultural College; Dr. Inez Prudent, Ohio State University; Mr. Kermit Schlamb, formerly Gordon Johnson Co.; Dr. Wm. J. Stadelman, Purdue University; Dr. Milo Swanson, University of California; Dr. A. R. Winter, Ohio State University.

Acknowledgment is also due Mr. Malcom Emmons, Photographer, Ohio Agricultural Extension Service and to all those who contributed photographs and gave permission to reproduce published materials.

Special acknowledgment is due Dr. A. R. Winter for the gift of his library of reprints in the area of poultry technology.

GEORGE J. MOUNTNEY

January, 1966

Contents

CHAPTER 1

The Poultry Industry

The ability of poultry to adapt to most areas of the world, the low economic value per unit, the rapid growth rate of poultry and the rapid generation time, all make poultry an ideal starting point for a beginning animal agriculture and a rich source of animal nutrients for human food. A poultry enterprise can be producing meat in eight weeks and eggs in 24. It has been estimated that chicken appears in the diet of more people throughout the world as a source of meat than the meat from any other animal. With the exception of strict vegetarians, there are few if any social or religious stigmas attached to the use of poultry in the diet.

The United States poultry industry is "one of the most amazing pieces of integrated work that has ever been done" (Blaxter 1961). A brief history and characterization of the industry should help to point out the research developments and circumstances which brought about the "poultry revolution."

Before 1930, most poultry was produced in small flocks as a side line farm enterprise usually to provide pin money for the housewife. Several turkeys or a pen of culled layers dropped off at the local poultry buyer before shopping provided the 5 to 10 dollars necessary to make the week's purchases. Each year the week before the opening of school, poultry buyers would prepare for heavy offerings of chickens. At that time, housewives would obtain the funds to purchase books, shoes, and school clothes by selling a few chickens. Broiler or fryer chickens were available fresh only during the late spring and summer months; frozen uneviscerated broilers or stewing chickens (New York dressed) supplied poultry meat the remainder of the year. Since 1930, conditions and research developments in the fields of genetics, nutrition, disease control, management, technology, and marketing have made the United States poultry industry the most efficient meat producer in the world (Table 1.1, Figs. 1.1, 1.2 and 1.3). Combs (1961) reported that more than 80% of the chicken consumed in the United States now comes from broilers.

In 1970, two companies handled 470 and 400 million pounds of dressed broilers, respectively. Another company reported that their poultry operations amounted to 100 million dollars, and still another company reported that they did 5 million dollars worth of business in canned poultry products alone. One company whose business is built almost entirely on selling fried chicken, became the second largest food handler in the world in 1970. Franchises of this organization

1

TABLE 1.1

EFFICIENCY WITH WHICH FARM ANIMALS PRODUCE FOOD PROTEIN [1]

Food Product	Level and/or Rate of Output	Protein Production (Gm./Mcal. of DE)
Eggs	200 eggs/yr	10.1
Broiler	3.5 lb./12 wk.; 3 lb. feed/1 lb. gain	11.9
	3.5 lb./10 wk.; 2.5 lb. feed/1 lb. gain	13.7
	3.5 lb./8 wk.; 2.1 lb. feed/1 lb. gain	15.9
Pork	200 lb.; 6 lb. feed/1 lb. gain	5.0
	200 lb./6 mo.; 4 lb. feed/1 lb. gain	6.4
	200 lb.; 2.5 lb. feed/1 lb. gain	8.7
	Biolog. limit (?); 2 lb. feed/1 lb. gain; no losses	12.1
Milk	7,936 lb./yr. (No concentrates)	10.5
	11,905 lb./yr.; (25% concentrates)	12.8
	20,000 lb./yr.; (50% concentrates)	16.3
	30,000 lb./yr.; (65% concentrates)	20.5
Beef	1100 lb./15 mo.; 8 lb. feed/1 lb. gain	2.3
	1100 lb./12 mo.; 5 lb. feed/1 lb. gain	3.2
	Highly intensive system; no losses	4.1

[1] These data represent the overall efficiency with which dietary energy is converted to food, as they include the energy cost of reproduction, rearing of breeding stock, and mortality as well as that of production itself. From Reid (1975).

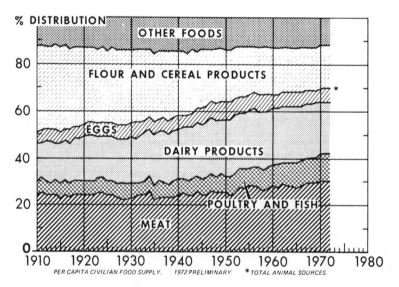

Courtesy U.S. Dept. Agr.

FIG. 1.1. DIET SOURCES OF PROTEIN

alone purchase 6–8% of the entire broiler production in the United States.

As a result of these advances in poultry production in the United States, it takes the work production equivalent of 14 min. to buy 1

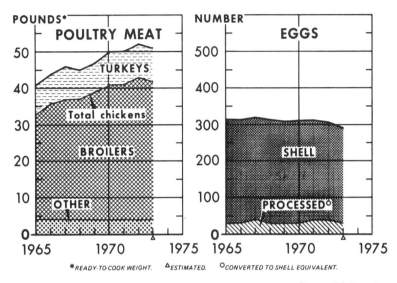

FIG. 1.2.   PER CAPITA CONSUMPTION OF POULTRY AND EGGS

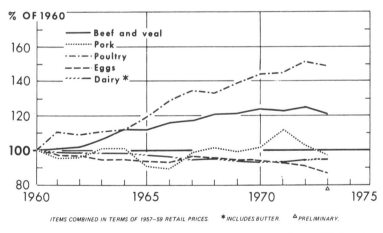

FIG. 1.3.   PER CAPITA CONSUMPTION OF SELECTED LIVESTOCK PRODUCTS

lb. of chicken and 17 min. for a dozen eggs, compared to France where 104 and 49 min. are required, and Russia where 241 and 162 min. are required.

GENETICS

Poultry Breeders Contributions to the Industry

Poultry were first selected and bred for exhibition. In the United States, the show bird era of the poultry industry lasted roughly from the late Nineteenth to the early Twentieth Century. Birds were selected and bred almost entirely for their show characteristics such as plumage color and patterns, stance, and conformation. Economic characteristics such as feed efficiency, egg production, hatchability, and increased meat production efficiency were neglected.

Gradually some breeders began selecting and breeding almost entirely for economic characteristics. At first, chickens were selected for general purpose to supply both meat and eggs. Then breeds began to be selected and bred specifically for meat or egg production and finally breeds, varieties, and strains were crossed to improve their ability to produce either meat or eggs.

Breeding for Egg Production

An important development in the field of poultry genetics was the recognition that like birds do not necessarily create like offspring but that if the genetic makeup of the birds could be determined by producing some offspring then rapid improvement could be made by selecting breeding stock on the basis of performance of offspring. This was known as progeny testing. To capitalize on this knowledge, the National Poultry Improvement Plan was developed in the 1930's. A principal feature of this Federal-State cooperative plan was that birds were selected for breeding on the basis of their offspring's performance.

Desirable traits for which breeder stock are selected to produce offspring for egg production are number, size, shape, and interior and shell quality of eggs produced as well as vigor of the birds, feed efficiency, and body size.

To test stocks developed by commercial breeders, random sample laying tests were set up by State agencies. In these tests, commercial breeding stocks are compared with each other under a standard carefully controlled set of conditions. Nordskog (1966) reported that such tests stimulate breeders to improve their stock, provide poultrymen with a basis of comparison for purchasing stock, and provide useful information on the best way to test birds for performance.

In the late 1930's, the breeding systems used to produce hybrid corn were successfully utilized by the poultry industry. Two separate lines of birds, often of different breeds, were inbred and offspring selected intensively for desired characteristics for several generations. Then to overcome the effects of inbreeding, the two lines were crossed to achieve hybrid vigor and intensify the desirable genes for the parent stock. Two major breeders in the industry today still use this system.

Another breeding system in current use is known as reciprocal recurrent selection. Under this system, the nonrelated strains are crossed and the parent lines of the strains that show good "combining ability" are kept. Then individuals are selected from each of these strains to improve combining ability further.

Breeding for Broiler Production

One of the first milestones in the broiler industry was the discovery by geneticists that family, as well as individual bird records are needed to develop high production. It was from this base that geneticists made an outstanding contribution by creating strains that could utilize feed efficiently and lay more eggs than their ancestors. The development of strains which were bred for high egg production and other strains bred for efficient production of high quality chicken meat followed. Although the production of chickens for meat was practiced to a limited extent for almost 60 yr., it has only been during the past 30 yr. that special emphasis was placed on producing birds with meat production characteristics only rather than using surplus cockerels and discarded laying hens as a source of poultry meat. Hodgson (1959) reported that "overshadowing all other developments in the production of poultry meat has been the evolution of the fast growing broiler bird through breeding experiments conducted by poultry scientists of the Department of Agriculture, state agricultural experiment stations, and private research institutions." The process has become so efficient that cockerels from production-type birds are destroyed at hatching time because they are no longer profitable sources of chicken meat. Laying hens are looked upon as a by-product, in many cases salvaged rather than produced as a source of meat.

Hughes (1960) reported that broiler strains "grow more rapidly and use feed more efficiently than birds with a less desirable genetic background." In addition, modern broilers are rapid feathering, have white feathers so that no dark feathers are present on the dressed carcass, and are uniform in size and conformation. They also have a high feed efficiency and a well-fleshed breast and thighs with a light covering of subcutaneous fat and a yellow skin color. Other characteristics important in broiler chicks are high livability, resistance to respiratory diseases and the ability to produce eggs of high fertility and hatchability since broiler stock must be able to reproduce at an economic cost. At the present time, white crossbreeds are the most common broiler stock. The sires, usually White Cornish (Fig. 1.4) are produced by one breeder while the dams, usually White Rocks or crosses (Fig. 1.5), are produced by another breeder.

Courtesy Vantress Farms, Division of International
Genetics Corp., Duluth, Ga.

FIG. 1.4 VANTRESS DOMINANT WHITE BREEDER COCKEREL. POPULAR
MALE LINE SIRES LARGE PERCENTAGE OF WORLD'S MEAT CHICKENS

To meet the specialized requirements of producing foundation stock for broiler producers, a specialized system of breeding and multiplying has evolved. Faber (1961) reports that primary breeders maintain numerous strains and thousands of birds for use in experimental and new mating combinations which are tested by the organizations' own geneticists, veterinarians and other experts to determine their performance as broiler chicks. Such breeding enterprises have decreased, but the few surviving have become larger and more efficient. Faber cites as an example a new crossbred female line developed over a five-year period by one breeder at a cost of a million dollars.

Primary breeders furnish multiplier farms with hatching eggs or chicks which are grown and mated to produce more breeding stock. These offspring or eggs produced by them are then sold to hatchery flock operators who in turn use the stock to produce eggs which are hatched and sold to broiler producers. Generally, the hatcheryman has a franchise arrangement with one primary breeder to supply pullet chicks and with another to supply cockerels. A recent survey disclosed that of 643 hatcheries answering a questionnaire, 280 had franchise arrangements. By using the fran-

Courtesy Arbor Acres Farm, Inc., Glastonbury, Conn.

Fig. 1.5. Arbor Acres "50" Broiler Breeder Hen, Industry's Most Widely Used Female Line for Production of Meat-Type Offspring

chise arrangements, primary breeders can establish a rigid system of quality control for furnishing vigorous, efficient, high quality broiler chicks to producers.

NUTRITION

Since feed costs constitute the major cost of producing poultry meat it is natural that considerable research should be concentrated on improving the efficiency of feed utilization (Fig. 1.6). Combs (1961) reported that in 1934 it required 14 weeks and 4 to 4½ lb. to produce a chicken broiler and in 1961, 8 weeks and 2 to 2.4 lb. of feed per pound of gain under commercial conditions. Schaible (1970) reported that it is now possible to produce broiler chickens with average weights of 3 lb. in 53 days with 2.2 lb. of feed per pound of gain.

The data in Table 1.2 illustrate the effects of improvements in breeding and feeding on the efficiency of broiler production.

Until the discovery of vitamins and naturally occurring sources of vitamins which could be included in poultry rations it was not possible to

TABLE 1.2

EFFECTS OF BREEDING AND FEEDING ON EFFICIENCY OF BROILER PRODUCTION[1]

Fast Growing Type Broiler—1956	Weight at 9 Weeks, Lb.	Feed Consumed Per Pound of Body-Weight Gain, Lb.
Fed 1956-type diet	2.64	2.5
Fed 1930-type diet	2.08	2.9
Slow growing type broiler—1930		
Fed 1956-type diet	2.38	2.8
Fed 1930-type diet	1.66	3.2

[1] U.S. Dept. Agr., Yearbook of Agriculture, 1959.

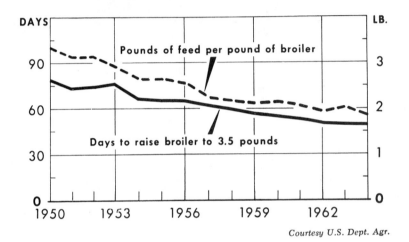

Courtesy U.S. Dept. Agr.

FIG. 1.6. EFFICIENCY GAINS IN BROILER PRODUCTION
Data from Maine broiler test.

produce broilers successfully year round in confinement. The period 1920–1940 has been called the vitamin era. Combs (1961) reports the following sequence of events. The first important discovery was that of McCollum in 1922 when vitamin D was discovered. It was at this point that cod-liver oil was first incorporated into broiler feeds and winter confinement rearing became possible. By 1927, thiamin had been isolated and during the 1930's several other B complex vitamins. Riboflavin, an especially critical nutrient in poultry rations, was isolated in 1933. Pantothenic acid, biotin, niacin, vitamin K, choline, pyridoxine, and vitamin E were all known by 1940. Since that time, folacin was isolated in 1946 and vitamin B_{12} in 1948. At the present time, there is some evidence that there are still additional unidentified growth and hatchability factors.

Considerable research on mineral requirements was conducted during the 1930's. During this same period the processing and nutritive value of soybean as a protein source for poultry was also under investigation. Stockstad and Jukes in 1950 demonstrated that the antibiotic, aureomycin, stimulated chick growth. Research workers at the Connecticut Agricultural Experiment Station formulated rations with low fiber and high energy ingredients in 1947. By 1955, the recognition of an energy protein balance brought about the use of stabilized fats. As a result of these and other research developments it has been possible to produce broilers on 1.04 lb. of feed per pound of broiler with experimental rations.

Growth rates and feed requirements for broilers, turkeys, and ducks are shown in Tables 1.3, 1.4, and 1.5.

TABLE 1.3

FEED CONVERSION AND CONSUMPTION FOR MIXED SEX COMMERCIAL BROILERS, 1963

Week	Feed Consumption per Broiler		Feed Conversion[1]	
	Weekly	Cumulative	Weekly	Cumulative
1	0.16	0.16	1.23	1.23
2	0.36	0.52	1.49	1.38
3	0.60	1.12	1.68	1.53
4	0.82	1.94	1.94	1.67
5	1.01	2.95	2.01	1.79
6	1.28	4.23	2.14	1.87
7	1.44	5.67	2.35	1.95
8	1.64	7.31	2.77	2.10
9	1.78	9.09	2.91	2.23

[1] Pounds of feed required to produce one pound of live weight. Reed and Skoglund (1963).

DISEASE CONTROL

Because of the relatively low economic value of individual broilers and the large numbers handled, disease control has changed from treatment of individual birds to flock treatments. With the development of vaccines and improved management practices, disease control has shifted to a prevention rather than a cure basis. As mass production and confinement rearing of broilers developed and more birds were grown in concentrated areas, new disease problems appeared or losses from old diseases began to increase. Even as late as 1956, Nordquist and Pals reported that "about 225 million chickens and 7.2 million turkeys died from diseases and other causes that year." Such figures do not include the losses in production, feed, labor, reduced market value and capital from those birds which recovered and were able to be salvaged. Byerley (1961) estimated the

TABLE 1.4

GROWTH RATE AND FEED CONSUMPTION OF STANDARD BELTSVILLE SMALL WHITE (BSW) TURKEYS RAISED IN CONFINEMENT ON MEDIUM-ENERGY DIETS[1]

Age (Weeks)	Toms			Hens			Both Sexes in Equal Numbers		
	Average Live Weight (Lb.)	Cumulative Feed per Bird to Date (Lb.)	Feed per Pound of Live Bird to Date (Lb.)	Average Live Weight (Lb.)	Cumulative Feed per Bird to Date (Lb.)	Feed per Pound of Live Bird to Date (Lb.)	Average Live Weight (Lb.)	Cumulative Feed per Bird to Date (Lb.)	Feed per Pound of Live Bird to Date (Lb.)
1/7 (1 day)	0.115	...	...	0.115	...	0.71	0.115	...	...
1	0.22	0.15	0.68	0.21	0.15	1.13	0.22	0.15	0.68
2	0.45	0.50	1.11	0.40	0.45	1.53	0.43	0.48	1.12
3	0.70	1.05	1.50	0.60	0.92	2.00	0.65	0.99	1.52
4	1.00	1.95	1.95	0.80	1.60	2.33	0.90	1.78	1.98
6	1.8	4.1	2.28	1.2	2.8	2.50	1.5	3.5	2.33
8	3.0	7.2	2.40	1.8	4.5	2.59	2.4	5.9	2.46
10	4.4	10.8	2.45	2.7	7.0	2.68	3.6	8.9	2.47
12	6.1	15.6	2.56	3.8	10.2	2.80	5.0	12.9	2.58
14	8.1	21.6	2.67	5.1	14.3	2.93	6.6	18.0	2.73
15[2]	9.0	24.9	2.77	5.7	16.7	3.08	7.4	20.8	2.81
16[2]	9.8	28.2	2.88	6.3	19.4	3.35	8.1	23.8	2.94
17	10.6	31.7	2.99	6.8	22.8	3.59	8.7	27.3	3.14
18	11.3	35.3	3.12	7.3	26.2	4.00	9.3	30.8	3.31
20	12.2	42.6	3.49	7.8	31.2	4.20	10.0	36.9	3.69
21[3]	12.9	46.7	3.62	8.3	34.9	4.40	10.6	40.8	3.85
22[3]	13.6	50.3	3.70	8.7	38.3	4.60	11.2	44.3	3.96
23[3]	14.4	54.7	3.80	9.1	41.9	4.80	11.8	48.3	4.09
24[3]	15.1	60.4	4.00	9.5	45.6	5.10	12.3	53.0	4.31
26	16.6	73.0	4.40	10.0	51.0	5.54	13.3	62.0	4.66
28	18.1	83.3	4.60	10.6	58.7	5.84	14.4	71.0	4.97
30	19.4	93.1	4.80	11.0	64.2	6.17	15.2	78.7	5.18
32	20.2	103.1	5.10	11.3	69.7	6.42	15.8	86.4	5.47
34[4]	21.0	113.8	5.42	11.5	73.8	6.70	16.3	93.8	5.75
36	21.4	123.0	5.75	11.7	78.4		16.6	100.7	6.07

[1] If growing conditions are optimal and high-energy diets are fed, weights about 1/6 higher and feed per pound of live turkey about 1/10 lower than those listed may be obtained at all ages with standard BSW turkeys. Weights about 1/8 higher and feed per pound of live turkey about 1/8 lower may be obtained with oversize BSW turkeys and those called Medium White.
[2] Ages at which small- or medium-type turkeys of both sexes usually are slaughtered as fryer-roasters, or "broilers."
[3] Ages at which BSW and medium-size turkeys usually are suitable for slaughter as mature roasters.
[4] Age at which BSW and other small-type turkeys may be said to attain maximum 1st-year breeding or "standard" weight.
From Agriculture Handbook 393, U.S. Dept. Agri., 1971.

TABLE 1.5

STANDARDS FOR GROWING WHITE PEKIN DUCKLINGS

Age	Live Weight, Lb.	Males: Feed Consumption Per Bird, Lb.	Feed Per Lb. Live Duckling, Lb.	Live Weight, Lb.	Females: Feed Consumption Per Bird, Lb.	Feed Per Lb. Live Duckling, Lb.
1 week	0.41	0.46	1.12	0.41	0.48	1.16
2 weeks	1.32	2.09	1.58	1.32	2.15	1.63
3 weeks	2.45	4.88	1.99	2.45	5.00	2.04
4 weeks	3.72	8.30	2.23	3.67	8.40	2.29
5 weeks	4.90	11.96	2.44	4.72	11.85	2.51
6 weeks	5.78	15.95	2.76	5.58	15.62	2.80
7 weeks	6.64	20.19	3.04	6.35	19.81	3.12
8 weeks	7.50	24.75	3.30	6.98	24.08	3.45
9 weeks	8.14	29.63	3.64	7.58	28.96	3.82

From data of Phillips and Snyder (1962).

overall losses caused by disease in the broiler industry alone amounted to around 85 million dollars.

Rapid expansion of the poultry industry was retarded until some of the more common diseases were eradicated or controlled because it was not possible to grow large numbers of birds in close confinement and in concentrated producing areas.

Poultry specialists of the Michigan State University (Ellis, Sheppard, and Weisner 1963) recommend the following vaccination program: (1) when the birds are 7 to 10 days old, give a vaccine for infectious bronchitis in the drinking water or apply a dust; (2) at 17 to 21 days of age, give the vaccine for Newcastle disease in the drinking water or else apply it as a dust or spray; (3) when 8 to 14 weeks old, vaccinate for fowl pox by individual wing-web; (4) at 10 to 16 weeks of age, give vaccine for epidemic tremor in drinking water; and (5) when 4 months of age and every 3 months thereafter, give the vaccine for Newcastle disease in the drinking water or apply it in a dust or spray.

One of the oldest and most troublesome diseases which has plagued the poultry industry is pullorum disease. According to Stafseth (1958), Rettger in 1900 discovered the cause of the disease, and in 1909 with Stoneburn discovered that it was a bacterial disease transmitted by the egg from infected hens. Jones in 1913, Gage and co-workers in 1914, and Rettger and co-workers in 1914 all contributed to the development of the macroscopic agglutination test by which infected chickens could be detected by testing for the presence of antibodies in the blood. Further tests were developed by Schaffer and co-workers in 1931, and by Coburn and Stafseth in 1931. The National Poultry Improvement Plan was inaugurated in the United States in 1935 for the purpose of controlling this disease.

Hoffman and Gwin (1954) reported that fowl typhoid is not only one of the more serious diseases affecting broilers but that it occurs wherever chickens are kept. Its history as reported by Stafseth (1958) includes reports of its occurrence in several European countries and in North and South America by Pfeiler and Rehse in 1913 and Van Straaten and te Hennepe in 1918. The fact that the causative organism *Salmonella gallinarum* could be transmitted by means of eggs was reported by Beaudette in 1925 and by Beach and Davis in 1927. Lambert in 1933 demonstrated that mortality could be reduced by selecting breeding stock for resistance. In 1946, Glover and Henderson reported what is believed to be the first outbreak in Canada.

Erysipelas infection is a disease of turkeys which can be transmitted to humans. It can survive for long periods under certain conditions and is also carried by birds, swine and sheep as well as turkeys.

Coccidiosis, like pullorum, is one of the oldest and most prevalent poultry diseases. Reid (1961) reported that in 1959 losses from coccidiosis amounted to about ten million dollars. Since the disease is most virulent among young chickens it is of particular importance to the broiler industry. According to Stafseth (1958), Johnson in 1923 and again in 1938, and Tyzzer and co-workers in 1932, did much to isolate the various species which cause this disease and to characterize the life cycles of the organisms. Johnson in 1927 was the first to report that some birds developed immunity when exposed continually to sublethal infections. A major contribution to the control of coccidiosis was the discovery of Delaplane and co-workers in 1947 that sulfaquinoxaline was an effective coccidiostat. Since that time, the use of coccidiostats in poultry rations has become standard practice.

Blackhead or infectious enterohepatitis is another protozoan disease which causes high mortality in turkeys and to a much lesser extent in chickens. Control of this disease was responsible in part for the rapid development of the turkey industry.

The avian leucosis complex which occurs in several forms is a major disease which causes large losses. It was first described in 1905 by Butterfield. Hutt and Cole in 1957 demonstrated that strains of birds could be bred which were resistant to the leucosis complex. Benton and Cover in 1957 reported that there was an increase in the incidence of visceral lymphamatosis in broilers and replacement birds. At the present time, the avian leucosis complex continues to be a cause of loss of both young and mature birds.

Marek's disease, originally considered to be part of the leucosis complex, and first characterized by Marek in 1907, is still a disease of major economic importance. During the past few years there has been outstanding progress which should lead to control of this disease. The first major development in a number of years which has led to partial control of the disease occurred in 1962 when it became possible to transmit the disease experimentally. By 1967 the causative agent, a herpes virus, was isolated and by 1969 the fact that feather follicles were the site where viral replication proceeded to completion was established. These findings led in turn to establishment of evidence that chickens could be immunized against Marek's disease and to the development of vaccines. Whether costs will permit widespread use of such vaccines must be established by further testing and refinements. It has been estimated that, when and if it becomes economical to vaccinate all broilers, the use of this one practice alone will result in adding as much as five percent more broilers to our total meat supply, simply by reducing mortality rates and condemnations.

Respiratory diseases are particularly troublesome to the broiler grower because they are highly contagious, at times cause a high mortality rate and are responsible for a high condemnation rate of poultry carcasses upon post-mortem inspection during processing.

Fowl pox is no longer a serious disease problem because it can be controlled by vaccination. The cause of this disease as reported by Stafseth (1958) was first demonstrated by Marx and Stricker in 1902. In 1923, de Blieck and van Heelsbergen reported the use of an anti-diphtherin for cutaneous vaccination. Woodruff and Goodpasture in 1931 developed a method for growing the pure virus on developing chick embryos. Since that time commercial vaccines have been made available.

Infectious coryza (commonly known as roup) is a highly contagious disease not readily controlled. As reported by Stafseth (1958), de Blieck in 1931 demonstrated that *Hemophilus gallinarum* was one of the organisms which plays a role in the disease. Nelson in 1935 and 1938 found that *Hemophilus gallinarum* was not the only organism involved and that there were three forms of the disease. These results were confirmed by Adler and Yamamoto in 1956.

In 1931, infectious bronchitis was first described by Schalk and Hawn. This disease can now be controlled by vaccination.

Chronic respiratory disease is caused by several microorganisms. It was first described by Delaplane and Stuart in 1943. Markham and Wong in 1952 suggested that the organism was one of a pleuropneumonia group. This fact was later confirmed by several other workers. Fahey and

Crawley in 1954 discovered that a virus could also cause the condition called chronic respiratory disease. In 1958, Gross reported that *Escherichia coli* is a complicating factor in cases of chronic respiratory disease. This disease continues to be one of the main reasons for condemnation of broiler carcasses.

Newcastle disease, so-called because Doyle in 1927 first isolated the causative organism from chickens near Newcastle-on-Tyne in England, is a troublesome respiratory disease. In 1940, a mild form of the disease was reported in California. It was characterized as a respiratory-nervous disorder and as pneumoencephalitis by Beach and Stover in 1942. By 1945, the disease was reported in the Eastern United States and by 1947 it had been observed in most regions of the United States. Van Roeckel in 1955 and Barger and co-workers in 1958 reported on vaccines developed to obtain immunity from the disease. Since that time both live and killed virus vaccines have been developed.

Infectious sinusitis, a disease of turkeys, was first found in 1905 by Dodd and in the United States by Tyzzer in 1926. In 1957, Hofstad demonstrated that the disease could be transmitted by eggs.

Infectious synovitis is a problem in broiler flocks. It was first reported by Wills in 1954 in Texas. Barger and co-workers in 1958 found that both chlortetracycline and oxytetracycline will reduce mortality.

Ornithosis (psittacosis) has been reported in poultry on several occasions. Irons and co-workers in 1951 and Andrews in 1957 reported outbreaks in workers in poultry plants caused by diseased birds.

THE COMMERCIAL HATCHERY INDUSTRY

Bennett and Warren (1939) report the following historic events in the growth and development of the hatchery industry in the United States (Figs. 1.7, 1.8). The first American incubator was patented in 1844 but it was not until 1870 that a second patent was issued to a Jacob Graves and he advertised baby chicks for sale. An improved incubator, the Monarch, was offered for sale in 1884. By this time small hatcheries had started. Their trading area was limited to the distance covered by a horse and wagon in a day. Joseph D. Wilson of Stockton, N.J., was the first to attempt shipment of baby chicks by express in 1892. In 1895, Charles A. Cyphers produced the first mammoth incubator which held 20,000 duck eggs. In 1918, Dr. S. B. Smith patented the forced draft incubator and in 1923 Ira M. Petersime invented the first electrically heated and controlled incubator. Also in 1918, the U.S. Post Office accepted chicks for shipment by mail for the first time. By 1939, the practice of sexing chicks had

Courtesy Arbor Acres Farm, Inc., Glastonbury, Conn.

FIG. 1.7 VANTRESS-ARBOR ACRES BROILER CROSS TYPIFIES MEAT
BIRDS NOW BEING PRODUCED BY U.S. BROILERMEN, AS WELL AS
OVERSEAS IN INCREASING QUANTITIES

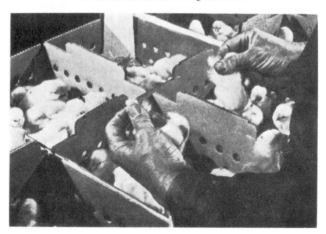

Courtesy Arbor Acres Farm, Inc., Glastonbury, Conn.

FIG. 1.8. IMPROVEMENTS IN PRODUCING HATCHING EGGS AND INCU-
BATING CHICKS WERE SOME OF THE EARLY DEVELOPMENTS RESPONSI-
BLE FOR THE BROILER INDUSTRY

Note the feathers on the wings of the day-old chicks. This is an
indication of rapid feathering, a desirable broiler characteristic.

been widely accepted and used. During the thirties improvements
in incubators and turkey hatching egg production made it practical
to hatch turkeys in incubators. According to the U.S. Department
of Agriculture there were 11,405 chick hatcheries operating in 1934,
by 1963 this number had decreased to 2900.

MANAGEMENT

Management involves taking all of the factors involved with production, processing and marketing and developing a tightly coordinated
systematic, smooth-running organization. To achieve this requires
millions of dollars worth of capital and a national organization. As
a result of these needs the organization of the industry is still moving
toward fewer owners with larger organizations, each controlling larger
portions of the market.

Although increased efficiency in poultry management has contributed
as much as other areas to rapid advances in the development of the poultry industry, changes were not brought about as much by inventions or

Courtesy Lancaster Poultry Co.

FIG. 1.9.   A BROILER FARM WITH HALF A MILLION ANNUAL CAPACITY

TABLE 1.6

GUIDE FOR BROODING CHICKS

(From day old to eight weeks)

Get Ready for Brooding

(1) Well in advance of the arrival of chicks, clean poultry house and equipment with lye water, a steam cleaner, or high pressure sprayer. Allow to dry, and disinfect interior of house thoroughly.

(2) Have feeders and waterers filled and brooder temperature at proper level before chicks arrive.

Brooding Temperature

(3) Brooder temperature should be 90 to 95° F. 2 in. above the litter for the first week. Reduce temperature 5 degrees per week until about 70°F. is reached. A good guide is to regulate the brooder temperature at a level at which chicks appear to be most comfortable.

Brooding Space

(4) Each chick should be allowed a minimum of 7 sq. in. of brooder space under the hover. For electric brooders, up to 10 sq. in. per chick may be needed.

(5) Where chicks are brooded under individual brooder stoves or units, allow a maximum of: 350 replacement chicks per brooder unit; 500 broiler chicks per unit.

(6) For chicks reared in confinement allow a minimum of $1/2$ sq. ft. of brooder room floor space per bird through six weeks, and a minimum of 1 sq. ft. per bird from 7 through 12 weeks.

Feeding-Drinking Equipment

(7) Allow chicks the following feeder space:

Day old through 2 weeks—100 linear inches[1] per 100 chicks.

3 weeks through 6 weeks—175 linear inches[1] per 100 chicks.

7 weeks through 8 weeks—300 linear inches[1] per 100 chicks.

Additional space should be provided in warm weather.

(8) Provide 100 chicks the following drinking space:

Day old through 2 weeks—20 linear inches[1] or two 1-gal. fountains.

3 weeks through 8 weeks—40 linear inches,[1] or two 3-gal. fountains.

Additional space should be provided in warm weather.

Management

(9) In cold weather, use a solid chick guard around the hover to keep chicks from straying and to prevent floor drafts. In warm weather, a wire guard may be used.

(10) Place guard 2 or 3 ft. from edge of hover. Gradually expand it and remove at end of one week.

(11) If roosts are to be used later for hens, provide them for the replacement chicks at 4 weeks of age. Allow 4 in. roosting space per chick.

(12) Provide at least 2 in. of suitable litter at the start. Sugar cane fiber, shavings, sawdust, crushed corn cobs, cottonseed hulls, peanut hulls, peat moss, flax shives, and others may be used when free from injurious materials and reasonably free from dust.

(13) Use all-night lights equivalent to 15 watts per 200 sq. ft. of floor space. This helps prevent pile-ups.

(14) Do not starve chicks—feed them as soon as possible. Sprinkle feed on paper, box lids, or filler flats under hover for first day or two. Use a commercial feed and follow program outlined by manufacturer. Have grit available at all times. Fine chick grain is sometimes given the first two days to prevent "pasting up."

(15) Prevent cannibalism by allowing plenty of floor space, reducing temperature rapidly, providing plenty of feeder space, covering windows to admit only subdued light. Use antipick salve if necessary.

[1] *For example, a 4-ft. hopper open to birds from both sides provides 96 linear inches of feeding space. Same principle applies to watering space.*

From Poultry Tribune, Watt Publishing Co., (Anon. 1965).

specific research developments as they were in the other areas. Although many management practices were considered and ready to be put into practice, developments had to wait until electricity was available, diseases could be controlled, and satisfactory rations and broiler strains could be developed. Perhaps the most important single labor-saving device was the ability to rear chickens in confinement. Another important development has been the ability to house thousands of birds in the same pen with a corresponding decrease in the hours of labor required to handle a thousand chickens or turkeys (Fig. 1.9).

Automatic feeders, lighting, delivery of feed in bulk quantities, waterers, ventilating systems, and medication dispensers have all brought about decreases in labor requirements. The development of large-scale central brooding systems with accurate thermostat controls also helped make large scale production possible. A guide for brooding chicks from day old to eight weeks is shown in Table 1.6.

One of the most important developments, which came as a result of the other advancements in the poultry industry, and the need for large amounts of capital to finance large scale production was the integration of various segments within the industry. Since feed was the largest single cost of production it was only natural that feed companies should obtain capital which was then loaned out usually in the form of feed and supplies for raising broilers or turkeys to producers. To protect their investments and insure good healthy chicks and a market for the broilers, hatcheries and processing plants soon became involved in integrated operations.

Extension workers at Ohio State University report two new developments. Computer programs using time-sharing techniques are now available to some poultrymen. An example of part of a print-out for a 25,000 bird flock estimating cost, income and profit for the 42nd to 56th day of the growing period is shown in Table 1.7. According to this print-out, the flock should have been sold or shipped to the processing plant on the 51st day to obtain maximum profits.

A second management development is the setting up of "package" deals for 200,000–300,000-bird egg production units which generally include poultry houses, cages, feed, water, and egg collection systems, and manure and environment control equipment along with an egg processing operation including egg washers, grading and packaging equipment—all in one package. Such operations require an investment of 1½ million dollars, 30–35 tons of feed and over 16,000 gal. of water a day which results in 75,000 lb. of manure and over 500 cases of eggs. There are also 4 to 5 miles of watering troughs to clean and 8 to 10 miles of feeders as well as 25 to 30 miles of egg gathering

TABLE 1.7

ECONOMIC PROJECTION—BROILERS (UNSEXED) INITIAL FLOCK = 25,000   CURVES: 111-211-311 DATE

42	22250	51516	6189	−471	0.248	−0.019	−9.605
43	22214	53241	7986	1173	0.319	0.047	23.467
44	22178	54901	8235	1279	0.329	0.051	24.893
45	22142	56666	8483	1365	0.339	0.055	26.252
46	22107	58205	8730	1460	0.349	0.058	27.549
47	22071	59848	10178	2251	0.407	0.110	50.952
48	22086	61486	10452	2873	0.418	0.115	52.327
49	21999	63118	11992	4266	0.480	0.171	76.181
50	21964	64834	12318	4431	0.493	0.177	77.243
51	21928	66544	12643	4595	0.506	0.184	79.236
52	21892	68243	12284	4072	0.491	0.163	69.046
53	21857	69946	12590	4223	0.504	0.169	70.372
54	21821	71638	12895	4372	0.516	0.175	71.693
55	21785	73324	11732	3044	0.469	0.122	49.108
56	21749	75005	12001	3154	0.480	0.126	50.069

[1] Includes 5% catching mortality.
Courtesy of Ohio State University.

belts and several hundred fans and electric motors to keep in operation. When such units are used one man can care for 100,000 birds.

PROCESSING POULTRY

Brant (1962) has reviewed the technological changes in poultry processing. Before the development of automobiles and trucks, poultry was shipped live in special railroad poultry cars to cities where they were slaughtered just before the consumer purchased them. Heavy losses caused by respiratory diseases forced the industry to kill and dress the poultry in the areas where it was produced and ship it to consuming areas in refrigerated cars. Ordinarily, the poultry were not eviscerated, but "New York dressed" with heads, feet and viscera intact (only the blood and feathers were removed). During the thirties, the use of power driven overhead conveyors, brain sticking and the use of agitated water for scalding gradually came into use. During this same period, some processors began to eviscerate poultry at the processing plant and freeze it. As a result practically all poultry is marketed in ready-to-cook form today.

Perhaps the most important development in the processing industry was the invention of the rubber picking finger. By the mid-forties rubber fingered picking machines were perfected to the point where much of the hand labor formerly used for pinning carcasses was eliminated.

Mandatory poultry inspection helped improve the quality of poultry received by consumers. Although poultry inspection was available on a voluntary basis for a number of years it was made mandatory in 1959 for all processors who sold birds in more than one state. To meet inspection requirements many plants had to modernize their facilities, improve the quality of processing, adopt better sanitation practices, and adopt strict quality control programs.

During the fifties, it was found that the shelf-life of carcasses could be extended by the addition of antibiotics. Unfortunately many of the results obtained in laboratories failed to materialize when adapted to plant conditions. Quick chilling of poultry as a means of extending shelf-life came into use and in the last few years the development of chilling equipment which chills carcasses in a continuous operation rather than in a batch or tank process has been adopted by the industry.

MARKETING POULTRY

Most of the advancements in the marketing of poultry are a direct result of improvements in processing and handling poultry and in technological advances made outside the poultry industry. With the advent of eviscerated poultry the cost of transportation was reduced because only the edible portions of the carcasses were shipped and shelf-life was increased because of better processing and sanitation practices. With the development of superhighways and modern motor trucks it became possible to ship eviscerated ice packed poultry several thousand miles in complete safety. A recent advancement has been the shipment of chilled poultry from a processing plant in Mississippi by truck to California and then by ship to Honolulu, Hawaii. Grading and standardization along with compulsory inspection have resulted in large quantities of uniformly high quality poultry meat being offered which consumers can purchase in complete confidence even though they may have little knowledge of poultry quality. The wide dissemination of Federal and Federal-State Market News reports and the increased use of telephones for reporting between different areas has resulted in reducing the variations in prices between different areas of production. Forecasts of broiler placements have helped to coordinate the supply of broilers and turkeys with the anticipated demand.

FUTURE POTENTIAL

One area in which considerable future progress will probably be made is increasing the size of production units further and in utilizing more automated equipment. However, Gordeuk (1963) predicts that "labor will become one of the lesser costs in food production and further commitment of resources to reduce the cost of labor will be relatively less important than the objective of getting optimum production per acre, and least cost per animal based on future performance." Although there surely will be further improvements in nutrition and breeding future gains will probably not be as rapid as those during the past 20 yr. Disease control and technology are two areas where all possibilities for reducing costs and increasing efficiency have not as yet been fully explored.

In 1969, the president of one of the nation's largest poultry combines was quoted as saying that "The industry has relied in the past on dramatic breakthroughs in technology. However, the industry has now run the gamut of nutritional and genetic and disease control breakthroughs. Improvement in production will come more slowly now. It will be necessary in the future to raise selling prices to cover the higher costs." Another industry leader also was of the opinion that the broiler industry could not hope to obtain increases in technology in the 1970's equivalent to those made in previous years.

At the present time it is not possible to forecast what the implications of the energy shortage will be on the poultry industry except that the shortage will contribute to the overall costs of things poultrymen buy and that these costs will need to be passed on to consumers in increased prices for poultry products. These changes could result in poultry products moving into a more favorable competitive position or it could raise the prices of poultry products more than the costs of competing meats.

Poultry Technology

Automation offers a means of increasing the efficiency of handling and processing poultry. Because of variations in size and shape of poultry carcasses, and the fact that they lack rigidity, it is difficult to position carcasses automatically and still more difficult to cut into the flesh with a machine. At the present time, there is a need for stunning birds while still in crates and then automatically hanging and bleeding them. On the other end of the line carcasses are still sorted and packed by hand. Further automation of cutting and packaging also offers opportunities.

Automatic materials handling and automated eviscerating systems have been the most recent advances in technology. Automatic live bird catching systems have not been perfected to the point where they are practical under commercial conditions.

The development of new food products from poultry meat shows considerable promise. At the present time, lack of a satisfactory method of automatically removing raw flesh from carcasses keeps the price of uncooked meat so high that chicken meat cannot compete with other meats for this use.

The poultry industry has not as yet utilized by-products as much as the meat packing industries. Since many so called by-products of the packing industry are already in surplus it is quite difficult to compete with products from this source unless special advantages can be demonstrated for using poultry by-products. Disposal of poultry manure may well become an important factor in limiting the size of poultry enterprises in some areas of the country.

Turkeys

An attempt is being made to produce 100-lb. turkeys. These birds could be cut into parts and sold as separate cuts of meat the same as lamb. Another advantage of such a strain would be the fact that they could be slaughtered at smaller weights to meet whatever weight range was needed.

Waterfowl

Ducks are produced primarily on Long Island in New York State and in the midwest (Fig. 1.10). Ziemba (1965) reported that the Long Island

Courtesy U.S. Dept. Agr.

Fig. 1.10. A Long Island Fresh Water Front Holding and Feeding Lot for Ducks

area is diminishing in importance because of high land costs, problems of pollution and the pressures resulting from urbanization. In 1964, seven midwest duckling producers grew 2,750,000 birds of an improved strain of white Pekin ducks noted for the high meat-to-bone ratio of the carcasses. These same producers are attempting to improve the strain by breeding for further improvements in meat to bone ratio, lower fat content, and an increase in egg production over the present 150 eggs a year average. Ducks are processed at exactly seven weeks and two days of age because at that time, just before the molting period, feather removal is easiest.

In the midwest area duck feet are frozen and shipped to the far East, eggs not used for hatching are sold to oriental markets for use as egg rolls and for pastry baking and the feathers are packed in 60-lb. bags for use in mattresses and bedding.

BIBLIOGRAPHY

ADLER, H. E., and YAMAMOTO, R. 1956. Studies on chronic coryza (Nelson) in the domestic fowl. Cornell Vet. *36*, 337–343.

ANDREWS, J. M. 1957. The importance of psittacosis in the United States. J. Am. Vet. Med. Assoc. *130*, 109–116.

ANON. 1965. Brooding guide. Poultry Trib. *71*, No. 2, 27.

ANON. 1969. Future shape of poultry industry outlined for agricultural marketers. Feedstuffs *41*, 12–14, 50–52.

ANON. 1971. 14 minutes = one lb. of chicken. Broiler Ind. *34*, No. 6, 14.

ANON. 1971. MD control may give us 15% more meat in 1972. Broiler Ind. *34*, No. 6, 24–26.

BARGER, E. H., CARD, L. E., and POMEROY, B. S. 1958. Diseases and parasites of Poultry, 5th Edition. Lea & Febiger, Philadelphia.

BEACH, J. R., and DAVIS, D. E. 1927. Acute infection of chicks and chronic infection of the ovaries of hens caused by the fowl typhoid organism. Hilgardia *2*, 411–424.

BEACH, J. R., and STOVER, D. E. 1942. Infectious avian encephalomyelitis. Calif. Cultivator *89*, No. 15, 387.

BEAUDETTE, F. R. 1925. The possible transmission of fowl typhoid through the egg. J. Am. Vet. Med. Assoc. *67*, 741–745.

BENNETT, B. H., and WARREN, C. C. 1939. The commercial hatchery industry in the United States. Proc. 7th World's Poultry Congress and Exposition, 360–364.

BENTON, W. J., and COVER, M. S. 1957. The increased incidence of visceral lymphamatosis in broilers and replacement birds. Avian Diseases *1*, 320–327.

BLAXTER, K. L. 1961. Efficiency of feed conversion by different classes of livestock in relation to food production. Federation Am. Soc. Exptl. Biol. Med. *20*, No. 1, 268–274.

BRANT, A. W. 1962. Technological changes in poultry processing affecting quality and costs. Presented at World's Poultry Science Association, Mexico City, Mexico (Mimeo).

BUTTERFIELD, E. E. 1905. Aleukaemic lymphadenoid tumors of the hen. Folia Haematol. *2*, 649–657.

BYERLEY, T. C.   1961.   The role of research in solving the poultry condemnation problem.   Proc. Disease, Environmental, Management Factors Related to Poultry Health.   USDA Agr. Res. Serv.; and Univ. Georgia.

COBURN, D. R., and STAFSETH, H. J.   1931.   A field test for pullorum disease. J. Am. Vet. Med. Assoc. 79, 241-243.

COMBS, G. F.   1961.   Quality and quantity of final product—poultry.   Federation Am. Soc. Exptl. Biol. Med. 20, 306-312.

DEBLIECK, L.   1931.   A haemoglobin bacteria causing coryza infection in the fowl.   Tijdschr. Diergeneesk. 58, 1-5. (Dutch)

DEBLIECK, L., and HEELSBERGEN, T. VAN.   1923.   Vaccination against diphtheria and fowl pox in chickens.   Deut. Tierarztl. Wochschr. 31, 85. (German)

DELAPLANE, J. P., BATCHELDER, R. M., and HIGGINS, J. C.   1947.   Sulfaquinoxaline in the prevention of Eimeria tenella infection in chickens.   North Am. Vet. 28, 19-24.

DELAPLANE, J. P., and STUART, H. O.   1943.   The propagation of a virus in embryonated chicken eggs causing a chronic respiratory disease of chickens. Am. J. Vet. Res. 4, No. 13, 325-332.

DÓDD, S.   1905.   Epizootic pneumo-enteritis of the turkey.   J. Comp. Pathol. Therapy 18, 239-245.

DOYLE, T. M.   1927.   A hitherto unrecorded disease of fowls due to a filter-passing virus.   J. Comp. Pathol. Therapy 40, 144-169.

ELLIS C. C., SHEPPARD, C. C., and WEISNER, E. S.   1963.   Vaccination of poultry. Mich. State Univ. Ext. Bull. 343.

ELVEHJEM, C. A., MADDEN, R. J., STRONG, F. M., and WOOLLEY, D. W.   1938.   The isolation and identification of the anti-black tongue factor.   J. Biol. Chem. 123, 137-149.

FABER, F. L.   1961.   The emerging structure of the broiler industry.   Agr. Mktg. 6, No. 1, 16-17.

FAHEY, J. E., and CRAWLEY, J. F.   1954.   Studies on a chronic respiratory disease of chickens.   II.   Isolation of a virus.   Can. J. Comp. Med. Vet. Sci. 18, No. 1, 13-21.

GAGE, G. E., PAIGE, B. H., and HYLAND, H. W.   1914.   On the diagnosis of infection with Bacterium pullorum in the domestic fowl.   Mass. Agr. Expt. Sta. Bull. 148.

GLOVER, J. A., and HENDERSON, W.   1946.   Fowl typhoid.   Report on a recent outbreak in Ontario.   Can. J. Comp. Med. Vet. Sci. 10, 241-249.

GOLDBLITH, S. M., and JOSLYN, M. A.   1964.   Milestones in Nutrition.   Avi Publishing Co., Westport Conn.

GORDEUK, A.   1963.   Farming and the feed industry 20 years from now.   Merck Agr. Mem. 8, 1-2.

GROSS, W. B.   1958.   Symposium on chronic respiratory disease of Poultry. II.   The role of Escherichia coli in the cause of chronic respiratory disease and certain other respiratory disease.   Am. J. Vet. Res. 19, 448-463.

GRUMBLES, L. C., DELAPLANE, J. P., and HIGGINS, T. C.   1948.   Sulfaquinoxaline in the control of Eimeria tenella and Eimeria necatrix in chickens on a commercial broiler farm.   Science 107, 196.

HODGSON, R. E.   1959.   Livestock production in transition.   In Food, The Yearbook of Agriculture.   U.S. Dept. Agr.

HOFFMANN, E., and GWIN, J. M.   1954.   Successful Broiler Growing.   Watt Publishing Co., Mount Morris, Illinois.

HOFSTAD, M. S. 1957. Egg transmission of infectious sinusitis in turkeys. Avian Diseases *1*, 165-170.

HUGHES, C. E. 1960. The commercial broiler. Armour's Analysis *9*, 1-8.

HUTT, F. B., and COLE, R. K. 1957. Control of fowl leukosis. J. Am Vet. Med. Assoc. *131*, 491-495.

IRONS, J. V., SULLIVAN, T. D., and ROWEN, J. 1951. Outbreak of psittacosis (ornithosis) from working with turkeys and chickens. Am. J. Public Health *41*, 931-939.

JANSEN, B. C. P. 1956. Early nutritional researches on beriberi leading to the discovery of vitamin B_1. Nutr. Abstr. Rev. *26*, 1-14.

JOHNSON, W. T. 1923. Avian coccidiosis. Poultry Sci. *2*, 146-163.

JOHNSON, W. T. 1927. Immunity or resistance of the chicken to coccidial infection. Oregon Agr. Expt. Sta. Bull. *230*, 1-31.

JOHNSON, W. T. 1938. Coccidiosis of the chicken with special reference to species. Oregon Agr. Expt. Sta. Bull. *358*, 1-33.

JONES, F. S. 1913. The value of the macroscopic agglutination test in detecting fowls that harbor *Bacterium pullorum*. J. Med. Res. *27*, 481-495.

LAMBERT, W. V. 1933. A preliminary study of the reaction of two disease resistant stocks of chickens after infection with their reciprocal pathogens. Iowa Acad. Sci. *40*, 231.

MCCOLLUM, E. V., SIMMONDS, N., BECKER, J. E., and SHIPLEY, P. G. 1922. Studies on experimental rickets. XXI. An experimental demonstration of the existence of a vitamin which promotes calcium deposition. J. Biol. Chem. *53*, No. 3, 293-312.

MARKHAM, F. S., and WONG, S. C. 1952. Pleuro pneumonia-like organisms in the etiology of turkey sinusitis and chronic respiratory disease of chickens. Poultry Sci. *31*, 902-904.

MARX, E. and STRICKER, A. 1902. Investigations on the contagious epithelioma of chickens. Deuts. Med. Wochschr. *29*, 79-80. (German)

NABER, E. C., TOUCHBURN, S. P., and MARSH, G. A. 1961. Ohio poultry rations. Ohio Agr. Ext. Bull. *343*.

NELSON, J. B. 1935. Cocco-bacilliform bodies associated with an infectious fowl coryza. Science *82*, 43-44.

NELSON, J. B. 1938. Studies on an uncomplicated coryza of the domestic fowl. IX. The cooperative action of *Hemophilus gallinarum* and the coccobacilliform bodies in coryza of rapid onset and long duration. J. Exptl. Med. *69*, 199-209.

NORDQUIST, A. V., and PALS, C. H. 1956. Economic losses from animal diseases and Parasites. *In* Animal Diseases, The Yearbook of Agriculture. U.S. Dept. Agr.

NORDSKOG, A. W. 1966. The evolution of animal breeding practices—commercial and experimental. World's Poultry Sci. *22*, No. 3, 207-216.

PFEILER, W., and REHSE, A. 1913. *Bacillus typhigallinarum alcalifaciens* and the contagious disease caused by this organism. Mitt. Kaiser Wilhelm Institut Landwirtschaft Bromberg, *5*, 306. (German)

PHILLIPS, H. S., and SNYDER, J. M. 1962. Standards for growing Long Island white Pekin ducklings. Magazine of Ducks and Geese. *462*, 26-31.

REED, W. S., and SKOGLUND, W. C. 1963. Growth and feed standards for broilers—1963. New Hampshire Agr. Expt. Sta. Bull. *478*.

REID, J. T. 1975. Energy cost of animal production enterprises. Presented at Am. Assoc. Advan. Sci. Meeting, New York, Jan. (Mimeo).

REID, W. M. 1961. Coccidiosis control. Proc. Disease, Environmental, Management Factors Related to Poultry Health. USDA Agr. Res. Serv. and Univ. Georgia.

RETTGER, L. F. 1900. Septicemia among young chickens. N.Y. Med. J. 71, 803-805.

RETTGER, L. F., KIRKPATRICK, W. F., and JONES, R. E. 1914. Bacillary white diarrhea of young chicks. Conn. Agr. Expt. Sta. Bull. 77, 263-309.

RETTGER, L. F., and STONEBURN, F. H. 1909. Bacillary white diarrhea of young chicks. Conn. Agr. Expt. Sta. Bull. 60. 33-57.

SAWYER, G. 1971. The Agribusiness Poultry Industry. Georgia Poultry Improvement Assoc., Oakwood, Georgia.

SCHAFFER, J. M., MACDONALD, A. D., HALL, W. J., and BUNYEA, H. 1931. A stained antigen for the rapid whole blood test for pullorum disease. J. Am. Vet. Med. Assoc. 79, 236-240.

SCHALK, A. F., and HAWN, M. C. 1931. An apparently new respiratory disease of baby chicks. J. Am. Vet. Med. Assoc. 78, 413-422.

SCHAIBLE, P. J. 1970. Poultry: Feeds and Nutrition. Avi Publishing Co., Westport, Conn.

SCOTT, M. L. 1965. Twenty-twenty is goal for '65. Poultry Meat 2, No. 1, 28-35.

STAFSETH, H. J. 1958. Advances in knowledge of poultry diseases over the past fifty years. Poultry Sci. 37, 741-775.

STOKSTAD, E. L. R., and JUKES, T. H. 1950. Growth-promoting effect of aureomycin on turkey poults. Poultry Sci. 29, 611-612.

TOBIN, B. F., and ARTHUR, H. B. 1964. Dynamics of adjustment in the broiler industry. Div. Res., Graduate School Business Admin., Harvard Univ.

TYZZER, E. E. 1926. The injection of argyrol for the treatment of sinusitus in turkeys. Cornell Vet. 16, 221-224.

TYZZER, E. L., THEILER, H., and JONES, E. E. 1932. Coccidiosis in gallinaceous birds. II. A comparative study of species of Eimeria of the chicken. Am. J. Hyg. 15, 319-393.

VAN ROECKEL, H. 1955. An evaluation of Newcastle Disease wing-web vaccine. Proc. 92nd Ann. Meeting Am. Vet. Med. Assoc. 324-326.

VAN STRAATEN, H., and TE HENNEPE, B. J. C. 1918. A Klein epidemic disease of chickens. Folia Microbiol. 5, 103. (German)

WILLS, F. K. 1954. Preliminary report on transmission of an agent producing arthritis in chickens. Texas Agr. Expt. Sta. Progr. Rept. 1674.

WITTER, R. L. 1971. Marek's disease research—history and perspectives. Poultry Sci. 50, 333-342.

WOODRUFF, A. M., and GOODPASTURE, E. W. 1931. The susceptibility of the chorio-allantoic membrane of chick embryos to infection with fowl pox virus. Am J. Pathol. 7, 209-222.

ZIEMBA, J. V. 1965. Duckling quality gains as techiques improve. Food Eng. 37, No. 1, 102-104.

CHAPTER 2

Quality Identification

INTRODUCTION

Quality has been defined by Kramer (1951) as "the sum of the characteristics of the given food item which influence the acceptability or preference for that food by the consumer." Since only those attributes or characteristics which have significance to users are important in marketing, theoretically there could be two or more sets of standards for the same commodity, depending on its use. Grades are used to classify a commodity into different levels or ranges of quality such as good, better, best or C, B, and A grades.

Grades are based on standards. Coles (1951) defines standards as "Descriptions of one or more characteristics of good which divide those on the market into two or more groups called grades." Commodities are compared against a standard or set of standards to determine their grade. Standards for poultry can be divided into three general groups—government standards, trade standards, and research standards.

Government standards are those developed by federal, state, county, or local agencies. They can be voluntary, as in the case of certain standards of quality, or compulsory as in the case of those issued under the Federal Food and Drug Act of 1938, or in the case of inspection of poultry processed for shipment between states.

Trade standards are those expressed or implied grade levels made up by individual companies. Although the consumer may not know the specifications for a particular trade standard she soon learns through use that a particular brand infers a certain minimum level of quality.

Research standards are often developed by research workers as a standard or control against which other batches of the product treated or handled in a slightly different manner can be compared.

A number of factors must be taken into consideration when developing standards and grades. Some of the more important listed by McCallister (1951) are: (1) base the standards on the quality of the product actually produced and marketed; (2) standards should be so constructed that they are useful to as many groups who will be using them as possible; (3) standards should reflect those characteristics that buyers recognize; and (4) standards should be such that they can be applied and still be uniform and dependable.

A number of state, county, and municipal laws influence quality identi-

27

fication. In many cases the only purpose is to eliminate the sale and use for food of all poultry which is unfit for human consumption; in other cases the laws are an attempt to standardize the different types of poultry offered for sale; and in a few cases laws act as trade barriers. Johndrew *et al.* (1972) classify the various types of laws affecting identification into the following groups.

Food and drug laws are similar to the Federal Food, Drug and Cosmetic Act. Their prime objective is to prevent the sale or consumption of poultry which is unfit for human consumption.

Licensing laws require dealers and poultry processors to obtain a license before buying and selling poultry. Generally the licensee must file a report of his activities or undergo inspection of his place of business or his records.

Standardization laws are an attempt to standardize the different types of poultry offered for sale in a given trading area or in a given political subdivision.

Laws pertaining to proof of ownership of poultry in transit are an attempt to guard against thievery and to provide a means of identifying the owner for law enforcement officers.

Laws limiting the hours of business make it unlawful to sell or offer poultry for sale at specified times.

Inspection laws require inspection of the poultry at some phase during processing or just prior to delivery or sale.

Laws governing the sale of imported poultry attempt to regulate the quality of poultry processed outside the jurisdiction of the state, country, or city where it is offered for sale or consumed.

UNITED STATES DEPARTMENT OF AGRICULTURE
GRADES AND STANDARDS

The first tentative standards and grades for live and dressed poultry were published in 1930 under an act of Congress in 1918 which gave the Secretary of Agriculture authority to establish grading services for agricultural products.

The U.S. Department of Agriculture Grades and Standards applied by qualified personnel provide as accurate and objective a method of identifying quality as can be devised for practical application. Within the limits of subjective evaluation, they are the same in all areas of the country and for all conditions and types of poultry marketed. The grades and standards are a matter of public record and are acceptable evidence in legal cases. They also serve as a basis for establishing state, trade and research specifications.

FIG. 2.1 THE U.S. DEPT. AGR. GRADE SHIELD (A) DENOTES THAT
A PRODUCT HAS BEEN GRADED FOR QUALITY, WHILE THE INSPECTION
MARK (B) INDICATES THAT IT HAS BEEN INSPECTED AND PASSED AS
WHOLESOME FOOD

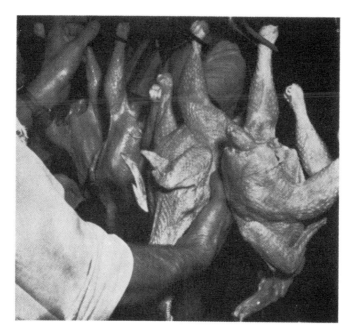

FIG. 2.2 IN EXAMINING POULTRY ON THE CONVEYOR LINE, THE U.S.
DEPT. AGR. GRADER MUST EVALUATE THE CARCASS AT A GLANCE,
KEEPING IN MIND EACH OF THE QUALITY FACTORS

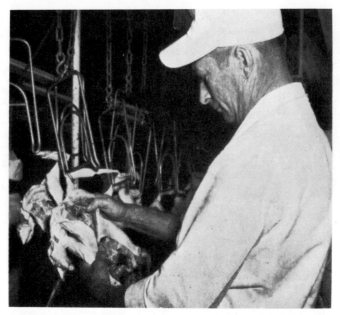

Courtesy U.S. Dept. Agr.

FIG. 2.3. A TECHNICALLY-TRAINED, LICENSED U.S. DEPT. AGR. INSPEC-
TOR EXAMINING A CARCASS, INSIDE AND OUT, ON THE PROCESSING LINE
TO ENSURE THE IT IS WHOLESOME FOR FOOD AND FREE OF ABNORMAL
CONDITIONS

Poultry are classified by the U.S. Department of Agriculture into kinds, classes, grades, weight ranges, condition, live, dressed, and ready-to-cook. Grading service is provided for the purpose of determining the class, quality, quantity, condition or any combination of the above (Figs. 2.1(A) and 2.2). Inspection service is provided for determining the condition and wholesomeness of poultry (Figs. 2.1(B) and 2.3).

Market Class

Before grading, poultry are divided into market classes according to their species, age, and sex (Table 2.1). In some cases their age is limited to a span of several weeks; in other cases they may be classified simply as young or old. Sex may not be specified where it has no effect on the market quality.

Species

For purposes of grading, poultry are classified into chickens, turkeys, ducks, geese, guineas, and pigeons. Each species has definite characteristics which influence cooking methods and organoleptic properties.

TABLE 2.1

MARKET CLASSES OF POULTRY

Species	Class	Sex	Age
Chicken	Cornish game hen	Either	5–7 weeks
Chicken	Broiler or fryer	Either	9–12 weeks
Chicken	Roaster	Either	3–5 months
Chicken	Capon	Unsexed male	Under 18 months
Chicken	Stag	Male	Under 10 months
Chicken	Hen or stewing	Female	Over 10 months
Chicken	Cock	Male	Over 10 months
Turkey	Fryer-roaster	Either	Under 16 weeks
Turkey	Young hen	Female	5–7 months
Turkey	Young tom	Male	5–7 months
Turkey	Yearling hen	Female	Under 15 months
Turkey	Yearling tom	Male	Under 15 months
Turkey	Mature or old	Either	Over 15 months
Duck	Broiler duckling	Either	Under 8 weeks
Duck	Roaster duckling	Either	Under 16 weeks
Duck	Mature or old	Either	Over 6 months
Goose	Young	Either	
Goose	Mature or old	Either	
Guinea	Young	Either	
Guinea	Mature or old	Either	
Pigeon	Squab	Either	
Pigeon	Pigeon	Either	

From U.S. Dept. Agr., Agriculture Handbook *31* (1956).

Sex

In many cases the various species of poultry are classified according to sex because sex has a definite influence on the quality of the resultant carcass. The flavor, tenderness, juiciness, conformation and finish of an old rooster are quite different from those of a stewing chicken or hen. In other cases where sex has little influence on the carcass, it may not be used as a basis for classifying birds. Two examples are broilers or fryers and geese. Some characteristics of poultry which can be used to determine sex are the larger head, comb and wattles and coarser appearance of males compared to females. Male feathers are long and pointed at the ends with long curved tail feathers in chickens and a curl in the tail feathers of male ducks. In females, the feathers are shorter with a blunt end and a short straight tail. Females have a finer bone structure and a more rounded body, a shorter keel and drumsticks and thighs comparatively shorter than males. The skin of males is coarser and the feather follicles are larger than females of the same lot. The feather tracts of females carry more fat than males.

Age

The degree of maturity also influences cooking methods and organoleptic qualities. There are a number of indications of the age of poultry.

Young chickens have a pliable, smooth, glossy comb with sharp points; young ducks have a pliable bill. Older birds have faded, worn, broken plumage except those which have recently molted. Old birds generally are darker in color and have a coarser texture and hardened muscle fibers, the end of the keel is hardened with no cartilage and the pinbones are not pliable. Young birds have smooth small scales on the shanks, a small, soft oil sac and spurs on the males are small and undeveloped. Young ducks and geese have a soft windpipe which is easily dented.

Grading Live Poultry

Sorting live poultry into United States grades is not practiced in most processing plants because of procurement practices in the industry. A processing plant purchases all broilers in a house on the basis of inspection of the birds on the farm. All birds that appear to be fit for slaughter are then hauled to the processing plant. It is the grader and inspector's responsibility to inspect and classify live birds before slaughter for condition to see that they are free of any condition which would render them unfit for slaughter.

United States Standards of quality for individual birds, nevertheless, can be used as criteria for inspecting and determining the quality of live poultry even though each bird in a flock is not individually inspected. Live poultry are examined for health and vigor, feathering, conformation, fleshing, fat, and freedom from defects (Table 2.2). Grading of live birds is not as accurate as grading dressed carcasses because feathers cover many defects on live birds.

Health and Vigor.—A bird of A or No. 1 quality is alert with bright eyes and appears to be vigorous and in good health. Such birds usually have a bright comb of good texture, glossy plumage, with clean dry feathers around the vent and close fitting around the body.

Feathering.—A or No. 1 quality birds are well feathered over all parts of their body, but they may have a slight scattering of pinfeathers. Birds with numerous pinfeathers, especially those just coming through the skin, bare backs, discolored areas or broken quills must be placed in the lower grades. One criterion sometimes used in judging feathering is whether normal scalding and picking operations will remove the pinfeathers.

Conformation.—Birds with good conformation generally have good flesh and fat covering. For example, for a carcass to have good fleshing over the breast the bird must have a long enough keel bone for the fleshing.

Conformation also refers to the presence or absence of such defects as dented breasts, keels that are crooked, knobby, V shaped or slab sided, narrow, crooked or hunched backs, deformed or swollen legs or wings and bodies that have a pronounced wedge shape.

TABLE 2.2

SUMMARY OF STANDARDS OF QUALITY FOR LIVE POULTRY ON AN INDIVIDUAL BIRD BASIS
(Minimum requirements and maximum defects permitted)

Factor	A or No. 1 Quality	B or No. 2 Quality	C or No. 3 Quality
Health and vigor	Alert, bright eyes, healthy, vigorous	Good health and vigor	Lacking in vigor
Feathering	Well covered with feathers showing luster or sheen	Fairly well covered with feathers	Complete lack of plumage feathers on back
	Slight scattering of pin feathers	Moderate number of pin feathers	Large number of pin feathers
Conformation	Normal	Practically normal	Abnormal
Breast bone	Slight curve, $1/8$-inch dent (chickens), $1/4$-inch dent (turkeys)	Slightly crooked	Crooked
Back	Normal (except slight curve)	Moderately crooked	Crooked or hunched back
Legs and wings	Normal	Slightly misshapen	Misshapen
Fleshing	Well fleshed, moderately broad and long breast	Fairly well fleshed	Poorly developed, narrow breast, thin covering of flesh
Fat covering	Well covered, some fat under skin over entire carcass	Enough fat on breast and legs to prevent a distinct appearance of flesh through skin	Lacking in fat covering on back and thighs, small amount in feather tracts
	Chicken fryers and turkey fryers and young toms only moderate covering	Hens or fowl may have excessive abdominal fat	
	No excess abdominal fat		
Defects	Slight	Moderate	Serious
Tears and broken bones	Free	Free	Free
Bruises, scratches, and calluses	Slight skin bruises, scratches, and calluses	Moderate (except only slight flesh bruises)	Unlimited to extent no part unfit for food
Shanks	Slightly scaly	Moderately scaly	Seriously scaly

From U.S. Dept. Agr., Agr. Handbook 31 (1972).

Fleshing.—Since poultry are purchased for the meat on the carcass both the amount and the distribution of fleshing are important criteria of qual- ity. Most flesh is found on the breast, thighs, and drumsticks. Examples of poor fleshing are those cases where the breast meat does not carry the width well back to the end of the keel, V or concave breasts, thin legs and drumsticks and backs that are not well fleshed.

Fat.—A carcass which lacks fat has a bluish appearance because some of the flesh shows through the skin. The skin between the heavy feather tracts and over the back are areas where lack of fat usually shows up most noticeably.

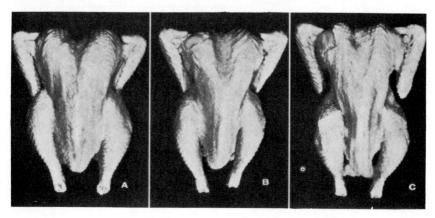

Courtesy U.S. Dept. Agr.

FIG. 2.4.   STEWING HENS OF U.S. DEPT. AGR. GRADES A, B, AND C QUALITY

Defects.—Common defects which lower the quality of live birds are such things as breast blisters, heavy calluses, insect bites such as those caused by lice or chiggers and discoloration caused by picking or scratch- es. Other defects are broken bones and flesh and skin bruises. Many of the above defects on live birds are hidden by feathers.

Reject.—The term reject refers to any bird which is unfit for human con- sumption.

Grading Ready-to-Cook Poultry

Dressed and ready-to-cook poultry are graded for class, condition and quality in that order. Summaries of specifications for standards of quality for the several classes of poultry are shown in Tables 2.3 and 2.4. Official United States grades for individually graded ready-to- cook poultry carcasses are U.S. Department of Agriculture Grades A, B, and C (Fig. 2.4). Wholesale grades are U.S. Extras, U.S. Standards, and U.S. Trades. Individual quality factors consist of conformation, fleshing, fat, freedom from pinfeathers and freedom from defects. The final quality of the bird will be determined by the individual factor applied to it which has the lowest rating. It should be emphasized that standards of quality apply to evaluation of individual birds or carcasses and that grades generally apply to wholesale lots of poultry. Tolerances have been set up to compensate for human error and variations in interpreting degrees of quality.

For the purpose of encouraging uniformity, specifications for weight have been set up for the various classes even though they are not included in the U.S. Grades.

Condition.—Condition refers to any characteristic which makes the carcass unfit for human consumption. These characteristics will be discussed in detail under poultry inspection.

Craftsmanship.—Dressed or ready-to-cook carcasses under certain conditions are returned for additional processing, or if this is not possible, they are classified as "No Grade." As such they cannot receive an official U.S. Grade. Some of these conditions are protruding pinfeathers, bruises which require trimming, lung, sex organs or parts of the trachea incompletely removed, vestigial or other feathers, extraneous material such as feces, blood, grease, feed, etc.

Conformation.—The same defects which are present on live birds are also found on dressed and ready-to-cook carcasses. For this reason, they will not be repeated here. A bird of A quality must have normal physical conformation with the exception of a slightly curved breastbone or other slight abnormality. Chickens, ducks, guineas, and pigeons may have as much as a $1/8$ inch dent in the breastbone and still qualify as A quality.

Fleshing.—Carcasses qualifying as A quality have "well-developed, moderately broad and long breasts, well-fleshed throughout the entire length, with the flesh carrying sufficiently well up to the crest of the breastbone so that the breastbone is not prominent. The legs are well covered with flesh."

Fat.—An A quality poultry carcass is well covered with fat over the breast, back, hips, and pinbones, except that chicken broilers or fryers and young tom turkeys may have only a moderate amount of fat covering. A hen, stewing chicken or fowl, although well covered with fat, is free from excessive abdominal fat.

Pinfeathers.—Pinfeathers are classified as protruding and non-protruding. Non-protruding pinfeathers are those which although visible have not as yet broken through the outer skin. Ready-to-cook poultry must be free of protruding pinfeathers "visible to an inspector or grader during an examination of the carcass at normal operating speed" before any quality designation can be assigned. Vestigal feathers (hairlike appendages) must also be considered when examining a carcass for pinfeathers.

TABLE 2.3

SUMMARY OF SPECIFICATIONS FOR STANDARDS OF QUALITY FOR INDIVIDUAL CARCASSES OF READY-TO-COOK POULTRY AND PARTS THEREFROM

(Minimum Requirements and Maximum Defects Permitted)   SEPTEMBER 1, 1965

Factor	A Quality	B Quality	C Quality
Conformation Breastbone	Normal Slight curve or dent	Moderate deformities Moderately dented, curved or crooked	Abnormal Seriously curved or crooked
Back	Normal (except slight curve)	Moderately crooked	Seriously crooked
Legs and Wings	Normal	Moderately misshapen	Misshapen
Fleshing	Well fleshed, moderately long, deep and rounded breast	Moderately fleshed, considering kind, class and part	Poorly fleshed
Fat covering	Well covered—especially between heavy feather tracts on breast and considering kind, class and part	Sufficient fat on breast and legs to prevent distinct appearance of flesh through the skin	Lacking in fat covering over all parts of carcass
Pinfeathers Nonprotruding pins and hair	Free	Few scattered	Scattering
Protruding pins	Free	Free	Free

Exposed flesh[1]

Carcass Weight		A Quality		B Quality		C Quality
Minimum	Maximum	Breast and Legs	Elsewhere	Breast and Legs[2]	Elsewhere[2]	
None	1½ lbs.	None	3/4"	3/4"	1½"	No Limit
Over 1½ lbs.	6 lbs.	None	1½"	1½"	3"	
Over 6 lbs.	16 lbs.	None	2"	2"	4"	
Over 16 lbs.	None	None	3"	3"	5"	
		Part (Slight trim on edge)		*Part (Moderate amount of the flesh normally covered)*		

	Weight	A Quality	B Quality	C Quality
Discolorations[3]				
None	1½ lbs.	½" 1"	¼" 1"	2" ½"
Over 1½ lbs.	6 lbs.	1" 2"	¼" 2"	3" 1"
Over 6 lbs.	16 lbs.	1½" 2½"	½" 2½"	4" 1½"
Over 16 lbs.	None	2" 3"	½" 3"	5" No Limit[4]
Disjointed bones		1	2 disjointed and no broken or 1 disjointed and 1 nonprotruding broken	No limit
Broken bones		None		No limit
Missing parts		Wing tips and tail[5]	Wing tips, 2nd wing joint and tail	Wing tips, wings and tail
Freezing defects (When consumer packaged)		Slight darkening over the back and drumsticks. Few small ⅛" pockmarks for poultry weighing 6 lbs. or less and ¼" pockmarks for poultry weighing more than 6 lbs. Occasional small areas showing layer of clear or pinkish ice.	Moderate dried areas not in excess of ½" in diameter. May lack brightness. Moderate areas showing layer of clear, pinkish or reddish colored ice.	Numerous pockmarks and large dried areas.

From U.S. Dept. Agr. Handbook 31 (1972).

[1] Total aggregate area of flesh exposed by all cuts and tears and missing skin.

[2] A carcass meeting the requirements of A quality for fleshing may be trimmed to remove skin and flesh defects, provided that no more than one-third of the flesh is exposed on any part and the meat yield is not appreciably affected.

[3] Flesh bruises and discolorations such as "blue back" (when permitted), are not permitted on breast and legs of A quality birds. Not more than one-half of total aggregate area of discolorations may be due to flesh bruises or "blue back" (when permitted), and skin bruises in any combination.

[4] No limit on size and number of areas of discoloration and flesh bruises if such areas do not render any part of the carcass unfit for food.

[5] In geese, the parts of the wing beyond the second joint may be removed, if removed at the joint and both wings are so treated.

TABLE 2.4

SUMMARY OF SPECIFICATIONS FOR STANDARDS OF QUALITY FOR INDIVIDUAL CARCASSES OF READY-TO-COOK TURKEYS AND GEESE

(Minimum requirements and maximum defects permitted)

Factor	A Quality	B Quality	C Quality
Conformation	Normal	Practically normal	Abnormal
Breastbone	Slight curve or dent	Dented, curved, slightly crooked	Seriously crooked
Back	Normal (except a slight curve)	Moderately crooked	Seriously crooked
Legs and wings	Normal	Moderately misshapen	Misshapen
Fleshing	Well fleshed, moderately long and rounded breast	Fairly well fleshed on breast and legs	Poorly fleshed
Fat covering	Well covered considering class	Sufficient fat on breast and legs to prevent a distinct appearance of flesh through skin	Lacking in fat covering over all parts of carcass
Pinfeathers	*Breast and legs* / *Elsewhere*	*Breast and legs* / *Elsewhere*	
Non-protruding pins and hair	Pract. free / Pract. free	Few scattered / Few scattered	Scattering
Protruding pins	Free / Free	Free / Free	Free
Cuts, tears, and missing skin[1]	Free / 3 in.	3 in. / 6 in.	No limit
Discolorations[2]	2 in. / 3 in.	3 in. / 6 in.	No limit[3]
Disjointed bones	1	1 or 2, if no broken bones	No limit
Broken bones	None	1 Non-protruding	No limit
Missing parts	Wing tips and tail	Wing tips, 2nd wing joint, and tail	Wing tips, wings and tail
Freezer burn	Few small ($^1/_4$ in. diam.) pockmarks	Moderate-dried areas not in excess of $^1/_2$ in. in diameter	Numerous pockmarks and large dried areas

From U.S. Dept. Agr. Agr. Handbook 31, (1972).

[1] Total aggregate area of flesh exposed by all cuts, tears, and missing skin.

[2] Flesh bruises and discolorations such as "blue back" not permitted on breast and legs of A Quality birds. Not more than one-half of total aggregate area of discoloration may be due to flesh bruises or "blue back" (when permitted), and skin bruises in any combination.

[3] No limit on size and number of areas of discoloration and flesh bruises if such areas do not render any part of the carcass unfit for food.

Defects.—The presence or absence of such defects as cuts, tears, broken bones, skin discoloration, flesh blemishes, bruises, abrasions, and freezer burn all influence the grade placed on a carcass, generally depending upon the severity of the defect and its location on the carcass.

Freezer burn is a discoloration and pock marking of the skin caused by dehydration of the skin during frozen storage.

POULTRY INSPECTION

The Poultry Products Inspection Act is "an Act of Congress which requires mandatory inspection by the U.S. Department of Agriculture of poultry and poultry products which move in interstate or foreign commerce or in designated major consuming areas." The Act is administered under the Meat and Poultry Inspection Program Animal and Plant Health Inspection Service. Inspection consists of "inspecting each bird processed to determine its wholesomeness and fitness for food, maintenance of prescribed sanitary standards, and supervision of the preparation and processing, labeling and packaging of poultry products packed at the official establishment" (Fig. 2.2).

The Federal Food, Drug and Cosmetic Act

In addition to compliance with the Poultry Products Inspection Act poultry are also under the jurisdiction of the Federal Food, Drug and Cosmetic Act after the product leaves the plant. The provisions of this Act are designed to prevent the sale of adulterated food including poultry. With the passage of the Poultry Products Inspection Act most inspection of poultry in the processing plant was taken over by the inspection service rather than the Food and Drug Administration.

Evidence of Disease.—Poultry is considered diseased if disease organisms or toxins dangerous to the consumer are present or the poultry contains morbid tissue caused by inflammation, degeneration or neoplasia or the animal shows evidence of a general systemic disturbance such as fever.

Sick birds should be condemned if possible before slaughter to prevent contamination of scald and chill water, processing equipment, and other carcasses. Evisceration and post-mortem inspection should follow immediately after slaughter and defeathering to prevent conditions which would prevent correlation of ante- and post-mortem findings, bring about conditions for contaminating healthy carcasses, and to prevent changes in the appearance or consistency of organs.

Ante-Mortem Inspection.—In processing plants having federal inspection, poultry arriving at a processing plant are inspected by lots before slaughter. The inspector observes the birds in the coops or batteries and separates them into four general categories according to their condition.

Birds in a dying condition which constitute the first category and those affected by disease to the point where they would be condemned on post-mortem inspection, the second classification, are condemned and destroyed without processing. The third group consists of those birds which show conditions which make them suspects for possible condemnation upon post-mortem inspection. Such birds are processed separately from healthy carcasses and receive special detailed inspection. The fourth group consists of those birds affected with or suspected of having a disease contagious to humans. After ante-mortem inspection all such live birds can be removed from the plant.

According to the U.S. Dept. of Agr. Meat and Poultry Inspection Manual (Anon. 1973) birds with any of the following conditions are considered as suspects: (a) dirty ruffled feathers; (b) swellings about the head and eyes or discharges from eyes and/or nostrils; (c) edema of the wattles; (d) lack of alertness or brightness of eyes, i.e., not showing normal prominence or luster, or the eyes may be off-shape or off-color such as showing cloudy cornea or pupil; (e) gaping or sneezing; (f) off-color diarrhea and/or collection of unusual amounts of fecal material on feathers about the vent; (g) skin lesions about the head and neck; (h) suppurating sores or visible swelling on body surfaces; (i) pinched appearing dehydrated shanks and those cold to the touch; (j) birds that are markedly lacking in flesh (referred to as "going light"); (k) birds that show lack of thrift and well-being by their posture and reluctance to move in response to normal stimuli; (l) birds which show central nerve disorders such as "wry neck" or lack of other muscular coordination in movement; (m) lameness; (n) birds which emit abnormal sickly squawks or sounds when disturbed or handled; (o) enlarged bones; (p) birds showing ascites.

According to the manual on Poultry Hygiene for Examination and Evaluation of Poultry and Poultry Products, published by the U.S. Department of Health, Education, and Welfare (1959), condemnation of live birds is recommended when the following conditions occur: (a) the bird is down, unable to stand; (b) a doughy feeling of the skin and flesh; (c) partial paralysis; convulsive movements, nervous disturbances; (d) greatly distended abdomen containing fluid; (e) unkept appearance, droopy or drowsy, with abnormally reddish purple or pale comb; (f) "droopy appearance and swollen or engorged, erect snood (turkeys)"; (g) emaciation; extreme thinness; extreme weakness; (h) difficult respiration accompanied by gasping, gurgling, shrill noises, by expulsion of blood; or by a discharge from the mouth, nostrils, or eyes; or by inflamed, swollen eyes; or by greatly swollen or discharging sinuses of the head; (i) extensive, numerous or repulsive scabs, nodules, blisters, open wounds, ulcers, abscesses, or multiple inflamed areas of skin or of underlying tissues; (*j*) multiple growths (tumors); (*k*) marked enlargement of the bones of the wings and legs.

Post-Mortem Inspection.—Carcasses receiving post-mortem inspection by the U.S. Department of Agriculture inspection service have the external surfaces, internal surfaces, and the visceral organs visually examined and the liver and spleen palpated. Carcasses then receive one of four dispositions. The carcass is passed as wholesome, affected visceral organs are discarded, the whole carcass is declared unwholesome and condemned, or dressing defects, severely damaged parts and nonmalignant tumors are trimmed from the carcass.

According to the manual on Poultry Hygiene for Examination and Evaluation of Poultry and Poultry Products published by the U.S. Department of Health, Education, and Welfare (Anon. 1959) it is recommended that carcasses with the following conditions be subject to condemnation: (*a*) yellow semisolid or solid accumulations of pus, fluid containing flaky substance, or slimy or stinking matter on the viscera, or in the body cavity of the crop; (*b*) numerous, extensive or repulsive growths inside the carcass; (*c*) emaciation, as evidenced by extreme thinness and little or no fat on the heart crown; (*d*) inflamed, abnormally red appearance of the lining of the body cavity and of the intestines; (*e*) marked engorgement of mesenteric veins with blood, indicating death other than by slaughter; (*f*) pronounced thickening of the lining of the body cavity or the walls of the intestines, or extensive adhesions (matting together) of the viscera and the lining of the body cavity.

Specific body organs also have evidences of disease processes which are cause for condemnation of the affected tissues.

BIBLIOGRAPHY

Anon. 1955. Federal Food, Drug, and Cosmetic Act and general regulations for its enforcement. U.S. Dept. Health, Education, Welfare.

Anon. 1957A. Poultry buying specifications for institutions. U.S. Dept. Agr., Agr. Marketing Serv. Leaflet.

Anon. 1957B. An Act to provide for the Compulsory Inspection by the United States Department of Agriculture of Poultry and Poultry Products. Public Law 85-172, 85th U.S. Congress.

Anon. 1959. Poultry hygiene. Part 1. Examination and evaluation of poultry and poultry products. U.S. Public Health Serv. Admin. Publ. 683.

Anon. 1961. Regulations governing the inspection of poultry and poultry products. U.S. Dept. Agr., Agr. Marketing Serv., Poultry Div.

Anon. 1973. Meat and Poultry Inspection Manual. U.S. Dept. Agr., Meat and Poultry Inspection Program, Animal and Plant Health Inspection Service.

Coles, J. V. 1951. Research in the improvement of standards and grades. *In* Market Demand and Product Quality. Mktg. Res. Workshop Rept. Mich. State Coll.

JOHNDREW, O. F., JR., HAUVER, W. E., JR., and KILPATRICK, L. 1972. Poultry
    Grading Manual. U.S. Dept. Agr. Marketing Serv., Poultry Div. Agr.
    Handbook 31.
KILPATRICK, L., and POND, T. H. 1958. Poultry grading and inspection. U.S.
    Dept. Agr., Agr. Mktg. Serv. Agr. Inform. Bull. 173.
KRAMER, A. 1951. What is quality and how it can be measured: From a
    food technology point of view. In Market Demand and Product Quality.
    Mktg. Res. Workshop Rept. Mich. State Coll.
McCALLISTER, K. J. 1951. Principles and practices in the development of
    standards for grades for agricultural products. In Market Demand and
    Product Quality. Mktg. Res. Workshop Rept., Mich. State Coll.

CHAPTER 3

Quality Maintenance

INTRODUCTION

Although the area of poultry technology is limited to the processing and handling of poultry after it leaves the farm, many factors influencing quality have already occurred before the birds are loaded for market. For this reason factors which influence quality during production are discussed as well as those occurring during marketing.

PRODUCTION FACTORS

With the initiation of compulsory inspection, many producers and processors found to their dismay that a new cost for handling and processing poultry had been added, that of condemnations. The majority of condemnations are largely results of pathological conditions, which in turn are influenced to a great extent by management practices. Schmittle (1961) reported that management practices are related to high condemnation rates and that a combination of poor management and adverse weather conditions leads to even higher condemnations.

Housing

Because temperature, humidity, and air movement are interrelated it is difficult to determine the effects of a specific variable on the quality of carcasses produced. The field of environmental physiology is one where considerably more information is needed. Abnormally high or low temperatures and humidity or rapid changes in temperature or humidity cause stresses on live broilers which make them less resistant to disease. Such extremes of temperature and humidity also set up other conditions within a poultry house which cause further stress situations.

Broilers and turkeys are housed to prevent abnormally high or low temperatures and to reduce wide fluctuations in temperature. A room temperature between 60° and 70°F. is generally considered the most desirable for poultry.

Ventilation.—Air movement helps to control the temperature and humidity inside poultry houses by removing heat and moisture from the house. Ventilation also helps to remove dust and fumes such as carbon dioxide, carbon monoxide, and ammonia. More information is needed on the effects of temperature, humidity, and the rate and amount of ventilation on the comfort of turkeys and broilers and on the role of air in the transmission of disease.

Clark *et al.* (1961) in a study of 53 Georgia broiler flocks reported that the following housing conditions were found to be correlated with high condemnations: inadequate ridge ventilators, houses longer than 150 ft., over 35 ft. wide, and houses located in low areas. Cover (1961) reported that in the Delmarva area condemnations were lower in narrow houses than wide ones and in houses having solid partitions between pens. These same conditions are also correlated with air movement and ventilation.

Insulation.—Insulation prevents the loss of warm air in winter and cool air in summer and helps to prevent wide fluctuations in temperature. Because the amount of moisture retained by air under a given set of conditions is influenced considerably by temperature, insulation helps to keep the inside of a poultry house dry. As a result of the insulation the air is warmer and retains more moisture than cold air which causes moisture to condense inside the house.

Litter.—Litter absorbs moisture when conditions in a poultry house are damp and releases it during dry periods. It also absorbs some gases and releases them when damp conditions occur and provides a good medium for the protection and growth of pathogenic organisms, especially when damp. Litter is a source of dust and irritation for growing birds when it becomes too dry; when too wet it is cold, damp and uncomfortable and adds an additional stress. Coarse, damp litter is also one cause of breast blisters in growing birds.

Disease Control

Condemnations because of disease cause the greatest loss of carcasses during inspection. In several surveys it was observed that those flocks with high condemnation rates did not have a satisfactory disease control program. Particular problems were lack of mortality records, houses not disinfected, high mortality during the first week, a disease outbreak during the fifth week, or a flock sick two weeks or longer. Other conditions found in flocks with high condemnation rates were the type coccidiostat used and early discontinuance of the coccidiostat, the combination of vaccines used, severe vaccine reactions, moderate to severe infestations of round worms and a persistance of disease symptoms up to the time of slaughter.

Schmittle (1961) reported that "respiratory diseases are the most important factor related to broiler condemnations."

Other Management Factors

On the basis of studies by Schmittle (1961) and Edgar *et al.* (1961) the following factors were also correlated with high condemnation rates: new, inexperienced growers; houses not prepared for chicks; houses not disinfected or not left vacant more than a week; chicks overcrowded under brooders; chicks started at 90°F. instead of 95°F.; and lack of heat during illness. Only three management practices related to feeding were observed. These were dirty feed bins, feeding chickens only once or twice daily, and poor feed conversion which is probably the combined result of disease outbreaks and other poor management conditions.

Wenger (1963) reported that with turkeys, clipping poults' wings at hatching time frequently caused infection of the joint to the point where the second joint of the wing also had to be removed at processing time and caused the grade of the carcasses to be lowered to B.

Breast blisters are frequently a cause of low grade carcasses. Koonz (1965) reported that selection, care and depth of litter, weight of birds at market time, control of disease, ventilation and other management factors all influence keel blister formation. Helbacka (1962) indicated that a considerable number of breast blisters may occur during transportation.

Insects such as lice, mites, ticks, and other insects can under certain conditions cause considerable damage to poultry by forming sores and lesions.

"Blue back" is a condition found on dark feathered varieties of turkeys. It is caused by broken pinfeathers and exposure to sunlight. These two conditions cause patches or blotches of blue pigment under the skin. Although it occurs mainly on the breast it can occur on any part of the skin. Harper et al. (1964) reported that a genetic condition different from "blue back" can also cause formation of melanin pigment in turkeys to the extent that the carcasses are downgraded.

MARKETING FACTORS

Loss in quality in market channels can be caused by handling live birds during the procurement operation, damage to the carcass during processing, and loss of quality because of poor or prolonged storage conditions. Although losses in quality during marketing generally do not result in condemnation of a whole carcass the monetary loss caused by a reduction in yield and grade are considerable.

Handling

Birds although small in size are awkward to handle because they are of an odd shape and they struggle and spread their wings when held by the feet. To prevent the escape of birds previously placed in crates, the crate opening is just slightly larger than the minimum size which is needed to allow entrance of the birds. Injury to a bird can result from careless handling of either individual birds or crates of birds.

Shrinkage

Shrinkage is the loss in weight of live poultry between the time it is picked up at the farm and delivered to the processing plant. King and Zwick (1950) reported that the following factors influence shrinkage: The time in transit from loading to market, the ration fed, the sex (males lose more weight than females), and changes in temperature and humidity. As the length of time from loading increases the shrinkage also increases but at a decreasing rate. The decreasing rate can probably be explained by the fact that birds generally struggle and excrete when picked up but relax as soon as they are placed in a crate. Birds fed on high fiber rations show the greatest shrinkage. High temperatures also increase the amount of weight lost; high humidity reduces it.

Simmons (1952) was unable to determine any relation between humidity and shrinkage but did find that increases in temperature cause an increase in shrink. Crowding in coops also appears to influence weight loss. In the same study, as the weight per coop increased from 45–49 lb. to 58–68 lb. shrinkage increased from 3.5 to 5.0%. The effects of time and distance on the weight losses of broilers are shown in Table 3.1.

TABLE 3.1

THE EFFECT OF TIME AND DISTANCE ON WEIGHT LOSSES OF BROILERS

Hours	Weight Loss,[1] %	Miles	Weight Loss,[2] %
2	1.1	1–25	1.1
6	2.9	26–50	1.1
10	3.7	51 and over	1.5
14	4.2	Average	1.3
18	4.6		

[1] Estimates by King and Zwick (1950).
[2] Data from Jewett (1960).

Bruises

Hood et al. (1955) in a study of broilers in marketing channels in Georgia reported that bruises were second only to fleshing as a defect and were responsible for over 11% of all broilers downgraded from A. Cox and May (1964) in a later study of broilers in marketing channels in Georgia reported that roughly 19% of all broilers had bruises and of this group 30–40% had bruises of sufficient size to cause a lowering of the grade of the carcass. Of the total bruised birds 11.6% were on the breasts and 7.5% on the legs. Jewett and Saunders (1960) in a study of 11 lots of Maine broilers reported that flesh bruises were responsible for 56% of all undergrades, with bruises on the breast the most common type of injury.

To reduce bruising, they recommended removal of feeders and waterers before catching, more care in catching birds, and more supervision in assembling broilers. Bruising was reduced 36% by slaughtering birds direct from the crates rather than transferring them to batteries. Kaiser and Smith (1958) estimated that 6.75% of Delaware broilers are downgraded because of bruising. Flocks with a large proportion of poorly fleshed birds tended to have fewer bruises than flocks with a higher proportion of well fleshed birds. Some breeds of chickens were found to bruise easier than others.

Hamdy *et al.* (1961A) reported that a sudden lowering of the environmental temperature reduced the susceptibility of birds to bruising and decreased the rate at which bruises healed. On the other hand, birds raised at high environmental temperatures bruised easily but the bruises healed quickly. Bruises on young birds healed faster than those on old birds.

Mountney *et al.* (1954) in a study of the market quality of Texas turkeys reported that bruises cause the greatest loss of quality during the marketing operation and that about eight per cent more hens than toms were downgraded because of bruises. Bruises were responsible for almost 23% of all undergrades.

As bruised tissue ages the blood oxidizes and the bruised area darkens in color from red to dark red or purple then to green or yellow. In carcasses the bruises change to dark red or purple. McCarthy *et al.* (1962) reported that bruised tissue has a greater permeability to penetration of dye and microorganisms than normal tissue. They observed that 61–74% of the bruises examined contained both aerobic and anaerobic bacteria. The age of the bruise, environmental conditions, particularly sanitation, the severity of the bruise, and the hemoglobin and its degradation products all had some influence on the microbial content. Hamdy *et al.* (1961B) reported that bruises which were injected daily with two milligrams of sodium ascorbate healed faster than those on non-treated birds.

Broken Bones

Broken bones are caused by rough handling during assembly or processing. If bones are broken while the bird is still alive a bruised area results. Broken bones are the third most important factor in causing downgrading of eviscerated carcasses (Hood *et al.* 1955). From samples taken from 24 processing plants, a breakdown of defects resulting in downgrading penalties is shown in Fig. 3.1.

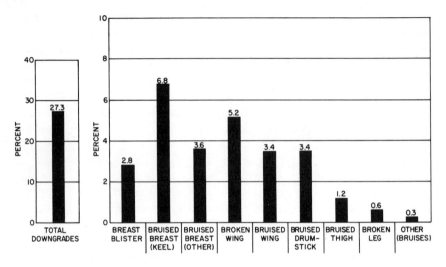

Courtesy U.S. Dept. Agr.

FIG. 3.1. PERCENTAGE OF TOTAL DEFECTS THAT RESULTED IN DOWNGRADING PENALTIES FOR 2400 SAMPLES (100 BIRDS EACH) IN 24 PLANTS, AND BREAKDOWN OF DEFECTS BY TYPE AND LOCATION

PROCESSING

Several conditions which result in grade losses or condemnations also occur as a result of processing.

Tears

Tears are often caused by birds crowding on top of each other or during processing. Poorly feathered birds are subject to more tears and scratches than well-feathered ones. Old injuries on turkeys from fighting or mating are an important cause of tears. The carcasses are either torn by pickers during dressing or trimmed by the inspector upon processing with resultant B or C grade carcasses.

Poor Bleeding

Improper slaughtering can cause incomplete bleeding and prolonged breathing so that the bird inhales water from the scalding tank. Such birds are considered contaminated and are subject to condemnation. Benjamin *et al.* (1960) reported that poorly bled carcasses have poor keeping quality, undesirable flavors and an unappetizing appearance. Such carcasses have red areas over the neck, shoulders, wings and feather follicles which discolor on storage and visceral blood vessels which are greatly engorged.

Rough handling causes an increase in excitement, temperature, and nervous tension (Reynolds *et al.* 1953). Birds in this condition do not bleed as rapidly or thoroughly as they should, scalding is not as effective, and feather removal is difficult. The final results of rough handling are an increase in processing costs and undergrades.

Overscalding

This condition generally results from stopping the conveyor line when carcasses are moving through the scalder. Such carcasses, as a result of being immersed in hot water for a prolonged period, are partially cooked and may be contaminated. The tissues of such carcasses cannot be properly cleaned and are susceptible to bacterial growth, decomposition, and deterioration. Overscalded carcasses are condemned.

Disfigurement

Occasionally a carcass has a bad tear opened by rubber picker fingers to the extent that the skin is torn off and the flesh is macerated. A similar condition sometimes occurs when the line stops and birds are left hanging in a picker with the fingers revolving.

Contamination

Sources for contamination are numerous. A common occurrence is the contamination of a carcass by oil or grease rubbed in the carcass and spread by picker fingers. Disposition of such carcasses depends upon the type and extent of contamination. Common contaminants are paint, grease, manure, and solvents. Carcasses contaminated with volatile oils and poisons are condemned.

STORAGE

The results of improper or prolonged storage can range from slight off-flavors to decomposed carcasses.

Freezer Burn

Cook and White (1939A) define freezer burn as "the development of lighter colored circular spots around feather follicles and discolored areas of irregular shape on the surface of the skin surface." Light colored spots are caused by uneven surface drying which depends upon temperature, relative humidity, air circulation, and the rate of movement of moisture from the interior of the product to the evaporating surface. Since most of the moisture in frozen products is in a solid state, little if any moisture moves to the surface to replace that lost by surface evaporation. It is believed that uneven desiccation of the skin occurs because of the layer of fat immediately under the skin.

Feather removal causes uneven desiccation to take place around the feather follicles. Loss of flavor, tenderness, and juiciness are the results of extreme freezer burn. Dried out meat becomes tough and hard to cook. Cook and White (1939A) also reported that "Severely freezer-burned muscle tissue contains only 50–55% moisture, whereas normal tissues contain about 72%." They stated that "the best way to reduce freezer burn was to store poultry wrapped in moisture vapor-proof paper at a low temperature and high humidity." Variations in below freezing temperatures are also reported to cause freezer burn.

Rancidity

Fresh, pure poultry fat is almost odorless, and tasteless. Cook and White (1939B) reported that "The free fatty acid content of poultry fat after storage varies somewhat between birds, but is usually low, and shows no relation to the storage condition at freezing temperatures. The storage temperature is the most important factor determining the extent of perox-ide-oxygen formation in poultry fat, the amount increasing with increase in storage temperature." Turkey fat is considerably more unstable than chicken fat.

Off-Flavors

Off-flavors can be caused by decomposition, rancidity, contamination, feed, and absorption of odors during storage.

Pink Meat in Cooked Poultry

Snyder and Orr (1964) described a condition in which the meat, especially white meat, turned pink after thorough cooking. Generally the color extends to a depth of about one-fourth inch and is found most often in young birds. The color is caused by a chemical reaction between carbon monoxide and nitric oxide, which are generated by the cooking flame, and the hemoglobin of the blood in the muscle tissue. Carboxy-hemoglobin and nitric oxide hemoglobin are formed. The pink color does not influence the edibility or palatability of the meat.

BIBLIOGRAPHY

BENJAMIN, E. W., GWIN, J. M., FABER, F. L., and TERMOHLEN, W. D. 1960. Marketing Poultry Products. John Wiley & Sons, New York.

CLARK, W. E., KIMSEY, J., MORRIS, D., and SCHMITTLE, S. C. 1961. Field study of broiler condemnation losses. Georgia Agr. Expt. Sta. Mimeo Ser. N.S. 119.

COOK, W. H., and WHITE, W. H. 1939A. Frozen storage of poultry. I. Freezer burn. Food Res. 4, 407–418.

COOK, W. H., and WHITE, W. H. 1939B. Frozen storage poultry. III. Peroxide oxygen and free fatty acid formation. Food Res. *4*, 433–440.

COVER, M. S. 1961. Survey of poultry condemnation. Symposium on Disease, Environmental, Management Factors Related to Poultry Health. Agr. Res. Serv., U.S. Dept. Agr. and Univ. Georgia.

COX, C. J., and MAY, K. N. 1964. Factors affecting bruising of commercial broilers. Georgia Agr. Expt. Sta. Tech. Bull. *N.S. 35*.

EDGAR, S. A., BREWER, R. N., MORA, E. C., and PRUETT, J. 1961. A preliminary report of activities in Alabama toward reducing losses from condemnation, particularly among broilers. Symposium on Disease, Environmental, Management Factors Related to Poultry Health. Agr. Res. Serv., U.S. Dept. Agr. and Univ. Georgia.

HAMDY, M. K., MAY, K. N., and POWERS, J. J. 1961A. Some physical and physiological factors affecting poultry bruises. Poultry Sci. *40*, 790–795.

HAMDY, M. K., MAY, K. N., POWERS, J. J., and PRATT, D. E. 1961B. Effect of ascorbate on healing of poultry bruises. Proc. Soc. Exptl. Biol. Med. *108*, 189.

HARPER, J. A., BERNIER, P. E., and BABCOCK, W. E. 1964. Skin melanization in turkeys. Poultry Sci. *43*, 577–583.

HELBACKA, N. V. 1962. Studies on bruising and breast blisters. Feedstuffs *34*, No. 21, 66–68.

HOOD, M. P., ROWAN, W. S., THOMPSON, D. W., and MIZE, J. J. 1955. Graded broilers in marketing channels in Georgia. Georgia Agr. Expt. Sta. Bull. *N.S. 7*.

JEWETT, L. J. 1960. Handling and processing broilers in Maine. Part 1. Cost and efficiencies in assembling live broilers for processing. Maine Agr. Expt. Sta. Bull. *592*.

JEWETT, L. J., and SAUNDERS, R. F. 1960. Handling and processing broilers in Maine. Part II. Quality losses in live broilers and methods of handling to reduce bruising and to improve efficiency. Maine Agr. Expt. Sta. Bull. *593*.

KAISER, W. K., and SMITH, R. C. 1958. Factors affecting the bruising of broilers. Delaware Agr. Expt. Sta. Tech. Bull. *323*.

KING, R. A., and ZWICK, C. J. 1950. Shrinkage of live poultry between farm and market. Conn. Agr. Expt. Sta. Bull. *270*.

KOHLS, R. L., and WALZ, T. C. 1952. Broiler trucker-buyers in Indiana. Purdue Univ. Agr. Expt. Sta. Bull. *580*.

KOONZ, C. H. 1965. Effect of processing factors on quality of poultry. *In* Food Quality. G. W. Irving and S. R. Hoover (Editors). American Association for the Advancement of Science, Publ. 77.

LONGHOUSE, A. D., and GARVER, H. L. Poultry environments. J. ASHRAE *6*, No. 7, 68–74.

McCARTHY, P. A., BROWN, W. B., and HAMDY, M. K. 1962. Microbiological studies of bruised tissues. Food Sci. *28*, 245–253.

MOUNTNEY, G. J., PARNELL, E. D., and HALPIN, R. B. 1954. Factors influencing the prices received for Texas turkeys. Texas Agr. Expt. Sta. Bull. *777*.

POMEROY, B. S. 1965. Protection of poultry product quality through preventative health measures. *In* Food Quality. G. W. Irving, and S. R. Hoover (Editors). American Association for the Advancement of Science, Publ. 77.

REYNOLDS, H. J., JOHNSON, G. W., ZEBARTH, R., and NICHOLS, W. 1953. Poultry

Processing Practices.   Gordon Johnson Co., Kansas City.

SCHMITTLE, S. C.   1961.   Field studies of broiler condemnation losses in Georgia.   Symposium on Disease, Environmental, Management Factors Related to Poultry Health.   Agr. Res. Serv., U.S. Dept. Agr.

SHACKELFORD, A. D., CHILDS, R. E., and HAMANN, J. A.   1969.   Determination of bruises on broilers before and after handling by live bird pickup crews. U.S. Dept. Agr. ARS, 52–47.

SIMMONS, W. M.   1952.   Shrinkage in shipment of live chickens.   In Farm Economics.   Agr. Econ. Dept., Cornell Univ.

SNYDER, E. S., and ORR, H. L.   1964.   Poultry meat-processing, quality factors, yields.   Ontario Agr. Dept. Publ. 9.

STADELMAN, W. J.   1965.   Genetic and environmental factors influencing eggs and poultry meat.   In Food Quality.   G. W. Irving, and S. R. Hoover (Editors). American Association for the Advancement of Science, Publ. 77.

WENGER, R. D.   1963.   Clipping poult wings.   Agr. Mktg. 8, No. 2, 3.

CHAPTER 4

Chemical and
Nutritive Characteristics

INTRODUCTION

Poultry meat is economical, quick and easy to prepare and serve and has a number of desirable nutritional and organoleptic properties (Table 4.1). Meat from poultry contains several important classes of nutrients, is low in calories, is a source of both saturated and unsaturated fatty acids, the fat contains essential fatty acids and the proteins are a good source of essential amino acids. The meat fibers are tender, easy to chew or grind, easy to digest and the flavor is mild and blends well with seasonings and other foods.

COMPOSITION OF POULTRY MEAT

Moisture Content

According to the U.S. Department of Agriculture, the edible portion of chicken broilers contains about 71% moisture; roasters, 66%; hens, 56%; and medium fat turkeys about 58%. Carcasses from young birds have a higher proportion of moisture to tissue than old ones.

Calories

Poultry meat is low in calories in relation to other nutrients present. For this reason, poultry is a good foodstuff for weight control diets, convalescents, and old people who are not physically active. By eating poultry meat as the source of proteins in a diet it is possible to reduce caloric intake, but at the same time help keep other nutrient requirements in proper balance. Broilers contain 151 calories per 100 gm. of meat, roasters 200, hens 302, and medium fat turkeys, 268 calories.

Proteins

Not only is poultry meat a good source of protein but it contains more proteins than red meats (Table 4.2). Scott (1956) reported that cooked poultry meat, excluding edible viscera, contains from 25–35% protein, depending upon the part of the carcass and the method of preparation. Beef contains 21–27%, pork 23–24% and lamb 21–24%.

Poultry meat contains high quality protein. It is easy to digest and contains all the essential amino acids presently known to be required in human diets. Scott (1959) reported that the amino acid composition of

TABLE 4.1

COMPARISON OF NUTRIENT COMPOSITION OF COOKED MEATS AND EGGS

Meat	Protein, %	Fat, %	Moisture, %	Food Energy Calories per Lb.	Riboflavin (B_2) % of Daily Needs For Avg. Adult Found in 1 Lb.
Turkey (roasted)					
White meat	34.3	7.5	58	923	15
Dark meat	30.5	11.6	57	1022	33
Chicken (roasted)					
White meat	31.5	1.3	68	621	11
Dark meat	25.4	7.3	67	754	22
Beef (cooked)					
Round steak	27.0	13.0	59	1049	8
Porterhouse Steak	23.0	27.0	49	1539	7
Rump roast	21.0	32.0	46	1701	6
Hamburger	22.0	30.0	47	1648	7
Pork (cooked)					
Ham	24.0	33.0	42	1800	9
Loin chops	23.0	26.0	50	1499	9
Lamb (cooked)					
Rib chops	24.0	35.0	40	1871	10
Shoulder roast	21.0	28.0	50	1539	8
Eggs (boiled) 8 = 1 lb.	13.4	10.5	74	648	56

Compiled from data of Scott (1956) and Poultry and Egg National Board by Chick Master Incubator Co. Ancn. (1958).

TABLE 4.2

COMPARISON OF AMINO ACID COMPOSITION OF VARIOUS ANIMAL FOODS
(Percentage of protein)

Amino Acid	Turkey[1]	Chicken	Beef	Pork	Milk	Eggs
Arginine	6.5	6.7	6.4	6.7	4.3	6.4
Cystine	1.0	1.8	1.3	0.9	1.0	2.4
Histidine	3.0	2.0	3.3	2.6	2.6	2.1
Isoleucine	5.0	4.1	5.2	3.8	8.5	8.0
Leucine	7.6	6.6	7.8	6.?	11.3	9.2
Lysine	9.0	7.5	8.6	8.0	7.5	7.2
Methionine	2.6	1.8	2.7	1.7	3.4	4.1
Phenylalanine	3.7	4.0	3.9	3.6	5.7	6.3
Threonine	4.0	4.0	4.5	3.6	4.5	4.9
Tryptophan	0.9	0.8	1.0	0.7	1.6	1.5
Tyrosine	1.5	2.5	3.0	2.5	5.3	4.5
Valine	5.1	6.7	5.1	5.5	8.4	7.3

[1] Average values for whole turkey (breast and leg). Scott (1959).

turkey is similar to chicken, beef, and pork. Since poultry contains a higher proportion of proteins than other meats, it also contains more amino acids.

Lipids

The fat content of poultry carcasses varies according to the age, sex, and species of poultry (Table 4.3). The part of the carcass from

TABLE 4.3

FATTY ACID COMPOSITION OF DIFFERENT SPECIES OF POULTRY

Species	No. of Lots	Iodine No.	Saturated Acids, %	Oleic Acid, %	Linoleic Acid, %	Linolenic Acid, %	Arachidonic Acid, %
Chicken	4	63–80	28–31	47–51	14–18	0.7–1.0	0.3–0.5
Turkey	6	73–79	28–33	39–51	13–21	0.8–1.3	0.2–0.7
Duck	1	87	27	42	24	1.4	0.20
Goose	1	67	30	57	8	0.4	0.05
Pigeon	1	82	23	56	17	0.7	0.04

From Mecchi et al. (1956).

which the fat is taken also influences the fat content considerably. Scott (1956) reported that cooked turkey skin contains 33.8% fat whereas the breast meat contains only 6.7–8.3%. Unlike red meats, most fat in poultry meat is found under the skin rather than distributed throughout the tissues. Cooked chicken breast meat contains only 1.3% fat; veal cutlets, 11%; beef cuts from 13–30%.

There is increasing evidence that not only the amount of fat in a diet but also the type of fat is important. One measure of the degree of saturation or unsaturation is the iodine number. Low iodine values indicate saturated fats, high ones unsaturated. Poultry meats contain a higher proportion of unsaturated fatty acids than the fats from red meats, but less than fats or oils of vegetable origin.

Poultry meats also contain less cholesterol, a fatty alcohol present in the arteries and veins of individuals suffering with atherosclerosis, than other foods of animal origin.

Vitamins

Bird (1943) reported that poultry meat is a good source of niacin and a moderately good source of riboflavin, thiamin, and ascorbic acid. Uncooked chicken livers contain 32,500 I.U. of vitamin A, 0.20 mg. of thiamin, 2.46 mg. of riboflavin, 11.8 mg. of niacin, and 20 mg. of ascorbic acid. Other edible parts of the carcass contain thiamin, riboflavin, and niacin, but in smaller quantities than found in liver.

POULTRY PRODUCTS NUTRITION LABELING

The Poultry and Egg Industry of America summarized the status of nutritional labeling as of January 1974.

USDA published regulations governing nutrition labeling of poultry in the Federal Register January 11, 1974. Nutrition labeling for poultry products is not mandatory unless:

1. A nutrient (vitamin, mineral or protein) is added to the products,
2. A claim is made on the label or in the advertising about the nutritional value of the product.

When poultry products are to be labeled with nutrition information, the USDA regulations specify the type of information, format on the labeling and how compliance is to be determined. USDA regulations are similar to those published by the Food and Drug Administration March 14, 1973 for food products other than meat and poultry.

The USDA regulations specifically require the company to have as a prerequisite to nutrition labeling a plant quality control system which will provide assurance that

1. The product will meet the labeling claims,
2. Product out of compliance will be held for disposition as determined by the USDA,
3. Plant personnel and USDA can monitor the system.

The system shall include as a minimum, a written description of

1. The methods used to maintain uniformity of raw ingredients,
2. The formulation for the product,
3. The handling and processing of the product,
4. A provision for chemical analysis of the finished product.

USDA defines a lot as "a collection of immediate containers for units of the same size of one product, type and style produced under uniform conditions and designated by a common container, code or marking."

A poultry product will be considered in compliance with the nutritional information on the labeling if the value obtained by analysis of a composite of 12 samples from the lot are

Equal to the value for added vitamins, minerals or protein, or

Equal to 80% of the value for naturally occurring vitamins, minerals or protein, and

Not over 20% in excess of the values given for calories, carbohydrate or fat.

The nutritional values to be used on the label will be determined by analyzing a composite of 12 randomly selected, immediate containers from a lot.

Compliance for product carrying approved nutritional labeling will be maintained through the quality control system and *verified* by analyzing a minimum of 12 containers from lots processed during the first year the labeling is approved. The purpose of this sampling during the first year is to determine whether the natural variations are within the 20–80% range referred to above, USDA's Irwin Fried said. Revisions of the sample requirements applicable after the first year will be published at a later date.

The PER (Protein Efficiency Ratio) for poultry and meat is considered by USDA to be equal to or better than casein. The U.S. RDA (Recommended Dietary Allowance) for protein for meat and poultry will be 45 gm.

The label may state "For Nutrition information write to _____." This statement does not subject the product to nutritional labeling requirements if

1. No mention of nutrition claim is made,
2. The reply to the requests conforms to USDA requirements,
3. No vitamin, mineral or protein is added to the product.

Nutritional information varying from USDA requirements may be sent to professionals if it is attached to the information which does conform to USDA requirements.

Any nutrient added to a poultry product for technical purposes and declared in the ingredient statement does not subject the product to mandatory nutrition labeling.

Another change USDA made will require information on nutrition on both raw and cooked products *if the product requires cooking before eating.* USDA regulations specify that *another column of figures shall be* used to give the nutritional values for the poultry product as cooked by a specific method which must be disclosed in a prominent statement immediately following the nutrition information. These values can be "best estimates" and are not subject to compliance testing.

Minerals

Harshaw (1942) reported that poultry meat contains sodium, potassium, magnesium, calcium, iron, phosphorus, sulfur, chlorine, and iodine.

POULTRY MEAT IN SPECIAL DIETS

Poultry meat is an ideal food for infants, young children, adolescents, adults, old people, convalescents, and those attempting to control their weight. Because of its high meat yield, low shrinkage during cooking and ease of cooking and serving, poultry meat fits well on the menu of restaurants, hotels, airlines, hospitals, schools, and institutions (Tables 4.4 and 4.5). The National Broiler Council (Anon. 1964) gives the following reasons why chicken is important in hospital diets.

Patients and staff like it and readily accept well-prepared chicken.

Chicken can be adapted to many special diets for all age groups. Because chicken is short-fibered, it is easy to digest, making it a favorite with all age groups and patients with special digestive problems.

Chicken drumsticks are easy to eat for patients who are too young or incapable of handling knives or forks.

Chicken can be adapted to many special diets for all age groups. For example, broiled and boiled chicken can be served in many variations that do not add calories but still have high patient acceptance.

The close tolerance on proportioned items makes it easier to use chicken for special diets than in the days when every portion had to be cut, weighed and checked.

The endless ways in which chicken can be cooked precludes menu monotony.

The task of the clinical dietitian and public health nutritionist is relatively simple when they teach the use of chicken compared to, for instance, the importance of liver in the diet. This is because most homemakers know how to cook chicken and their families accept it readily.

In terms of the cost per pound of edible meat and the nutrient return for the money spent, chicken is your best buy today.

Chicken also lends itself well to a portion of low-sodium diets.

POULTRY FLAVOR

Although most people purchase chicken because it tastes good, the term flavor has different meanings to different people. Flavor is made up of a combination of taste, aroma, body, and mouth satisfaction.

TABLE 4.4

COMPARATIVE YIELDS OF EDIBLE PORTIONS OF CHICKEN, EGGS, TURKEY AND SOME CUTS OF BEEF AND PORK

Kind of Meat, All Better Than Avg.	Avg. Live Wt., Lb.	Dressing Loss, Lb.	Avg. Carcass, Lb.	Carcass, % Cuts Sold, Bone In, Lb.	Bone, Lb.	Edible Muscle Fat and Suet, Lb.	Edible Portion After Cooking, Lb.	Edible Portion Compared to Carcass %
Beef	950	380 or 40%	570	485 or 85%	80 or 14%	410 or 72%	220 plus fat	40
Pork	220	71 or 31%	149	120 or 80%	16 or 13%	78 or 52%, plus 30 lb. lard	47	32
Lamb	85	43 or 51%	42	36 or 87%	6.7 or 16%	30 or 72%	20	48
Poultry	3.5 to 21	23–31%	2.5 to 16	100%	22–32%	70–78%	...	46–59%
Eggs, 8 per lb.	1.0	0	1.0	1.0 or 100%	0.11 or 11%	0.89 or 89%	Boiled 0.89 or 89%	89

Chick Master Incubator Co., Anon. (1958).

TABLE 4.5

COMPARATIVE YIELDS OF EDIBLE PORTION OF THE WHOLE CARCASS

Kind of Meat	Average Weight Raw Ready-to-Cook (Bone in), Lb.	Bone, Lb.	Edible Portion Only, Lb.	Average Cooked Edible Portion After Cooking, Lb.	Edible Portion Compared Ready to Cook, %
Beef					
Chuck roast, 8 samples	4.16	1.70	2.46	1.63	39.2
Round roast, 2 samples	3.8	.0	3.8	2.13	56.0
Pork					
Rib and loin chops, 2 samples	1.97	0.89	1.08	0.74	37.6
	Avg Live Wt.				
Chickens*					
60 broilers	3.43	2.57	0.82	1.75	50.2
Cut-up legs and thighs		0.81	0.19	0.62	53.3
Breasts		0.64	0.10	0.54	63.4
20 Hens	5.2	3.56	0.9	2.66	52.2
20 Roasters	6.8	5.07	1.18	3.72	51.3
Turkeys					
6–12 Weeks	7.67	5.59	1.23	4.27	46.0
6–18–20 Weeks	14.40	10.56	1.98	8.60	46.2
4–26 Weeks	20.43	15.75	3.89	11.86	58.7
Eggs, 8 = 1 lb.	...	1.0	0.11	0.89	89.0

Chick Master Incubator Co., (Anon. 1958).
  * Compiled from data of Alexander and Schopmeyer (1949), Brown and Bean (1962), Scott (1956) and Tadle, Lewis, Winter and Jaap (1955).

Taste includes combinations of the basic sweet, sour, salty, and bitter sensations which humans experience. Aroma includes those sensations perceptible to the nose while the term body or texture is used to describe whether the food is tough, tender, chewy, stringy, or viscous. Mouth satisfaction includes stimulation of salivation, smoothness, and other pleasant sensations associated with flavor.

A number of variables are involved in flavor research. The sex, age, genetics, attitudes, and ethnic and sociological backgrounds all influence individual's likes or dislikes for foods. The flavor of the product tested, in this case poultry, can also be influenced by the age, breed, storage, rations, processing, additives, cooking, and methods of serving the bird.

There are still a number of questions which need to be answered by additional research such as: Can we breed chickens for flavor? Can we fortify chicken broth and poultry products with combinations of flavor precursors such as ammonia, hydrogen sulfide, lactic acid, and other compounds? What effects do specific types of microorganisms have on flavor? What effect does pH have?

Although considerable work, both fundamental and applied, has been carried out on flavor research, a number of problems remain unsolved. The effects of age, ration, and strain have been studied by Hanson *et al.* (1960), who compared the flavor of different breeds of chickens representative of commercial production in 1930 and 1956, and also fed rations used in 1930 and 1956. After making 600 flavor comparisons on almost 2000 carcasses cooked by five methods, they reported that no differences in flavor were noted in carcasses cooked by four methods and only inconsistent differences were found in the fifth method. They concluded that "the modern bird has as much chicken flavor as the old style bird."

Fry *et al.* (1958) in a study of the effects of age, sex and hormonization on the flavor of chicken meat reported that taste panels could pick up differences in chicken broths between 6- and 10- to 14-week-old carcasses, but that age had no appreciable effect when comparing 10- to-14-week-old birds. They also reported that the flavor of baked chicken was influenced chiefly by age. Leong *et al.* (1958) reported that stabilized inedible choice white grease is not likely to have an adverse effect on flavor. As a result of these and other studies, Lineweaver (1961) concluded that age, sex, variety, and production conditions do not have too much influence on flavor under ordinary conditions.

Pippen *et al.* (1954) found that although fat contributes to the aroma of chicken broth it does not have much effect on flavor. Chicken meat was found to be a better source of flavor than bones, skin, or a mixture of the three.

Pippen and Klose (1955) reported that chicken immersed in cold water for prolonged periods loses flavor but under normal conditions of chilling flavor loss is no problem.

Some fundamental research has been underway to isolate and identify the chemical compounds which are responsible for the flavor of poultry meat (Figs. 4.1 and 4.2). Bouthilet (1949) isolated and characterized a flavor constituent which "appears to be a weak acid produced in the flesh during cooking." Bouthilet (1950) reported that volatile compounds responsible for the flavor of chicken could be stripped from a broth and concentrated by means of a fractionating column and then recombined to produce a broth undistinguishable from natural chicken broth. Bouthilet (1951A) demonstrated the presence of ammo-

Courtesy Ohio Agr. Research and Development Center

FIG. 4.1. GAS CHROMATOGRAPHS ARE NOW BEING USED TO STUDY THE COMPONENTS OF CHICKEN FLAVOR

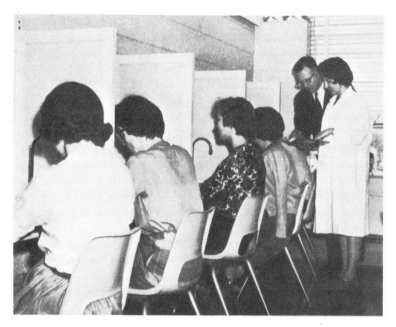

Courtesy Ohio Agr. Research and Development Center

FIG. 4.2   A TASTE PANEL TASTING BROTH MADE FROM YOUNG BROILERS AND OLD HENS

nia in the volatile fraction and reported that sulfur compounds are also responsible for part of the flavor. In later work (1951B), he reported that the "meaty flavor" of chicken is found in the meat fibers and has properties similar to glutathione.

Pippen *et al.* (1958) in a study of volatile carbonyl compounds of cooked chicken were able to separate 18 different compounds. Pippen *et al.* (1960) postulated that diacetyl contributes substantially to a "transient buttery-oily type aroma observed in cooked chicken."

Wasserman (1972A) presented an excellent review on flavor components in the aroma of meat and poultry with particular emphasis on thermally produced flavor components. He reported that species differences are of special importance since beef, pork, chicken, duck, guinea, and fish all have different but characteristic flavors and different chemical compositions. Variation also occurs among strains and individual animals within the same strain. Various organs and tissues within the same animal also have markedly different characteristics. Hydrogen ion concentration and chemical changes which are influenced by starvation, a low nutritional plane, emotional state, and

TABLE 4.6

CHEMICAL COMPOUNDS IDENTIFIED IN CHICKEN

Compound	I_E on Unknown[1]	I_E on Known[1]	Previously Reported
Alcohols			
Saturated			
n-Butanol	5.00	5.00	
n-Pentanol	6.07	6.08	
n-Hexanol	7.13	7.15	
n-Heptanol	8.16	8.19	
n-Octanol	9.19	9.24	×
Unsaturated			
2-Methyl-3-buten-2-o	3.80	3.79	
1-Penten-3-ol	5.11	5.10	
3-Penten-2-ol	5.21	5.29	
1-Octen-3-ol	8.12	8.18	
Linalool	9.07	9.00	
trans-2-Octenol	9.75	9.73	
α-Terpineol	10.43	10.49	
Benzyl alcohol[2]	Not determined	Not determined	
1-Phenyl-1-propanol[2]	Not determined	Not determined	
Phenylethyl alcohol[2]	Not determined	Not determined	
Acids			
Phenol[2]	Not determined	Not determined	
p-Cresol[2]	Not determined	Not determined	
Heterocyclics			
n-Pentylfuran[2]	6.00	6.00	×
2-Methylpyrazine[2]	6.31	6.34	
Lactones			
γ-octalactone[2]	Not determined	Not determined	
Ketones			
Saturated			
Acetone	1.00	0.98	
2-Butanone	2.15	2.21	×
2-Heptanone	5.47	5.47	×
Unsaturated			
4-Hexen-3-one	5.53	5.54	×
3-Buten-2-one	2.85	2.83	
Aldehydes			
Saturated			
n-Valeraldehyde	3.29	3.29	×
n-Hexanal	4.48	4.44	×
n-Heptanal	5.46	5.47	×
n-Octanal	6.49	6.52	×
n-Nonanal	7.57	7.62	×
Monounsaturated			
2-Methylcrotonaldehyde	Not determined	Not determined	
trans-2-Hexenal	5.80	5.85	×
trans-2-Heptenal	6.83	6.83	×
trans-2-Octenal	7.87	7.87	×
trans-2-Nonenal	8.92	9.00	×
trans-2-Decenal	9.95	9.97	×
trans-2-Undecenal	11.02	11.10	×
Diunsaturated			
2,4-Heptadienal	8.48	8.45	×
2,4-Nonadienal	10.49	10.64	
2,4-Decadienal	11.60	11.69	×
Aromatic			
Benzaldehyde	8.75	8.81	×
Piperonal	15.41	15.42	
Hydrocarbons			
p-Xylene[2]	5.00	5.08	×
o-Xylene[2]	5.46	5.57	×
Limonene	5.61	5.70	×
Naphthalene[2]	10.81	10.95	×
Methylnaphthalene[2]	Not determined	Not determined	

[1] I_E's were determined on a 200-ft × 0.03-in. Carbowax 20M open tubular column.
[2] Tentative identification.
From Wilson and Katz (1972) with permission of American Chemical Society.

other factors also influence flavor and aroma as well as the characteristics of the fat fed to animals. Conventionally raised chickens have a more characteristic "chicken" flavor than those produced in a germ-free environment.

Other factors observed which influence flavor are aging and its influence on carbohydrate breakdown, protein denaturation, and fat breakdown. The method of cooking such as stewing compared to roasting also has a profound effect on aroma and flavor.

TENDERNESS

Although the results of a number of experiments on the factors believed to influence tenderness in poultry have been reported, it is still not possible to explain why under certain conditions some carcasses are tender and some are tough even though they are from the same lot and have been treated identically.

Age clearly influences tenderness. Peterson et al. (1959) reported that toughness of cooked muscle increased with age in both dark and light muscle and that exercise or treatment with stilbesterol or testosterone had no effect on muscle toughness. Dodge and Stadelman (1959) reported that the age of birds and the class of poultry appeared to be important factors in post-mortem tenderization. Shrimpton (1960) observed a difference in tenderness between birds 2, 6, and 18 months old with the young birds having the most tender meat. He also reported that no broilers were tough regardless of the post-mortem treatment they received. Shrimpton and Miller (1960) found that the most tender meats came from birds in the fastest growing groups and the toughest from the slowest groups.

The effects of rations have not been clearly demonstrated. Goertz et al. (1961) observed that generally tenderness scores and shear values were similar regardless of the cereal grains fed both singly and in combination. Mellor et al. (1958) reported that fasted broilers had a higher muscle glycogen level than groups fed a sugar-broiler mash mixture. Carcasses with high concentrations of glycogen had lower shear values than muscles with low glycogen concentrations. Morrison et al. (1954) found no significant differences between breeds or crosses in tenderness. Stadelman (1963) expressed the opinion that degree of finish is responsible for differences in breed and sex.

A number of factors occurring after slaughter have been shown to influence tenderness in one way or another. Shrimpton (1960) reported that increasing the scalding temperature delayed the breakdown of glycogen with a similar delay in formation of lactic acid. Klose et al. (1956) observed that high scalding temperatures, long scalding temperatures, and beating by picking machines have an adverse effect on tenderization. Dodge and Stadelman (1960) reported that under normal processing conditions, struggling had little effect on tenderization. Dodge and Stadelman (1959) also observed that the time of aging, the temperature of aging, and the media in which the carcasses were aged appear to influence tenderness. May *et al.* (1962) reported that carcasses aged at 32° and 66°F. were more tender than those aged at 98.6°F. but that all carcasses approached the same degree of tenderness after eight hours aging regardless of temperature. Huffman *et al.* (1961) demonstrated that 100 p.p.m. of crude papain injected before slaughter not only brought about additional tenderization but caused overtenderization.

Freezing and cooking also influence tenderness. Koonz *et al.* (1954) reported that cutting the muscles and freezing interfere with tenderness. Stadelman and Wise (1961) demonstrated that cooking before freezing and gamma irradiation have a minor effect on tenderness. Nembutal extends the period of maximum toughness. Cooking before carcasses have had a chance to pass completely through rigor has also been reported by some workers to cause tough muscles.

A comprehensive review of factors influencing meat tenderness in avian species has been compiled by Marion (1967).

BIBLIOGRAPHY

ALEXANDER, L. M., and SCHOPMEYER, G. E. 1949. Yield of edible portion of chicken and various meats cooked by different home methods. Food Technol. *3*, 263-268.

ANON. 1958. What is an egg worth? Chickmaster Incubator Co., Cleveland.

ANON. 1964. Chicken Packs Profit Punch. National Broiler Council, Richmond, Va.

ANON. 1972. Information panel and nutrition labeling. Federal Register *39*, No. 8, 1611-1614.

BIRD, H. R. 1943. The nutritive value of eggs and poultry meat. Poultry Egg Nat. Board Nutr. Res. Bull. *5*.

BOUTHILET, R. J. 1949. A note on the nature of a flavor constituent from poultry meat. Food Technol. *3*, 118-119.

BOUTHILET, R. J. 1950. Chicken flavor: Separation and concentration of its volatile components from broth. Food Res. *15*, 322-325.

BOUTHILET, R. J. 1951A. Chicken flavor: The fractionation of the volatile constituents. Food Res. *16*, 137-141.

BOUTHILET, R. J. 1951B. Chicken flavor: The source of the meat flavor component. Food Res. *16*, 201-204.

BROWN, P. B., and BEAN, H. W. 1962. The yield of edible meat from different market classes of chickens. Poultry Sci. *31*, 232-234.

DODGE, J. W., and STADELMAN, W. J. 1959. Post-mortem aging of poultry meat and its effect on the tenderness of breast muscles. Food Technol. *13*, 81-84.

DODGE, J. W., and STADELMAN, W. J. 1960. Variability in tenderness due to struggling. Poultry Sci. *39*, 672-677.

FRY, J. L., BENNETT, G., and STADELMAN, W. J. 1958. The effect of age, sex and hormonization on the flavor of chicken meat. Poultry Sci. 37, 331-335.

GOERTZ, G. E., WEATHERS, B., HARRISON, D. L., and SANFORD, P. E. 1961. Tenderness scores and Warner-Bratzler shear values for broilers and Beltsville white turkeys fed different cereal grains. Poultry Sci. *40*, 488-493.

HANSON, H. L. *et al.* 1960. The flavor of modern and old-type chickens. Poultry Sci. *38*, 1071-1078.

HARSHAW, H. M., 1942. Physical and chemical composition of chickens and turkeys. U.S. Dept. Agr., Bur. Animal Ind., Animal Nutr. Div. 7.

HUFFMAN, D. L., PALMER, A. Z., CARPENTER, J. W., and SHIRLEY, R. L. 1961. The effect of ante-mortem injections of papain on tenderness of chickens. Poultry Sci. *40*, 1627-1630.

KLOSE, A. A., HANSON, H. L., POOL, M. F., and LINEWEAVER, H. 1956. Poultry tenderness improved by holding before freezing. Quick Frozen Foods *18*, 95.

KOONZ, C. H., DARROW, M. I., and ESSARY, E. O. 1954. Factors influencing tenderness of principal muscles composing the poultry carcass. Food Technol. *8*, 97-100.

KOONZ, C. H., STRANDINE, E. J., and GRAY, R. E. 1963. A study of factors responsible for keel blisters in poultry. Poultry Sci. *42*, 1281. (Abstr.)

LEONG, K. C., SUNDE, M. L., BIRD, H. R., and WECKEL, K. G. 1958. Taste panel evaluation of the effect of added fat on the flavor of chicken meat. Poultry Sci. *37*, 1170-1172.

LINEWEAVER, H. 1961. Chicken flavor. *In* Proc. Flavor Chemistry Symposium. Campbell Soup Co., Camden, N.J.

LINEWEAVER, H. L., and PIPPEN, E. L. 1961. Chicken flavor. *In* Proc. Flavor Chemistry Symposium. Campbell Soup Co., Camden, N.J.

LOWE, B. 1958. Experimental Cookery. John Wiley and Sons, New York.

MARION, W. W. 1967. Meat tenderness in the avian species. World's Poultry Sci. J. *23*, No. 1, 6-19.

MAY, K. N., SAFFLE, R. L., DOWNING, D. L., and POWERS, J. J. 1962. Interrelationships of post-mortem changes with tenderness of chicken and pork. Food Technol. *16*, 72-78.

MCCARTHY, P. A., BROWN, W., and HAMDY, M. F. 1963. Microbiological studies of bruised tissues. J. Food Sci. *28*, 245-253.

MECCHI, E. P. *et al.* 1956. The role of tocopherol content in the comparative stability of chicken and turkey fat. Poultry Sci. *35*, 1238-1246.

MELLOR, D. B., STRINGER, P. A., and MOUNTNEY, G. J. 1958. The influence of glycogen on tenderness of broiler meat. Poultry Sci. *37*, 1028-1033.

MORRISON, M. A., SAUTER, E. A., McLAREN, B. A., and STADELMAN, W. J. 1954. Some factors affecting yield and acceptability of chicken broilers. Poultry Sci. *33*, 1122-1125.

PETERSON, D. W., SIMONE, M., LILYBLADE, A. L., and MARTIN, R. 1959. Some factors affecting intensity of flavor and toughness of chicken muscle. Food Technol. *13*, 204-207.

PIPPEN, E. L., CAMPBELL, A. A., and STREETER, I. V. 1954. Flavor studies: origin of chicken flavor. J. Agr. Food Chem. *2*, 364-367.

PIPPEN, E. L., and EYRING, E. J. 1957. Characterization of volatile nitrogen and volatile sulfur fractions of cooked chicken and their relation to flavor. Food Technol. *11*, 53–56.

PIPPEN, E. L., EYRING, E. J., and NONAKA, M. 1960. The occurence and flavor significance of acetoin in aqueous extracts of chicken. Poultry Sci. *39*, 922–924.

PIPPEN, E. L., and KLOSE, A. A. 1955. Effects of ice water chilling on flavor of chicken. Poultry Sci. *34*, 1139–1146.

PIPPEN, E. L., NONAKA, M., JONES, F. T., and STITT, F. 1958. Volatile carbonyl compounds of cooked chicken. I. Compounds obtained by air entrainment. Food Res. *23*, 103–113.

SCOTT, M. L. 1956. Composition of turkey meat. J. Am. Dietet. Assoc. *32*, 941–944.

SCOTT, M. L. 1958. Composition of turkey meat. II. Cholesterol content and fatty acid composition. J. Am. Dietet. Assoc. *34*, 154–156.

SCOTT, M. L. 1959. Composition of turkey meat. III. Essential amino acid composition. J. Am. Dietet. Assoc. *35*, 247–249.

SHRIMPTON, D. H. 1960. Some causes of toughness in broilers. I. Packing station procedure, its influence on the chemical changes associated with rigor mortis and on tenderness of the flesh. British Poul. Sci. *1*, 101–110.

SHRIMPTON, D. H., and MILLER, W. S. 1960. Some causes of toughness in broilers, II. Effects of breed management and sex. British Poultry Sci. *1*, 111–121.

STADELMAN, W. J. 1963. Relation of age, breed, sex and feeding practices on poultry meat tenderness. Proc. Meat Tenderness Symposium. Campbell Soup Co., Camden, N.J.

STADELMAN, W. J., and WISE, R. G. 1961. Tenderness of poultry meat. I. Effect of anesthesia, cooking and irradiation. Food Technol. *15*, 292–294.

TADLE, J., LEWIS, M. N., WINTER, A. R., and JAAP, R. G. 1955. Cooked edible meat in parts of chicken. I. Broilers. J. Am. Dietet. Assoc. *31*, 597–600.

WASSERMAN, A. E. 1972. Thermally produced flavor components in the aroma of meat and poultry. J. Agr. Food Chem. *20*, No. 4, 737–741.

WILSON, R. A., and KATZ, I. 1972. Review of literature on chicken flavor and report of isolation of several new chicken flavor components from aqueous cooked chicken. J. Agr. Food Chem. *20*, No. 4, 741–747.

CHAPTER 5

Measuring Yields
and Characteristics

INTRODUCTION

Yields of poultry vary considerably among lots even at the same stage of processing. At the present time, many measurements, especially on methods of taking yields of cut-up parts, cooking yields, and meat yields have not been standardized. As a result it is often difficult to obtain comparable sets of data from different experiments. Because of lack of standardization in obtaining yields and individual carcass variations, average values serve only as rough guides. Quality control methods based on statistical analysis are just beginning to appear in poultry processing operations. The data in Tables 5.1 through 5.18 show the various losses from different species of poultry caused by slaughtering, eviscerating, cutting up, cooking, and deboning.

PROCESSING SHRINKAGES

Shrinkages during processing are influenced by the kinds and classes of poultry, the age, sex, size and breeding. In general, shrinkage is greater in young birds and light weight ones than in older or heavier birds. Blood generally amounts to from 3.3 to 4.8% and feathers from 4.8 to 8.5% of the total carcass weight.

PROPORTIONS OF DIFFERENT PARTS OF CARCASSES

The increased use of poultry parts sold in separate packages of a given weight, the use of certain parts for ready-to-serve convenience items, and the problem of portion control when poultry is served in large quantities has created a need for more information for use in quality control methods in poultry processing and marketing. The results of such information are valuable for uniform portion and weight control and for predicting the yields and proportions of various parts of carcasses to the whole weight. The yield can also be predicted within various tolerances. A practical application of such a system is the problem of packing poultry drumsticks in one pound cartons. Unless the drumsticks have been sized previously it is difficult to add the last drumstick in such a manner that the weight of the contents is exactly a pound plus a small tolerance, or if the net weight comes out at a pound the last drumstick is much smaller than the others in the pack.

TABLE 5.1

WEIGHTS OF THE SEVERAL PARTS OF VARIOUS KINDS OF POULTRY PROCESSED AT ONTARIO[3] COMMERCIAL PROCESSING PLANTS

| Kind | Sex | Age, Weeks | No. of Birds | Average Weight, Lb. | | | | | Giblets | | | | Total[1] Ready-to-Cook | Chilled[2] Carcass and Neck | Water Uptake in Cooling |
				Live	Hot Dressed	Heads	Legs	Carcass and Neck	Hearts	Liver	Gizzard	Total			
Chicken broilers	Male	8.5	105	3.8	3.5	0.1	0.2	2.7	0.02	0.08	0.07	0.17	2.9	2.7	0.02
	Female	8.5	105	3.0	2.8	0.1	0.1	2.1	0.02	0.07	0.07	0.15	2.3	2.2	0.04
	Male	10.6	100	5.4	5.1	0.1	0.2	4.0	0.02	0.10	0.08	0.21	4.2	4.1	0.13
	Female	10.6	100	4.1	3.8	0.1	0.2	3.0	0.01	0.08	0.09	0.19	3.2	3.1	0.03
Capons	Male	18.7	104	8.7	7.8	0.2	0.3	6.2	0.03	0.14	0.17	0.35	6.5	6.3	0.10
Turkeys B.B.W.	Male	26.0	100	27.0	25.0	0.5	0.5	20.8	0.11	0.51	0.34	0.96	21.7	21.6	0.80
	Female	23.0	100	16.2	14.9	0.3	0.4	12.3	0.06	0.27	0.25	0.59	12.9	12.8	0.50
Turkey broilers B.B.W.	Male	16.4	100	12.0	10.8	0.4	0.4	9.1	0.05	0.15	0.17	0.38	9.5	9.6	0.50
	Female	16.4	100	8.0	7.4	0.2	0.2	6.1	0.13[4]		0.12	0.25	6.4	6.4	0.50
Pekin ducks	Male	7.6	100	5.8	5.0	0.2	0.1	3.8	0.04	0.19	0.10	0.33	4.1	4.0	0.20
	Female	7.6	100	5.5	4.7	0.2	0.1	3.6	0.04	0.17	0.10	0.31	3.9	3.7	0.10
Pheasants	Male	21.0	79	3.1	2.8	0.1	0.1	2.3	0.01	0.05	0.05	0.13	2.5	2.4	0.10
	Female	21.0	75	2.4	2.1	0.1	0.05	1.8	0.01	0.04	0.05	0.10	1.9	1.9	0.10

From Snyder and Orr (1964), Ontario Agr. College.
[1] Ready-to-cook = carcass + neck + giblets.
[2] Cooled by procedure prevailing in each plant.
[3] Under supervision of authors.
[4] Hearts and livers.

TABLE 5.2

WEIGHT OF THE SEVERAL PARTS AND DRESSING PERCENTAGES OF POULTRY PROCESSED AT DEPARTMENT OF POULTRY SCIENCE

| Kind | Sex | Age, Weeks | No. of Birds, Lb. | Average Weight of, Lb. | | | | As a Percentage of Life Weight | | | As a Percentage of Dressed Weight | |
				Live	Hot Dressed	Carcass[1]	Total[2] Ready-to-Cook	Hot Dressed	Carcass[1]	Total[2] Ready-to-Cook	Carcass[1]	Total[2] Ready-to-Cook
Roasters	Male	16	29	8.2	7.3	5.4	6.0	89.5	66.3	73.2	74.1	81.7
White Rock fowl	Female	49	100	7.2	6.7	4.9	5.3	92.2	67.3	73.2	73.0	79.4
White Leghorn fowl	Female	50	100	3.5	3.1	2.2	2.3	89.9	62.6	66.4	69.6	73.8

(Continuation of table — turkey varieties)

Kind	Sex	No.	No.						Chilled Carcass and Neck	Carcass and Neck	Total Giblets	Total Ready-to-Cook	Chilled Carcass
Turkey broilers (small white)	Male	17	18	15.7	13.7	10.7	11.8	87.8	68.2	75.7	4.9	77.7	86.2
	Female	17	30	10.7	9.4	7.3	8.1	87.7	68.2	75.5	5.6	77.8	86.0
Large white X	Male	29	8	25.7	23.9	19.4	21.3	92.8	75.3	82.6	4.2	81.2	89.1
Small white turkeys	Female	29	11	14.6	13.5	11.0	11.9	92.5	75.5	81.6	5.1	81.7	88.2
Large white X	Male	29	8	28.6	26.4	21.3	23.4	92.3	74.4	81.2	4.5	80.5	88.6
Bourbon Red turkeys	Female	29	8	15.4	14.3	11.5	12.5	92.8	74.7	81.4	3.8	80.4	87.8
Bourbon Red X	Male	29	8	24.8	22.8	18.4	20.2	92.0	74.2	81.4	4.0	80.6	88.4
Small white turkeys	Female	29	8	13.8	12.7	10.2	11.1	92.1	74.3	80.9	3.5	80.7	87.9
Bourbon red turkeys	Male	29	19	22.9	21.0	16.6	18.4	91.7	72.4	80.3	3.4	78.9	87.5
	Female	29	7	13.3	12.2	9.6	10.5	91.9	72.3	79.5	6.5	72.3	86.5
Color-strain	Male	24	19	24.0	22.0	17.4	19.3	91.8	72.8	80.3	4.7	79.3	87.5
Cross turkeys	Female	22	33	15.3	14.2	11.3	12.4	92.5	73.7	81.1	4.9	79.7	87.7

From Snyder and Orr (1964), Ontario Agr. College.
[1] Carcass only (giblets and necks not included except W.L. fowl which includes carcass and neck).
[2] Includes carcass, neck, and giblets (before chilling).

TABLE 5.3

DRESSING PERCENTAGES OF THE SEVERAL KINDS OF POULTRY PROCESSED AT ONTARIO COMMERCIAL PROCESSING PLANTS[1]

Kind	Sex	Hot Dressed	Heads	Legs	Carcass and Neck	Heart	Liver	Gizzard	Total	Total Ready-to-Cook	Chilled Carcass and Neck
					(As a Percentage of Live Weight)	*Giblets*					*(As a % of Dressed Wt.)*
Chicken broilers	Male	92.1	2.7	5.3	72.2	0.5	2.1	1.9	4.6	76.7	72.8
	Female	91.8	2.9	4.8	71.5	0.5	2.3	2.3	5.1	76.6	72.9
	Male	94.5	2.6	4.7	74.2	0.4	1.9	1.6	3.9	78.2	76.4
	Female	92.6	2.5	3.9	73.8	0.4	2.3	2.3	4.7	78.5	74.8
Capons	Male	90.3	2.4	3.9	68.9	0.4	1.7	2.0	3.6	75.7	71.5
	Female	92.6	1.8	1.7	77.0	0.4	1.7	1.6	3.6	80.6	80.1
Turkeys B.B.W.	Male	92.0	1.5	2.7	75.8	0.4	1.7	1.4	3.2	79.4	78.7
	Female	89.9	3.7	3.1	75.8	1.7[2]		1.5	3.5	79.0	80.1
Turkey broilers B.B.W.	Male	92.8	2.8	2.6	77.0	0.7	1.3	1.8	3.2	80.1	80.5
	Female	85.8	4.3	2.1	64.4	0.7	3.3	1.5	5.5	70.1	67.9
Pekin ducks	Male	84.8	4.0	2.0	64.7	0.6	3.0	1.9	5.7	70.3	64.7
Pheasants	Male	91.7	3.0	2.4	76.8	0.5	1.9	1.8	4.7	81.1	78.9
	Female	90.8	2.8	2.1	75.1	0.5	1.8	2.2	4.5	79.6	78.8

From Snyder and Orr (1964), Ontario Agr. College.
[1] Refer to Table 5.1 for any explanations.
[2] Hearts and livers.

TABLE 5.4

AVERAGE WEIGHT OF LIVE, READY-TO-COOK;[1] COOKED EDIBLE PORTION, PARTS AND BONES OF POULTRY PROCESSED AT DEPARTMENT OF POULTRY SCIENCE

Kind	Sex	No. of Birds	Average Weight of, Lb.										Cooking Loss		
			Live	Ready-to-Cook Carcass	Cooked Carcass	White Meat	Dark Meat	Skin	Separable Fat	Total Edible Meat	Carcass Bones	Loss in[3] Deboning	Drippings	Evaporation	Total
Roasters	Male	10	8.6	5.8	4.0	1.3	1.2	0.4	...	3.0	0.7	0.3	0.3	1.6	1.8
White Rock fowl	Female	10	7.0	5.1[2]	3.3[2]	1.1	0.9	0.3	...	2.5[2]	0.5	0.1	0.9	0.9	1.9
White Leghorn fowl	Female	10	3.5	2.3[2]	1.3[2]	0.5	0.3	0.1	...	0.9[2]	0.2	0.1	0.2	0.8	0.9
Turkey broilers (Small white)	Male	18	15.7	11.2	8.1	3.3	1.8	0.6	...	5.7	1.7	0.7	0.7	2.4	3.1
	Female	30	10.7	7.6	5.5	2.3	1.3	0.4	...	4.0	1.0	0.4	0.5	1.5	2.1
Large white X	Male	8	25.7	19.5	13.3	5.8	2.9	1.2	0.7	10.7	1.8	0.7	2.4	3.7	6.1
Small white turkeys	Female	11	14.6	11.1	7.4	3.2	1.8	0.7	0.3	5.8	1.0	0.5	1.6	2.0	3.5
Large white X	Male	8	28.6	21.4	14.4	5.9	3.4	1.3	0.9	11.5	2.1	0.8	3.1	3.7	6.9
Bourbon Red turkeys	Female	4	15.4	11.4	7.6	3.2	1.9	0.7	0.3	6.0	1.1	0.5	1.7	2.2	3.8
Bourbon Red X	Male	8	24.8	18.5	12.8	5.3	3.1	1.1	0.7	10.2	1.8	0.7	2.2	3.4	5.6
Small white turkeys	Female	8	13.8	10.2	7.0	2.9	1.7	0.7	0.3	5.5	1.0	0.6	1.4	3.2	3.2
Bourbon Red turkeys	Male	19	22.9	16.6	11.6	4.5	2.9	1.1	0.5	8.9	1.9	0.7	2.0	3.0	5.0
	Female	7	13.3	9.7	6.5	2.5	1.7	0.6	0.2	5.0	1.0	0.5	1.5	1.6	3.1
Color-strain	Male	19	24.0	18.1	12.8	5.4	3.3	0.8	...	9.5	2.3	1.0	2.2	3.0	5.2
Cross turkeys	Female	33	15.3	11.7	8.0	3.4	2.2	0.6	...	6.1	1.3	0.6	1.7	1.9	3.6

From Snyder and Orr (1964), Ontario Agr. College.
[1] Defrosted weight.
[2] Neck included.
[3] Includes waste + evaporation.

TABLE 5.5

AVERAGE LIVE, DRESSED, DRAWN, AND COOKED WEIGHTS OF COOKED CARCASSES OF GEESE

Age in Weeks	No. of Birds	Live Weight, Lb.	Dressed Weight, Lb.	Drawn Weight, Lb.	Cooked Weight, Lb.	Total Edible Meat, Lb.	Total Bones, Lb.	Drip-pings, Lb.
8	4	9.0	8.0	6.2	4.2	3.0	1.2	1.1
10	4	9.8	8.5	6.7	4.6	3.4	1.2	1.2
12	4	11.4	10.0	8.0	5.4	4.1	1.3	1.6
13	4	13.2	11.4	9.0	5.5	4.2	1.3	1.6
14	4	11.4	9.9	7.8	5.2	3.7	1.2	1.7
19	4	12.7	11.1	8.7	5.3	3.9	1.1	1.7

From Snyder and Orr (1964), Ontario Agr. College.

TABLE 5.6

PERCENTAGE OF VARIOUS PARTS OF GEESE AT SEVERAL AGES
(Based on chilled weights)

Age in Weeks	No. Birds	Feet, %	Head, %	Neck, %	Total Giblets, %	Remaining Carcass, %	Total Drawn Weight, %	Waste, %	Wing Tips, %
8	12	3.6	5.8	4.4	7.6	65.2	77.3	22.9	1.7
10	24	3.6	6.4	4.4	6.5	68.5	79.4	20.4	1.6
12	18	3.4	6.3	4.1	6.7	68.1	78.9	21.0	1.5
13	33	3.3	6.6	3.8	6.7	68.4	78.6	21.4	1.5
14	38	3.2	6.4	3.9	6.3	68.1	78.4	21.6	1.4
19	13	2.7	6.1	3.5	5.5	69.5	78.5	21.6	1.2

From Snyder and Orr (1964), Ontario Agr. College.

TABLE 5.7

PERCENTAGE OF EDIBLE MEAT AND BONES OF COOKED CARCASSES OF GEESE

Age in Weeks	Per Cent Total Edible Meat of			Percentage Bones of Live Weight
	Live Weight	Chilled Weight	Total Drawn Weight	
8	33.4	37.3	48.2	13.0
10	34.4	39.6	49.7	12.3
12	35.9	40.9	51.1	11.0
13	31.8	36.7	46.4	9.5
14	32.6	37.6	47.3	10.2
19	31.1	35.1	44.8	8.5

From Snyder and Orr (1964), Ontario Agr. College.

Walters, May, and Rodgers (1963) in an attempt to relate the weights and sizes of broiler parts to carcass weights have used statistical quality control procedures so that a processor can predict with a fair degree of accuracy, the relation of the total carcass weight of broilers to the weight or size of any part of the carcass commonly removed in a cut-up operation (Fig. 5.1). With this method not only the average weight of all the parts can be predicted, but also the number of parts which will fall into certain ranges.

Table 5.8

WEIGHT RANGE AND VARIATION OF BROILER PARTS FROM 32–36 OUNCE CARCASSES

Part	Weight Range for 95% of the Parts, Oz.	Weight Variation for 95% of the Parts, Oz.	Average Part Weight, Oz.
Wing	2.0– 2.9	0.9	2.5
Drumstick	2.3– 3.3	1.0	2.8
Thigh	2.9– 4.4	1.5	3.7
Back	3.7– 5.7	2.0	4.7
Breast	9.3–12.8	3.5	11.1

Source: Walters, May, and Rodgers (1963).

Another method sometimes used is the range between the high and low values. Since there is often quite a difference between these extremes the range serves only as a rough guide.

Winter and Clements (1957) have reported on a comparative study of the distribution of cut-up parts for broilers, turkeys, ducks, and geese. Breast meat made up the largest portion of large turkeys, ducks, and geese and the legs and thighs the largest portion of broilers and small turkeys. Giblets amounted to four per cent of the weight of large turkeys and 10.7% of the weight of 11-lb. geese.

MOISTURE ABSORPTION DURING WASHING AND CHILLING

The losses in weight and variations in the rate at which moisture is released from poultry carcasses chilled in a slush ice mixture and then stored in crushed ice are problems of considerable magnitude in the poultry industry. Not only is there considerable variation in the amount of water absorbed during washing and chilling, but it is also difficult to predict the amount and the rate of loss during the period the carcasses are stored in crushed ice. In an attempt to standardize the amounts of moisture absorbed during the essential washing and chilling operations, the U.S. Department of Agriculture has set up regulations which limit the weight increases permitted during these operations for carcasses packed for consumer use or feezing. They are:

Ready-to-cook weight:

Turkeys—20 lb. or over	4.5%
Turkeys—10–20 lb.	6.0%
Turkeys—under 10 lb.	8.0%
Chickens—5 lb. and under	8.0%
All other kinds and weight of poultry	6.0%

If the poultry is to be ice packed, the maximum weight increase is 12%. The losses in weight during the period after chilling and before actual re-

TABLE 5.9

MAXIMUM MOISTURE ABSORPTION AND RETENTION LIMITS FOR ALL CLASSES OF POULTRY, OTHER THAN TURKEYS,
TO BE CONSUMER PACKAGED, FROZEN OR COOKED AS WHOLE POULTRY

Average Ready-to-Cook Carcass Weight Prior to Final Washer (Less Necks and Giblets)	Average Percent Increase in Weight Over Weight of Carcass Prior to Final Washer (Less Necks and Giblets)	
	Zone A[1]	Zone B[1]
Chickens 4¹/₄ lb. and under	8.0	8.7
Chickens over 4¹/₄ lb. and all other classes of poultry other than turkeys	6.0	6.7

[1] Product shall be retained if, out of five consecutive tests more than one test exceeds the Zone A limits or any test exceeds the Zone B limits. These zone limits were based on a statistical analysis of variation between individual birds with regard to moisture absorption. With these limits the chance of passing a lot with average moisture at or above the Zone A limit is less than 15 percent. A lot with average moisture at or above the Zone B limit would have virtually no chance of passing.
From U.S. Dept. of Agr.

TABLE 5.10

MAXIMUM MOISTURE ABSORPTION AND RETENTION LIMITS FOR ALL TURKEYS TO BE CONSUMER PACKAGED,
FROZEN OR COOKED AS WHOLE POULTRY

Average Ready-to-Cook Carcass Weight Prior to Final Washer (Less Necks and Giblets)	Average Percent Increase in Weight Over Weight of Carcass Prior to Final Washer (Less Necks and Giblets)	
	Zone A[1]	Zone B[1]
8 lb. 8 oz. and under	8.0	9.0
8 lb. 9 oz.–15 lb. 15 oz.	6.0	6.4
16 lb.–16 lb. 15 oz.	5.8	6.05
17 lb.–17 lb. 15 oz.	5.5	5.75
18 lb.–18 lb. 15 oz.	5.3	5.55
19 lb.–19 lb. 15 oz.	5.1	5.35
20 lb.–20 lb. 15 oz	4.9	5.15
21 lb.–21 lb. 15 oz.	4.8	5.05
22 lb.–22 lb. 15 oz.	4.6	4.85
23 lbs–23 lb. 15 oz.	4.5	4.75
24 lb.–26 lb. 15 oz.	4.4	4.65
27 lb. and over	4.3	4.55

[1] Product shall be retained if, out of five consecutive tests, more than one test exceeds the Zone A limits or any test exceeds the Zone B limits. These zone limits were based on a statistical analysis of variation between individual birds with regard to moisture absorption. With these limits the chance of passing a lot with average moisture at or above the Zone A limit is less than 15 percent. A lot with average moisture at or above the Zone B limit would have virtually no chance of passing.
From U.S. Dept. of Agr.

tail sale are sufficient to compensate for the additional moisture previously absorbed. Henry and Fromm (1958) reported that even under the most favorable conditions of moisture absorption a processor could only receive 3 to 12 cents per hundred pounds additional income by excessive water chilling.

Brant (1963) has reported on the research on chilling poultry and on some of the factors which influence moisture absorption and loss. Car-

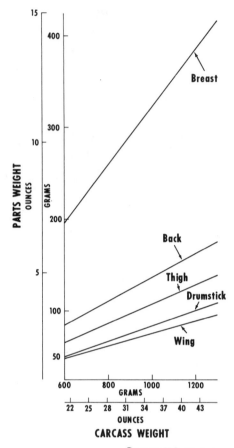

Courtesy U.S. Dept. Agr.

FIG. 5.1. RELATIONSHIP BETWEEN MEAN WEIGHT OF BROILER PARTS
AND CARCASS

casses absorb from 2.00–3.25% moisture during washing. The period of time carcasses are left in the chilling solution influences the amount of water absorbed. The longer the immersion period the greater the increase in moisture. The rate of absorption is fastest during the first few hours but carcasses can continue to absorb moisture for as long as seven days. Agitation of the slush/ice water mixture has little if any effect on moisture absorption but movement of the carcasses has a pronounced effect. Absorption of as much as 22.7% moisture in 30 min. using a tumbling type chiller has been reported. The temperature of the chilling mixture ap-

TABLE 5.11

PERCENTAGE DISTRIBUTION OF CUT-UP PARTS IN DIFFERENT SPECIES OF READY-TO-COOK POULTRY

Kinds	Number of Birds	Average Age, Weeks	Average Live Weight, Lb.	Legs and Thighs, %	Breast, %	Back and Ribs,[1] %	Wings, %	Neck, %	Gizzard, %	Liver, %	Heart, %
Broilers											
Male	10	10	3.9	34.1	25.4	17.0	13.3	3.5	3.5	2.6	0.6
Female	10	10	3.0	32.4	25.7	16.6	13.6	4.1	4.1	2.8	0.7
Turkeys											
Small											
Male	10	16	10.0	29.3	28.3	19.9	13.0	3.3	3.8	2.3	1.0
Female	10	16	7.0	29.0	29.9	20.0	12.0	3.7	3.8	2.1	0.4
Large											
Male	10	28	22.0	24.1	41.3	18.4	9.5	3.4	1.8	1.1	0.4
Female	10	28	14.0	25.5	35.5	20.6	11.3	2.4	2.8	1.6	0.3
Ducks											
Male	10	7.5	7.1	23.4	29.7	23.0	10.6	5.4	4.3	2.7	0.9
Female	10	7.5	6.3	23.5	30.1	23.6	10.8	4.7	3.9	2.5	0.9
Geese	20	10–12	10.8	21.9	23.8	21.3	16.0	6.3	6.3	3.5	0.9

From Winter and Clements (1957).
[1] Ribs separated from breast and attached to back. Pelvic meat attached to thighs.

TABLE 5.12

PERCENTAGE YIELDS OF POULTRY COOKED BY DIFFERENT METHODS[1]

Cooking Method	Average	Range
Chicken		
Broiled	74	82–62
Fricassee	82	82–81
Fried	79	83–74
Roasted	72	83–61
Stewed or braised	68	77–51
Breast	81	93–73
Drumstick	73	76–68
Thigh	72	76–68
Wing	92	94–84
Back	76	84–68
Ribs	84	85–82
Neck	89	92–86
Turkey		
Roasted under 5 lb.	79	82–73 without giblets
over 5 lb.	72	82–56 without giblets
Boiled or stewed	71	74–68 without giblets
Steamed	69	75–65 without giblets
Pressure cooked	72	74–70 with giblets
Duck, not reported	82	85–74
Gosling, roasted	66	72–61

Compiled from Agricultural Handbook No. 102, Food Yields, U. S. Dept. Agr.
[1] Computed from ready-to-cook weights.

pears to have some effect on moisture absorption but reports are conflicting as to whether it causes a gain or loss.

Polyphosphates added to the chilling solution, generally at a level of six per cent, influence the amount of moisture absorption and the rate of loss. In general, moisture absorption is not as great during chilling when polyphosphates are added and moisture losses are less than with untreated groups during storage in crushed ice. Cooking losses have been reported to decrease slightly in some cases and not at all in others. However, carcasses treated with polyphosphates have a bluish color, a slippery texture and a slightly different flavor and texture upon cooking.

Draining after chilling causes a rapid loss of moisture for the first few hours. After 18 hr. in cellophane bags at 34°F., moisture losses in one experiment amounted to four per cent. However, it appears that in most cases an equilibrium is reached when the absorbed moisture content reaches six per cent.

Absorption of moisture is greatest in the skin, muscle, bone, and fatty tissue in that order. Carcasses high in fat absorb less moisture than those containing less fat.

With the exception of phosphate-treated carcasses, moisture absorption appears to have little effect on cooking losses or the quality of the cooked meat.

In 1971, the European Economic Community, an important consuming group for U.S. processed poultry, announced that immersion chilled poultry would not be purchased after January 1, 1977, mainly because such poultry could be insanitary. As a result, several symposia have been held on this subject. Thompson *et al.* (1974) in a review of chilling poultry meat reported that, compared with immersion chilling, spray chilling results in a 1–3% moisture uptake with considerable variability, and dry chilling under experimental conditions results in a 1% loss and under commercial conditions, from 5–8%. On the other hand, immersion chilled broilers lost more weight from cooking than dry chilled ones.

Brant (1974) summarized the present status of poultry chilling by reporting "that the objections to in-line immersion chilling of poultry cannot be supported by carefully conducted research on properly operated equipment. All alternative chilling procedures so far proposed are less efficient, do not improve the sanitary quality of the carcasses without extravagant use of water or require greater capital outlay."

COOKING LOSSES AND COOKED EDIBLE MEAT YIELDS

Lowe (1958) reported a number of factors which influence cooking losses. They are the degree of fatness, distribution, post-mortem stage, age, size, and cooking times. Other factors which she considered impor-

TABLE 5.13

PERCENTAGE OF EDIBLE MEAT YIELDS OF POULTRY COOKED BY DIFFERENT METHODS[1]

Cooking Method	Average	Range
Chicken		
Fricassee	66	69–63 with skin, without giblets
Roasted	62	69–58 without skin or giblets
Breast	86	92–71 fricassee with skin
Drumstick	68	74–58 fricassee with skin
Thigh	79	82–74 fricassee with skin
Wing	56	71–44 fricassee with skin
Back	58	67–48 fricassee with skin
Ribs	47	55–39 fricassee with skin
Neck	59	73–44 fricassee with skin
Turkey		
Roasted	71	88–57 with skin, without giblets
Boiled or stewed	65	72–60 without skin, with neck and giblets
Pressure cooked	55	56–54 without skin, with neck without giblets
Breast	89	92–86 with skin
Drumstick	69	73–63 with skin
Thigh	81	84–76 with skin
Wing	63	69–55 with skin
Foreback	59	67–48 with skin
Rearback	64	77–54 with skin

Compiled from Agricultural Handbook *102*, Food Yields, U. S. Dept. Agr.
[1] Computed from cooked weights.

Table 5.14

AVERAGE WEIGHTS OF LIVE, READY-TO-COOK,[1] COOKED EDIBLE PORTION,[2] PARTS AND BONES OF VARIOUS KINDS OF POULTRY PROCESSED IN ONTARIO COMMERCIAL PLANTS

Kind	Sex	No. of Birds	Method of Cooking	Average Weight of, Lb.											
				Live[4]	Ready-to-Cook[1] (Carcass and Neck)	Cooked[2]	White Meat	Dark Meat	Skin	Neck Meat	Total Edible Meat	Carcass Bones	Neck Bones	Total Bones	Loss[3] in Deboning
Chicken broilers	Male	6	Rotisserie	—	2.8	2.1	0.6	0.5	0.2	0.04	1.5	0.4	0.02	0.5	0.1
		9	Roasted	—	2.5	1.9	0.6	0.5	0.1	0.05	1.4	0.4	0.02	0.4	0.2
		15	Combined	3.8	2.6	2.0	0.6	0.5	0.2	0.05	1.4	0.4	0.02	0.4	0.1
	Female	7	Rotisserie	—	2.3	1.7	0.5	0.4	0.2	0.04	1.3	0.3	0.02	0.4	0.1
		8	Roasted	—	2.0	1.5	0.5	0.4	0.1	0.03	1.0	0.3	0.02	0.3	0.1
		15	Combined	3.1	2.1	1.6	0.5	0.4	0.1	0.04	1.1	0.3	0.02	0.3	0.1
Chicken broilers	Male	7	Rotisserie	—	3.9	2.8	0.9	0.8	0.2	0.06	2.0	0.6	0.03	0.6	0.1
		3	Roasted	—	4.1	2.9	0.9	0.8	0.2	0.07	1.9	0.6	0.04	0.6	0.3
		10	Combined	5.5	4.0	2.8	0.9	0.8	0.2	0.06	2.0	0.6	0.03	0.6	0.2
	Female	3	Rotisserie	—	3.0	2.1	0.7	0.6	0.2	0.05	1.6	0.4	0.02	0.4	0.03
		7	Roasted	—	2.9	2.1	0.7	0.5	0.1	0.06	1.4	0.4	0.03	0.4	0.1
		10	Combined	4.1	2.9	2.1	0.7	0.5	0.2	0.05	1.5	0.4	0.02	0.4	0.1
Capons		6	Rotisserie	—	5.7	4.1	1.5	1.3	0.3	—	3.2	0.8	—	—	0.3
		6	Roasted	—	5.9	4.2	1.5	1.3	0.3	—	3.1	0.7	—	—	0.3
		12	Combined	8.7	6.2	4.2	1.5	1.3	0.3	—	3.1	0.8	—	—	0.3
Turkey broilers	Male	8	Roasted	12.4	9.4	6.8	2.7	1.7	0.4	0.16	5.0	1.3	0.09	1.4	0.3
	Female	8	Roasted	7.9	6.1	4.6	1.8	1.2	0.3	0.10	3.3	0.8	0.05	0.9	0.3
Pekin ducks	Male	10	Roasted	5.8	3.4	2.0	0.6[5]	0.5	0.2	—	1.4	0.4	—	—	0.1
	Female	10	Roasted	5.6	3.2	1.8	0.6	0.5	0.2	—	1.3	0.4	—	—	0.2
Pheasants	Male	5	Roasted	3.0	2.4	1.7	0.8	0.4	0.1	0.03	1.3	0.2	0.01	0.2	0.2
	Female	5	Roasted	2.5	1.9	1.3	0.6	0.3	0.1	0.02	1.0	0.2	0.01	0.2	0.1

From Snyder and Orr (1964), Ontario Agr. College.
[1] Defrosted weight (carcass + neck in all except capons and ducks which are less neck).
[2] Includes carcass + neck with exception of capons and ducks in which necks are not included.
[3] Includes waste + evaporation.
[4] Live weight for individual birds cooked on rotisserie and roasted not available.
[5] Breast meat.

Table 5.15

PERCENTAGE RELATIONSHIP OF COOKED EDIBLE PORTION, PARTS AND BONES TO LIVE WEIGHT OF VARIOUS KINDS OF POULTRY PROCESSED IN ONTARIO COMMERCIAL PLANTS

Kind	Sex	Method[1] of Cooking, %	Cooked Carcass[2] and Neck, %	White Meat, %	Dark Meat, %	Skin, %	Neck Meat, %	Total Edible Meat, %	Carcass Bones, %	Neck Bones, %	Total Bones, %	Total Loss[3] in Deboning, %
Chicken broilers	Male	Combined	51.9	15.3	13.5	4.2	1.3	36.8	10.9	0.7	11.6	3.5
Chicken broilers	Female	Combined	52.7	17.0	13.8	5.1	1.4	37.4	11.0	0.8	11.7	3.6
Chicken broilers	Male	Combined	51.8	16.9	14.4	4.1	1.2	36.6	11.0	0.7	11.8	3.4
Chicken broilers	Female	Combined	51.2	17.2	13.6	4.5	1.4	36.8	10.2	0.7	10.8	2.7

(Continuation of table from preceding page)

Kind	Sex		As a Percentage of Live Weight — Cooked Carcass	White Meat	Dark Meat	Skin	As a Percentage of Ready-to-Cook Weight — White Meat	Dark Meat	Skin	Separable Fat	Total Edible Meat	Carcass Bones
Capons	Male	Combined	47.9	17.6	14.7	3.5	35.8	8.7	···	···	···	3.4
Turkey broilers	Male	Roasted	54.8	21.8	14.1	3.4	40.6	11.0	0.7	11.7	1.4	2.5
	Female	Roasted	57.7	22.3	15.1	3.5	42.2	10.7	0.7	11.4	1.3	3.6
Pekin ducks	Male	Roasted	34.2	10.7[4]	9.0	4.3	24.1	7.8	···	···	···	2.6
	Female	Roasted	33.2	10.1	8.7	4.2	23.0	7.1	···	···	···	3.0
Pheasants	Male	Roasted	57.7	26.0	13.7	3.2	44.1	7.9	0.5	8.4	1.2	5.1
	Female	Roasted	52.7	24.0	12.3	3.0	40.4	6.8	0.4	7.2	1.0	5.0

From Snyder and Orr (1964), Ontario Agr. College.
[1] See Table (5.14) for number and method of cooking.
[2] For capons and ducks—carcass only, necks not included.
[3] Includes waste + evaporation.
[4] Breast meat.

TABLE 5.16

PERCENTAGE RELATIONSHIP OF COOKED EDIBLE PORTION, PARTS AND BONES TO LIVE AND READY-TO-COOK WEIGHT OF POULTRY PROCESSED AT DEPARTMENT OF POULTRY SCIENCE

Kind	Sex	As a Percentage of Live Weight — Cooked Carcass	White Meat	Dark Meat	Skin	Separable Fat	Total Edible Meat	Carcass Bones	As a Percentage of Ready-to-Cook² Weight — Cooked Carcass	White Meat	Dark Meat	Skin	Separable Fat	Total Edible Meat	Carcass Bones
Roasters	Male	46.4	15.7	14.5	4.4	···	34.7	8.7	68.2	23.1	21.3	6.5	···	51.0	12.9
White Rock fowl	Female	46.9[1]	16.3	13.3	4.4	···	35.2[2]	7.6	63.9[1]	22.4	18.2	6.0	···	47.9[1]	10.3
White Leghorn fowl	Female	38.0[1]	13.3	9.9	3.1	···	27.3[1]	7.2	58.3[1]	20.5	16.5	4.8	···	51.4	11.1
Turkey broilers	Male	51.5	21.1	11.8	3.9	···	36.7	10.6	72.2	29.7	16.5	5.3	···	52.9	14.9
Small white	Female	51.6	22.6	12.5	4.7	2.7	37.5	9.7	72.8	29.7	17.6	5.5	3.5	55.1	13.7
Large white X	Male	51.6	21.6	11.4	4.7	1.8	41.4	6.9	68.6	30.0	15.1	6.3	2.4	53.0	9.2
Small white turkeys	Female	50.7	20.5	12.0	4.7	3.0	40.1	7.2	68.6	28.6	15.9	6.2	4.1	54.0	9.7
Large white X	Male	50.3	20.6	11.8	4.4	1.8	40.1	7.5	67.1	27.6	16.3	6.3	2.4	52.6	9.7
Bourbon Red turkeys	Female	49.7	21.4	12.2	4.9	2.9	39.3	7.1	66.5	28.8	16.6	6.0	3.9	52.6	10.0
Bourbon Red X	Male	51.7	20.9	12.4	4.9	1.9	41.2	7.1	69.6	28.1	16.6	6.3	3.6	55.5	9.9
Small white turkeys	Female	51.1	19.0	12.4	4.6	2.7	40.1	8.0	68.8	28.8	16.6	6.7	3.7	53.9	9.5
Bourbon Red turkeys	Male	50.5	18.8	12.9	3.3	1.5	39.3	7.5	68.8	26.3	17.5	6.4	2.1	54.3	11.1
Bourbon Red turkeys	Female	49.1	22.6	13.9	4.0	···	37.9	9.6	67.8	26.0	17.4	4.4	···	52.4	10.4
Color-strain	Male	53.5	22.6	13.9	···	···	39.9	9.6	70.9	30.0	18.4	···	···	52.8	12.8
Cross turkeys	Female	52.6	22.1	14.2	···	···	40.2	8.6	68.8	29.0	18.6	5.3	···	52.6	11.1

From Snyder and Orr (1964), Ontario Agr. College.
[1] Neck included.
[2] Defrosted ready-to-cook weight.

tant are covered vs. uncovered pans, basting, breast up or down, double vs. single cooking periods, time and temperature of cooking and the stage of doneness.

Winter and Clements (1957) reported that from an edible yield standpoint the best yields come from large turkeys with 1.76 lb. of ready-to-cook meat required for each pound of cooked edible meat, followed by small turkeys which require 1.85 lb., chicken broilers, 1.94 lb., chicken breasts, 1.58 lb., giblets, 1.71 lb. and the legs and thighs of turkeys and chicken 1.75 and 1.88 lb., respectively.

Swickard, Harkin and Paul (1954), in a study of the quality of Leghorn hens, reported that before cooking 27 to 30-month old hens had higher prepared carcass yields than 18 to 20-month old ones but after cooking the older hens had lower carcass yields. Grade A carcasses had the lowest percentage cooked carcass yield and Grade C ones the highest.

MEASURING SOME CHARACTERISTICS OF FATS

The term rancidity is used to describe any disagreeable off-flavor or odor in fats and oils; however, from a chemical viewpoint it is considered to be the oxidation of unsaturated fatty acids with resultant secondary products and off-odors. Rancidity can be caused by the absorption of odors, enzymatic action, microorganisms, and oxidation. Because poultry fats contain unsaturated fatty acids, rancidity causes off-odor and -flavors in poultry under some conditions.

The peroxide values or substances in fat which oxidize potassium iodide are generally used as a test for rancidity and fat stability, but the best tests for rancidity are flavor and odor. Unfortunately there is not very good agreement between organoleptic scores and peroxide values.

Oxidative rancidity is caused by oxygen in the atmosphere reacting with the unsaturated bonds in the fats or oils. In addition to the type of fat, air, temperature, metals, light, and surface area all influence the rate of development and extent of rancidity.

MEASURING TENDERNESS

Since tenderness consists of several factors it is difficult to develop an objective measurement which will measure tenderness in the same way it is viewed by the consumer. Generally a taste panel can be used to evaluate tenderness. One approach to the problem has been for panel members to count the number of chews required before swallowing. Fairly good correlations have been obtained between taste panels and both the Warner Bratzler and Lee Kramer shear presses (Figs. 5.2 and 5.3). The Warner Bratzler press does not always work as well as the Lee Kramer

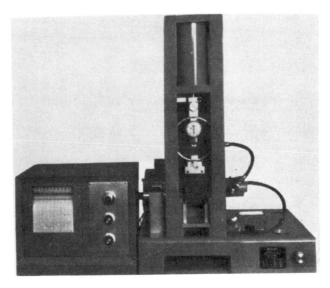

Courtesy Allo Precision Metals Engineering, Inc.

FIG. 5.2.   A HYDRAULIC RECORDING SHEAR PRESS

press for poultry work because of the problem of obtaining a large enough sample and because it measures in pounds rather than grams. Although several other instruments have been developed to measure tenderness such as food grinders which measure the energy required to grind a standard amount of tissue and a recording strain gage denture tenderometer which utilizes a set of dentures, the Warner Bratzler and Lee Kramer presses are still the most used instruments.

TESTS FOR FLAVOR

Tests for flavor according to Dawson *et al.* (1963) can be divided into those which test for differences in flavor and those in which preferences are expressed for a particular flavor or characteristic. Tests for differences include the triangle, paired-comparison, duo-trio, multiple-comparison, descriptive-term, profile, and dilution tests. Generally, such tests are conducted under carefully controlled laboratory conditions with trained panels able to reproduce results with a high degree of accuracy. Data from such panels are generally analyzed statistically to determine whether the results can be reproduced and with what degree of accuracy. Despite the above conditions tasting is nevertheless subjective because the data are based on human judgments.

TABLE 5.17

PERCENTAGE RELATIONSHIP OF COOKED EDIBLE PORTION, PARTS AND BONES TO READY-TO-COOK[1] WEIGHT OF VARIOUS KINDS OF POULTRY PROCESSED IN ONTARIO COMMERCIAL PLANTS

Kind	Sex	Method of Cooking	Cooked Carcass[2] and neck, %	White Meat, %	Dark Meat, %	Skin, %	Neck Meat, %	Total Edible Meat, %	Carcass Bones, %	Neck Bones, %	Total Bones, %	Loss in[3] Deboning, %	Cooking Loss		
													Drippings, %	Evaporation, %	Total, %
Chicken broilers	Male	Rotisserie	73.2	20.0	18.3	7.4	1.8	53.6	15.7	0.9	16.6	3.0	...	...	26.7
		Roasted	76.2	23.7	20.3	5.0	2.1	52.8	15.7	1.1	16.8	6.6	5.3	18.4	23.7
		Combined	75.0	22.1	19.4	6.0	1.9	53.1	15.7	1.0	16.7	5.1	...	...	25.0
	Female	Rotisserie	76.2	25.4	20.5	8.0	2.1	56.0	15.4	1.1	16.5	3.7	...	...	23.8
		Roasted	74.2	23.2	18.9	6.6	1.9	50.6	15.8	1.1	16.9	6.7	8.3	17.5	25.8
		Combined	75.2	24.3	19.7	7.3	2.0	53.3	15.6	1.1	16.7	5.2	...	...	24.8
Chicken broilers	Male	Rotisserie	72.4	23.9	20.1	6.1	1.7	51.9	15.5	1.0	16.5	3.9	...	...	27.6
		Roasted	69.1	21.9	19.0	4.4	1.7	47.0	14.5	1.0	15.5	6.6	13.4	17.4	30.8
		Combined	71.4	23.3	19.8	5.6	1.7	50.4	15.2	1.0	16.2	4.7	...	...	28.6
	Female	Rotisserie	71.7	24.6	20.1	8.5	1.9	55.1	14.5	0.8	15.2	1.3	...	...	28.3
		Roasted	72.1	24.0	18.8	5.4	2.1	50.3	14.2	1.0	15.2	4.8	12.3	15.6	27.9
		Combined	72.0	24.2	19.2	6.3	2.0	51.8	14.3	1.0	15.2	3.7	...	...	28.0
Capons		Rotisserie	74.4	24.7	22.9	4.6	...	55.8	12.1	...	...	5.1	...	...	25.6
		Roasted	66.7	25.8	20.4	5.2	...	49.7	12.7	...	...	4.9	9.4	23.9	33.3
		Combined	70.4	25.2	21.6	4.9	...	52.6	13.4	...	...	5.0	...	...	29.6
Turkey broilers	Male	Roasted	72.0	28.6	18.5	4.5	1.8	53.3	14.4	1.0	15.4	3.3	5.4	22.6	28.0
	Female	Roasted	75.0	28.9	19.6	4.5	1.7	54.8	13.9	1.0	14.8	4.7	6.2	18.8	25.0
Pekin ducks	Male	Roasted	60.7	18.5[4]	15.2	7.4	...	41.5	13.4	...	...	4.4	21.7	17.6	39.3
	Female	Roasted	57.8	17.7	15.2	7.3	...	40.1	12.5	...	...	5.2	24.4	17.7	42.1
Pheasants	Male	Roasted	72.9	32.9	17.4	4.0	1.5	55.8	10.0	0.6	10.6	6.5	12.9	14.1	27.0
	Female	Roasted	68.1	31.1	15.9	3.9	1.3	52.3	8.8	0.6	9.3	6.5	20.3	11.6	31.9

From Snyder and Orr (1964), Ontario Agr. College.
[1] Ready-to-cook = defrosted drained weight of carcass and neck, with exception of capons and ducks in which necks are not included.
[2] Necks not included in capons and ducks.
[3] Includes waste + evaporation.
[4] Breast meat.

Courtesy Ohio Agr. Ext. Service

FIG. 5.3.   A WARNER BRATZLER SHEAR PRESS

Palatability tests are used in quality control work and in research and the development of new products to measure differences in preparation and serving, to determine differences in processing and varieties, and to attempt to characterize or describe flavors for promotion and advertising.

Preparation of Sample

Samples are cooked and the degree of doneness is measured by determining a given period of time, a particular internal temperature or by tenderness such as whether thigh joints can be pierced with a skewer or the wing joints are soft. Generally salt or seasoning is not added during cooking. After cooking, each carcass should be carved in the same manner and each judge should receive a sample from the same relative position of the

Table 5.18

PERCENTAGE RELATIONSHIP OF DEBONING AND COOKING LOSSES TO READY-TO-COOK[1] WEIGHT AND PER CENT JELLY AND FAT IN DRIPPINGS OF VARIOUS KINDS OF POULTRY PROCESSED AT DEPARTMENT OF POULTRY SCIENCE, O.A.C., 1962–63

Kind	Sex	Deboning Loss, %			Cooking Loss, %			Percentage in Drippings	
		Waste	Evaporation	Total	Drippings	Evaporation	Total	Jelly	Fat
Roasters	Male	1.1	3.4	4.5	5.1	26.6	31.7	53.1	46.9
White Rock fowl	Female	0.8	1.4	2.2	17.6	18.5	36.1	27.3	72.7
White Leghorn fowl	Female	0.6	3.8	4.4	7.6	34.1	41.7	37.4	62.6
Turkey broilers	Male	1.1	4.9	6.0	6.1	21.7	27.8	82.1	17.9
(small white)	Female	1.2	3.9	5.1	7.3	19.9	27.2	74.1	25.9
Large white X	Male	0.5	3.3	3.8	12.2	19.2	31.4	37.0	63.0
Small white turkeys	Female	0.3	4.1	4.4	14.7	18.2	32.9	19.1	80.9
Large white X	Male	0.4	3.6	4.0	14.7	17.6	32.5	35.1	64.9
Bourbon Red turkeys	Female	0.3	3.7	4.0	14.6	18.9	33.5	14.9	85.1
Bourbon Red X	Male	0.3	3.7	4.0	11.9	18.4	30.3	33.0	67.0
Small white turkeys	Female	0.2	5.2	5.5	14.0	17.1	31.2	20.9	79.1
Bourbon Red turkeys	Male	0.1	4.4	4.5	12.2	17.9	30.2	28.8	71.2
	Female	0.3	5.0	5.3	15.6	16.5	32.1	22.9	77.1
Color-strain	Male	1.1	4.3	5.4	12.4	16.7	29.1	59.6	40.4
Cross turkeys	Female	1.0	4.1	5.1	14.7	16.4	31.2	34.1	65.9

From Snyder and Orr (1964), Ontario Agr. College.
[1] Defrosted ready-to-cook weight as in Table (5.4).

carcass each time. The carved meat can be served with toothpicks. Clean glass rods have been used for sampling drippings. Generally, discussion is prohibited until after judging has been completed. To remove flavors from the mouth soda crackers, raw apple and dry bread with black coffee have been used. Reference samples are frequently used for a standard of comparison.

Triangle and Duo-Trio Tests

Triangle and duo-trio tests are used to evaluate the difference between two treatments or between a reference standard and different treatments. In the triangle test, two samples are alike and one is different. The judges determine which sample is different from the other two. The triangular test has been reported to be more efficient statistically than paired comparison tests, but the paired comparison tests are more economical.

Paired Comparison Tests

With this type of test panel members determine whether two samples are from the same or different treatments. Since the test consists of direct comparisons it requires only a short memory span on the part of the participants.

Multiple-Sample Tests

With this type of test a number of treatments can be compared to a standard. Advantages of the multiple sample test are that smaller differences can be detected, it gives additional information on the relationship of the samples and it requires fewer samples and less time than the other methods.

Ranking

Ranking consists of placing the samples numerically in order of some given characteristic such as increasing saltiness or decreasing preference. Ranking is easier to use and does not require as highly trained a panel as some of the other methods. It eliminates the tendency to prefer certain scoring ranges. Ranking is generally used when several samples are tested for an individual quality criteria.

Scoring

Numerical scores are given to products with different degrees of a quality attribute. Descriptive terms have been used to describe the flavor of poultry; however, in some cases this has suggested the possibility of off-flavors which would not ordinarily be considered. Several workers have used scores varying from 0–3 to 0–50. Generally a sample which received 0 is considered inedible. Some of these same scores have been used to score flavor and aroma.

Dilution Tests

Dilution tests can be used to determine the smallest amount of a substance which can be detected when diluted with a solvent. They have been used with chicken broth.

BIBLIOGRAPHY

ANON. 1950. Review of literature on methodology in palatability testing. Bur. Human Nutr. Home Econ., U.S. Dept. Agr., Agr. Res. Serv.

ANON. 1952. Conversion factors and weights and measures for agricultural commodities and their products. U.S. Dept. Agr., Production Mktg Admin.

ANON. 1960. The Science of Meat and Meat Products. American Meat Institute Foundation (Editors). W. H. Freeman & Co., San Francisco.

ANON. 1963. An introduction to taste testing of foods. Merck Tech. Bull. Merck & Co., Rahway, N.J.

ANON. 1974. Part 381—Poultry products inspection regulations. Federal Register 37, No. 95, 9722.

BRANT, A. W. 1963. Chilling poultry. A review. Poultry Process. Mktg. 69, No. 5, 14-22.

BRANT, A. W. 1974. Chilling poultry meat. 6. The current status of poultry chilling in Europe. Poultry Sci. 53, 1291-1295.

DAWSON, E. H., GROGDON, J. L., and McMANUE, S. 1963. Sensory testing of differences in taste. I. Methods. Food Technol. 17, No. 9, 45-51.

HENRY, W. R., and FROMM, D. 1958. Economic aspects of prolonged broiler chilling. N. Carolina State Coll. A. E. Inform. Ser. 67.

LOWE, B. 1958. Experimental Cookery, 4th Edition. John Wiley & Sons, New York.

McCALLISTER, K. J. 1951. Principles and practices in the developments of standards for grades for agricultural products. In Market Demand and Product Quality. Rept. Mktg. Res. Workshop, Michigan State Coll. Dept. Agr.

MINOR, L. J., DAWSON, L. E., and PEARSON, A. M. 1964. Cooked meat yields from roasters and heavy light hens. Food Technol. 18, 153-156.

PECOT, R. K., and WATT, B. K. 1956. Food yields summarized by different stages of preparation. U.S Dept. Agr., Agr. Res. Serv., Agr. Handbook 102.

STADELMAN, W. J. 1974. Chilling poultry meat. 1. Why the surge of interest? Poultry Sci. 53, 1267-1268.

SNYDER, E. S., and ORR, H. L. 1964. Poultry meat—processing, quality factors, yields. Ontario Dept. Agr., Publ. 9.

SWANSON, M. H., CARLSON, C. W., and FRY, J. L. 1964. Factors affecting poultry meat yields. North Central Res. Publ. 158.

SWICKARD, M. T., HARKIN, A. M., and PAUL, B. J. 1954. Relationship of cooking methods, grades, and frozen storage to quality of cooked mature Leghorn hens. U.S. Dept. Agr., Tech. Bull. 1077.

THOMPSON, J. E., WHITEHEAD, W. K., and MERCURI, A. J. 1974. Chilling poultry meat—a literature review. Poultry Sci. 53, 1268–1281.

WALTERS, R. E., MAY, K. N., and RODGERS, P. D. 1963. Relations of weights and sizes of broiler parts to carcass weights. U.S. Dept. Agr., Agr. Mktg Serv., Mktg. Res. Rept. 604.

WATT, B. M., and MERRILL, A. L. 1963. Composition of foods—raw, processed, prepared. U.S. Dept. Agr., Agr. Handbook 8.

WINTER, A. R., and CLEMENTS, P. 1957. Cooked edible meat in ready-to-cook poultry. J. Am. Dietet. Assoc. 33, 800–802.

CHAPTER 6

Microbiology of
Poultry Meat

INTRODUCTION

Several hundred different species of microorganisms have been reported on poultry meat. One team of workers alone, Gunderson, Rose and Henn (1947) isolated 186 strains of bacteria representing 19 different genera.

Microorganisms found on poultry can be divided into two general groups, those which can produce disease in humans, generally referred to as pathogens, and those not associated with a recognized disease which are designated as non-pathogenic organisms.

PATHOGENIC ORGANISMS

Pathogens can be divided further into those which produce diseases by invading the body and producing an infection and those which produce toxins or poisons in the food itself. *Salmonella* and *Streptococci* are examples of organisms which cause infections. *Staphylococcus* and *Clostridium* are examples of types of organisms which cause disease by producing toxins which are consumed with contaminated food.

Poultry are known to be carriers of a number of organisms pathogenic to humans. Galton and Arnstein (1960) have reported that "In the United States domestic fowl are the most frequent vehicle of dissemination in outbreaks of food-borne infections, and the Salmonellas, followed by paracolons (Arizona group), are the most important organisms implicated in these outbreaks."

Ingalls (1950) stated that at least 26 diseases reported to occur in poultry can also cause disease in man. However, despite the large number of pathogenic organisms found in poultry which are transmissable to man, poultry is believed to play a very minor role in the transmission of diseases of human beings. Probably the main reason for the small incidence of human infection is because poultry meat is eaten only after thorough cooking.

Bacteria

Reports by a number of workers have shown that fowl are the largest single source of *Salmonella* in the United States. For this reason *Salmonella* is probably the most important group of bacteria found in poultry which can cause human illness. Ingalls (1950) in a review of literature reported that *Salmonella orangienburg, S. typhimurium, S. montevideo, S. newport, S. enteritidis, S. anatum,* and under certain conditions, *S. gal-*

88

linarium and *S. pullorum* may cause gastrointestinal disturbances in human beings. Since 1950, the time of their report, a considerable number of other *Salmonella* organisms have also been found to cause disease in humans.

Other bacterial diseases transmissible to humans from poultry are paracolon infections, erysipelas, staphylococcal infections, streptococcal infections, tuberculosis, brucellosis, listerosis, tularemia, pasteurellosis, pseudotuberculosis, diphtheria, anthrax, botulism, and leptospirosis.

Viruses

Several virus organisms which can cause diseases are also found in poultry. Newcastle disease has been reported by several workers to cause conjunctivitis in humans. Psittacosis-ornithosis infections transmitted to humans from poultry have been reported in several processing plants. Symptoms in humans vary from mild influenza-like attacks to fatal illness. Equine encephalomyelitis has also been reported in several species of poultry.

Fungi

Favus, thrush, aspergillosis, and histoplasmosis have all been reported in poultry. These organisms are considered to be only a minor hazard to poultry workers.

Other Parasites

Poultry mites and lice frequently cause skin irritation and sometimes sores on poultry carcasses. The protozoan organisms causing toxoplasmosis have also been found in several species of poultry.

SPOILAGE ORGANISMS

Non-pathogenic organisms can be divided into those groups which cause food spoilage and those which do not bring about conditions generally considered as spoilage in foods. Because most non-pathogens live in soil, water, or air they are as a group more resistant than most pathogens. In general organisms produce spoilage by bringing about chemical changes in one or more of the three major nutrients, the carbohydrates, fats, and proteins; in other cases they bring about desirable changes such as fermentation reactions.

Microflora on Poultry Carcasses

Walker and Ayres (1956) in a study of microorganisms found on poultry in six Iowa processing plants reported that live poultry generally had from 600 to 8100 organisms per square centimeter of skin area and that

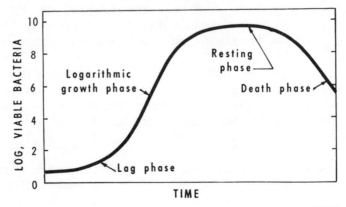

From Elliott and Michener, U.S. Dept. Agr. (1965)

FIG. 6.1.   A TYPICAL BACTERIAL GROWTH CURVE

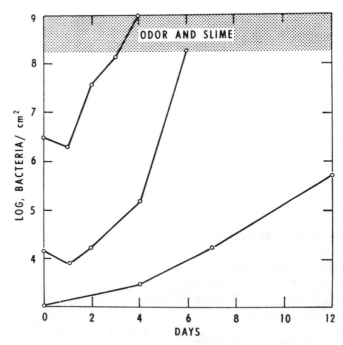

From Elliott and Michener, U.S. Dept. Agr. (1965)
and data of Ayres et al. (1950)

FIG. 6.2.   EFFECT OF INITIAL BACTERIAL LOAD ON SHELF-LIFE OF
CHICKEN MEAT AT 40°F.

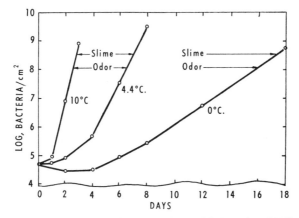

From Elliott and Michener, U.S. Dept. Agr. (1965)
and data of Ayres et al. (1950)

FIG. 6.3. EFFECT OF STORAGE TEMPERATURE ON GROWTH OF
BACTERIA ON CHICKEN MEAT

after processing and evisceration carcasses had from 11,000 to 93,000 organisms per square centimeter. In a later paper, Walker and Ayres (1959) reported that live turkeys generally had from 750 to 41,000 organisms per square centimeter.

The bacterial population also influences the point at which spoilage is observed organoleptically (Figs. 6.1, 6.2 and 6.3). Elliott and Michener (1961) in a review of microbiological standards for foods reported that off-odors appeared from poultry carcasses when the log of the number of bacteria reached from 6.5 to 8.0 per sq. cm. Slime formation occurred when the number of organisms reached a log concentration of 7.5 to 9.0 per sq. cm.

Ayres, Ogilvy and Stewart (1950) identified the following genera on eviscerated cut-up poultry; *Pseudomonas, Micrococcus, Achromobacter, Flavobacterium, Alcaligenes, Proteus, Bacillus, Sarcina, Streptococcus, Eberthella, Salmonella, Escherichia, Aerobacter, Streptomyces, Penicillium, Oospora, Cryptococcus,* and *Rhodotorula.*

These workers reported that immediately after processing chromogenic bacteria represented about 50–60% of the microflora on the carcass, *Pseudomonas,* colorless cocci, and closely related forms about 20–25% and the remaining 20–25% of the organisms consisted of miscellaneous bacteria. After storage chromogens and miscellaneous bacteria accounted for less than one per cent of the total organisms present. *Pseudomonas* and *Alcaligenes* were found to be the principal organisms found on slime spoiled carcasses (Fig. 6.4).

Nagel, Simpson, Ng, Vaughn, and Stewart (1960) in a study of the mi-

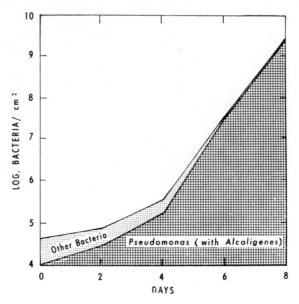

From Elliott and Michener, U.S. Dept. Agr. (1965)
and data of Ayres et al. (1950)

Fig 6.4.   Floral Changes During Spoilage of Chicken Meat
at 40°F.

croflora of spoiled cut-up, tray packed fryers from six different states re-
ported that from 103 isolates 88 of the cultures belonged to the genus
Pseudomonas, two belonged to the genus *Aeromonas* and 13 were of the
Achromobacter-Alcaligenes group.

Sources of Contamination

Walker and Ayres (1956) reported that soil and fecal material on the
feet and feathers of birds and their intestinal contents were the main
sources of contamination but that the processing line was their main
means of dissemination.   They concluded that any practice which
would limit contact with these contaminants would, as a result, keep
bacterial counts low.   Other sources of contamination can be water
supply, humans, air, equipment, packaging material, and ice.

Nagel, Simpson, Ng, Vaughn, and Stewart (1960) reported that the geo-
graphical location, location of the cut-up operations and antibiotics did
not influence the distribution of the genera of spoilage organisms encountered in their study.

TABLE 6.1

SALMONELLA SEROTYPES ISOLATED FROM TEN FLOCKS AT VARIOUS STAGES OF PROCESSING

S. enteriditis Serotype	Feces at Plant Entrance	Carcasses During Processing Before First Incision	Carcasses During and After Evisceration	Edible Viscera	Plant Environ- ment[1]
Group I[2]					
blockley	1	2	4	1	3
bredeney	4	26	6	5	0
heidelberg	3	17	3	4	2
litchfield	1	0	9	1	2
montevideo	1	6	9	9	8
thompson	1	3	6	5	13
typhimurium	1	0	2	1	2
Group II[3]					
eimsbuettel	0	0	1	0	0
lexington	0	1	0	0	0
schwarzengrund	0	1	0	0	0
Group B, non-motile	0	0	0	1	0

[1] Tables, tubs, conveyors, knives, saws, and gutter water.
[2] Isolated from feces of chickens entering plant.
[3] Not isolated from feces of chickens entering plant.
From Morris and Wells (1970).

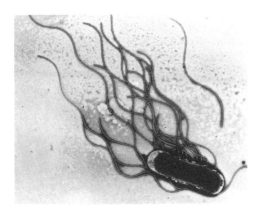

Courtesy U.S. Dept. Agr.

FIG. 6.5.   A *SALMONELLA* MICROORGANISM MAGNIFIED BY AN ELECTRON MICROSCOPE

The scalding operation is one area where bacterial contamination is spread during processing. The range in numbers of bacteria in water used for scalding varies considerably depending upon temperature, amount of use, cleanliness of the tank, and carcasses and the rate of overflow. In a review of this work Thompson and Kotula (1959) have reported studies in which counts as high as 292 million bacteria have been reported to ranges as low as 400–2500 per ml.

Thompson and Kotula (1959) using water in a scald tank contaminated with *Streptococcus fecalis* as a tracer organism reported that kosher style cut chickens (trachea, esophagus and the carotid artery and jugular vein severed) had only about one sixth as many test organisms in the wing air sac areas as chickens in which only the skin, artery and vein were severed.

The skin of broilers apparently acts as a barrier to microorganisms during processing. Mundt, Stokes, and Goff (1954) reported that almost all muscle tissue from carcasses processed at both high and low scald temperatures and several temperatures of chilling were sterile.

Scald temperatures may have some effect on shelf-life. Essary, Moore, and Kramer (1958) reported no difference between the types of organisms found on carcasses scalded at 128° and 138°F. Ziegler and Stadelman (1955) reported an extension of one day in shelf-life of carcasses scalded at 128°F. compared with those scalded at 140°F.

Kidneys and livers of healthy carcasses are sometimes a source of bacterial contamination. Essary and Howes (1960) reported that 42% of plates inoculated with bacteria from kidneys and 84% of plates inoculated with bacteria from livers were negative for bacterial growth. Removing kidneys from fryers during evisceration extended shelf-life for 1.27 days.

May, Irby, and Carmon (1962), in a study of the keeping quality of the skin, muscle, and kidney tissue which was aseptically removed from 102 fresh commercially processed ready-to-cook broilers, found that after storage at 39.2°F. skin tissue spoiled first in 75% of the cases while muscle tissue had the longest shelf-life. These workers suggested that tissue samples, especially kidneys, could be used to estimate shelf-life because they have the same rate of spoilage as the rest of the carcass.

The effect of chilling on bacterial populations depends to a large extent upon the conditions under which the carcasses are chilled. Kotula, Thompson, and Kinner (1962) compared bacterial counts obtained from carcasses chilled in a standard non-agitated chill tank, a rocker or oscillating vat type chiller and a counter-flow tumble type chiller. Bacterial numbers increased during a six-hour chill period in the standard non-agitated chill tank, they stayed about the same in the rocker type chiller and decreased in the counterflow-tumble type chiller. They suggested that these differences might be caused by the degree of agitation and the location of the entrance of the chilling media into the tanks of on the line chillers. Walker and Ayres (1956) reported that the median number of organisms stayed almost the same during chilling in a chill tank in which the slush ice was agitated with air.

Determining Bacterial Numbers

Several methods have been developed for taking samples for bacteriological examination from poultry carcasses. The two most generally used are the swab technique (Fig. 6.6) and the rinse method. Although there are some individual variations in using these methods depending upon the worker the general principles are the same. Mallmann, Dawson, Sultzer, and Wright (1958)[1] gave the following descriptions of the two methods.

"**Swab Technique.**—The swab on a wooden applicator consisted of firmly twisted cotton forming a swab about $3/_{16}$ in. in diameter and $3/_4$ in. long. The swabs were sterilized by dry heat. Prior to swabbing, each swab was moistened in sterile saline and pressed free of excess moisture. Approximately 4 sq. in. of the skin surface of each half bird, just above the thigh, was swabbed 3 times in different directions, rotating the swab in the process. The applicator stick was broken off aseptically about 1 in. above the swab, the swab being placed in a tube containing 10 ml. of sterile saline. The tube was vigorously shaken by striking it against the palm of the hand for 2 min. to disperse the cotton. Serial dilutions were made from the diluent and plated in the appropriate medium.

"**Rinse Methods.**—Each half bird was placed aseptically in a sterile 1 gal. glass jar and 400 ml. of sterile saline was then added. This volume was chosen in order to have adequate washing action; it approximates the average weight of the half birds. The jar was then vigorously shaken by means of a reciprocal shaker for 2 min. at 200 oscillations per minute. Serial dilutions of the diluent were made for plating."

Fromm (1959) made a quantitative comparative analysis of the cotton swab, alginate swab, spot plate, tissue sample, and rinse techniques to determine the efficiency of removal of bacteria from the skin of broiler carcasses. He reported that when accuracy, variability and the ease and speed of manipulation were considered the alginate swab was considered the method of choice; however, there was little difference in the results obtained by the use of alginate and cotton swabs.

Ayres, Walker, Fanelli, King, and Thomas (1956) reported that, although there is a constant relationship between the numbers of organisms removed by the rinse and swab techniques, the counts were always at a lower level when the rinse method was used. They also reported that the swab method was easier to use.

Mallmann, Dawson, Sultzer, and Wright (1958) found that results with the swab sampling method in which a four square inch sample was used were quite variable. They reported that although swab counts paralleled the rinse counts there was considerable variation from sample

---

[1] Reprinted from Food Technology *12*, 122–126, March 1958. Copyright 1958 by the Institute of Food Technologists and reprinted by permission of copyright owner.

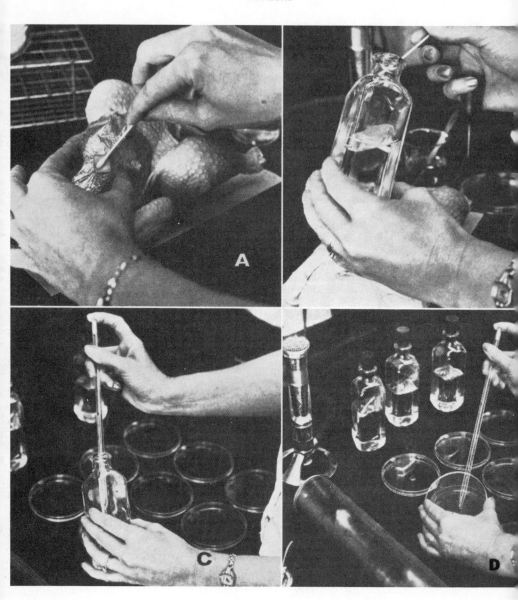

FIG. 6.6 STEPS IN DETERMINING BACTERIAL NUMBERS

(A) Taking the sample, (B) breaking the swab in diluting fluid, (C) taking the diluted sample, (D) transferring the sample to plates,

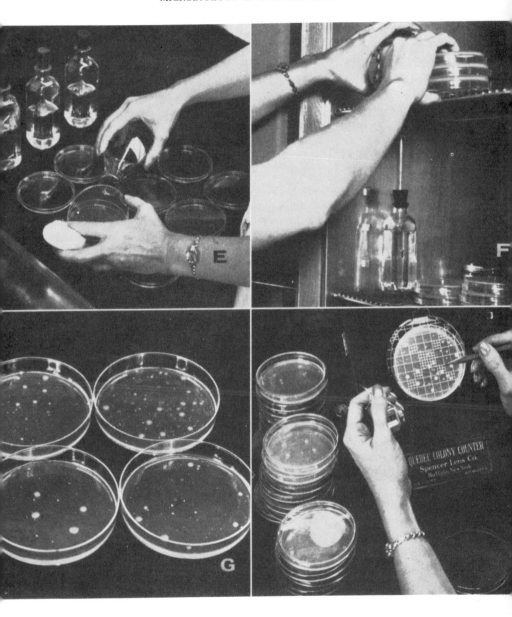

ON A POULTRY CARCASS

(E) pouring agar into plates, (F) incubation, (G) plates after incubation showing colonies, (H) counting colonies with a colony counter.

to sample with the rinse counts. Kinsley and Mountney (1966) have indicated that the size of the area sampled had considerable influence on the number of organisms recovered. Although the number of organisms recovered increased as the size of the template increased, the number of organisms recovered per square centimeter declined as the size of the template increased over two square centimeters. This effect of template size may explain the differences in results obtained by the two groups, Fromm and Mallmann, and Dawson, Sultzer, and Wright.

Goresline and Haugh (1959) developed a chart for determining the surface area of chicken parts. With their system, a piece of chicken is placed in a suitable container holding a diluent equal to three times the weight of the part. Then by locating the weight of the part on a chart and following lines the surface area in square centimeters can be determined and used with the counts to calculate the number of organisms per square centimeter found on the particular part.

Mercuri and Kotula (1964) were able to obtain good correlations between the log of bacteria per milliliter obtained by breast swabs and from drip obtained from tray-packed cut-up fryer chickens at several periods of storage.

Diluents.—Generally sterile distilled water is used as a diluent for making serial dilutions with poultry meat. However, work by Straka and Stokes (1957) demonstrated that the use of diluents can lead to large errors in the quantitative determination of bacterial numbers by plating methods. As many as 40 to 60% of the bacteria are destroyed within 20 min. in water and after standing for an hour as many as 40 to 90% are killed. When phosphate dilutions were used as many as 20–30% of the organisms were killed in a 20 min. period. A 0.5% peptone solution in water caused little or no loss within the limits of normal variation upon standing for periods up to an hour.

Media.—Kinsley and Mountney (1966) using inoculum from chilled poultry carcasses with low, medium and high bacterial loads brought about by different storage periods compared counts using tryptone glucose agar, heart infusion agar, eugon agar, and trypticase soy agar. Counts were slightly higher with heart infusion agar than with the other media; however, the differences in counts among the several agars were not statistically significant.

Incubation Temperatures.—Kinsley and Mountney (1966) observed that highest counts in the majority of cases were obtained by incubation at 68°, 50°, and 86°F. in that order. If only one set of counts are to be made, 68°F. is generally recommended.

Rapid Tests.—A number of attempts have been made to obtain estimates of bacterial numbers immediately after sampling. In general, these have consisted of the use of metabolic indicators, or counting or estimating the number of organisms on a microscopic slide.

Metabolic Indicators.—Mallmann, Dawson, Sultzer, and Wright (1958) developed a method utilizing phytone-nacconol broth designed to be selective for gram negative organisms which indicated bacterial growth by the reduction of triphenyl tetrazolium chloride. A phytone-nacconol reduction time of 24 hr. or a plate count of 10^3 organisms per square centimeter indicates a sanitary processing operation.

Slime Smears.—Ziegler, Spencer, and Stadelman (1954) developed a method in which samples of bacteria are collected by drawing a wire loop from the pectoral feather tract just under the wing and then transferring the organisms by spreading them uniformly over a glass slide. By taking daily samples an abrupt change in the number of organisms can be observed which is indicative of spoilage or approaching spoilage.

Ultraviolet Light.—Cotterill (1956) demonstrated that ultraviolet light could be used to detect advanced stages of spoilage as indicated by the presence of fluorescence from colonies of *Pseudomonas fluorescens*, a small gram negative rod which produces a fluorescent pigment.

RETARDING THE GROWTH OF MICROORGANISMS

A number of methods to delay spoilage of poultry have been tested. Of these methods low temperature remains the most dependable and widely used method.

Temperature

A number of studies to determine the effect of temperature on growth of bacteria on poultry carcasses have been made. These studies have been reviewed by Dawson and Stadelman (1960). When carcasses are stored close to 32°F. it takes approximately 18 days for spoilage to occur; when stored at 37°F. it takes 11 days and at 68°F. only 2 days.

Hydrogen Ion Concentration

The pH of the chilling media has some influence on bacterial counts. Murphy and Murphy (1962) patented a method where carcasses were immersed in lactic, citric or hydrochloric acid. Under some conditions they were able to obtain a longer shelf-life than when the carcasses were treated with an antibiotic. Carcasses immersed in a 0.12% concentration of lactic acid had a total bacterial count of 400 compared with a control group which had 130,000 organisms. Mountney, Blackwood, Kinsley, and

O'Malley (1964) demonstrated that hydrochloric acid in dilute amounts can reduce bacterial counts. Perry, Lawrence, and Melnick (1962) reported that sorbic acid is an effective preservative when a 7.5% solution is sprayed onto the chilled poultry parts at 140°F. in a ratio of 70 : 20 : 10 propylene glycol, water, and glycerin. With this treatment and previous immersion for two hours in a five per cent solution of NaH_2PO_4 shelf life was extended ten days.

Silliker *et al.* (1957) reported on a unique method for delaying spoilage by the use of *Lactobacilli*. In their patent they reported that when *Lactobacillus* cells were added to chill water at a concentration of 100 million cells per milliliter shelf-life was increased as much as three days, the equivalent of adding ten parts per million of aureomycin to chill water. Mold growth was also less than with aureomycin treated carcasses.

Phosphates have also been used to extend shelf-life by reducing bacteria counts. Spencer and Smith (1962) have reported that a commercial mixture of polyphosphates, applied by adding a commercial mixture to the chill water at a rate of ten ounces per gallon and then immersing carcasses for six hours, increased shelf-life one to two days.

Preservatives

Of the materials tested for use in preserving chilled poultry carcasses, antibiotics have received the most attention. Unfortunately, although both chlortetracycline and oxytetracycline have been accepted as food preservatives by the United States Food and Drug Administration with tolerances on poultry meat not to exceed seven parts per million their ability to extend the shelf-life of poultry carcasses in commercial operations has certain limitations. According to Vaughn and Stewart (1960) various difficulties may be encountered. Some problems are: (1) it has not been possible to duplicate the results of many laboratory tests in extending shelf life under commercial conditions; (2) it appears that antibiotic resistant strains of bacteria have developed; (3) antibiotics are only effective against some bacteria; and (4) antibiotics have no effect on yeasts and molds which are also a part of the microflora of poultry carcasses.

In commercial practice antibiotics are generally added to slush ice at a concentration of ten parts per million and the carcasses are chilled in this mixture for about two hours. Citric acid is added to the antibiotic mixture to act as a chelating agent and sodium chloride to help as a dispersing agent.

Experiments have also been conducted to determine the effect of chlorine and iodine on bacterial growth. Dawson and Stadelman (1960) summarized the work done in this field. Although carcasses immersed in chill water containing 20 parts per million chlorine had lower bacterial counts than control groups the first few days of storage, shelf-life was not prolonged. However, in another study chlorine increased the shelf-life of chicken fryers two days.

Although iodine has been tested as a method of reducing bacterial counts numbers of bacteria were not reduced.

Carbon Dioxide

Ogilvy and Ayres (1951) studied the effect of carbon dioxide on prolonging the storage life of cut-up chicken. They reported that the effectiveness of carbon dioxide in inhibiting slime-forming organisms and increasing shelf-life improved as the carbon dioxide concentration increased. Both carbon dioxide concentrations between 0 and 25% and temperatures between 32° and 50°F. influenced bacterial growth. Concentrations of carbon dioxide above 25% caused discoloration.

MICROBIOLOGY OF POULTRY MEAT PRODUCTS

Cooked boned poultry meat can, if improperly handled, be a source of contamination for any of the numerous food products prepared from poultry meat and other ingredients. Not only is the surface area of the cooked meat increased and contaminated by deboning and dicing but the meat is then mixed with other ingredients usually of such a nature that they provide a good bacterial media for growth.

Boned Chicken

Gunderson, McFadden, and Kyle (1954) reported the following sequence of contamination in producing deboned poultry meat. The cooking process lowers the bacterial load, during cooling bacterial counts increase and then increase further at a rapid rate during the deboning operation. Handling, prolonged holding periods during boning, and build-up of contamination on equipment during the day all contributed to high bacterial counts.

Creamed Chicken

Straka and Combes (1952) reported that containers of creamed chicken should not be held for more than two hours before being placed in the freezer and that if the quick frozen samples are thawed at 77°F. over a 10 to 11 hr. period excessive counts should not be encountered.

Chicken Pies

Hucker and David (1957) in a study of commercial frozen chicken pies reported that about half had coliform types of organisms present. When these pies were held at 70° or 90°F. it took about ten hours for an increase in total flora.

Poultry Stuffing

Castellani *et al.* (1953) investigated the effects of roasting time and temperatures on elimination of *Streptococcus faecalis*, *Streptococcus liquefaciens*, and *Salmonella pullorum*. They reported that a temperature of 165°F. in the center of the stuffing during roasting appeared to be sufficient to kill the test organisms and allow a modest margin of safety. During the early stages of roasting active bacterial growth occurred. They concluded that the initial temperatures of the stuffing and the carcass have considerable effect on the time required to reach a lethal temperature. Longree *et al.* (1958) investigated the effect of using various ingredients on bacterial growth in stuffings. They reported that in general bacterial growth decreased as pH decreased. Apricots, cranberries, orange juice, and raisins caused considerable reductions in bacterial counts. High bacterial counts were observed when eggs, giblets and oysters were included in the stuffing. Counts were lowest in white bread stuffings and highest in corn bread stuffings.

Chicken Salads

Chicken salads have been a common cause of food poisoning because of unsanitary methods of preparation and insufficient refrigeration. Weiser, Winter, and Lewis (1954) recommended that cooked and deboned chicken should be refrigerated at 45°F. or lower in shallow pans as soon as produced and as soon as it is incorporated in chicken salad it should be refrigerated under the same conditions until served.

BIBLIOGRAPHY

AYRES, J. C., OGILVY, W. S., and STEWART, G. F. 1950. Post-mortem changes in stored meats. I. Microorganisms associated with development of slime on eviscerated cut-up poultry. Food Technol. 4, 199–205.

AYRES, J. C. *et al.* 1956. Use of antibiotics in prolonging storage life of dressed chicken. Food Technol. 10, 563–568.

CASTELLANI, A. G., CLARKE, R. R., GIBSON, M. I., and MEISNER, D. F. 1953. Roasting time and temperature required to kill food poisoning microorganisms introduced experimentally into stuffing in turkeys. Food Res. 18, 131–138.

COTTERILL, O. J. 1956. Use of ultraviolet light to determine the apparent condition of fresh poultry. Poultry Sci. 35, 1138 (Abstr.)

DAWSON, L. E., and FARMER, E. H. 1958. Influence of packaging material and temperature on shelf-life of poultry meat. (Unpublished.) Cited in Mich. State Univ. NCM-7 Tech. Bull. 278.

DAWSON, L. E., and STADELMAN, W. J. 1960. Microorganisms and their control on fresh poultry meat. Mich. State Univ. NCM-7 Tech. Bull. 278.

ELLIOTT, R. P., and MICHENER, H. D. 1961. Microbiological standards and handling codes for chilled and frozen foods. A review. Appl. Microbiol. 9, 452–468.

ESSARY, E. O., and HOWES, C. E. 1960. Bacterial flora of poultry kidneys and effects of kidney removal on yield and shelf-life. Poultry Sci. 39, 56–59.

ESSARY, E. O., MOORE, W. E. C., and KRAMER, C. Y. 1958. Influence of scald temperatures, chill times, and holding temperatures on the bacterial flora and shelf-life of freshly chilled, tray-pack poultry. Food Technol. 12, 684–687.

FROMM, D. 1959. An evaluation of techniques commonly used to quantitatively determine the bacterial population on chicken caracasses. Poultry Sci. 38, 887–893.

GALTON, M. M., and ARNSTEIN, P. 1960. Poultry diseases in public health, review for epidemiologists. U.S. Dept. of Health, Education and Welfare, Public Health Service Publ. 767. Communicable Disease Center, Atlanta, Georgia.

GORESLINE, H. E., and HAUGH, R. R. 1959. Approximation of surface areas of cut-up chicken and use in microbiological analysis. Food Technol. 13, 241–243.

GUNDERSON, M. F., McFADDEN, H. W., and KYLE, T. S. 1954. The Bacteriology of Commercial Poultry Processing. Burgess Publishing Co., Minneapolis.

GUNDERSON, M. F., ROSE, K. D., and HENN, M. J. 1947. Poultry boning plants need bacteriological control. Food Ind. 19, 1516–1517, 1609–1610.

GUNDERSON, M. F., SCHWARTZ, P. M., and ROSE, K. D. 1946. How much dressed poultry is as clean as it looks? U.S. Egg Poultry Mag. 52, 389–391, 418, 422, 424–425.

HUCKER, G. J., and DAVID, E. R. 1957. The effect of alternate freezing and thawing on the total flora of frozen chicken pies. Food Technol. 11, 354–356.

INGALLS, W. L. 1950. The public health aspects of poultry diseases. Proc. Am. Vet. Med. Assoc. 282–291.

KINSLEY, R. N., and MOUNTNEY, G. J. 1966. A comparison of methods used for the microbiological examination of poultry carcasses. Poultry Sci. 45, 1211–1215.

KOTULA, A. W., THOMPSON, J. E., and KINNER, J. A. 1962. Bacterial counts associated with the chilling of fryer chickens. Poultry Sci. 41, 818–821.

LALLY, M. 1963. Why you need a laboratory to control your product. In Proc. Inst. Am. Poultry Ind. Fact Finding Conf., Kansas City. (Mimeo)

LONGREE, K. et al. 1958. Bacterial growth in poultry stuffings. J. Am. Dietet. Assoc. 34, 50–57.

MALLMANN, W. L., DAWSON, L. E., SULTZER, B. M., and WRIGHT, H. S. 1958. Studies on microbiological methods for predicting shelf-life of dressed poultry. Food Technol. 12, 122–126.

MAY, K. N. 1974. Chilling poultry meat. 3. Changes in microbial numbers during final washing and chilling of commercially slaughtered broilers. Poultry Sci. 53, 1282–1285.

MAY, K. N., IRBY, J. D., and CARMON, J. L. 1962. Shelf-life and bacterial counts of excised poultry tissue. Food Technol. 16, 66–67.

MERCURI, A. J., and KOTULA, A. W. 1964. Relation of "breast swab" to "drip" bacterial counts in tray-packed chicken fryers. J. Food Sci. 29, 854–858.

MORRIS, G. K., and WELLS, J. G.   1970.   *Salmonella* contamination in a poultry processing plant.   Appl. Microbiol. *19*, 795-799.

MOUNTNEY, G. J., BLACKWOOD, U. B., KINSLEY, R. N., and O'MALLEY, J. E.   1964. The effect of 2 hepta-5-methylbenzimidazole and hydrochloric acid on the growth of microflora found on poultry carcasses.   Poultry Sci. *43*, 778-780.

MUNDT, J. O., STOKES, R. L., and GOFF, O. E.   1954.   The skin of broilers as a barrier to bacterial invasion during processing.   Poultry Sci. *38*, 799-802.

MURPHY, J. F., and MURPHY, R. E.   1962.   Method of treating poultry.   U.S. Pat. 682,302, Mar. 13.

NAGEL, C. W. *et al.*   1960.   Microorganisms associated with spoilage of refrigerated poultry.   Food Technol. *14*, 21-23.

OGILVY, W. S., and AYRES, J. C.   1951.   Post-mortem changes in stored meats. II.   The effect of atmospheres containing carbon dioxide in prolonging the storage life of cut-up chicken.   Food Technol. *5*, 97-99.

PERRY, G. A., LAWRENCE, R. L., and MELNICK, D.   1962.   Extension of shelf life of poultry by processing with sorbic acid.   Food Technol. *18*, 101-107.

SILLIKER, J. H. *et al.*   1957.   Poultry Chilling, U.S. Pat. 681,190, Aug. 30.

SPENCER, J. V., and SMITH, L. E.   1962.   The effect of chilling chicken fryers in a solution of polyphosphates upon moisture uptake, microbial spoilage, tenderness, juiciness and flavor.   Poultry Sci. *41*, 1685. (Abstr.)

STRAKA, R. P., and COMBES, F. M.   1951.   The predominence of micrococci in the flora of experimental frozen turkey meat steaks.   Food Res. *16*, 492-493.

STRAKA, R. P., and COMBES, F. M.   1952.   Survival and multiplication of *Micrococcus pyogenes* Var. *aureus* in creamed chicken under various holding, storage, and defrosting conditions.   Food Res. *17*, 448-455.

STRAKA, R. P., and STOKES, J. L.   1957.   Rapid destruction of bacteria in commonly used diluents and its elimination.   Appl. Microbiol. *5*, 21-25.

THOMPSON, J. E., and KOTULA, A. W.   1959.   Contamination of the air sac areas of chicken carcasses and its relationship to scalding and method of killing.   Poultry Sci. *38*, 1433-1437.

VAUGHN, R. H., and STEWART, G. F.   1960.   Antibiotics as food preservatives. J. Am. Med. Assoc. *174*, 1308-1310.

WALKER, H. W., and AYRES, J. C.   1956.   Incidence and kinds of organisms associated with commercially dressed poultry.   Appl. Microbiol. *4*, 345-349.

WALKER, H. W., and AYRES, J. C.   1959.   Microorganisms associated with commercially processed turkeys.   Poultry Sci. *38*, 1351-1355.

WEISER, H. H., WINTER, A. R., and LEWIS, M. N.   1954.   The control of bacteria in chicken salad. I.   *Micrococcus pyogenes* Var. *aureus*.   Food Res. *19*, 465-471.

ZEIGLER, F., SPENCER, J. V., and STADELMAN, W. J.   1954.   A rapid method for determining spoilage in fresh poultry meat.   Poultry Sci. *23*, 1253-1255.

ZIEGLER, F., And STADELMAN, W. J.   1955.   (a) The effect of different scald water temperatures on the shelf life of fresh non-frozen fryers.   Poultry Sci. *34*, 237-238.

CHAPTER 7

Water Supply, Plant Layout
and Sanitation

THE USE OF WATER IN POULTRY PROCESSING

Water is required in poultry processing operations for scalding, for washing carcasses and equipment, for manufacturing ice, for slush ice chilling after processing, for cooking when further processing is practiced, for washing plant equipment, for carrying wastes through disposal lines, and for the use of plant personnel. Porges and Struzeski (1962) reported that in plants with disposal systems which carry solid wastes with water (flow-away systems) 8000 gal. of water are required for each 1000 birds processed and for non-flowaway systems 4500 gal.

WATER QUALITY

Water can be classified several ways according to quality. One method of classification is according to its source. In general, the source from which the water is drawn is also related to its quality.

Water can be obtained from either ground water or surface water supplies. Wells are the principal source of ground water and streams, lakes, and reservoirs are the main source of surface water. Weiser *et al.* (1971) give the following advantages of ground water: (1) ground water is usually clearer than surface water; (2) it contains fewer microorganisms; (3) the mineral content is usually uniform when taken from a single well; and (4) the water temperature remains relatively constant.

Disadvantages of ground water supplies are: (1) supplies are generally not adequate for large consumers; (2) its source and supply are sometimes uncertain; (3) calcium and magnesium compounds are more likely to be present in ground water supplies than in surface supplies; (4) iron and manganese are often problems as well as hydrogen sulfide; (5) it usually costs more to pump well water than surface water; and (6) the quality of water from two wells in the same area can vary greatly.

Contamination is often a problem with surface water. Mud, organic matter, chemicals, sewage, manufacturing plant wastes, and other materials often make it necessary for surface water supplies to receive extensive treatment before use. The problem of surface water contamination is increasing at an alarming rate all over the United States.

Hardness

Water hardness refers to the amount of calcium and magnesium salts present in the water, although other minerals are often present along with these salts. The effect of hardness becomes most noticeable in the reduced foaming and cleansing action of soaps and the formation of precipitates or curds. In fact, the ability of water and soap to form a lather is sometimes used as a test to determine water hardness. Hardness decreases the wetting action of water which is required in scalding.

A report by the Association of Food Industry Sanitarians (Anon. 1952) gives the following criteria for water hardness.

Calcium Carbonate, p.p.m.[1]	Hardness Classification
Less than 50	Soft
50–100	Slightly hard
100–200	Hard
Above 200	Very hard

[1] 17.7 p.p.m. = 1 grain per U.S. gallon.

Hardness can be subdivided further into temporary and permanent hardness. Temporary or carbonate hardness is that portion of the hardness which can be precipitated out by boiling. It is caused by the bicarbonates of the calcium and magnesium. The accumulation of boiler scale caused by hard water frequently makes it necessary to install water softening equipment in poultry processing plants.

Permanent hardness is caused by the presence of calcium and magnesium sulfates and chlorides. Although these salts do not precipitate upon boiling when the water evaporates they become concentrated and precipitate as a hard scale.

Other minerals can also influence the quality of water and the uses which can be made of the water. The following analyses generally are made to determine the quality of water for industrial use: total hardness, calcium hardness, magnesium hardness, alkalinity, sulfates, chlorides, iron, manganese, silica, nitrates, organic matter, turbidity, sediment, color, and odor. From this information the type and cost of treatment required for specific uses can be determined.

Wholesomeness

Wholesomeness refers to the quality of water for use in direct contact with foodstuffs and for human consumption. In addition to its chemical quality it includes freedom from objectionable microorganisms, organic matter, colors and undesirable flavors, and odors.

Since water, especially if it contains organic matter, makes an ideal vehicle for the transmission and dissemination of microorganisms which are pathogenic to humans, the number and types of microorganisms found in a sample are important. Coliform organisms are used as an index of the possible presence of pathogenic bacteria. Not over one coliform organism per 100 ml. of water should be present.

Non-pathogenic organisms can cause under some conditions off-odors and-flavors in water. Slime formations in pipes are sometimes caused by bacteria and can cause clogging of valves.

pH

The pH of water is influenced by the mineral content of the water. Extremes in pH can cause corrosion of pipes and equipment and also influence the cleansing action of detergents.

SEWAGE DISPOSAL

Ross and Kahle (1959) have estimated that liquid wastes from processing poultry can exceed 100,000 gal. daily in a large slaughtering operation. Such sewage contains various quantities of manure, blood, feathers, fleshings, and miscellaneous organic material. Under conditions of good processing plant management where solids and waste matter are kept to a minimum the waste water from processing 1000 birds is roughly equal to the domestic sewage from 150 people but when blood and manure are included the sewage load may be equivalent to as many as 600 people. Because of the amount and strength of sewage from processing poultry and the demand on the sewage system processing plants are not always welcome in many municipalities. Fortunately, manure as a plant waste in broilers and turkey processing plants has almost disappeared and is becoming an almost negligible problem in plants processing fowl because birds are no longer held in feeding stations. Data showing the strength of sewage from various types of waste materials in poultry processing plants are presented in Tables 7.1, 7.2, and 7.3.

TABLE 7.1

STRENGTH OF SEWAGE FROM VARIOUS TYPES OF WASTE MATERIALS IN POULTRY PROCESSING PLANTS

Type of Waste	Water per 1000 Birds, Lb.[1]	BOD, P.P.M.	BOD per 1000 Birds, Lb.
A. Processing waste water only	29,000	515[2]	15
B. Blood	150		45
Processing waste including blood	29,150	2050[2]	60
C. Manure	12,000		75
Processing waste including manure	41,000	2200	90
D. Processing waste including blood and manure	41,150	3300	135

From Kahle and Gray (1957).
[1] One gallon per-pound live weight for processing and 0.4 gal. per pound live weight for washing batteries.
[2] BOD in parts per million not given until waste materials are combined with processing waste water.

Measuring Characteristics of Poultry Processing Wastes

The U.S. Environmental Protection Agency (EPA) recommends the following measurements to determine the characteristics of wastewater from meat processing operations.

Biochemical Oxygen Demand (BOD).—The biochemical oxygen demand analysis is an attempt to simulate the effect a waste will have on the dissolved oxygen of a stream by a laboratory test. It has been the most widely used method for estimating the strength of domestic or other biodegradable wastes. It must be applied with greater caution to many industrial wastes since the presence of certain compounds can inhibit the test. Although it is a useful measurement in characterizing industrial wastes, its use in monitoring is limited because of the five days required to run the test. It is expected, however, that BOD will continue to be a standard for regulatory agencies for many years. Therefore, an understanding of this parameter is essential.

The BOD test gives an indication of the amount of oxygen needed to stabilize or biologically oxidize the waste. The BOD test will measure the biodegradable organic carbon, and under certain conditions the oxidizable nitrogen present, in the waste. The measurement of oxidizable nitrogen may be avoided by adding inhibitors for the nitrifying bacteria. The ammonia content of the waste should be measured separately. Ammonia is also important to maintain the oxygen balance in the steam because, after the carbon has been oxidized, the nitrifying bacteria begin using oxygen (for 1 mg. NH_4^+, bacteria need 4.56 mg. O_2) for oxidizing the ammonia. The advantage of the BOD test is that it measures only the organics which are oxidized by the bacteria. The disadvantage of the BOD test is the time lag between sampling and results of the analysis (5 days for BOD_5) and the difficulty in obtaining consistent repetitive values. It is possible that organics not degraded in a BOD bottle will be oxidized in an environment by bacteria which are acclimatized to that environment. Normally, the BOD bottle is not shaken and the CO_2 produced accumulates in the bottle. Both shaking and CO_2 accumulation influences the test results. A further disadvantage of BOD is the poor reproducibility of the test. The BOD of the same sample computed by two different laboratories seldom agrees within 10 percent.

Manometric methods used to determine BOD are more reproducible. The mixture is usually stirred and the CO_2 is adsorbed by a strong basic solution. For individual BOD analyses, the BOD bottle method is the only economically feasible method. If BOD is to be continuously monitored, the use of the Hach type of apparatus of the electrolysis BOD device should be considered. The use of the Warburg apparatus

TABLE 7.2

MEASURED WATER USE FOR POULTRY PROCESSING, GOLD KIST POULTRY PROCESSING PLANT,
DURHAM, N. CAROLINA, JULY 1969

Process	Source	Flow Rate (Gpm)	Total Volume (Gal.)
Killing station		2.0	1,080
Scalder	Fresh	38.7	20,898
Pickers	Fresh	38.0	20,520
Feather flume	Fresh	94.3	50,922
	Chiller effluent	54.6	—
	Re. offal water	111.7	—
Neck scalders	Fresh	1.5	810
Whole bird washers	Fresh	37.3	20,142
Defeather cleanup hose			
(1 @ 1 hr.)	Fresh	34.0	2,040
"Hang-back" belt	Fresh	9.1	5,460
Eviscerating trough			
(a) Hand wash outlets	Fresh	285.0	153,900
(b) Side pan wash	Fresh	90.0	48,600
Final bird wash	Fresh	100.0	54,000
Lung vacuum pump effluent	Fresh	14.2	7,668
Gizzard machine and giblet flumes	Fresh	360.0	194,400
Evisc. cleanup hose			
(2 @ 30 min. each)	Fresh	72.0	2,040
Giblet chiller	Fresh and ice	4.5	2,430
Neck cutter	Fresh	4.0	2,160
Chillers	Fresh and ice	72.1	38,934
Packing ice	Ice	15 lb./box	6,111
Bird pickup			
(10% in chillers)	Fresh	—	8,640
Packing cleanup hoses			
(3 @ 10 min. each)	Fresh	102.0	1,020
By-product cleanup hoses			
(1 and 10 min.)	Fresh	34.0	340

From Crosswhite *et al.* (undated).
Normal processing day runs from 7:00 a.m. to 4:00 p.m.   725,600
                                                                                        (1,340) gpm
Water meter readings: (a) Processing (7:00 a.m. to 4:00 p.m.)   = 725,600 gpd
                      (b) Cleanup (4:00 p.m. to 7:00 a.m.)   = 112,200 gpd
                                                        Total   = 837,800 gpd
Undetermined process water: 850,000 − 837,800   = 12,200 gpd
Note: Cleanup hoses are used to rinse off equipment at break periods and lunch during processing operation.

is justified for research purposes but probably not for routine measurements of BOD.

Acids and Alkalies.—The pH in a biological system, such as in surface water or treatment plants, is an important factor because a sudden change can cause serious damage. The measurement used to determine the required dosage of neutralizing agent, either $Ca(OH)_2$ or H_2SO_4, is termed acidity or alkalinity, respectively.

The acidity measures the capacity to donate protons. Acidity is attributible to the unionized portions of weakly mineral acids, hydrolizing salts and mineral acids. Mineral acids are probably the most significant group. It is difficult to predict neutralization requirements

TABLE 7.3

BENCHMARK DATA ON WATER AND WASTE, GOLD KIST POULTRY PROCESSING PLANT,
DURHAM, N. CAROLINA, DEC. 1969

			Solids			
	BOD	COD	Total	Dissolved	Suspended	Grease
Scalder entry	1,182	2,080	1,873	1,186	687	350
Scalder exit	490	986	1,053	580	473	200
Whole bird wash	108	243	266	185	81	150
Final bird wash	442	662	667	386	281	580
Giblet chiller	2,357	3,959	2,875	1,899	976	1,320
Chiller No. 1	442	692	776	523	253	800
Chiller No. 2	320	435	514	331	183	250
Feather flume	590	1,078	894	382	512	120
Eviscerating flume	233	514	534	232	302	430
Plant effluent	560	722	697	322	375	150

From Crosswhite *et al.* (undated).

when diverse forms of mineral acidity are prevalent. Microbial systems may reduce acidity in some instances through biological degradation of organic acids.

Alkalinity, or the ability of wastewater to accept protons, is significant in the same general way as acidity, although the biological degradation process does offer some buffer capacity by furnishing carbon dioxide as a degradation end-product to the system. Alkalinity can be due to the presence of HCO_3^-, CO_3^{--}, or OH^-. It has been estimated that approximately 0.5 lb. of alkalinity (as $CaCO_3$) is neutralized for each pound of BOD removed. Excess alkalinity often has to be removed by neutralization.

Suspended Solids.—Suspended solids represent the undissolved substances in the wastewater retained on a 0.45 micron filter. The residue retained on the filter is dried in an oven at 105°C. Non-homogenous particulate matter should be excluded from the sample. Analysis for suspended solids should begin as soon as possible since preservation of the sample is not practical.

The use of glass filters has increased considerably and these filters appear to give comparable results to the millipore filters. The glass fiber filters have one advantage over combustible materials, such as the millipore. Since the glass fibers are non-combustible at the temperatures used for determination of volatile suspended solids, the same crucible used for suspended solids determinations can be employed directly for determining volatile content. The combustible materials must be placed in a crucible and the final weight must be corrected to account for combustion of the filter.

Settleable Solids.—The term "settleable solids" applies to solids in suspension that will settle under quiescent conditions. Only the coarser suspended solids with a specific gravity greater than that of water will settle. The test for settleable solids is conducted in an Imhoff cone, allowing a one hour settling time. Samples should be at room temperature and the test conducted in a location away from direct sunlight. The settled solids volume is measured and reported in terms of milliliters or settleable solids per liter. The settleable solids test is important since it serves as the principal means to establish the need for and assist in the design of sedimentation facilities. This test is widely used in sewage and industrial waste treatment plant operation to determine the efficiency of sedimentation units.

Oil, Grease and Immiscible Liquids.—Oil, grease and immiscible liquids can produce unsightly conditions and in most cases the quantities permitted in wastewater are restricted by regulatory agencies. In sewer systems the presence of oils and immiscible liquids, such as naphthene and ether, may cause explosive conditions. Wastes from the meat-packing industry, particularly where fats are involved from the slaughtering of sheep and cattle, have resulted in serious decreases in the capacity of sewers. In treatment plants, wastewater with a high grease content may cause trouble with aerobic biological treatment.

The term, grease, applies to a wide variety of organic substances that may be extracted from aqueous solution or suspension by hexane. Hydrocarbons, esters, oils, fats, waxes, and high molecular weight fatty acids are the major materials dissolved by hexane. These materials have a "greasy feel" and are associated with problems in aerobic waste treatment.

Fats, oils, and waxes are esters. Fats and oils are esters of the trihydroxy alcohol, glycerol; while waxes are esters of long-chain monohydroxy alcohols. The glycerides of fatty acids that are liquid at ordinary temperatures are called oils and those that are solids are called fats. The term, oil, also represents a wide variety of substances ranging from low to high molecular weight hydrocarbons of mineral origin, spanning the range from gasoline through heavy fuel to lubricating oils.

It should be emphasized that oils and greases of vegetable and animal origin are generally biodegradable and, in an emulsified form, can be successfully treated by a biological treatment facility. On the other hand, oils and greases of mineral origin may be relatively resistant to biodegradation and will require removal by methods other than biological treatment. Unfortunately, a satisfactory method of distinguishing between oils and greases of vegetable and animal origin and those of mineral origin is not readily available.

Pathogenic Wastes.—Wastewaters that contain pathogenic bacteria can originate from livestock production (cattle, poultry, swine, lab animals), tanneries, pharmaceutical manufacturers and food processing industries. Pathogenic bacteria in wastewaters may be destroyed by the process of chlorination.

The bacteriological safety of a wastewater is normally measured by the number of fecal coliform bacteria present. Coliform bacteria are not pathogenic but are an indication of the probability that pathogenic bacteria are present. Examples of pathogenic bacteria are *Salmonella, Shigella, Leptospira and Vibrio.* To this group of undesirable pathogens also can be added the enteric viruses and parasites, such as *Endamoeba histolytica.*

Toxic Materials and Heavy Ions.—For biological waste treatment plants, the maximum tolerable concentrations of toxic materials have been reported for many materials. Occasionally, treatability studies have to be made to determine the maximum allowable concentration of the toxic substance in a biological treatment system. In general, the threshold toxicity levels for biological treatment systems are higher than the allowable standards for surface waters. Establishing maximum concentrations for toxicants in biological treatment plants is useful only if the amount of toxicant is reduced during the treatment, as is the case with phenols. Often, it is necessary to decrease the concentration of the toxic material by pre-treatment. However, it is necessary to guard against the so-called synergistic effect of certain materials. One plant may be allowed to discharge zinc below the toxic level, while another plant may be allowed to do the same with copper. The resulting combination of both discharges will have a synergistic effect, and may cause biological deterioration in the receiving stream or the municipal treatment system.

Ammonia nitrogen is present in many natural waters in relatively low concentrations while industrial streams often contain exceedingly high concentrations of ammonia. Nitrogen in excess of 1600 mg/liter has proven to be inhibitory to many microorganisms present in the activated sludge basin. Sulfides are present in many wastewaters either as a mixture of HS^--H_2S (depending on pH), sulfonated organic compounds, or metallic sulfides.

The influence of heavy metals on biological unit processes has been the subject of many investigations. Toxic thresholds for Cu, Zn, and Cd, have been established at approximately 1 mg/liter.

Nutrients—Nitrogen and Phosphorus.—When effluents are discharged into lakes, ponds, and surface streams, the presence of nitrogen and phosphorus is particularly undesirable since it enhances eutrophication and stimulates undesirable algae growth. Industrial wastes containing insufficient nitrogen and phosphorus for biological development in waste treatment systems require addition of these nutrients in forms such as anhydrous ammonia and phosphoric acid.

The chemical form in which nutrients are present may differ and vary with the degree of treatment. Nitrogen can be present as ammonia, nitrate, nitrite and organic nitrogen in the form of proteins, urea and amino acids. Phosphorus can be present as ortho phosphates (for example $Na_3(PO_3)_6$) or organic phosphorus.

Color and Turbidity.—Color and turbidity present aesthetic problems. Low concentrations of compounds such as lignins and tannins will impart color to natural waters and may be intensified when combined with other materials. An example of this is iron and tannin which combine to form iron-tannate—a common base of blue-black ink.

It is possible to differentiate between the true and apparent color of a sample. True color is due to matter which is in true solution, while apparent color includes the effects of matter in the suspended and colloidal states as well. Examples of true color constituents are soluble dyes used in industry. Constituents which cause apparent color are usually finely divided metal hydroxide particles.

Total Dissolved Solids.—Total dissolved solids can be obtained by evaporating a sample of filtrate on a water bath. After the wastewater is evaporated, the dish is dried in an oven at a temperature of 105° or 180° C. When total solids are measured, large floating particles should be removed from the sample. Oil and grease present in the sample should be included and dispersed by blending before evaporating.

Some materials, such as metallic hydroxides, will retain an associated water of hydration at 105° C., resulting in an apparent higher measurement of solids. At 180° C. organic matter can be reduced by volatilization, but is not completely destroyed, some chloride and nitrate salts may be lost and bicarbonate may be converted to carbonate which may be partially decomposed to oxide or to basic salts. In general, waters containing considerable organic matter, or those with pH greater than 9, should be dried at the higher temperature. The report should indicate the drying temperature used in the analysis.

Characteristics of Poultry Wastes

Porges and Struzeski (1962) have reviewed the work done on determining the characteristics of poultry wastes. Poultry manure and blood because of their high BOD place the greatest stress on a disposal system. Manure, feathers and dirt accumulated from battery room operations have been reported with a 5-day BOD of 32 lb. and a suspended solids content of 35 lb. per 1000 chickens. Another study indicated that wastes from battery room operations were 36 lb. for a 5-day BOD waste and 40 lb. of suspended solids. When the battery wastes were removed by dry cleaning these amounts were reduced to 5 lb. BOD and 6 lb. of suspended solids per 1000 chickens per day.

Chicken blood has been reported to have a five-day BOD of 92,000 mg/liter. Approximately 70% of such blood is drainable. Drainable blood has a 17.4 BOD per 1000 chickens. Another study demonstrated that BOD and suspended solid loads can be reduced by 15 and 6 lb., respectively, when some of the blood is recovered.

Waste solids from evisceration and cutting operations amount to 6 to 8 lb. BOD when the waste solids are collected in containers.

BOD values for flow-away plants amount to 25 lb. when blood is recovered and 41 lb. when it is part of the waste. Nonflow-away systems have an average BOD load of 23–35 lb. Suspended solids from flow-away plants averaged 13 lb. with blood recovery and 23 lb. without blood recovery. Nonflow-away plants averaged 12 and 21 lb., respectively. The composition of combined poultry wastes is shown in Table 7.4.

TABLE 7.4

COMPOSITION OF COMBINED POULTRY PLANT WASTES

Five-day BOD, mg./l.	150–2400
COD, mg./l.	200–3200
Suspended solids, mg./l.	100–1500
Dissolved solids, mg./l.	200–2000
Volatile solids, mg./l.	250–2700
Total solids, mg./l.	250–3200
Suspended solids, % of total solids	20–50
Volatile solids, % of total solids	65–85
Settleable solids, ml./l.	1–20
Total alkalinity, mg./l.	40–350
Total nitrogen, mg./l.	15–300
pH	6.5–9.0

From Porges and Struzeski (1962).

Separating and Handling Poultry Wastes

Because of the large volume and the characteristics of poultry wastes considerable time and effort can be spent to reduce the pollutional load so that the amount of waste material requiring treatment can also be reduced.

Careful use of water not only reduces the amount and cost of water required for processing but also the amount which must be disposed as sewage. In some cases water can be reused, especially if it is chlorinated.

In the receiving and holding areas, dry scraping and cleaning of manure and feathers prevents them from being washed down the drain. Blood can be collected from the killing area before hosing, and bleeding time can be extended as long as possible during slaughter to reduce the amount of blood carried over to the scalder.

Feathers are a particular nuisance in plants because they clog screens and become matted. Eviscerating room wastes such as tissues, grit, and feed wastes are also a problem. They require a fine-mesh screen to keep them from draining down the sewer. In many plants wastes are now moved to a central disposal area by flow-away troughs. Grease can be removed by means of traps.

Untreated or inadequately treated wastes increase the treatment load in the following ways: (1) reduce oxygen available; (2) cause an increase in solids; (3) cause an increase in floating matter; (4) bring about an increase in coliform and possible pathogenic organisms; (5) increase odors; and (6) increase the inorganic content of the material.

Methods of Waste Treatment

Most processing plants discharge poultry wastes to municipal treatment facilities. To take advantage of such facilities, plants are generally required to use prescribed methods which will keep solids and feathers to a minimum. In some cases charges for use of sewage disposal facilities are made according to the BOD demand of the sewage.

Trickling filters and activated sludge processes have not been utilized to a great extent for treatment of poultry wastes. In some areas stabilization ponds have been used with success. Disposal of wastes by irrigation is another method sometimes used.

In-Plant Waste Conservation Factors

Steffen (1973A) listed the following considerations for in-plant waste conservation and the factors which should be considered in determining the degree of pretreatment prior to discharge to a city sewer.

With increasing demands for improved quality in wastewater effluent, whether discharged to a watercourse or to a city sewer, in-plant waste conservation and water reuse are becoming more advantageous than ever, if the processor intends to remain economically competitive.

Here are eight simple rules that govern in-plant waste conservation:

(1) Use water wisely—only enough to get the job done.
(2) Keep waste solids in bulk whenever possible, for disposal as a solid or as a concentrated sludge, without discharging to the sewer.

(3) Clean with high pressure and minimum water volume (small hoses). Use the right detergents in the right proportions to clean well with minimum rinsing.

(4) Recycle water as much as possible, within the limits of USDA regulations. Some reconditioning, such as cooling or screening, may be necessary for recycling in some instances. Thus, provide the lowest quality of water consistent with the job.

(5) Use the minimum pressure and volume for washing product, consistent with quality control. High pressure in washing product may drive soil into the product and also wash away valuable edible protein and fat.

(6) Control volume, temperature and pressure automatically. Dependence upon manual regulation can lead to waste.

(7) Use valves that shut off automatically when the water is not needed.

(8) Study each process independently. General rules alone will not do the job.

In-Plant Pretreatment Factors

The degree of pretreatment, prior to discharge to a city sewer, depends upon several factors, as outlined by Steffen (1973B):

(A) Maximum concentrations of pollutional ingredients established as guidelines by the Federal Environmental Protection Agency and the owners of the public sewer and treatment facility into which effluent is discharged.

(B) The economic possibilities of reducing the municipal or sanitary district charges and surcharges by pretreatment.

(C) The possibilities that the charge and surcharge rates may be increased in the future.

(D) The marketability or cost of disposal of residual greases and sludges from the pretreatment facility.

(E) The local and state tax situation for amortizing the cost of pretreatment facilities and whether or not they will be placed on the property tax rolls.

(F) The cost (labor, power and chemicals) of operating the pretreatment facilities. In some states licensed operators and detailed daily records may be required. This is a trend in pretreatment. Thus the simplest facilities may be the best, and first cost may be a less important consideration than operating costs.

(G) The performance of *pilot scale* pretreatment facilities on *your* wastewater. Dependence on data from "similar processing plants" is dangerous. Most manufacturers of such equipment have pilot plants available for rental.

PLANT LAYOUT

A number of criteria are used in designing a poultry processing plant. Among the more important considerations are construction, cost, sanitation, adequacy of facilities for personnel, efficiency of the facility and equipment layout, and ease of maintenance. Another important consideration is whether the design of a proposed plant meets the requirements of the U.S. Department of Agriculture Poultry Inspection Service. Illustrations of a typical poultry processing plant handling 1500 birds per hour are shown in Figs. 7.1 and 7.2.

Most plants have eight general work areas. These are a receiving, hanging, and slaughtering, defeathering, eviscerating, packaging, refrigeration room, and shipping area. In addition, storage areas, offices, toilets, lockers, machinery rooms (which may contain heating and refrigeration equipment), and refuse rooms are considered as auxiliary rooms.

Receiving and Holding Areas

The receiving dock is separated from processing areas by a masonry wall. This area sometimes includes the killing area and bleeding tunnel but generally only provides space for unloading full coops, hanging live birds onto the defeathering conveyor and for loading empty coops.

Dressing Area

In this area, killing, bleeding (separated from the defeathering area by a masonry wall), scalding, picking, pinning, and washing operations are carried out. After completing these operations, workers transfer the carcasses to another conveyor line which transports the carcasses to the eviscerating room. Dressing rooms require good ventilation and continuous removal of feathers, water and other waste. The atmosphere is one of high humidity caused by hot water in the scalder, spray from pickers and wet feathers with blood and dirt scattered over the area from birds struggling and pickers slinging material over the walls and ceiling. For these reasons dressing rooms should be designed so they can be easily washed down.

Eviscerating Room

Carcasses move into the eviscerating room on a separate conveyor track from the dressing room. Blood, feathers, and manure are scrubbed and washed from the carcasses before they are hung on the eviscerating shackles. In this area, viscera are removed, the edible viscera are separated from inedible, then trimmed and cleaned and the inedible viscera are discarded. Postmortem inspection is carried on during this operation, followed by the grading and chilling operations.

Packaging Area

Frequently the packing area adjoins and is part of the eviscerating area when carcasses are ice-packed. If carcasses are wrapped individually or further processed (cut-up, filleted, etc.) packaging is generally carried out in a separate room.

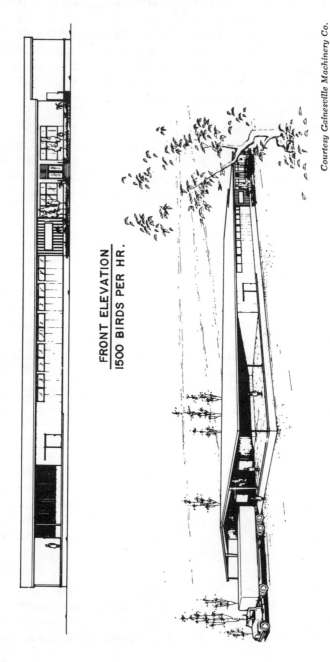

FRONT ELEVATION
1500 BIRDS PER HR.

Courtesy Gainesville Machinery Co.

FIG 7.1.   A MODERN POULTRY PROCESSING PLANT

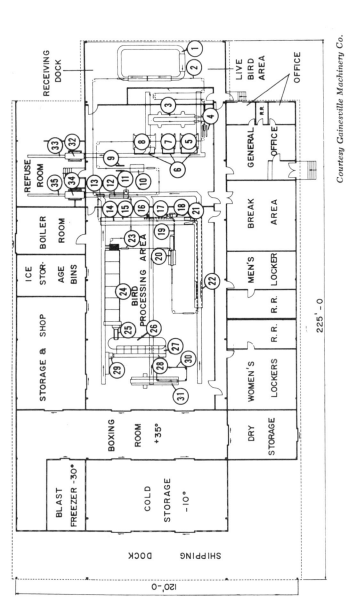

Courtesy Gainesville Machinery Co.

Fig. 7.2. A Typical Poultry Processing Plant Handling 1,500 Birds Per Hour

Equipment: 1, Coop conveying system; 2, overhead picking conveyor with automatic shackles; 3, turnabout scalder; 4, hock steamer; 5, hock picker; 6, feather pans; 7, picker; 8, roto-disc picker; 9, singer; 10, outside bird washer; 11, simplex automatic hock cutter; 12, belt-type rehang conveyor; 13, automatic shackle trip–drops feet into gutter; 14, overhead eviscerating conveyor with automatic shackles; 15, eviscerating trough; 16, heart and liver stations; 17, automatic gizzard splitter; 18, gizzard peeling machines; 19, giblet flume trough; 20, giblet washing and wrapping table; 21, automatic head cutter; 22, combination bird washer; 23, automatic shackle trip–drops birds into chiller; 24, automatic continuous chiller; 25, belt conveyor; 26, automatic bird sizer; 27, packing bins; 28, packing conveyor; 29, scale; 30, drip line; 31, packaging table; 32, feather separator; 33, feather conveyor; 34, offal separator; 35, offal conveyor.

Refrigerated Rooms

This area includes freezers and chill rooms where poultry can be chilled, frozen, and held in storage until ready for delivery.

Auxiliary Rooms

A number of auxiliary rooms are required in a processing plant for offices, offal, cleaning equipment, boiler room, refrigerating equipment, maintenance work rooms, toilets, dressing rooms, lunch room, maintenance work, and for storage of supplies.

Structural Materials

Concrete, concrete block, brick, glazed tile, and structural steel are the principal materials used for the construction of poultry processing plants.

Floors

Floors in processing areas should be constructed of smooth, troweled, reinforced concrete. Floors should be sufficiently smooth to permit ready cleaning and sloped so that water runs off without collecting in puddles or depressions. To minimize the hazard of accidental falls all floors in the "wet" work areas should have an abrasive substance incorporated in the wearing surface. Floor drains and gutters should be sloped to provide a sufficient flow of water to wash away processing wastes and designed so as to avoid sewer line siphonage or backup. Traps should be installed to prevent the entrance of rodents, insects and sewer gas into the building. They should also be designed for easy cleaning and inspection.

Walls, Posts, and Doors

These parts of the buildings should be smooth and made of materials which are impervious to moisture to at least six feet above the floor so they can be washed down with water and easily cleaned. Above six feet they should be constructed of materials that are smooth and moisture resistant.

Ceilings

Ceilings should be constructed of a smooth moisture resistant material, preferably light in color and sealed and finished in such a manner as to prevent dirt or dust from sifting through.

Plumbing

Plumbing systems should be designed in such a manner to prevent contamination through cross-connections, back-siphonage, back-flow, leakage, or condensation. Overhead drainlines and piping should be installed in such a manner that leakage does not occur and condensation will not contaminate food products, supplies or equipment.

Non-potable water lines should be plainly marked and separated from potable ones. Hose connections with steam and hot water mixing valves should be placed at strategic locations throughout the plant for use in cleaning. Hot water at a temperature of at least 130°F. should be available for cleaning.

Ventilation

Effective ventilation is required to remove dust, moisture, vapors, gases, and odors. A filtered air positive pressure-type system provides clean air from the outside and prevents recontamination of the plant with dust and dirt from the outside. Counter-flow air systems (from finished product area to raw or non-processed area) should be used.

Lighting

Recommendations for lighting include at least 50 foot-candles in inspection areas, 30 foot-candles in other working areas and 5 foot-candles 30 inches above the floor in other areas.

Childs and Rogers (1958) reported that fluorescent lighting is preferred over incandescent lights because (1) it is about three times as efficient, (2) it is the nearest thing to daylight of any practical lighting system, (3) it gives off far less heat than incandescent light, and (4) it diffuses light more effectively.

Equipment Design

Proper design of equipment allows easy adjustments, cleaning, inspection, safe operation, maintenance, and replacement of parts. In addition, proper equipment installed for maximum efficiency provides "work-station layouts so that products and all equipment are positioned to permit smooth hand motion patterns, minimum 'reach' distances, and reduction of the frequency of 'search' or 'fumble' elements" (Figs. 7.3, 7.4, and 7.5). Suspension of light pieces of equipment from the ceiling to eliminate legs on the floor is recommended in order to facilitate clean-up. An equipment maintenance chart for poultry processing equipment is shown in Table 7.5 and ownership and operating costs for various types of equipment in Table 7.6.

Plant Safety

The poultry industry has one of the highest accident rates of all food processing industries. For this reason plant safety should be given careful consideration in designing and operating a poultry processing plant.

TABLE 7.5

EQUIPMENT MAINTENANCE CHART

Equipment	Daily	Weekly	Monthly	Yearly
Conveyors	Check line speed and drive synchronization. Replace missing shackles. Replace defective shackles.	Check oil level in gear box. Check oil level in fluid drive coupling. Grease and clean entire drive unit. Check drive lugs—tighten retaining bolts. Check belt tension. Oil conveyor rollers if needed.	Remove excess conveyor chain. Check rises for wear—replace if necessary. Check drive lugs for wear—replace if necessary. Check corner wheels for proper chain contact. Grease corner wheels. Check bearings and shaft on drive unit. Clean and grease variable speed sheave. Every 3 months steam clean and re-oil chain.	Change oil in gear box. Remove and clean chain and track—re-oil. Replace all belts. Disassemble and clean drive unit.
Scalders	Clean pump impellers and check agitation.	Check belts on scalder pumps. Check pump packing for leakage. Clean and check controls and thermometers.	Check pulleys and belts for wear. Grease pumps. Check impeller for excessive wear.	Replace belts on pumps. Have controls cleaned and reset by manufacturer. Have steam valves serviced by manufacturer.
Quill pullers	Grease bearings. Check springs. Check guards for breakage.	Grease chain and check for wear. Check belt tension. Check height adjustment mechanism.	Check rollers for wear. Replace when needed. Check bearings for wear.	Change oil in gear box. Replace belts, chain and sprockets.
Pickers	Grease reel bearings, preferably immediately after clean-up. Replace worn and broken fingers.	Grease Jackshaft bearings. Check belt tension. Check reel speed during plant operation. Grease adjustment mechanism.	Check pulleys for wear—use gage. Grease, oil. Lift gear box.	Replace all belts. Replace pulleys.

Equipment				
Neck and hock scalders	...	Check guide bars for location and water flow. Check machine for correct position under conveyor.	Check controls. Check steam hose.	Grease—oil gear box. Have steam controls serviced by manufacturer.
Singers	...	Grease lift mechanism.	Check burner adjustment.	...
Washers	...	Check belts and grease chain. Clean water sprays.	Grease bearings.	Replace all fingers. Replace belts. Replace chain and sprockets.
Water flush trough	...	Clean all openings.	Check for leaks. Check trough for height and proper slope.	...
Headcutter	Hone Cutter.	Clean water spray nozzles. Check rollers to see if they rotate freely. Check springs. Check blade adjustment.	Replace blade.	...
Neck cutter	Grease daily.	Hone cutter. Check and clean water spray nozzles. Check roller chain tension. Check gear box for oil level and water seepage.	Check brass guide for wear and replace when necessary. Clean and grease variable speed sheave. General over-all machine inspection.	Replace belts. Change oil in gearbox.
Packing tables	Check belt alignment when running.	Grease bearings. Lubricate chain. Clean sprays on belt washer.	Clean and grease variable speed pulleys.	Drain and refill gear box. Replace drive belts. Replace sprockets and chain if necessary.
Giblet wrapping table	Check belt alignment while running.	Grease bearings. Lubricate chain. Clean spray nozzles on belt washer.	Clean and grease variable speed pulley.	Drain and refill gear box. Replace drive belts. Replace sprockets and chain if necessary.

TABLE 7.5 (*continued*)

EQUIPMENT MAINTENANCE CHART

Equipment	Daily	Weekly	Monthly	Yearly
Spin chill	Check pulley and belt alignment. Check plastic guide rollers for alignment and excessive wear.	Check elevator for tension. Check belts for wear. Check for loose, missing, or bent elevator flights. Grease all bearings.	Grease and check oil in gear box. Check belt tension. Check alignment of reel with tank openings. Check reel for damage. Check bearing and seal on impeller. Inspect roller chain.	Drain and refill gear boxes. Replace all belts. Check sprockets for wear.
Liqui-flash freezer	Check glycol mixture for water content or freeze point. Check height liquid in main tank. Check operation of reclaimer.	Clean filters in reclaimer. Clean perforated pans and screens. Check liquid flow to perforated pans. Check for glycol leakage. Check liquid height on conveyor.	Check all belt tension. Check tension on main conveyor. Check pump packing. Grease pumps. Check oil in gear boxes. Clean and grease variable speed sheave. Grease all bearings. Check for loose flights.	Change gear box oil. Check glycol for contamination. Replace all drive belts.
Giblet chiller	Check reel alignment.	Check elevators for loose or broken flights. Check guide rollers on reels.	Check brass end plates for wear. General machine inspection. Check lift mechanism. Check drive chain and sprockets. Check belt tension.	Drain and refill gearbox. Replace drive belts.
Gizzard skinner	Oil bearings.	Check rollers for wear. Check bearings and combs for adjustment. General machine inspection.	...	...

Electric motors	...	...	Visual inspection. Check for overheating.	Remove from machine. Disassemble, clean, replace ball bearings and reassemble.
Giblet film pak	Remove oven. Remove excess film from under oven and guide rails. Spray guide rails and underside oven with silicone spray. Grease main shaft bearings. Check sharpness of knife. Check freeness of film tracking rollers. Check tension of knife drive chain.	Grease reeves pulley. Clean and oil motor adj. worm gear. Grease all bearings. Inspect for damaged buckets.	Inspect main chain and buckets. Check and add oil to gear box.	Change oil in gearbox.
Giblet pumping system	Inspect tubing for kinks and snags. Clean and sanitize pumping system (see manual). Reverse pump impellers.	Check vacuum in relief valves.	Check tightness of motor-to-pump drive chains. Make visual inspection of all parts.	...
Shackle cleaner and sanitizer	Flush tank after use.	...	Grease lift gear box.	...

Courtesy of Gordon Johnson Industries, Earnshaw (1963).

TABLE 7.6

OWNERSHIP AND OPERATING COSTS FOR ONE UNIT EACH OF VARIOUS TYPES OF EVISCERATING EQUIPMENT IN POULTRY PROCESSING PLANTS

Item	Unit[1]	Initial Cost[2] dollars	Expected Life, years	Ownership Cost Depreciation[3] dollars	Ownership Cost Interest[4] dollars	Ownership Cost Insurance and Taxes[5] dollars	Ownership Cost Total, dollars	Operating Cost Power[6]	Operating Cost Maintenance	Operating Cost Total	Total Annual Cost	Total Cost per Hour[7]
Bird washer (inside and outside)												
Single line	1	1166.00	10	116.60	29.15	46.64	192.39	…	23.32[10]	23.32	215.71	0.11
Double line	1	1231.36	10	123.14	30.78	49.25	203.17	…	24.63[10]	24.63	227.80	0.11
Catwalk, 18-in. width	1	10.33	10	1.03	0.25	0.41	1.69	…	0.21[10]	0.21	1.90	…
Cleanup equipment, hot-water type	1	355.68	5	71.14	8.89	14.23	94.26	…	28.45[11]	28.45	122.71	0.06
Conveyor, eviscerating with shackles on 6-in. centers												
Single track	100-ft. section	1962.22[8]	9	331.46	49.05	78.48	459.00	11.11	156.27[11]	168.08	627.09	0.31
Dual tracks	100-ft. section	3547.76[8]	9	625.14	88.68	141.90	855.72	22.22	283.82[11]	306.04	1161.78	0.58
Single track, dual shackles (equivalent to 2 lines)	100-ft. section	2725.00[8]	9	436.46	68.12	109.00	613.58	11.11	218.00[11]	229.11	842.69	0.42
Flume, giblet	1	95.40	10	9.54	2.39	3.82	15.75	…	1.91[10]	1.91	17.66	0.01
Giblet wrapping table (10-ft. long)	10-ft. section	2142.96	10	214.30	53.57	85.72	353.59	10.00	171.44[11]	181.44	535.03	0.27
Gizzard peeler												
Manual ejecting	1	667.80	3	222.60	16.70	26.71	266.01	20.00	54.42[11]	73.42	339.43	0.17
Automatic ejecting	1	694.30	3	231.43	17.36	27.77	276.56	20.00	55.54[11]	75.54	352.10	0.18
Gizzard splitter, mechanical	1	3339.00	3	1113.00	83.48	133.56	1330.04	50.00	267.12[11]	317.12	1647.16	0.82
Gizzard washer, mechanical	1	141.32	3	47.11	3.53	5.65	56.29	10.00	11.31[11]	21.31	77.60	0.04
Head cutter, mechanical												
Single line	1	1729.56	3	576.52	43.24	69.18	688.94	30.00	138.36[11]	168.36	857.30	0.43
Double line	1	2856.70	3	952.23	71.42	114.27	1137.92	60.00	228.54[11]	288.54	1426.46	0.71
Knives												
6-in. blade	Dozen	21.20	1/4	84.80	1.07	0.85	86.72	…	150.00[2]	150.00	236.72	0.12
5-in. blade	Dozen	12.86	1/4	51.44	0.64	0.51	52.59	…	150.00[2]	150.00	202.59	0.10
Knife holder	1	6.86	10	0.69	0.17	0.27	1.13	…	0.14[10]	0.14	1.27	…
Lung removal equipment												
Hand rake	Dozen	24.00	1	24.00	1.20	0.96	26.16	…	0.48[10]	0.48	26.64	0.01
Vacuum system (4 nozzles)	1	4611.00	5	922.20	115.28	184.44	1122.92	600.00	368.88[11]	968.88	2190.80	1.10
Neck cutter, mechanical	1	3704.70	3	1234.90	92.62	148.19	1475.71	20.00	296.38[11]	316.38	1792.09	0.90
Scissors, curved blade	Dozen	50.50	1/12	606.00	2.53	2.02	610.55	…	150.00[2]	150.00	760.55	0.38
Scissors, 6-in.	Dozen	40.75	1/4	163.00	2.04	1.63	166.67	…	150.00[2]	150.00	316.67	0.16
Sharpener												
Mechanical	1	145.04	5	29.01	3.63	5.80	38.44	0.20	11.60[11]	31.60	70.04	0.04
"Steel"	1	3.50	1	3.50	0.18	0.14	3.82	…	0.07[10]	0.07	3.89	…
Shears, neck cutting	Dozen	27.00	1/12	324.00	1.35	1.08	326.43	…	150.00[2]	150.00	476.43	0.24
Trough, waste disposal (35-in. width)	10-ft. section	253.40	10	25.34	6.34	10.14	41.82	…	5.07[10]	5.07	46.89	0.02
Trough components												
Downspout with end	1	48.76	10	4.88	1.22	1.95	8.05	…	0.98[10]	0.98	9.03	…
Gizzard removal and trim station	1	45.58	3	15.19	1.19	1.82	18.20	…	0.91[10]	0.91	19.11	0.01
Hand-wash station	1	9.94	5	1.99	0.25	0.40	2.64	…	0.80[10]	0.80	3.44	…
Heart and liver removal and trim station	1	40.28	3	13.43	1.01	1.61	16.05	…	0.81[10]	0.81	16.86	0.01
Inspection station	1	329.00	10	32.90	8.23	13.16	54.29	…	6.58[10]	6.58	60.87	0.03
Trough end section	1	7.42	10	0.74	0.19	0.30	1.23	…	0.15[10]	0.15	1.38	…
Trough legs	1 pair	14.84	10	1.48	0.37	0.59	2.44	…	0.30[10]	0.30	2.74	…

From U. S. Dept. Agr. Mktg. Res. Rept. 549, 1962.

[1] Based on most common sale unit. [2] Includes installation cost. [3] Straight-line depreciation for the number of years shown. [4] 5% of average investment (computed at 50% of initial investment). [5] 4% of initial investment. [6] Estimated at $0.02 per kw.h. [7] Based on 2000 hr. operation per year. [8] Single track at $19.62 per ft., dual track at $17.74 per ft. of each track, and single track dual shackles at $27.25 per ft. [9] Estimated life of trolleys 3 yr., shackle chains and cables 5 yr., all other components 10 yr. [10] Based on an estimated 2% of initial cost. [11] Based on an estimated 8% of initial cost. [12] Estimated at 100 hr. per year per dozen sharpened.

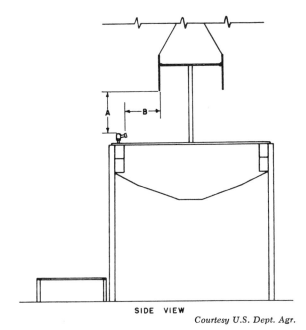

SIDE   VIEW

Courtesy U.S. Dept. Agr.

FIG. 7.3.   A DIAGRAM SHOWING PROPER RELATIVE HEIGHTS FOR WORK
STATIONS ALONG THE EVISCERATING LINE

Dimensions for Various Workstations

	2 Point		3 Point	
Station	A	B	A	B
Open cut, tail split	7.5″	10.5″	9″	10.5″
Open cut, vent	7.5″	10.5″	9″	10.5″
Open cut, body incision	7.5″	10.5″	9″	10.5″
Draw viscera	7.5″	10.5″	10.5″	10.5″
Lung & reproductive organ removal	14.5″	7″	14.5″	7″
Cut & lower neck bone	14.5″	7″		
Crop removal	13.25″	9″		
Final inspection	10.75″	10″		

Westerman (1963) has discussed a number of important safety factors
to be considered in food manufacturing and processing plants.   These
apply equally well to poultry processing operations.

A nearby fire department and an eight-inch or larger water main connected to a dependable water supply are essential not only in case of fire
but also for low insurance rates.   Hydrant threads should match those of
the fire department.

A hospital, clinic, or doctor's office should be located nearby, especially

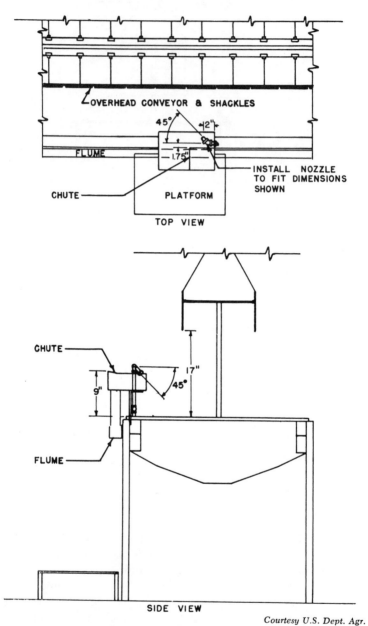

OVERHEAD CONVEYOR & SHACKLES

45°

2"

FLUME

1.75"

INSTALL NOZZLE
TO FIT DIMENSIONS
SHOWN

CHUTE

PLATFORM

TOP VIEW

CHUTE

17"

45°

9"

FLUME

SIDE VIEW

Courtesy U.S. Dept. Agr.

FIG. 7.4.   LAYOUT DETAILS FOR A HEART AND LIVER TRIM STATION

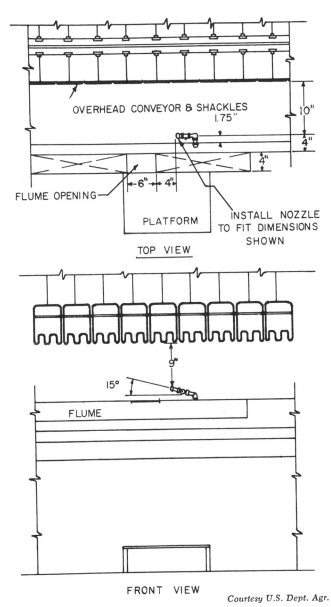

FIG. 7.5. LAYOUT DETAILS FOR A GIZZARD TRIM AND WASH STATION

Courtesy U.S. Dept. Agr.

since most processing plants are not large enough to justify a doctor or nurse at the plant.

Poultry plants should be constructed of fire resistant materials and auxiliary buildings such as those for crate and pallet storage should be located away from the main food plant so that if they catch fire they will not endanger other buildings.

Electrical wiring should be installed with materials and methods approved by the National Fire Protection Association. Standby power should be available for refrigeration systems.

All moving parts of machinery should have adequate guards to prevent injury to personnel. In some cases emergency switches should be located within easy reach.

Fire extinguishers should be conspicuously displayed within easy reach at strategic locations throughout the plant.

Temporary wiring should be removed or replaced by permanent wiring as fast as conditions permit. Wires hanging on nails or hooks or cord that has been damaged should be discarded as soon as observed. Grounding connections should be checked periodically. Fuse boxes should be checked at frequent intervals to determine whether blown fuses have been replaced with new ones of the correct size. Portable power tools should be grounded.

Rubbish in the plant and surrounding areas and weeds should all be eliminated since they are not only a source of fire but because they also harbor insects and rodents.

Common safety violations found on inspection of poultry processing plants by Occupational Safety and Health Administration (OSHA) and listed by the Poultry and Egg Institute of America are:

Grate missing over floor drain area.
No guardrail, toeboards, or stair handrail on three loading platforms.
No guard on cooling fans in holding shed.
Permanent type electrical outlets in truck maintenance shop were wired with temporary-type wiring.
Grinder in plant maintenance shop had no tool rest and guard.
Noise level in picking room seemed too high without ear protection.
Conveyor turn guards missing in two locations.
Temporary wiring to electrical shocker should be replaced with properly installed hook-up.
Electrical switch boxes shall be properly maintained. Keep covers in place.
Stapling machine in box room shall be effectively grounded.
Exhaust fan in women's toilet shall be repaired.
A covered receptacle shall be provided for women's toilet.
All v-belts within seven feet of floor or working platform shall be guarded. Violations observed in box room, compressor room, picking room, and ice machine.
A nip point guard shall be installed at pulley of gib belt.

All fans within seven feet of floor or working platforms shall be completely covered with a wire mesh of less than ½ inch in diameter. Violations observed at cooling shed, and box room.

Several pedestal fans are inadequately guarded.

Stairwell at box room shall be properly enclosed.

Exits for plant and freezer shall be provided with emergency lighting.

PLANT SANITATION

According to the U.S. Department of Agriculture poultry inspection service manual (Anon. 1964B):

Premises should be kept free from refuse, waste materials, and all other sources of objectionable odors and conditions. Batteries and dropping pans shall be cleaned regularly and the manure removed from the plant daily. Scalding tanks shall be completely emptied and thoroughly cleaned as often as may be necessary, but not less frequently than once a day when in use. Wetting agents added to scald water shall not exceed one per cent.

All equipment and utensils, such as tables, bins, trays, knives, chilling equipment, conveyor belts, and flumes, shall be maintained in a clean condition throughout the operating day and shall be thoroughly cleaned at least once daily. Thorough cleaning involves the removal of soil, grease, and other debris by use of water, steam, or hot water, followed by scrubbing with hot water and a cleaning agent and then thorough rinsing with clean water to remove any residues of cleaning agents. The use of litmus paper is an effective means of determining the presence of alkali or acid residues resulting from the use of cleaning agents. Only those compounds which have received prior approval shall be used.

Only scouring pads of the non-corrosive type and of such composition as will result in no contamination of products by fine particles of the pads can be considered satisfactory for cleaning equipment and utensils. Fine wire brushes or steel wool shall not be used on the products or on equipment which will come in contact with the product.

Chilling or defrosting tanks shall be emptied after each use. They shall be thoroughly cleaned at least once daily when in use except that when the same poultry is held therein in excess of 24 hr. the tanks shall be thoroughly cleaned after the poultry is removed therefrom and prior to re-use.

Conveyor trays or belts which come in contact with raw products shall be completely washed and sanitized after each use.

Personnel.—All persons coming in contact with exposed poultry products or poultry products handling equipment shall wear clean garments and suitable head coverings to prevent hair from falling into poultry products; and shall keep their hands and fingernails clean at all times while thus engaged.

All persons with infected cuts, boils, or open sores on their hands shall not handle dressed poultry or poultry products or poultry products handling equipment.

Cleaning

A special cleaning crew, usually on the night shift, should be assigned the task of cleaning and sanitizing the processing plant after each day's work. Cleaning should be their main task but they can also serve as night watchmen, sharpen knives and make minor equipment repairs and adjustments. Because feathers and offal must be removed continuously, one man must be assigned this job during working hours.

A good cleaning arrangement consists of a team of three men, one of whom is designated leader. One man removes the bulk of the feathers from equipment in the defeathering room, the second man places the feathers and coagulated blood in containers and the third member moves the containers to the offal room or truck, When most of the work is completed, two members of the team move to the eviscerating room to start dismantling equipment and removing offal. Next one of the workers moves to the packing room.

One man in the defeathering room overflows the scalder and then adds detergent to the circulating scald water. Pumps can be left operating 20 to 30 min. during which time he can rinse the bleeding area. Next all walls and equipment are scrubbed down with a brush or preferably a steam gun. After walls and equipment are cleaned, the floor is the last area for cleaning. Remaining debris should be swept into piles and put into containers for removal to the offal room. The floor can then be scrubbed with a stiff bristle deck scrub brush and a heavy duty alkaline material. Finally, the floor should be thoroughly rinsed with very hot water to remove grease.

In the eviscerating room, small equipment should be assembled in one place so the remaining equipment can be rinsed with tepid water. All equipment should be scrubbed with an alkaline detergent to emulsify fat and loosen dried-on blood. If the detergent remains on the equipment for several minutes, it will clean better than when it is removed immediately. Clean only 10 to 15 sq. ft. at a time, then rinse. Clean the floor the same as in the defeathering room. Dry all knives, shears, etc., with a cloth towel to prevent rust.

To remove mineral and protein films, stainless steel equipment can be washed with an acid detergent once a week. Acid detergents corrode galvanized and aluminum surfaces.

Sanitizing

Just before processing operations start for the day, all equipment surfaces should be sanitized by applying a 200 p.p.m. chlorine solution with a compression-type garden sprayer. Make sure that all surfaces are wet thoroughly.

Chlorination.—Chlorine is an ideal sanitizer for use in food processing plants because it deteriorates rapidly when it comes in contact with organic matter and it leaves no residue in or on food products. A chlorinator can be attached to the plant water line to increase the concentration of chlorine.

Chlorination has made it possible to increase the efficiency of processing plants. Processed carcasses stay fresh longer and have better flavor and appearance when they reach the consumer. In-plant chlorination decreases the number of bacteria on carcasses and equipment, eliminates slime, corrosion and plant odors, and reduces clean-up time and labor by approximately a third. A concentration of 20 p.p.m. of chlorine kills more organisms that 10 p.p.m. but 45 p.p.m. is only slightly more effective than 20 p.p.m. which is the concentration generally recommended. Chlorine reduces bacteria counts by as much as 90% on equipment and working surfaces.

Chlorine in concentrations above 20 p.p.m. causes eye and nasal irritations. In-plant chlorination reduces the number of infections from open sores. High concentrations of chlorine when used in vats with antibiotics will inactivate the antibiotic. Because chlorine breaks down rapidly in the presence of organic matter, it cannot be used as a substitute for cleanliness.

Detergents and Sanitizers.—The U.S. Department of Agriculture defines detergents as "mixtures of chemicals that change the characteristics of dirt and soil so that they can be separated from the surface of equipment with a solvent, usually water."

Detergents are classified as alkaline or acid types. Common alkaline detergents are sodium carbonate, sodium hexametaphosphate, sodium hydroxide, sodium metasilicate, sodium or potassium soaps, tetrasodium pyrophosphate, and trisodium phosphate.

Acid detergents are used primarily for removing scale caused by the minerals found in hard water. They are generally mineral or organic acids.

Sanitizers are compounds used to kill bacteria, fungi, and other microorganisms which remain on the surface of equipment after it has been cleaned. The more common ones are chlorine, hydrogen peroxide, iodine, and quaternary ammonium compounds.

Table 7.7 lists the soil characteristics of various food components; Table 7.8, the functions of chemicals used as cleaning compounds; and Table 7.9, the properties of detergents.

Insect Control

An insect control program includes proper construction of buildings and equipment, elimination of attractants, control of stored items, temperature and moisture control, and area control.

Flies are generally the greatest problem encountered in and around

TABLE 7.7

SOIL CHARACTERISTICS

Component on Surface	Solubility Characteristics	Ease of Removal	Changes Induced by Heating Soiled Surface
Sugar	Water soluble	Easy	Carmelization, more difficult to clean
Fat	Water insoluble, alkali soluble	Difficult	Polymerization, more difficult to clean
Protein	Water insoluble, alkali soluble, sl. acid soluble	Very difficult	Denaturation, much more difficult to clean
Salts			
Monovalent	Water soluble, acid soluble	Easy	
Polyvalent (i.e., $CaPO_4$)	Water insoluble, acid soluble	Difficult	Interactions with other constituents, more difficult to clean

From Harper (1968).

TABLE 7.8

FUNCTIONS OF CHEMICALS USED AS CLEANING COMPOUNDS

Class of Compound	Major Functions
Basic alkalies	Soil displacement—emulsifying, saponifying, and peptizing.
Complex phosphates	Soil displacement by emulsifying and peptizing; dispersion of soil; water softening, prevention of soil depositions.
Surfactants	Wetting and penetrating soils; dispersion of soils and prevention of soil redepositions.
Chelating compounds	Water softening; mineral deposit control. Soil displacement by peptizing; prevention of redeposition.
Acids	Mineral deposit control; water softening.

From Harper (1968).

TABLE 7.9

PROPERTIES OF DETERGENTS

	Strong Alkalies	Mild Alkalies	Poly-Phosphate	Mild Acids	Strong Acids	Surfactants
Sequestering	0	+	++++	0	0	0
Wetting	+	++	+	+	0	++++
Emulsifying, suspending	+	++	++	0	0	++++
Dissolving	++++	+++	++	+++	++++	+
Saponifying	++++	+++	0	0	0	+
Peptizing	++++	+++	+	++	+++	0
Dispersion	++	+++	+	+	0	+++
Rinsing	+++	+++	++	+	0	++++
Corrosion	++++	++ to +++	0	++	++++	0

Key: Degrees of Activity
Extreme ++++
High +++
Medium ++
Low +
None 0

From Harper (1968).

poultry processing plants. Control consists of eliminating all breeding areas such as drainage, manure, offal, blood, stagnant water, and other organic matter. Chlorate, polyborate, borax, and other commercial preparations can be dusted or sprayed on breeding places to prevent development of fly larva. Any organic materials which have odors should be eliminated when possible.

Good plant construction for fly control consists of tight fitting screens on all openings into the plant. When doors or openings into buildings must be kept open for extended periods or are opened and closed frequently specially designed fans can be used to help reduce the number of insects which enter.

Insofar as possible, flies should be killed before they enter the plant by the use of insecticides in breeding areas. Inside buildings a space spray should be used after working hours so that all dead flies can be removed and the residual insecticides washed from equipment before resuming processing operations.

Roaches can become a problem in plants. Plant construction is of particular importance in roach control. All possible holes, cracks, and crevices should be sealed and warm moist areas should be eliminated where possible. Equipment should be installed in such a manner that it is easy to sweep or clean underneath and remove any waste food materials.

Rodent Control

Continuous preventative control is the best way to control rodents. St. Aubin (1963) lists three steps for control: these are (1) bar entry, (2) remove sources of food and shelter and (3) destroy those animals already present inside the buildings.

All hiding places in the area should be removed. Areas conducive to harboring rodents are old lumber, machinery, equipment, trash, and brush. Once all areas harboring rodents have been removed, the existing rodents can be killed by gassing underground burrows and closing them off.

Construction of buildings should be such that they are rodent-proof. All outside doors should be fitted with self-closing devices. For an efficient job of rodent proofing all entries larger than one-fourth inch must be sealed to prevent entry. Doors and frames should be of metal or metal covered to prevent the entrance of animals by gnawing. Eaves of buildings are entryways for rats and squirrels. Other areas commonly used for entry of rodents are crevices in walls, around pipes, wires, cracks in foundations, sidewalk gratings, floor drains, fan openings, mail drops, and transoms.

Food supplies attract rodents.   Good plant sanitation requires prompt disposal of refuse, viscera, blood, and other waste materials to prevent them from serving as a food source.   All foodstuffs should be kept covered and stored at least 18 in. away from walls and 8–10 in. from the floor.   A border of white paint 18 in. from the wall serves as a constant reminder to keep stored materials away from the wall.

Trapping and poisoning are the two most common methods of destroying rodents inside plants.   In some plants, poisoning is not used because of the chance of accidental contamination of food materials.   Common wood snap traps are widely used and work well; however, to be successful they must be serviced every day to remove dead animals, reset and rebaited and then relocated as needed.   Nuts, meats, peanut butter, and apples are good materials for bait.

Poisoning inside buildings in addition to the hazards created by the possibility of food contamination creates the additional problem of rodents dying in holes, walls, and other inaccessible areas and causing offensive odors.   Bait stations help reduce the hazards involved in the use of poisons.   The areas should be checked frequently to remove dead animals and to change or replace bait.

Hazards from Pesticides

Poultry and poultry carcasses can be contaminated with harmful chemicals as a result of feeding, or coming in contact with materials on the farm, or become contaminated during processing while moving through marketing channels.

The following types of chemical residues and some of the problems with them are taken as excerpts from the USDA Meat and Poultry Inspection Manual.

Chlorinated Hydrocarbons.—These compounds accumulate and are stored in animals'fat, and act as stimulants or depressants of central nervous systems.

Organo-phosphates.—They inhibit acetylcholinesterase and other cholinesterases. Their biological action results from acetylcholine accumulation at nerve endings, causing first stimulation and then paralysis of all nerve synapses and motor endings, except termination of sympathetic fibers.

The organo-phosphates include parathion, methylparathion, ronnel,malathion, ethion, dioxathion (Delnav®), mevinphos (phosdrin®), and naled (Dibron®).

Carbamates.—Many carbamic esters have pesticidal action. Like the organo-phosphates they inhibit cholinesterase. Most common carbamates are carbaryl (Sevin®) and pyrolan (Pyrolan®).

Fungicides.—These compounds are widely used for treating seed grains. Treated grains used for feeding animals raised for food (livestock and poultry), cannot be diverted without approval.

Since residue tolerance is not established in meat or edible organs from livestock or poultry fed treated seed grains, such practice is considered unsafe.

Fungicides include captan, thiram, ceresan M®, and zineb.

Herbicides.—They include: ammate, borax, dinitro-compounds, chlorobenzoic acids, arsenicals, sodium chlorate, phenols, and hormone types.

Metals.—*Arsenic.*—It is used as a component of pesticides, herbicides, and in combination with sodium, copper, and lead. It remains in the soil for long periods.

Lead.—Metallic lead and its alloys and salts frequently produce poisoning in cattle. Most animals are susceptible, but swine and goats appear rather resistant. Sources of lead are paints, pesticides, wet cell batteries, industrial contamination, etc.

Mercury.—This is a cumulative poison and is found in fungicides, antiseptics, and corrosives (mercuric chloride).

Selenium.—Intoxication (alkali disease) results from insecticides or seleniferous soil, water, or plants (Rocky Mountain and Great Plains areas).

When poultry and poultry carcasses are found contaminated they should be condemned and destroyed. The U.S. Department of Agriculture has compiled a list of chemical compounds which are approved for use under the U.S. Department of Agriculture poultry and poultry products inspection and grading programs. This list includes the general trade name of all compounds which have been approved for use and conditions limiting the use of each compound. This publication provides a good guide for the proper use of chemicals needed for operation of a poultry processing plant.

The use of medications in feeds just before slaughter has also created problems. The Food and Drug Administration (1964) has issued the following suggestions to avoid illegal drug residues in poultry carcasses which might make the carcasses subject to condemnation: (1) Comply strictly with withdrawal requirements before slaughter. Do not assume that the required withdrawal time will pass between sale of your poultry and slaughter. Be safe—take the birds off medicated feeds sufficiently ahead of sale. (2) Use medicated feeds only for purposes and the type of poultry—broilers, layers, turkeys—indicated on the label. (3) Follow feeding instructions exactly. (4) Heed all warning statements on the feed label. (5) Do not give any other drugs to birds on medicated feeds without first checking with a veterinarian. (6) Follow label directions when adding a drug to poultry drinking water. (7) Do not permit feeds to become contaminated with other drugs, chemicals or pesticides. (8) Never mix a drug or chemical into a feed unless so authorized under State and Federal law. (9) Instruct all feed handlers to follow label directions.

BIBLIOGRAPHY

ANON. 1952. Sanitation for the Food Preservation Industries. Association of Food Industry Sanitarians (Editors). McGraw-Hill Book Co., New York.

ANON. 1955. Poultry Ordinance, 1955 Edition. U.S. Dept. Health, Education, Welfare, PHS Bur. State Serv. Publ. 444.

ANON. 1957. Poultry Plant Sanitation, Supplement No. 1., Institute of American Poultry Industries, Chicago.

ANON. 1964A. Regulations governing the inspection of poultry and poultry products. U.S. Dept. Agr., Agr. Mktg. Serv., Poultry Div.

ANON. 1964B. Poultry Inspector's Handbook. U.S. Dept. Agr., Agr. Mktg. Serv., Poultry Div., Inspection Branch.

ANON. 1964C. Protect the public health. U.S. Dept. Health, Education, Welfare, Food Drug Admin. 0-719-963.

ANON. 1964D. Poultry Plant Sanitation. Tech. Rept., Klenzade Products, Beloit, Wisconsin.

ANON. 1964E. Sani-Facts. Tech. Rept., Wyandotte Chemicals Corp., Wyandotte, Mich.

ANON. 1973A. Handbook for Monitoring Industrial Wastewater. U.S. Environmental Protection Agency, Washington, D.C.

ANON. 1973B. Accepted meat and poultry equipment. Sci. Tech. Serv., Meat Poultry Inspection Program, Animal Plant Health Inspection Serv., USDA.

ANON. 1973C. Meat and Poultry Inspection Manual. Sci. Tech. Serv., Meat Poultry Inspection Program, Animal Plant Health Inspection Serv., USDA.

ANON. 1973D. List of chemical compounds authorized for use under USDA poultry, meat, rabbit and egg products inspection program. Sci. Tech. Serv., Meat Poultry Inspection Program, Animal Plant Health Inspection Serv., USDA.

CHILDS, R. E., REED, M. J., and HAMANN, J. A. 1970. Guidelines for poultry-processing plant layouts. USDA Agr. Res. Serv. in cooperation with College of Agriculture Experiment Stations. Univ. Georgia Mktg. Res. Rept. 878.

CHILDS, R. E., and RODGERS, P. D. 1958. Methods and equipment for icepacking poultry. U.S. Dept. Agr. Mktg. Res. Rept. 242.

CHILDS, R. E., and WALTERS, R. E. 1962. Methods and equipment for eviscerating chickens. U.S. Dept. Agr., Agr. Mktg. Serv. Res. Rept. 549.

CROSSWHITE, W. M., CARAWAN, R. E., and MACON, J. A. (Undated) Water and waste management in processing. N. Carolina State Univ. (mimeo).

DODDS, D. D. 1963. Electricity in food processing operations. In Food Processing Operations, Vol. I. M. A. Joslyn and J. L. Heid (Editors). Avi Publishing Co., Westport, Conn.

EARNSHAW, G. 1963. Maintenance schedules No. 1 and 2 (Poultry Process. Equipment). Tech. Bull., Gordon Johnson Industries, Kansas City.

HARPER, W. J. 1968. Cleaning compounds—characteristics and functions. Ohio State Univ. Dept. Food Sci. (mimeo).

KAHLE, H. S., and GRAY, L. R. 1957. Utilization and disposal of poultry by-products and wastes. U.S. Dept. Agr., Mktg. Res. Rept. *143*.

KAPLOVSKY, A. J. 1958. Problems in handling poultry wastes. Food Technol. *12*, 180–182.

PORGES, R., and STRUZESKI, E. J. JR. 1962. Wastes from the poultry processing industry. Robert A. Taft Sanitary Engineering Center, Cincinnati, Tech. Rept. *W62-3*.

ROSS, F. M., and KAHLE, H. S. 1959. Irrigation as a low cost method of sewage disposal for the poultry processor. U.S. Dept. Agr., Mktg. Res. Rept. *306*.

ST. AUBIN, F. E. 1963. Three simple steps control rodents. Food Eng. 35, 56–59.

STEFFEN, A. J. 1973A. Elements of in-plant water conservation for poultry processors. Proc. Poultry Egg Inst. Fact Finding Conf., New Orleans. (mimeo).

STEFFEN, A. J. 1973B. Elements of pre-treatment of poultry processing wastewater prior to discharge into a city sewer. Proc. Poultry Egg Inst. Fact Finding Conf., New Orleans. (mimeo).

VAUGHN, R. H. 1963. Food plant sanitation. *In* Food Processing Operations, Vol. I. M. A. Joslyn and J. L. Heid (Editors). Avi Publishing Co., Westport, Conn.

WEISER, H. H., MOUNTNEY, G. J., and GOULD, W. A. 1971. Practical Food Microbiology and Technology, 2nd Edition. Avi Publishing Co., Westport, Conn.

WESTERMAN, C. M. 1963. Plant safety in food products manufacture. *In* Food Processing Operations, Vol. I. M. A. Joslyn and J. L. Heid (Editors). Avi Publishing Co., Westport, Conn.

CHAPTER 8

Processing
Fresh Poultry

ASSEMBLING

Whenever possible, broilers are caught at night for loading. At that time they are easier to catch, struggle less, settle down in the coops faster and in summer the weather is cooler at night. Loading schedules should be arranged so that the birds arrive at the plant within an hour before they are to be unloaded for slaughter.

Turkeys and fowl are caught and handled whenever they are needed for processing. This is normally the afternoon before slaughter since turkeys sometimes must be caught on open pasture and hens are removed from laying cages or a laying house.

Mountney and Gardner (1957) reported one method of assembling broilers commonly used in Texas. A catching crew of 4 or 5 men is responsible for the loading. Before the birds are caught, all feeders, waterers and other equipment are moved to one corner of the house and the lights turned out or dimmed to prevent birds from becoming excited. Then two men catch broilers by the shanks, four in each hand. The birds are then handed to two other men who carry them to the truck outside the house; there the truck driver and a helper place them in coops and arrange them on the truck. The truck driver is responsible for seeing that the birds are properly crated and loaded and that they arrive at the plant on schedule and in good condition. Generally a representative of the feed company financing the operation is present to observe the loading.

Hale *et al.* (1973) reported that other catching methods in various stages of development include transporting birds from the house to the truck by vacuum, special conveyor systems, enlarging and redesigning coops and trucks, and designing completely new total mechanized systems for producing, harvesting, and transporting birds.

WEIGHING

Bulk weighing is now used almost exclusively in weighing birds. A truck loaded with empty crates is weighed at the public scale nearest the farm. Then the truck proceeds to the farm and the broilers are loaded into the crates which are left on the truck. Only 1 or 2 rows of crates are removed from the truck for loading. The load of poultry is weighed again at the public scales nearest to the processing plant or at the plant.

Shrinkage

Contract hauling is practiced extensively in broiler areas. In some areas a shrinkage of four per cent during hauling is permitted; in other areas only three per cent is permitted. Shrinkage above the maximum level is borne by the seller or hauler. In a few cases broilers are paid for on a delivered-to-the-plant basis. The paying price is determined by the weight of the birds when they are unloaded at the plant. This method eliminates the problem of who pays for shrinkage, how much the hauler should be paid and the responsibility for the birds during assembly. To compensate for hauling charges and loss in weight, the paying price on such a transaction is generally a cent a pound over the on-the-farm market price.

SLAUGHTERING AND DEFEATHERING

Slaughtering and defeathering consist of hanging, sometimes stunning, bleeding, scalding, picking, and washing.

Receiving and Hanging

After weighing, the truck parks alongside the unloading dock where an overhead conveyor carries the shackles from the dressing room out onto the dock. The loaded crates of broilers are moved off the trucks onto roller conveyors and pushed to the processing line. There several men remove the birds from the crates and shackle them for slaughter. As the crates are emptied, they are conveyed back to the truck on roller conveyors and reloaded.

When the coops are built onto the truck as permanent equipment, in some plants the birds are removed from the coops on one side and then the truck is turned around for removing birds from the other side; in other plants two conveyors are used so birds can be unloaded from both sides at the same time.

Slaughtering

Slaughtering involves stunning and bleeding. In most cases the birds are bled without stunning. In those cases where carcasses are stunned, the method of stunning should be such that the heart action is not destroyed.

Stunning.—Stunning with an electric shocker is frequently used when slaughtering turkeys and occasionally with other types of poultry to prevent struggling. Stunning also relaxes the muscles which hold the feathers. Generally turkey wing and tail feathers are pulled from the carcass immediately after stunning and bleeding if the feathers are to be sold.

Other types of poultry are scalded with the wing and tail feathers intact.

Mountney, Gardner, and Gayvert (1956) have demonstrated that shocking reduces the rate of bleeding with turkeys, but that the total amount of blood lost is the same as other methods of slaughter if the bird is given sufficient time for complete bleeding.

Mountney and Parnell (1958) reported that shockers can be a knife which has an electric current in the blade or an electric plate or wands which touch the heads of the birds as they move along the conveyor. To obtain a current supply, one electric line is attached to the track and another one to the shocking device. When the circuit is completed by touching the bird's head the current runs through the bird and stuns it. The size of the electrical charge can be regulated according to the size and species of poultry being slaughtered.

Carbon dioxide immobilization is still in the experimental stages. As yet it has not been possible to utilize carbon dioxide slaughtering in poultry plants. The concentration of CO_2 required must be carefully controlled, otherwise the bird will be killed. Drewniak, Baush, and Davis (1955) reported that practical limits for stunning turkeys varied from 73 to 75% concentration but the optimum times for exposure varied for males, females and different varieties. Kotula, Drewniak, and Davis (1957) have reported evidence to indicate that carbon dioxide speeds up the rate of bleeding of chickens.

Piercing the cerebellum of the brain either by running a knife through the eye or through the roof of the mouth was once a common method of stunning poultry. This method has largely been replaced by the use of electric stunning in slaughtering turkeys and by severing the jugular vein only in the case of other poultry.

Bleeding

There are several ways of cutting poultry so that they can be bled. "Modified kosher" killed birds are those where the jugular vein is severed just below the jowls so that the windpipe and esophagus remain uncut. According to Jewish law the windpipe must pop out in true kosher slaughtering. The name comes from the use of "kosher" slaughtering for dispatching poultry to be consumed by orthodox Jewish people. Another method, decapitation, although it can be considered as a method of slaughter, is seldom used. A third method, usually used when carcasses are pierced through the brain, consists of severing the veins in the roof of the mouth. This method of slaughter has just about passed out of existence.

Of the three methods "modified kosher" slaughter is the most widely used in modern processing operations because it is easier to obtain good bleeding and leaves the head and neck intact for use in suspending the carcass for later eviscerating operations.

Newell and Shaffner (1950) reported that between 34 and 50% of the total blood of the body of chickens is lost during the bleeding phase of the killing operation, but that considerable variation exists. They also reported that birds which are decapitated lose less blood than those slaughtered by "kosher" killing or those stuck and then pierced through the brain.

Davis and Coe (1954) in later work on factors influencing bleeding reported that debraining before cutting the carotid arteries and jugular veins was of little value during the first 20 sec. of bleeding other than for immobilizing the bird. They also substantiated part of the work of Newell and Shaffner (1950) that decapitating the birds decreased the flow of blood.

Automatic killers are now coming into general use where the birds are first electrically stunned to immobilize them and for better positioning on an automatic killing machine.

By law, any animal ". . . stunned, by electrical, chemical, gunshot, or other methods . . . shall be unconscious when shackled, hoisted, or cut." The one exception is when ritual slaughter is being carried out.

Scalding

The U.S. Department of Agriculture (1953) published a discussion of the considerations involved in the use of various methods of scalding poultry.

Poultry immersed in water heated to 160°–180°F. for 30 to 60 sec. is considered to be hard-scalded. The flesh of carcasses scalded in this manner expands and becomes slightly puffy under the skin so that the carcass appears plump. It is easier to remove the feathers from carcasses scalded at this temperature than those scalded at lower temperatures but the flesh of such poultry is "doughy" and lifeless and the skin becomes discolored soon after processing. As a result the carcass must be kept covered with a packaging material or moist with ice or water.

Hard-scalding is used mostly for waterfowl because it is the only satisfactory way to release feathers and the skin of waterfowl does not discolor as readily as do other species of poultry. Hard-scalding of poultry other than waterfowl is not considered a desirable practice.

Carcasses scalded in water of 138°–140°F. for 30 to 75 sec. are generally considered as subscalded. Such carcasses have the outer layer of skin broken down but the flesh is not affected as in hard-scalding. The main advantage of subscalding is easy removal of feathers and a uniform skin color; however, the skin surface is moist and sticky and will discolor if not kept moist and covered.

Semi-scalding, often called soft- or slack-scalding, is carried out at 123°–130°F. for 90–120 sec. The proper combination of water and temperature is particularly important in this temperature range because too high a temperature for too long a time will cause patches of the skin to peel off leaving blotchy, unsightly areas when the skin becomes dry. The chief advantage of the semi-scald method is that it leaves the skin intact and so permits more diverse methods of chilling and packing. Its disadvantage is that it is harder to remove feathers and more hand pinning is required or additional pickers must be installed on the processing line.

To overcome some of the disadvantages of semi-scalding the hocks and necks are sometimes scalded separately at a higher temperature after the rest of the carcass has been picked. As a result the neck and hock feathers can be removed by pickers and the skin is removed only on the neck and hocks.

Generally scalding carcasses in the range between 130° and 138°F. should be avoided because the temperature is too hot to keep all of the skin intact and too low to remove all of the epidermal layer of skin. As a result blotches and unsightly patches are formed if the skin dehydrates.

Recently, a new "semi-scald" system was developed. It is now in use in a number of plants. Since the scalders are completely enclosed, blood and feathers are not splashed around the room and humidity, water sprays, and noise and odor levels are greatly reduced. With this process, the carcasses are showered with hot water and then conveyed through humidity cabinets where they are sprayed with steam at 140° F.

Feather Release

During the past few years several studies have been made in an attempt to determine some of the factors which affect feather release mechanisms. Pool et al. (1954) observed that the force required to remove feathers from turkey carcasses decreased as the scalding temperature increased. They also concluded that scalding temperature is of more importance than scalding time. Klose and Pool (1954) as a result of further work stated that their studies suggested that turkeys scalded at 140° F. are acceptable for frozen storage if proper moisture control is maintained. Klose, Mecchi, and Pool (1961) in work with chickens reported that scalding resulted "in a reduction of feather pulling force ranging from 30% at 122° F. to over 95% at 140° F." Anesthetizing the bird also reduced the feather pulling

FIG. 8.1.   AN AUTOMATIC, ON-THE-LINE RUBBER-FINGERED FEATHER
PICKER

force 25-50%. When the anesthetized birds were slaughtered and scalded there was generally a greater reduction than when either one was used alone.

Knapp and Newell (1961) reported that it required more force to pull feathers from males than females and that fasting for eight hours increased the force required to remove feathers. Exercise for 90 sec. also increased the force required to remove feathers, while tranquilizers and scalding time in most cases decreased the force required for removal.

Automatic rubber-fingered feather pickers are shown in Figs. 8.1 and 8.2.

Wax Picking

After waterfowl carcasses have been scalded and rough picked they are usually dipped in wax to remove pinfeathers (Fig. 8.3). Because of better processing methods and equipment, wax picking (with the possible exception of its use for picking waterfowl) has been replaced by other methods. Generally the carcasses are dropped into a tank of hot wax while suspend-

FIG. 8.2. A CYCLO-MATIC PICKER WITH AUTOMATIC LOADING CON-
VEYOR, DRESSED BIRD CONVEYOR, AND FEATHER REMOVAL CONVEYOR

ed on shackles by the head and feet, removed, and dipped a second time.
Then they are immersed in cold water to harden the wax. When the wax
is properly hardened it peels off in large pieces pulling out small feathers
with it thus leaving a clean carcass. Although the wax can be reclaimed it
must be heated to kill microorganisms; otherwise it serves as a source of
contamination.

Picking

In processing plants, carcasses are carried by a conveyor line while
hanging by the feet through rubber-fingered pickers which beat and rub
the feathers from the carcass. A steady stream of water washes the feathers away and acts as a lubricant. To remove feathers from all areas the
direction and location of the fingers relative to the carcass are changed as
the poultry move along the line and pass through different pickers. In
some cases the carcasses are also reversed so they move through some
pickers hanging by the head.

Singeing

After picking and pinning carcasses are singed to remove hair-like appendages called filoplumes. Each carcass passes through a sheet of flame
as it moves along the conveyor line.

FIG. 8.3. WATERFOWL ARE DIPPED TWICE IN A SPECIAL WAX TO ASSIST REMOVAL
OF PIN FEATHERS AND DOWN

Washing

Finally the carcasses are washed with a stream of water and scrubbed with rubber fingers at the same time. Scrubbing not only loosens and removes soiled areas but also reduces the number of microorganisms found on carcasses.

Removing Shanks and Oil Glands

Where possible these two operations are generally carried out in the dressing room immediately after the carcasses are washed. Shanks can be removed by knives, saws, manually operated shears, or mechanized shears. Childs and Walters (1962) reported that an operator using a knife could handle more carcasses than with shears, but that the knife was a continuous hazard for the operator.

In the same study it was observed that the most efficient method of removing the oil gland was to suspend the carcasses by the hocks rather than by the neck. With this method some skilled operators could achieve a rate of 40 birds a minute.

EVISCERATION

The methods of eviscerating poultry vary considerably not only among different areas and for different species of poultry, but also among different plants. Childs and Walters (1962) conducted a detailed time and motion study of the methods and equipment used for eviscerating chickens. Most of the methods described here are taken from the results of their study because they represent the methods in most common use.

Positioning

Separate conveyor lines are used for dressing and eviscerating. Two lines have several advantages over one continuous line. If one line stops the other operation can continue until the poultry on the line is completely dressed, the eviscerating line is not contaminated with filth from the dressing line and generally the dressing line can operate faster than the eviscerating line. In some plants, one dressing line supplies up to four eviscerating lines. Where batch pickers are used the birds can be transferred to operators for hanging on the eviscerating line by means of a belt system. Most broiler carcasses are positioned for evisceration by hanging both hocks on a shackle. This position is called two-point suspension. Turkeys are usually suspended by both the hocks and neck hanging on the shackle. This position is called three-point suspension.

Opening the Body Cavity

The opening knife cuts are made either with a slicing motion or with a stabbing motion which can be used only with two-point suspension. The vent can be removed by cutting around it with a knife or a pair of scissors.

Removing the Viscera

Since most poultry processing plants now operate under government inspection it is important that the viscera be removed carefully and intact to avoid contaminating the carcass and to facilitate inspection. To retain the identity of the viscera with the carcass and to be in a position for easy inspection, the viscera are generally left hanging outside the body but still attached to the carcass. Childs and Walters (1962) describe the method as follows:

The evisceration is performed by supporting the bird with one hand and inserting the fingers of the other hand through the incision in the abdomen. The three middle fingers (sometimes the middle finger, too) extended, slide past the viscera until the heart is reached. They are then partly closed in a loose grip, followed by a gentle twisting action, and the viscera are slipped out of the body and released.

Automatic eviscerators are now available which can eviscerate 40 carcasses a minute on a 2400-per-hour line; however, Hale *et al.* (1973) reported that ones currently in commercial operation cannot completely draw out the viscera and some carcasses are missed.

Inspection

Carcasses should pass by the inspector positioned in such a manner that the overhead light illuminates the body cavity so that the carcass does not need to be tilted or turned. Guide rails help steady shackles and carcasses during inspection and S hooks with swivels make it possible for the inspector to turn the carcass.

Processing Giblets

The heart and liver are removed from the remaining viscera by cutting or pulling them loose. As soon as they are removed the gall bladder is cut or pulled from the liver and the pericardial sac and arteries are cut from the heart. More edible tissue is lost by cutting than by pulling.

The gizzard is generally removed by first cutting it loose in front of the proventriculus and then cutting both incoming and outgoing tracts. Then it is split open with scissors, emptied, washed, and the lining removed on a gizzard peeler.

Removing Lungs

Lungs can be removed with either a hand rake or a vacuum system. Vacuum removal is the most efficient method and is used in most large plants.

Decapitating

Heads can be removed manually by pulling, with a V-shaped slot with tension obtained from the pull of the conveyor, with a revolving drum, or by means of other mechanical devices.

Removing Crop, Windpipe and Neck

Several methods are used to remove the crop, windpipe, and neck. One method consists of cutting the neck from the back close to the body with a pair of shears, then pulling and removing the crop and windpipe. The neck is then cut off with a knife or mechanical device.

Courtesy W. F. Altenpohl, Inc.

FIG. 8.4.   AN AUTOMATIC SIZING SYSTEM WHICH SORTS CARCASSES
INTO PREDESIGNATED WEIGHTS

Wrapping and Stuffing Giblets

Giblets are generally moved from processing to packing stations by a flume conveyor or pump.   They are wrapped in 9 x 12 in. sheets of parchment paper, parchment bags or film and then stuffed in the body cavity of the carcass.   It is easier to stuff giblets when the carcasses are warm but when tumbling type chillers are used it is necessary to wait until carcasses are chilled because the tumbling action causes giblets to fall out.   Chilling before stuffing helps to increase shelf-life.

SORTING CARCASSES

After carcasses are removed from the eviscerating line they are hung on a sorter which passes over a row of chill tanks and drops the carcasses in the vat according to predesignated weight classifications (Fig. 8.4).

CHILLING

Poultry carcasses can be chilled in cold running tap water, crushed ice, slush ice, slush ice agitated with compressed air or a circulating pump or in an on-the-line chiller.   According to U.S. Department of Agriculture regulations carcasses must be chilled to at least 40° F. internal temperature.   Cold running tap water is satisfactory for preliminary chilling but it generally is not cold enough to chill carcasses to 40° F. and the amount of water required prohibits its use.

Crushed ice and water chill faster than crushed ice alone because with water the carcasses are completely immersed in the cooling medium. By agitating the water, the rate of cooling is increased further.

The water can be agitated by placing a perforated galvanized pipe in the bottom of the chill vat and pumping air through the slush ice or by circulating the water from the bottom to the top of the vat with a pump.

To eliminate batch operations in which birds must be placed in chill tanks, held for a few hours and then removed, continuous on-the-line chillers have been developed. These fall into four classifications: "drag" chillers, parallel-flow tumble chillers, counterflow tumble chillers, and oscillating vat chillers. Kotula, Thompson, and Kinner (1960) have described these systems.

"Drag" chillers consist of two vats in which carcasses, suspended on shackles are dragged through the cooling medium. The size of the vats depends on the rate at which carcasses are transported through the chiller. The first vat has a 50 ft. trough which contains water at about 41° F. The second vat contains slush ice at 32°–33° F. The second vat is S-shaped and contains 200 lineal feet of cooling area.

Parallel-flow tumble systems for chilling also consist of two metal tanks about 26 ft. long depending on capacity. A cylindrical revolving drum tumbles the birds in the coolant and recirculated water provides a current to move the carcasses along the drum at a given rate of speed. The first tank uses tap water and the second tank contains slush ice.

Counterflow tumble chillers are essentially the same as the parallel-flow system except that the water circulates in the opposite direction of the carcasses. The carcasses are moved along the drum by a helical drive.

Oscillating vat chillers consist of two tanks. Tap water is used in the first one for precooling and water in the second tank is cooled to 33°–35° F. with ice. The tanks are rocked from side to side on eccentric rollers to agitate the carcasses (Fig. 8.5).

ICE PACKING IN BOXES

According to Childs and Rodgers (1958) the ice-packing operation consists of receiving, storing, setting up, and distributing boxes. The operation also includes removing chilled carcasses from chill vats, packing them in containers, weighing the boxes of poultry and recording identifying information on the box, capping poultry boxes with crushed or flake ice, closing and securing box lids, and stacking boxes preparatory to shipment. Generally 30 to 35 lb. of crushed ice are placed on top of the birds in each box. In some operations after the ice has been placed on top of the poultry, the boxes are closed automatically.

Hale et al. (1973) reported that most processors now supply carcasses iced or dry packed with CO_2.

Courtesy Big Dutchman/Barker

FIG. 8.5. A CONTINUOUS ROCKER-CHILLER SHOWING FIVE REGULAR SECTIONS—ONE DRIVE TANK—INGOING END PLATE—TRANSFER CONVEYOR END SECTION, AND WATER CIRCULATING SYSTEM

PROCESSING WATERFOWL

Ducks

Ziemba (1965) describes the methods used to process ducklings. Ducks are delivered in open trucks in lots of 600 and processed at the rate of 600 per hr. After delivery they are weighed and then held for 1 to 2 hr. to settle down before slaughter. Carcasses are scalded twice in rocker scalders, first at 140° F. for two and a half minutes and then at 142°-145° F. Next they are picked on batch type pickers which hold 20 birds per lot. After drying the carcasses are dipped in wax at 195° F. and then cooled in water at 55° F. Wax is removed by a wax stripping machine and the remainder by pinners. Next the ducks are eviscerated and chilled in a continuous chiller and then packaged in Cryovac and frozen at −28° F. for 24 hr.

Geese

For processing, birds are delivered to a holding corral. Then they are forced to swim through a canal to clean their feathers. After hanging on the conveyor line they are stunned and bled with an electric knife and then scalded at 150°–154°F. in a homemade rocking scalder.

Flight and shoulder feathers are removed as soon as the carcasses leave the scalder. Then carcasses are released automatically from shackles and dropped into a hopper. At preset intervals the hopper drops groups of carcasses into a centrifuge-type picker to remove the remaining feathers. Any remaining pinfeathers left by the picker are removed with an on-the-line picker after which the carcasses are dried with a jet of compressed air and hung in a triangular suspension with the breast down. Then the carcasses are dipped in molten wax at 220°F. for 3 to 5 sec., cooled, redipped at 160°F. for 3 to 5 sec. and dipped in cold water to harden the wax. The head is removed from the shackle which breaks the wax so it can be stripped from the carcass in several large pieces. The remaining wax is removed by a drum picker and then the carcasses are dipped in water at 180°F. to tighten the skin. Tightening the skin makes it easy for pinners to remove the remaining pinfeathers. Carcasses are then eviscerated and inspected.

Geese are generally slaughtered at 17 weeks of age at which time they generally average 6 to 7 pounds live weight. Dressing yields generally are about 70% with a pick up of about 4.5% during chilling.

BIBLIOGRAPHY

ANON. 1953. Considerations in the use of hard-scald, subscald, and semi-scald methods in dressing poultry. U.S. Dept. Agr. Mimeo.

CHILDS, R. E., REED, M. J., and HAMANN, J. A. 1970. Guidelines for poultry-processing plant layouts. USDA Agr. Res. Serv. in cooperation with Coll. Agr. Expt. Stations, Univ. Georgia. USDA Mktg. Res. Rept. 878.

CHILDS, R. E., and RODGERS, P.D. 1958. Methods and equipment for icepacking poultry. U.S. Dept. Agr. Mktg. Res. Rept. 242.

CHILDS, R. E., and WALTERS, R. E. 1962. Methods and equipment for eviscerating chickens. U.S. Dept. Agr. Mktg. Res. Rept. 549.

DAVIS, L. L., and COE, M. E. 1954. Bleeding of chickens during killing operations. Poultry Sci. 33, 616–619.

DREWNIAK, E. E., BAUSH, E. R., and DAVIS, L. L. 1955. Carbon dioxide immobilization of turkeys before slaughter. U.S. Dept. Agr. Circ. 958.

HALE, K. K., THOMPSON, J. C., TOLEDO, R. T., and WHITE, H. D. 1973. An evaluation of poultry processing. A special report. Univ. Georgia Coll. Expt. Sta. Committee Poultry Processing Ind. Univ. Georgia Coll. Agr., Athens.

KLOSE, A. A., KAUFMAN, V. F., and POOL, M. F. 1971. Scalding poultry by steam at subatmospheric pressures. Poultry Sci. 50, 302.

KLOSE, A. A., MECCHI, E. P., and POOL, M. F. 1961. Observations on factors influencing feather release. Poultry Sci. *40*, 1029-1036.

KLOSE, A. A., and POOL, M. F. 1954. The effect of scalding temperature on the quality of stored frozen turkeys. Poultry Sci. *33*, 280-289.

KNAPP, B. G., and NEWELL, G. W. 1961. Effect of selected factors on feather removal in chickens. Poultry Sci. *40*, 510-517.

KOTULA, A. W., DREWNIAK, E. E., and DAVIS, L. L. 1957. Effect of carbon dioxide immobilization on the bleeding of chickens. Poultry Sci. *36*, 585-589.

KOTULA, A. W., and HELBACKA, N. V. 1966A. Blood retained by chicken carcasses and cut-up parts as influenced by slaughter method. Poultry Sci. *45*, 404-410.

KOTULA, A. W., and HELBACKA, N. V. 1966B. Blood volume of live chickens and influence of slaughter technique on blood loss. Poultry Sci. *45*, 684-688.

KOTULA, A. W., and HELBACKA, N. V. 1968. Chicken blood volume: The hematocrit and comparison of I^{131} and evans blue methods. Poultry Sci. *47*, 26-31.

KOTULA, A. W., THOMPSON, J. E., and KINNER, J. A. 1960. Water absorption by eviscerated broilers. U.S. Dept. Agr. Mktg. Res. Rept. *438*.

MOUNTNEY, G. J., and GARDNER, F. A. 1957. Processing Texas broilers. Texas Agr. Expt. Sta. Bull. *857*.

MOUNTNEY, G. J., GARDNER, F. A. and GAYVERT, R. A. 1956. The influence of electric shock on turkey bleeding. Poultry Sci. *29*, 271-275.

MOUNTNEY, G. J., and PARNELL, E. D. 1958. Proper slaughtering for good carcass quality. Poultry Process. Mktg. 64, No. 11, 14-15.

NEWELL, G. W., and SHAFFNER, C. S. 1950. Blood loss by chickens during killing. Poultry Sci. *29*, 217-275.

POOL, M. F., MECCHI, E. P., LINEWEAVER, H., and KLOSE, A. A. 1954. The effect of scalding temperature on the processing and initial appearance of turkeys. Poultry Sci. *33*, 274-279.

RASKOPF, B. D., and MILES, J. F. 1966. Labor efficiency in broiler processing plants in the south. Tenn. Agr. Expt. Sta., Knoxville, Southern Coop. Ser. Bull. *112*.

ZIEMBA, J. B. 1965. Duckling quality gains as techniques improve. Food Eng. *37*, 102-104.

CHAPTER 9

Packaging

INTRODUCTION

Packaging of poultry products is done for both aesthetic and utilitarian purposes. Dichter (1952) reported that packaging provides a number of functions in addition to purely utilitarian ones. Among these are adding shape and character to otherwise amorphous products, assuring the consumer that the merchandise has not been previously handled by another shopper and that the merchandise in the package is as nearly as possible in the same condition as when originally packaged. Packaging also helps to assure the consumer of product cleanliness.

Utilitarian functions derived from packaging are assemblage of a number of small units into one larger easier to handle unit, protection from physical damage, dehydration, oxygen, and other gases and protection from odors, microorganisms, dirt, filth, insects, and other contaminants. Packaging is also used to distinguish different units of a product into single or multiple portions and for heat-and-serve meals, in which case the package also serves as the container for heating and serving the meal.

Uncooked poultry products are packaged in many forms such as refrigerated ice packed, dry packed, whole, parts, cut-up, and deboned. Frozen poultry is packaged as whole, parts, cut-up, or deboned products. Other poultry products include complete ready to heat-and-serve dinners, chicken pies, chicken a-la-king, turkey steaks, turkey rolls, canned products, and in various other forms.

TRENDS IN POULTRY PACKAGING

The majority of chickens are delivered to stores as ice-packed, or dry packed whole carcasses, where the carcasses are individually packaged and cut into portions according to the demands of the clientele of the particular trading area. Most turkeys are delivered frozen and sealed in plastic bags. Turkeys, chickens, and parts are also displayed packed in ice.

Plant Versus Supermarket Packaging

Recent attempts have been made to perform the cutting and packaging services at the processing plant. However, the rapid dehydration of cut-up poultry and the resultant loss in weight have discouraged many retail stores from handling chilled poultry that has been cut up and packaged at

TABLE 9.1

PERCENTAGE OF TRAYS OF FROZEN CUT-UP POULTRY ARRIVING WITH TORN FILM OVERWRAPS AT 3 WILMINGTON SUPERMARKETS, BY TYPE OF FILM, SUMMER 1962[1]

Store	1-mil Irradiated Polyethylene (%)	1-mil Polyethylene (%)	1-mil Polypropylene (%)	½-mil Cast Polyvinyl Chloride (%)	1-mil Extruded Polyvinyl Chloride (%)
A	12.5	6.9	9.7	20.8	11.1
B	[2]	0	4.2	22.2	4.2
C	18.0	10.4	9.7	43.8	16.7
Avg of 3 stores	13.8	6.2	7.1	30.4	9.5

[1] Average of 4 shipments in store A and 3 shipments in stores B and C.
[2] In one shipment the film on 71% of the packages was torn. The master container in which they were delivered was crushed and broken, apparently the result of abnormally rough treatment.

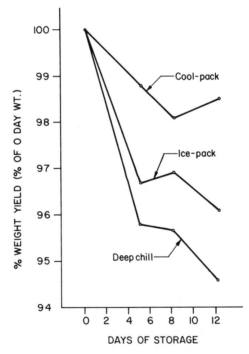

From Gardner and Nichols (1971)

FIG. 9.1. WEIGHT YIELD AS AFFECTED BY PACKAGING TREATMENT AND LENGTH OF STORAGE AT 35° F

the processing plant. Jordan and Saunders (1958) in a study of the costs of these services reported that there were lower labor rates, more sanitary conditions, more uniform packaging, a higher quality product, the elimination of certain inconveniences for the retailer and brand identification for the processor when these services were performed at the processing plant. On the other hand, the loss in weight from dehydration increased, more expensive packaging materials were required and more frequent deliveries to stores were necessary to help reduce weight loss. These workers reported that fryers cut up in supermarkets lost 1.8% in weight from dehydration whereas those cut up in a Delmarva processing plant lost 5.0%. Mountney and Branson (1958) in a survey of 2000 consumers at the Texas State Fair reported that consumers prefer carcasses cut into 10 or 13 pieces rather than 6 pieces. Such processing increases the dehydration rate by increasing the number of parts. This cutting up increases surface areas exposed for dehydration and increases the chances for bacterial contamination.

Fresh Versus Frozen Poultry

Considerable controversy still exists regarding the value of marketing fresh or frozen poultry. Proponents of merchandising frozen broilers argue that frozen broilers have a longer shelf-life, equilibrating supply and demand is easier and freezing would create no problem for the housewife since many already freeze broilers at home. Proponents of fresh poultry argue that freezing adds extra costs of freezing, requires better packaging, requires handling in and out of storage, and requires storage and transportation in a frozen state. Since broilers are no longer a seasonal commodity, frozen poultry brought from storage for sale must still compete with the fresh poultry in the market. Recently a compromise between fresh and frozen poultry has been tried in which the cut-up parts have been held at temperatures just above freezing. Using this method with the aid of good packaging, the shelf-life and high quality of poultry can be maintained for several weeks.

BULK CONTAINERS

Bulk containers commonly used for handling chilled poultry are wooden wire-bound crates, corrugated paraffin lined containers, polyethylene coated cardboard containers, and metal containers, either in the form of wire baskets or sheet metal. Wire baskets and sheet metal containers are reusable; the other types are discarded after one trip. Generally these containers hold 60 to 70 lb. of chicken and 20 to 30 lb. of ice. Size is limited primarily by the weight one workman can handle.

Wire-bound Wood Crates

The Package Research Laboratory (Anon. 1962) reported that 63 million wire-bound wooden crates were furnished to the industry in

1962 for packing iced poultry. They cite these advantages for these containers: (1) Easy to handle. Cleats on the side provide easy handles. (2) Easy to stack because they are easy to hold and the boxes will not collapse under heavy weight. (3) The size and shape are such that rapid and easy packing is possible. (4) There is good drainage and ventilation of melted ice from the crates. (5) The crates are resistant to moisture damage.

Disadvantages of this type container are: (1) Water may drip onto the crates below. (2) It requires a paper liner. (3) Ice must be removed before the chickens are removed. (4) The problem of disposal of boxes creates a problem since they cannot be baled and the wires remain when the crates are burned.

Plastic and Wax Impregnated Fiberboard Containers

Hale and Chapogas (1963) reported that fiberboard boxes come in three different designs: (1) the one-piece regular slotted container which is closed by folding side flaps over end flaps; (2) the one-piece container with interlocking top in which the overlapping top portion is scored so it can be folded and interlock with the opposite flaps; and (3) the full telescope container.

All of these are available with a paraffin coating and the telescope model is also available with polyethylene coating.

Fiberboard containers have a uniform tare weight, they do not present the disposal problem of wirebound wooden boxes, they eliminate water dripping during handling and it is easier to remove chickens from cartons with the telescope design because they can be turned upside down and opened from the bottom. The ice stays in the top portion of the container. Fiberboard boxes are slightly smaller in size than wire-bound boxes so that they cannot hold as much ice and chickens and they are difficult to handle because the handholds are not as convenient as those on wooden crates.

A recent development has been the use of a corrugated shipping container with a polyethylene interior liner, spot laminated to high-absorbant paper toweling. Water dripping from the carcasses is absorbed by the toweling. This helps maintain a humid atmosphere which retards evaporation. The liner is disposable but the cases can be used over. The main advantage claimed for cases of this design is a reduction in shipping and handling costs because ice is not required and less dehydration occurs than when no ice is used.

Metal Containers

In some areas wire baskets and sheet metal containers are used for packing poultry. Generally they are lined with a disposable polyethylene liner. Wire baskets hold 30 to 35 lb. of ice and 65 lbs. of poultry.

The main advantage of such containers is their low cost since they can be reused many times. Primary disadvantages result from the high initial cost and the need for return. Under field conditions, many of these containers become lost or stolen.

TRAY PACKING

Refrigerated cut-up poultry is packaged in trays made from fiber backing board, pulp cardboard or plastic trays or in rectangular cardboard boxes. Sometimes pads are used in the bottom to absorb moisture. Poultry packed in this manner and then overwrapped with a plastic film are known as traypacks. Heitz (1958) reported that over 80% of the chickens sold in 1958 were sold as cut-up tray-packed fryers or parts.

Packing

In packing cut-up poultry, the neck, giblets, and back are placed in the bottom of the tray. Then the wings are placed parallel to the front sides of the tray and the breast is placed over the back. The thighs are then tucked along each side of the breast toward the back of the tray.

Overwrapping

A tray size of $5^{1}/_{2}$ x 8 in. with inch sides is recommended for cut-up frying chickens and one 5 x 10 in. for baking hens. A film 15 x 16 in. is recommended for wrapping frying chickens and 17 x18 in. for baking hens (Table 9.2).

TABLE 9.2

APPROXIMATE FILM SHEET SIZES FOR WRAPPING FRESH WHOLE, OR CUT-UP READY-TO-COOK POULTRY IN RETAIL STORES FOR SELF-SERVICE, AND SIZES FOR DIRECT WRAPS (CLOSE FITTING) ON READY-TO-COOK FROZEN POULTRY

Items		Size of Sheets, In.				
		For Wrapping Whole Fresh Poultry in Retail Stores for Self-Service		For Wrapping Cut-up Poultry Alone or Poultry in Trays for Self-Service		For Direct, Close-Fitting Wraps on Frozen Ready-to-Cook Whole Birds
Kind	Class	From	To	From	To	Sheet Size and Size Ranges
Poultry	Broilers	16 x 18	18 x 20	14 x 16	18 x 20	14 x 16
	Fryers	16 x 18	18 x 22	16 x 18	18 x 20	16 x 18
	Roasters	18 x 20	20 x 22	16 x 18	20 x 20	18 x 20–20 x 20
	Fowl	18 x 20	20 x 22	16 x 18	20 x 20	16 x 18–18 x 20
Ducks	Duckling	18 x 20	20 x 22	16 x 18	20 x 20	20 x 20
Turkeys	Small	22 x 26	26 x 30	22 x 26	26 x 30	25 x 28
	Medium	26 x 30	30 x 34	26 x 30	30 x 34	29 x 32
	Large	30 x 34	34 x 38	30 x 34	33 x 36	32 x 35

From U.S. Dept. Agr., Agr. Handbook 25 (1951).

TABLE 9.3

SOME SIZES FOR PAPERBOARD CARTONS, CORRESPONDING CARTON LINERS AND CARTON OVERWRAPS FOR CARTONING FROZEN WHOLE OR CUT-UP READY-TO-COOK POULTRY

| Frozen Items That Are Cartoned | Dimensions (Sizes), In. | | | | | | |
| | Carton (I.D.) | | | Film Overwrap | | Film Liner | |
	Length	Width	Height	Length	Width	Length	Width
Whole Long Island ducks	11	6	$3^1/_2$	$20^3/_4$	$16^1/_2$	17	17
Whole roaster							
(a) Regular carton	9	4	$5^1/_4$	$20^1/_4$	15	17	17
(b) 1-piece tuck carton	$9^1/_2$	$5^1/_2$	4	...	...	17	17
Whole fryer, 2-piece carton	$7^3/_4$	5	2	...	...	17	17
Whole broiler, 2-piece carton	$7^1/_4$	$4^1/_4$	2	...	...	10	13
Cut-up fowl	$7^3/_4$	$5^3/_4$	$2^5/_{16}$	$17^3/_4$	11	17	17
Cut-up broilers or fryers	$7^7/_8$ or	$4^1/_2$ or 6	$2^3/_8$ or	$15^1/_2$	$11^3/_4$	10	13
	$6^3/_4$		$1^5/_8$ –3	$15^1/_2$	$11^3/_4$	10	13
Parts (under 1 lb.)	5	4	$1^3/_4$	$13^1/_4$	$7^3/_4$	10	13
Parts							
1 lb. thighs, wings, etc.	$6^1/_2$	4	$1^3/_4$	13	$9^1/_4$	10	13
2 lb. backs	$7^7/_8$	5	$2^3/_4$	$17^3/_4$	11	17	17
Livers (10 oz.)	5	3	$1^1/_2$	$10^1/_2$	$7^1/_4$	10	13
Won ton soup and chicken chow mein	$5^1/_4$	4	$1^3/_4$	$10^1/_2$	$7^1/_4$	10	13

U. S. Dept. Agr., Agr. Handbook 25 (1951).

Sizes for paperboard cartons, corresponding carton liners and carton overwraps for cartoning frozen whole or cut-up ready-to-cook poultry are shown in Table 9.3.

Transparent Plastic Films

Stokes (1961) reported that a number of different films are used for prepackaging poultry. Among them are Mylar, a polyester film, CryOvac "L" a shrinkable irradiated polyethylene film, Saran "S" a polyvinylidene chloride, Pliofilm, a rubber hydrochloride and cellophane. Harwell, Anderson, Shaffer, and Knowles (1953) reported that according to several manufacturers Pliofilm and cellophane represent about 98% of the films used in packaging retail meat. In a study of packaging and displaying meats in self-service meat markets these workers made the following recommendations: (1) apply the board or tray as the package is wrapped; (2) use film presheeted to the proper size; (3) store the film properly for ease in handling; and (4) use a diagonal instead of a square wrap to conserve wrapping material.

To prevent loss and deterioration to the film, they recommended storage at the proper temperature and humidity and storage in the original containers. Large inventories of films should be avoided and care should be taken to avoid damage to the film by dropping or mishandling. Films should be kept on horizontal racks to prevent telescoping during handling.

An additional item of expense is the cost of rewrapping. Dobbins and Hoecker (1951), in a study of costs for rewrapping meats, reported that discoloration was responsible for removing 1.7% of the poultry from the display case, unattractive packages for 49.7%, broken film for 11.5% and spoilage for 4.7%.

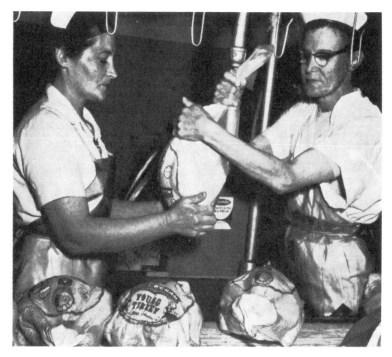

Courtesy U.S. Dept. Agr.

FIG. 9.2.   IN PACKAGING SOME POULTRY, A VACUUM IS USED TO DRAW AIR FROM
THE BAG BEFORE SEALING

Plastic Trays

Recently a package called Chil-pak was placed on the market consisting
of a transparent lid and a yellow tray both made from polystyrene.   It can
be used for either fresh or frozen poultry.   The lids are both crimped and
heat sealed so that it is possible to chill the carcasses after packaging.
Finally the trays are stacked in master cartons for holding or distribution.

PACKAGING FROZEN POULTRY

Plastic Bags

Frozen whole poultry carcasses are packed in plastic bags, generally
heat shrinkable (Figs. 9.2, 9.3, 9.4, and 9.5).   The carcasses are placed
in the bag, the air is evacuated, the bag sealed with a metal clip,
the tail of the bag trimmed and finally the wrapped carcass is immersed
in water at 195°–200° F.   The package shrinks up to 50% in size and

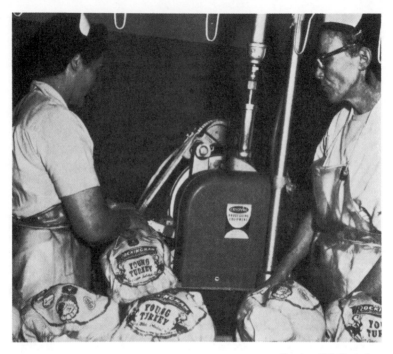

Courtesy U.S. Dept. Agr.

FIG. 9.3.   THIS MACHINE ATTACHES A METAL SEAL TO THE BAG CONTAINING THE
TURKEY AND CUTS OFF THE BAG'S LOOSE END

molds itself to the contour of the product.   Care must be taken to
see that the air is completely exhausted from the package before sealing
and shrinking.   Sizes of round-end film bags for ready-to-cook turkeys
are shown in Table 9.4.

Plastic envelopes are being used for "boil in the bag" foods and experiments are underway to use plastic in place of cans for packaging some
items.

TABLE 9.4

SIZES OF ROUND-END FILM BAGS FOR READY-TO-COOK TURKEYS

Relative Sizes of Different Classes of Turkeys	Dimensions of Bags, in.	
	Length	Width
Small hens	18	12
Medium hens and small toms	24	14
	20	14
Very large hens and medium toms	24	16
Large toms	26	18
Very large toms	27	20

U.S. Dept. Agr., Agr. Handbook *25*, 1951.

Courtesy U.S. Dept. Agr.

FIG. 9.4. A MOMENTARY DIP IN HOT WATER SHRINKS THE PLASTIC FILM SURROUNDING TURKEYS TO REMOVE AIR POCKETS AND WRINKLES

Boxes

Frozen food products manufactured from poultry meat are cartoned in waxed cardboard boxes and then overwrapped and heat sealed either with waxed paper or cellophane. Fiberboard boxes laminated on one or both sides with aluminum so they will withstand oven temperatures are also being used. Boxes laminated on both sides with aluminum foil can withstand oven temperatures as high as 475°F. and those with single laminations can withstand temperatures as high as 425°F. for a half hour with a moist product.

Individual cartons of frozen food are generally packed in standard corrugated fiberboard shipping containers.

Aluminum Containers

Aluminum containers have found widespread use for packaging precooked frozen foods. According to Tressler (1968) aluminum foil is highly resistant to many corrosive chemicals found in foods and is non-toxic. Aluminum is also light in weight, has a high thermal

Courtesy U.S. Dept. Agr.

FIG. 9.5. PACKAGED CHICKENS REACH THE END OF THE MOVING
BELT, WHERE EACH IS EXAMINED FOR TORN OR BROKEN BAGS BEFORE
GOING INTO A LIQUID FREEZE TANK

conductivity, high light reflectivity, does not burn and is grease- and
oilproof. It is not affected by sunlight and does not absorb moisture
vapors and odors. It is attacked by strong mineral acids and weak
alkaline products. With recent developments it is now possible to
print directly on aluminum.

Edible Coatings

Several workers have investigated the use of liquid coatings, which dry
or harden after application, as a means of preventing dehydration or as a
method of applying preservatives to poultry. Pearce and Lavers (1949)
dipped poultry carcasses in solutions of an extract of Irish moss seaweed at
212°F. to extend shelf-life. Coating the carcasses with Irish moss extract
containing six per cent sodium chloride approximately doubled the storage

life. Meyer, Winter and Weiser (1959) reported that agar and carrageenin gels increased the keeping time of chicken necks when antibiotics were mixed with the coatings. Westveer (1958) reported the development of an experimental resin film which melts at 325°F. for use as a coating for frozen meats. The coating material was peeled from the meat after thawing. Woodmansee and Abbott (1958) reported that a coating of mixed acetylated monoglycerides applied as a dip at 200°F. for one second reduced dehydration of chicken drumsticks as much as 23.9% after 10 days storage at 40°F. Mountney and Winter (1961) reported that chicken drumsticks dipped in 3 coats of a 4% calcium alginate coating stored 12 days at 35°F. lost 7.6% less moisture than untreated control parts.

BIBLIOGRAPHY

Anon. 1951. Recommended specifications for standard packs, containers, and packaging materials for poultry and poultry products. U.S. Dept. Agr., Production Mktg. Admin., Agr. Handbook 25.

Anon. 1962. Some factors affecting poultry packaging. Package Research Laboratory, Bull. 378 (revised).

Anon. 1964. Modern Packaging Encyclopedia. Modern Packaging, New York.

Dichter, E. 1952. What packaging really means. Paraffined Carton Research Council, Bull., Chicago, Ill.

Dobbins, C. E., and Hoecker, R. W. 1951. Costs of and reasons for rewrapping prepackaged meats, poultry, and cheese, U.S. Dept. Agr., Production Mktg. Admin., Agr. Inform. Bull. 77.

Gardner, F., and Nichols, J. 1971. Product quality and consumer preferences as affected by alternative methods of handling and packaging chicken. Texas Agr. Mktg. Res. Develop. Center Tech. Rept. MRC-71-2, College Station, Texas.

Hale, P. W., and Chapogas, P. G. 1963. New shipping containers for short hauls of icepacked poultry. U.S. Dept. Agr., Agr. Mktg. Serv. Res. Rept. 584.

Harwell, E. M., Anderson, D. L., Shaffer, P. F., and Knowles, R. L. 1953. Packaging and displaying meats in self-service meat markets. U.S. Dept. Agr., Production Mktg. Admin. Rept. 44.

Heitz, G. A. 1958. The tray pack operation. Am. Poultry Ind. Inst. Fact Finding Conf. Mimeo.

Jordan, M. P., and Saunders, R. F. 1958. Retailers or processors, who will tray pack fresh fryers? Maine Farm Res. 6, 14–17.

Meyer, R. C., Winter, A. R., and Weiser, H. H. 1959. Edible protective coatings for extending the shelf life of poultry. Food Technol. 13, 146.

Mountney, G. J. and Branson, R. B. 1958. Consumers preferences for selected poultry products and merchandising practices, Texas Agr. Expt. Sta. Progr. Rept. 2066.

Mountney, G. J., and Winter, A. R. 1961. The use of a calcium alginate film for coating cut-up poultry. Poultry Sci. 40, 28–34.

PEARCE, J. A., and LAVERS, C. G. 1949. Frozen storage of poultry. V. Effects of some processing factors on quality. Can. J. Res. *F 27*, 253.

SAUNDERS, R. F., and JORDAN, M. P. 1960. Tray packing fresh fryers at the store and plant levels. Maine Agr. Expt. Sta. Bull. *588*.

SMITH, H. D., and STILES, J. D. 1958. Comparative costs of cutting and packaging chicken in the retail store versus the processing plant. Univ. Maryland Misc. Publ. *331*.

STOKES, D. R. 1961. Possibilities and problems of prepackaging poultry at the processing plant level. Presented at Southeastern Poultry Egg Assoc., Processor Packaging Workshop. Mimeo.

STOKES, D. R., KOTULA, A. W., MERCURI, A. J., and BUXTON, F. K. 1964. Evaluation of specified shrink films for prepackaging frozen cut-up chickens at the processing plant. USDA Agr. Mktg. Serv., Mktg. Res. Rept. *662*.

THOMPSON, J. E., MERCURI, A. J., and RISSE, L. A. 1968. Shipping containers for ice-packed poultry. Effect on microbial counts and weights of poultry and ice. USDA Agr. Res. Serv., Mktg. Res. Serv. Rept. *811*.

TRESSLER, D. K. 1968. The packaging of precooked and prepared frozen foods. *In* the Freezing Preservation of Foods, 4th Edition, Vol. 4. D. K. Tressler, W. B. Van Arsdel, and M. J. Copley (Editors). Avi Publishing Co., Westport, Conn.

WABECK, C. J., LISKA, B. J., and STADELMAN, W. J. 1967. Studies with corrugated and wirebound containers for packaging fresh poultry. Poultry Sci. *46*, 1195–1199.

WESTVEER, W. M. 1958. Personal communication. Dow Chemical Co., Midland, Mich.

WOODMANSEE, C. W., and ABBOTT, O. J. 1958. Coating subscalded broiler parts in order to afford protection against dehydration and skin darkening in fresh storage. Poultry Sci. *37*, 1367.

CHAPTER 10

Refrigerated Storage

INTRODUCTION

Poultry meat can be refrigerated in either cool or frozen storage. Cool storage is considered to be storage at temperatures above freezing usually in the range of 32° to 45°F. and frozen storage 0°F. or below, usually in the range of −40° to 0°F. Crushed ice, mechanical refrigeration, or a combination of the two are used as the source of refrigeration for cool storage and liquefied gases and mechanical refrigeration for frozen storage.

REFRIGERATION REQUIREMENTS

According to McCoy (1963) proper refrigeration requires a controlled temperature, proper air circulation, proper moisture control and some contol of the air composition.

Controlled temperatures are required to prevent losses in quality caused by fluctuating temperatures and to predict shelf life with some degree of accuracy.

Proper air circulation is required to cool the poultry and maintain a uniform temperature throughout the storage area and to help control mold growth.

Proper moisture control is important to prevent undue losses of moisture, especially in the presence of rapidly circulating air, to prevent excessive condensation on refrigerating coils, and to retard mold growth in above freezing areas. Generally, most systems represent a compromise between extremes of high humidities which prevent dehydration and low humidities which prevent mold growth.

Control of air composition is necessary to maintain reasonably high humidities at low temperatures and to provide fresh air free of odors and undesirable gases.

Cool Storage

The temperature at which poultry is held during cool storage determines to a large extent its shelf-life. Carcasses held at 32°F. will remain edible for several weeks while those held at 60°F. will remain edible only a matter of hours.

Storage in Crushed Ice

The majority of broilers produced in the United States and a large portion of the fowl are packed in crushed ice for delivery to stores. Naden

167

and Jackson (1953) in a comparison of the merits of wet- and dry-packed chilled poultry gave the following advantages in favor of ice-packed poultry: (1) the freshness quality of the chicken is maintained longer; (2) drying out is prevented; (3) the keeping time is longer; (4) and a more attractive display is possible.

Disadvantages are: (1) the chicken picks up weight from water, which the customer buys; (2) keeping the chicken wet is an unsanitary procedure; and (3) the ice and water hide quality defects.

On the other hand, Baker (1957) reported that there was no difference in bacterial counts or appearance of any consequence between dry-packed and ice-packed broiler halves. Members of a taste panel preferred dry-packed cooked broiler halves over ice-packed halves in general surface appearance, aroma, flavor, and juiciness of the flesh. McKee, Conkey, and Carlson (1959) reported that wet-packed acronized carcasses had the lowest bacterial counts, dry-packed next, and untreated dry-packed carcasses had the highest counts of the three treatments.

Mechanical Refrigeration

Mechanical refrigeration can hold a set temperature indefinitely; however, poultry stored in this manner requires some sort of packaging to prevent dehydration. The cost of equipment for mechanical refrigeration is quite high when compared to ice. Generally, a combination of the two methods is used in marketing poultry. The carcasses are delivered to the supermarket from the processing plant packed in ice, removed from the ice, packaged, or cut up and then offered for sale in refrigerated show cases in the store.

FREEZING POULTRY

Poultry can be frozen in air, or liquid or on refrigerated plates. Poultry can also be either sharp or quick frozen. According to Sawyer, Midura, and Vondell (1960) sharp freezing consists of freezing at $-10°F$. or lower without mechanically agitating the air. Tressler et al. (1968) define sharp freezing as freezing with temperatures between $+5°$ F. and $-20°$ F. Under these conditions it takes from 3 to 72 hr. for the product to freeze.

A number of specifications have been suggested to make the term "quick frozen" more meaningful. Among those listed by Tressler and Evers (1957) are (1) that rate of freezing which results in the product being completely frozen in 90 min. or less, (2) that rate of freezing which moves through the product at a rate of 0.3 cm. per min. or faster and (3) a rate of freezing which results in passage through the zone of maximum crystal formation in 30 min. or less. An important, difference in the products frozen by these methods is in the size of the ice crystals. Larger ice crystals are formed during sharp freezing than during quick freezing.

Since there is a high correlation between the size of ice crystals formed during freezing and the quality of the frozen product, small ice crystals formed by quick freezing are the most desirable. Although a small amount of exudation of body fluids, commonly called "drip," occurs when poultry is thawed, it is not as much a problem with poultry as with other products. The temperature range between 31°–25°F. called by Birdseye the "zone of maximum crystal formation" is the range in which large ice crystals form when poultry meat is frozen slowly. The faster the poultry carcasses pass through the zone of maximum crystal formation, the smaller the crystals in the frozen product and the less the "drip."

Three general temperature changes occur during freezing. First the temperature is gradually lowered to the freezing point, then the product freezes and finally the product is subcooled. After freezing the carcasses can be held in storage at temperatures of 0°F. and lower, providing the temperature is held reasonably constant.

According to Nicholas (1945), several factors influence the rate of freezing. They are: (1) The size and shape of the package. Small packages freeze faster than large ones. (2) The size and shape of the product. Thin flat packages freeze faster than round ones. (3) The medium in which the foods are packed. Products packed in liquid have lower freezing points than those packed dry. (4) The amount of food being frozen. Freezing capacity is a matter of the capacity of the compressors rather than the number of cubic feet of area in the freezer. (5) The amount of wrapping or packaging material. Wrapping materials retard the rate of heat transfer.

Sawyer, Midura and Vondell (1960) reported that well packaged turkeys and cut-up chicken stored at 0°F. will remain in good condition for one year, when stored at 10°F. they will remain in good condition only six months, and when held at 20°F. only three months. These temperatures are higher than those at which poultry is commonly stored. A survey by Tressler (1965) indicated that in most cold storage warehouses, poultry is stored at −10°F. or lower.

Changes in Quality of Frozen Poultry During Storage

Poultry can deteriorate in quality during freezing or during frozen storage. The conditions under which the carcasses are frozen can influence the color of the carcass, drip, and bone darkening.

Carcass Color.—Slow freezing and scalding at 140°F. cause dark frozen carcasses. Klose and Pool (1956) reported that when the outer layer of skin is removed from poultry carcasses by scalding at 140°F., the carcasses

TABLE 10.1

POULTRY STORING CHART

Product	Storage Period (To Maintain Its Quality) Refrigerator 35°–40° F. Days	Freezer 0° F. Months
Fresh Poultry		
Chicken and turkey	1-2	12
Duck and goose	1-2	6
Giblets	1-2	3
Cooked poultry		
Pieces (covered with broth)	1-2	6
Pieces (not covered)	1-2	1
Cooked Poultry dishes	1-2	6
Fried chicken	1-2	4

Source: U.S. Dept. Agr.

have a darkened appearance upon freezing which is caused by an increased transparency of the skin. This increased transparency of the skin permits the penetration and partial absorption of light.

Fast freezing results in lighter colored carcasses than slow frozen ones. During slow freezing the skin dries, shrinks, becomes more transparent and as a result has a darker appearance than if the same carcass were frozen rapidly. Light colored frozen carcasses are generally considered to be more desirable than dark colored ones. During slow freezing, large ice crystals are formed with a resulting transparent surface layer and a darker appearance on the surface of the frozen carcass. A major part of the darkening takes place in the skin and the remainder in the surface layer of the flesh. The rate of freezing of the flesh below the surface has no effect on the surface color. Although well-finished carcasses are desirable, fat acts as an insulator and retards the freezing rate.

Marion and Stadelman (1958) in a study at the Indiana State Fair of consumer's preferences for the color of frozen turkeys reported that from a possible six choices the greatest preference was for the two darkest colored carcasses followed by the lightest colored one. These results contradict the general belief that light colored carcasses are preferred by consumers.

Tenderness and Flavor.—Dawson, Davidson, Frang, and Walters (1958) reported that when carcasses were held 6 or 24 hr. before freezing the breast muscles were more tender than those of fryers held only 40 min. before freezing.

Carlin, Lowe, and Stewart (1949), in a study comparing the effects of aging carcasses without freezing and with aging, freezing and thawing, found that there was no difference in aroma or flavor but that there was a tendency for the birds that had been frozen to be less juicy than those only aged and not frozen. These workers reported that tenderness was increased by both aging and freezing.

Klose, Campbell, Pool, and Hanson (1961) reported that turkey carcasses held one hour and then held frozen at 27°F. for three days provided "adequate tenderization and no adverse flavor changes were noted after 14 days at 27°F." When the birds were frozen before the onset of rigor, wide differences in the rate of thawing did not adversely affect tenderness.

Marion and Stadelman (1958) studied the effects of liquid freezing, plate freezing and freezing with moving air on drip, total cooking loss and tenderness of the *pectoralis major* muscles of chicken fryers, fowl, turkey fryers and mature turkey hens. The method of freezing had no effect on any of the above variables.

Klose, Pool and Lineweaver (1955), in a study of the effect of fluctuating temperatures on frozen turkeys, reported that excess fluctuations caused an accumulation of frost on the package but did not affect the eating quality.

Mountney, Branson, and Hurley (1960) conducted a study of the ability of 1500 visitors to the Texas State Fair to distinguish by tasting between cooked chicken which had been held in frozen storage and freshly slaughtered cooked chickens. Cut-up, quick frozen chickens packaged in paraffin coated cartons with cellophane overwraps and stored at 0°F. were used. These workers concluded that under the conditions of their experiment "there was enough difference in the flavor of stored frozen chicken to create a slight resistance towards this product."

Bone Darkening.—Woodroof and Shelor (1948) reported that chilling before freezing will not prevent bone darkening, but storing at temperatures below —15°F. lowers it or prevents it entirely.

Brant and Stewart (1949) reported that freezing rate, temperature of storage, length of storage period and temperature fluctuations apparently will not reduce or eliminate bone darkening. Cooking immediately after thawing reduces the severity but methods by which the carcass is cooked have no effect.

POULTRY PLANT FREEZING REQUIREMENTS

A modern poultry processing plant requires efficient freezing facilities, adequate freezer storage space and adequate ice-making equipment. Freezing at the plant is desirable. When the carcasses are packaged at the processing plant and then transported to a cold storage warehouse for freezing, considerable bloody water accumulates in the bottom of the bag.

Still Air Freezing

Freezing with still air results in a slow frozen product because the air is not moved away from the poultry as it becomes warmed after removing heat from the product. Despite this limitation, still air freezing is used in home freezers and small freezer operations with satisfactory results providing appearance is of no concern.

Frozen carcasses are usually held in holding freezers after they have been quick frozen. Such freezers generally have a temperature of around —20°F. which may rise to around 0°F. when loaded with an incoming product. Generally, the air is not circulated in holding freezers.

Blast Freezing

Freezing with a continuous blast of cold air is the most prevalent method used in freezing poultry. With this system air is moved around the products at 1300–1500 f.p.m. Kohlenberger (1960) gives the following advantages of the blast freezer compared to liquid freezing: (1) air blast systems are more flexible because they can freeze other products in addition to poultry; (2) different methods and types of materials handling equipment can be used; (3) the freezer can be overloaded because the air temperature rises and freezing occurs at slightly higher temperature and

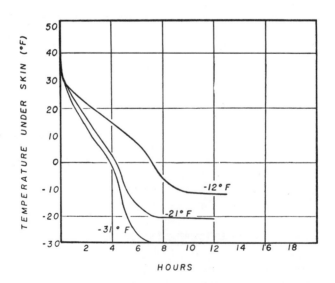

Courtesy Refrigeration Research Foundation

Fig. 10.1. Effect of Temperature of Air Blast (600 f/m) on Freezing Rate of 14-Week-Old Tom Turkeys in Open Tunnel

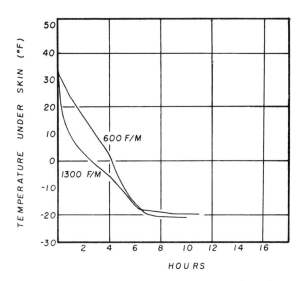

FIG. 10.2. EFFECT OF AIR VELOCITY ON FREEZING RATE OF 14-WEEK-OLD TOM TURKEYS IN AIR BLAST AT −21° F IN OPEN TUNNEL

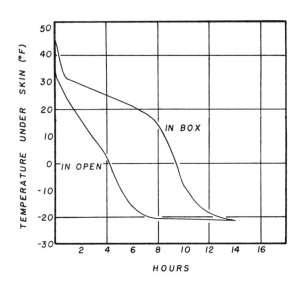

FIG. 10.3. OPEN VS BOX FREEZING OF 14-WEEK-OLD TOM TURKEYS IN BLAST TUNNEL AT −21°F, 600 F/M

higher plant capacity; and (4) the plant capacity is higher with air blast freezers.

Van den Berg and Lentz (1958) in a study of factors affecting the freezing rates and appearance of eviscerated air blast frozen poultry reported that the color of eviscerated vacuum packed poultry depended upon the freezing rate. The lightness of color increased rapidly when air velocity was increased from 0 to 700 f.p.m. or when the temperature with a velocity of 500 f.p.m. was lowered from 10°F. to —20°F. Beyond these ranges of temperature and velocity improvement in color was relatively small. Boxing and close stacking of boxed poultry for freezing resulted in non-uniform appearances and long freezing times.

Liquid Freezing

Liquid freezing entails immersing the product after packaging in circulating super-cooled solutions of calcium chloride, glycols, or other appropriate solutions until a crust is formed and then completing the freezing in a conventional freezer. Kohlenberger (1960) reported the following advantages for liquid freezing: (1) The finished product has a good color. (2) It operates at higher suction pressure.

He cited as disadvantages: (1) a lack of flexibility; (2) greater floor requirements; (3) the need for finish freezing after the surface is frozen; (4) larger cartons because the bird is "sprawled out" during freezing; (5) contamination if the bag is broken; (6) dripping brine from the package; and (7) loss and contamination of the brine.

Lentz and van den Berg (1957) in a study of liquid immersion freezing using methanol at —20°F. reported that it takes an immersion period of 20 min. for 4- to 6-lb. chickens and 40 min. for 15-lb. turkeys to obtain optimum appearance. The initial temperature of the carcass influences the freezing rate and appearance of the carcass after freezing but Cryovac packaging has no affect. The appearance in storage changes in two weeks when the carcasses are frozen at 20°F., in six weeks when frozen at 0°F. and the color holds indefinitely when frozen at —20°F.

Freezing With Liquefied Gases

During the past few years the process of freezing foods with liquid nitrogen, nitrous oxide, and carbon dioxide has been re-examined due to the reduced costs of these gases brought about by large scale production. At the present time, the cost of freezing by this method is higher than by other methods; however, proponents of this system claim that the resulting products are of higher quality and, because of the rapid freezing, produc-

Courtesy U.S. Dept. Agr.

Fig. 10.4. Trays of Prepared Packaged Poultry Dinners and Poultry Pies Are Placed in a Plate Freezer Where they Are Quick-Frozen Before Being Loaded into Trucks for Shipment to Wholesale and Retail Outlets

tion is increased. Some products which cannot be frozen by other methods can be frozen by the use of liquefied gases.

Gunning (1963) reported that cut-up fryers, packaged in preformed aluminum trays, can be frozen to a center temperature of 29°F. in $2^1/_2$ to 5 min. compared with brine immersion freezing which takes 80 min. to achieve the same temperature. With liquefied gas freezing, the product is frozen completely rather than just the surface. In addition to the advantage of rapid freezing, the poultry is cooled to a much lower temperature during freezing than can be done by other freezing methods.

Other advantages of liquified gas freezing, in this case liquid nitrogen, were cited by Kivert and Sills (1972). They include a $1/_3$ less original investment cost, a labor requirement of approximately one man per day including cleaning, almost no maintenance problems, less dehydration of the poultry, less drip because of small ice crystals, poultry with better surface color, no bone darkening, reduced bacterial counts, and a system which requires $1/5$ less space than conventional systems.

Plate Freezing

Plate freezing is adapted only to packaged poultry (Fig. 10.4). Plates which contain a refrigerant flowing through them come into contact with the package so that there is a direct transfer of heat from the package to the plate. Generally plate contact is made with both the top and bottom of the package.

BIBLIOGRAPHY

ANON. 1960. Home freezing of poultry. U.S. Dept. Agr. Home and Garden Bull. 70.

ANON. 1973. Information Bulletin. Refrigeration Research Foundation, Colorado Springs, Colo.

BAKER, R. C. 1957. Determining the keeping quality of ice-packed and dry-packed poultry. Poultry Sci. 36, 859-864.

BRANT, A. W., and STEWART, G. F. 1949. Bone darkening in frozen poultry. Food Technol. 4, 168-174.

CARLIN, F., LOWE, B., and STEWART, G. F. 1949. The effect of aging versus aging, freezing and thawing on the palatability of eviscerated poultry. Food Technol. 3, 156-159.

DAWSON, L. E., DAVIDSON, J. A., FRANG, M., and WALTERS, S. 1958. The effects of time interval between slaughter and freezing on toughness of fryers. Poultry Sci. 37, 231-235.

GUNNING, P. V. 1963. How to flash freeze poultry. Presented at Inst. Am. Poultry Ind. Fact Finding Conf., Kansas City. Mimeo.

KIVERT, A. N., and SILLS, J. T. 1972. Liquid nitrogen freezing counters rising labor, raw material cost. Quick Frozen Foods 34, No. 11, 55-57, 84.

KLOSE, A. A., CAMPBELL, A. A., POOL, M. F., and HANSON, H. L. 1961. Turkey tenderness in relation to holding in and rate of passage through thawing range of temperature. Poultry Sci. 40, 1633-1636.

KLOSE, A. A., and POOL, M. F. 1956. Effect of freezing conditions on appearance of frozen turkeys. Food Technol. 10, 34-38.

KLOSE, A. A., POOL, M.F., and LINEWEAVER, H. 1955. Effect of fluctuating temperatures on frozen turkeys. Food Technol. 9, 372-376.

KOHLENBERGER, C. R. 1960. Refrigerating criteria for modern poultry processing. Natl. Assoc. Pract. Refrig. Eng., Operating Data 1, 8-11.

LENTZ, C. P., and VAN DEN BERG, L. 1957. Liquid immersion freezing of poultry. Food Technol. 11, 247-250.

MARION, W. W., and STADELMAN, W. J. 1958. Effect of various freezing methods on quality of poultry meat. Food Technol. 12, 367-369.

McCOY, D. C. 1963. Refrigeration in food processing. In Food Processing Operations. M. A. Joslyn and J. L. Heid (Editors). Avi Publishing Co., Westport Conn.

McKee, R. C., Conkey, J., and Carlson, J. A. 1959. A study of the comparative shelf life of wet and dry-packed poultry. Poultry Sci. 38, 260-271.

Mountney, G. J., Branson, R. E., and Hurley, W. C. 1960. The effect on flavor of holding frozen chicken for selected periods. Poultry Sci. 29, 287-289.

Naden, K. D., and Jackson, G. A. Jr. 1953. Some economic aspects of retailing chicken meat. Calif. Agr. Expt. Sta. Bull. 734.

Nicholas, J. E. 1945. Freezing rates of foods. Penn. Stat College Agr. Expt. Sta. Bull. 471.

Sawyer, F., Midura, T., and Vondell, R. M. 1960. Handling and merchandising frozen food. Univ. Mass. Coop. Exten. Serv.

Stutts, H. P. 1961. Bibliography of frozen foods. U.S. Dept. Agr., Misc. Publ. 868.

Tressler, D. K. 1965. Personal communication. Westport, Conn.

Tressler, D.K.,Van Arsdel, W. B., and Copley, M. J. 1968. The Freezing Preservations of Foods, 4th Edition, Vol. 1. Avi Publishing Co., Westport, Conn.

van den Berg, L., and Lentz, C. P. 1958. Factors affecting freezing rate and appearance of eviscerated poultry frozen in air. Food Technol. 12, 183-185.

Woodroof, J. G., and Shelor, E. 1948. Prevention of bone darkening in frozen-packed chickens. Food Ind. 20, No. 1, 48-52, 154, 156.

CHAPTER 11

Canning Poultry
Products and Processing Soups

INTRODUCTION

Many canned poultry products are available to the American housewife (Figs. 11.1 and 11.2). Among them are whole fowl, broilers, and disjointed chickens packed in broth or gravy, boned poultry meat, turkey breasts, chicken liver products, stews, chicken a-la-king, chicken and dumplings, chicken and noodles, chicken fricassee, broth, chicken chop suey and chow mein, and potted chicken. A number of different soups are also available in canned, dehydrated, and frozen forms. Examples are chicken, chicken rice, chicken gumbo, chicken consommé, chicken vegetable, cream of chicken, turkey noodle, and turkey vegetable.

The increased use of poultry in canned form is illustrated in Fig. 11.3.

DEVELOPING CANNED PRODUCTS

A number of steps are required for developing, producing, and marketing a new canned product. Strandine (1963) reported the following procedures: (1) formulation of satisfactory recipe for a product that can be manufactured and sold competitively; (2) small scale panel-testing to determine variations in consumer preferences; (3) determination of proper and safe cooking schedules; (4) incubation storage studies at elevated temperatures of inoculated packs or cans to determine safety of cook; (5) U.S. Department of Agriculture approval of name of product, label copy, and ingredient list; (6) pilot scale production of approved product; (7) large scale consumer research testing of new product; (8) setting up commercial scale production; and (9) advertising, promotion, distribution, and sales of products.

GENERAL RECOMMENDATIONS FOR CANNING POULTRY

Only well-fleshed and finished poultry carcasses which are clean and well picked, as found in those of high quality, should be used for canning. Particular care should be taken to see that the dressed carcasses are not held for long periods under conditions which cause an increase in bacterial numbers. Carcasses should be kept under refrigeration and canned as quickly as possible after they have passed through rigor. Frozen car-

Courtesy Ohio Agr. Ext. Service

FIG 11.1.   CANNED POULTRY PRODUCTS

Courtesy Ohio Agr. Ext. Service

FIG. 11.2.   BABY FOOD CONTAINING POULTRY MEAT

casses should be thawed in water between 40° and 60°F. Iron and copper equipment which comes in contact with the broth or meat should be avoided because these metals sometimes cause discoloration of the meat. Different classes of poultry and those of the same class which vary considerably in size should be cooked in separate batches containing approximately the same size and age birds to ensure uniform cooking and packing. The same broth can be used up to four times providing the fat is removed each time before a new batch is cooked. Using broth more than four times results in a bitter flavor. After filling and sealing cans they should be washed to remove dirt and grease.

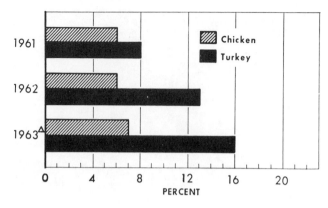

Courtesy U.S. Dept. Agr.

FIG. 11.3. PERCENTAGE OF POULTRY CANNED OR USED IN PREPARED
FOOD

Based on data from federally inspected slaughtering plants.
Δ, Partly forecast.

Marion *et al.* (1964) carried out a series of investigations on the pretreatment and processing methods for canned whole chickens.   They
made the following conclusions: "(1) An autoclaving temperature of
240°F. for 75 min. was superior to 250°F. for 65 min. in producing an acceptable product.   (2) Sixty-five and 75 min. at 240°F. for broilers and
hens canned in 404 x 700 and 412 x 704 cans, respectively, were shown to
be adequate autoclaving times for producing a sterile product.   (3) Pretreatment of broiler carcasses with saline soaking solutions at 35°F. generally improved sensory scores and resulted in higher moisture and salt levels in the meat of the final product.   (4) An eight-hour soaking period in
5% saline resulted in slightly improved sensory ratings, while longer soaking periods with up to 10% saline solutions either improved or did not adversely affect product quality."

EQUIPMENT REQUIRED FOR CANNING POULTRY PRODUCTS

Continental Can Co. (Anon. 1965A, B) suggested the following
equipment to be used for canning poultry products:

4 400-gal. stainless metal steam jacketed kettles (if chickens are pre-
cooked)

6 exact weight type scales (5-lb. capacity)

2 hoist and track work over retorts and kettles

2 agitating steam jacketed kettles for gravy

3 vertical three-crate retorts[1]
12 retort crates

Estimated Requirements of Accessory Equipment

1 stainless metal holding table for pre-cooked pieces
4 15 x 3 ft. stainless metal cutting tables
1 filled can washer
5 poultry trucks (500-lb. capacity)
4 wire pre-cooking baskets
closing machine
empty can washer
can runways

NOTE: Facilities such as refrigeration, incubation, can storage, and requirements needed to meet inspection standards are additional. Miscellaneous equipment such as sanitary collection pans, waste cans, and boning knives are also additional.

The data in Table 11.1 show the comparative tin plate basing weights for different sizes of metal cans for cooked poultry and cooked poultry products.

RECENT DEVELOPMENTS IN CANNING POULTRY

Milleville (1964) reported on an improved method of the Smith-Ball canning process which works well in the canning of some poultry products. With this improved method the ingredients are first heated to 255°F. in a pressurized chamber which prevents the products from boiling. The chamber is designed so that the canning equipment and workmen perform the filling, sealing, and partial cooking operations inside the chamber area.

Advantage claimed for this type of process is that the product can be heated before canning which prevents overheating on the outside of the can and possible underheating in the center when the food is first placed in the can for sterilization. As a result large institutional-size cans of foods which formerly required long processing times can be processed as easily as smaller cans which require less than 15 min. One of the products scheduled for production is a one-half roasted chicken packed in gravy.

CANNING POULTRY AND POULTRY PRODUCTS

The following formulas, processing times, and temperatures are intended only as guides in canning poultry because many other factors are in-

---

[1] Retort capacity—1125 cans; retort cycle—125 min.

TABLE 11.1

COMPARATIVE TIN PLATE BASING WEIGHTS FOR DIFFERENT SIZES OF METAL CANS FOR COOKED
POULTRY AND COOKED POULTRY PRODUCTS

Can Identification[1]	Trade Name	Can Maker's Description	Weight per Base Box,[2] Lb.	Equivalent Weight per Square Feet, Lb.	Approximate Thickness, In.	Tin Coating or Type of Finish for Cans for Each Product
Whole chicken with bone						
Regular 3-lb., 2-oz.	No. 3 cyl.	404 x 700	100	0.4592	0.0110	No. 50 electrolytic
Regular 4-lb., 8-oz.		411 x 708	100	0.4592	0.0110	or 1.25 hot dipped
Jumbo 4-lb., 8-oz.		415 x 708	100	0.4592	0.0110	tin plate and
Regular 4-lb., 12-oz.		100 x 112	100	0.4592	0.0110	enameled
Boned chicken or boned turkey						
Small 6-oz.		208 x 212	100	0.4592	0.0110	Enamel-lined
Jumbo 6-oz.		303 x 113	100	0.4592	0.0110	
Regular 1-lb.	No. 303	303 x 406	100	0.4592	0.0110	
Regular 2-lb. 3-oz.	No. 3	404 x 414	100	0.4592	0.0110	
Smoked turkey (boned and sliced)						
Regular 6-oz.		307 x 112	85	0.3903	0.0094	Enameled outside and inside
Chicken fricassee						
Regular 1-lb.		303 x 402	85	0.3903	0.0094	C-enamel lined or plain interior
Chicken a-la-king						
Regular 8-oz.	8 Z short	211 x 300	85	0.3903	0.0094	C-enamel lined or
Regular 11-oz.	No. 1	211 x 400	85	0.3903	0.0094	plain interior
Regular 13½-oz.	No. 211 cyl.	211 x 400	85	0.3903	0.0094	
Regular 1-lb.		303 x 402	85	0.3903	0.0094	
Boneless chicken with jelly						
Regular 8-oz.	8 Z short	211 x 300	85	0.3903	0.0094	C-enamel lined or
Regular 12-oz.		404 x 115	85	0.3903	0.0094	plain interior
Chicken or smoked turkey spreads						
Regular 5-oz.		208 x 208	85	0.3903	0.0094	Enameled outside
Regular 6-oz.		307 x 112	85	0.3903	0.0094	and inside
Chicken broth						
Regular 10½-oz.	No. 1	211 x 400	85	0.3903	0.0094	C-enamel lined or
Regular 1-lb.	No. 303	303 x 406	85	0.3903	0.0094	plain interior
Regular 1-lb., 4-oz.	No. 2	307 x 409	85	0.3903	0.0094	
Regular 3-lb., 1-oz.	No. 3 cyl.	404 x 700	90	0.4133	0.0099	
Regular 6-lb., 3-oz.	No. 10	603 x 700	100	0.4592	0.0110	
Chicken noodle soup						
Regular 10½-oz.	No. 1	211 x 400	85	0.3903	0.0094	C-enamel lined or
Regular 15-oz.	No. 300	300 x 407	85	0.3903	0.0094	plain interior
Cream of chicken soup						
Regular 1-lb.	No. 303	303 x 406	85	0.3903	0.0094	C-enamel lined or plain interior
Chicken gumbo soup						
Regular 1-lb., 4-oz.	No. 2	307 x 409	85	0.3903	0.0094	C-enamel lined or plain interior
Smoked turkey split pea soup						
Regular 3-lb., 3-oz.	No. 3 cyl.	404 x 700	90	0.4133	0.0099	C-enamel lined or plain interior
Chicken rice soup						
Regular 6-lb., 10-oz.	No. 10	603 x 700	100	0.4592	0.0110	Plain 1.25 pound hot dipped tin plate, body C-enamel. No. 50 electrolytic tin plate end

From U.S. Dept. Agr., Agr. Handbook 25, 1951.
[1] Net weights will not be constant and will depend upon the consistency of the product. It is generally considered that in order to avoid a charge of slack fill, a can must be filled to not less than 90% of its total capacity.
[2] Means the weight of 112 sheets, each being 14 x 20 in. in size.

volved in preparation such as the level of tenderness desired, age, size, and condition of the poultry, as well as the amount of broth, gravy, gelatin, and similar types of materials used.

A flow sheet for canning boned chicken, disjointed chicken, whole chicken, chicken a-la-king and chicken broth is shown in Fig. 11.4.

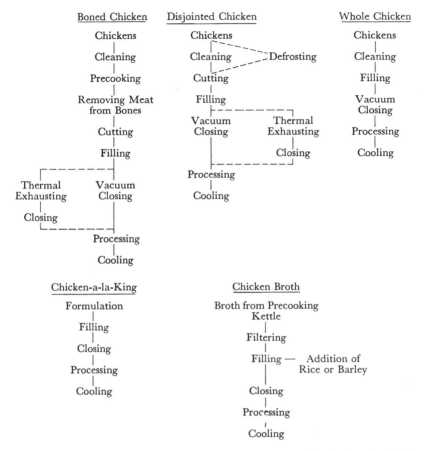

Fig. 11.4.   Flow Sheet for Boned Chicken, Disjointed Chicken, Whole Chicken, Chicken-a-la-King, and Chicken Broth

Canning Whole Chicken

Canned chicken usually contains a chicken with chicken broth but without giblets.   Mature poultry is generally considered better for canning than younger birds because young tender carcasses generally disintegrate during the cooking process.

Continental Can Co. (Anon. 1965A) suggests the following procedures for preparing whole chicken for canning:

Chicken.—The thoroughly cleaned and eviscerated birds intended for canning must have the necks and the neck skin or flap removed prior to placing the bird into the can.   This is for the purpose of permitting unobstructed circulation of the brine or broth through the body cavity during processing.

Broth.—Chicken broth obtained from pre-cooking birds in simmering water with the addition of two per cent salt by weight may be used to complete the fill. However, most packers add hot two per cent brine or hot water and salt tablets to the raw chicken after placing in the can. A broth results during the processing.

Canning Operation

The specific canning procedures recommended by the Continental Can Co. (Anon. 1965A) are as follows:

Cans.—Cans made from fully enameled electrotin plate are recommended. The empty cans should be protected from dampness and steam and kept as clean as possible during storage. The can handling methods should be designed to prevent scratching or denting, particularly of the flange. Prior to filling, they should be spray washed with a relatively large volume of water at a minimum temperature of 180°F.

Filling.—Filling of the cans is a hand operation. Entrapped air which may cause subsequent buckling and underprocessing can be avoided by first placing approximately 8 oz. of brine or broth in the can. The raw bird of the correct weight and size is then placed neck end first into the can. The neck is added last in such a manner that it cannot interfere with circulation of the packing medium. The can is filled to an exact predetermined weight with broth or brine. A net weight of 3 lb. 4 oz. for the 404 x 700 cans and a net weight of 4 lb. for the 412 x 704 cans is suggested.

A broth or brine temperature of approximately 120°F. is suggested if the cans are to be closed in a vacuum seamer. A minimum broth or brine temperature of 180°F. is suggested when a "Steam-Vac" closure is used.

If long narrow birds are used, it may be necessary to sever the tail bone and end of the leg bone to permit closure of the can.

Closing.—If mechanical vacuum closure is employed, a minimum machine vacuum of 12 in. and a maximum machine vacuum of 15 in. is suggested. This is a critical machine vacuum and is required to prevent buckling during processing or paneling after cooling. "Steam-Vac" closure may be used provided the product is closed at a minimum average temperature of 120°F. obtained by the use of hot broth or brine at a minimum temperature of 180°F.

Filled Can Washing.—It is desirable to pass the cans through a detergent spray wash after closure to remove grease and bits of adhering product. The cleaning operation should consist of a pre-rinse in water at 150°F., then a suitable detergent spray wash, followed by a rinse in fresh water at 150°F. It is important that the retorts be clean to avoid the necessity of cleaning cans after processing.

Processing.—The processing of whole chicken is extremely critical and is based on the following assumptions which must be followed to prevent under-processing and also to attain acceptable quality.

(1) The weight of the birds at the time of canning should not exceed the fill-in weights given for the size can to be used. This is very critical; if heavier birds are used, spoilage may occur.

(2) The bird should not fit the can so tightly as to prevent circulation between the can wall and the bird.

(3) There should be an opening through the body cavity to permit free circulation of the packing medium during processing. The neck of the bird is placed in such a position that it cannot possibly obstruct the circulation of the brine. This is best done by placing the neck around the legs so that it is locked in place to one side of the cavity opening.

(4) The cans are processed with the legs in a down position; that is, with the bottom end up if the birds were placed in the can neck down as suggested. Processing with the legs down aids in preventing under-processing and permits the packing medium to cover the legs during the process which minimizes shrinkage of the meat from the bone.

It is important that there be no delay between the can closing and processing operations. The following is a partial list of can sizes, maximum fill-in weights of chicken, approximate net weights, and suggested processes for whole chicken in broth or brine.

Can Size	Fill-In Weight of Chicken, Oz.	Net Weight Lb.	Oz.	Initial Temp.,* °F.	Time at (Min.) 240°F.
404 x 700	28–33	3	4	100	80
412 x 704	36–46	4	0	100	95

* The initial temperature is the average temperature of the can contents at the time steam is turned on for the process.

Cooling.—Immediately after processing, the cans should be pressure cooled. A retort pressure of 10 lb. maintained either by means of steam or air is suggested for the first 5-min. period of cooling. The retort pressure may then be dropped to 5-lb. pressure and held for a period of 5 min. before completely releasing the pressure. Paneling may occur if the pressure is maintained for too long a period. Water cooling should be continued to an average temperature of 95°–105°F. If cooling is extended to a temperature below 95°F. external rusting of the container may occur. Casing cans, when the content temperature is substantially above 100°F. may produce thermophilic bacterial spoilage or injury.

Chicken Broth

American Can Co. (Anon. 1958A) suggests the following procedures for canning chicken broth.

Preparation.—Chicken broth is prepared from the stock obtained in pre-cooking chickens for canning as boned chicken or chicken a-la-king. This stock or broth may be fortified by boiling chicken skins and bones in a small amount of water in a pressure cooker for 3 or 4 hr. at 220°F. This extract is added to the broth in the tanks where the chickens have been pre-cooked. Chicken broth should be strained through sterilized muslin or some other suitable filter to remove small bone fragments and bone marrow which, if included, would detract from the clarity of the product. The broth is then seasoned as desired before canning.

Some packers add a teaspoonful of dry barley or rice (regular or converted) to each small can and a proportionate amount to larger cans before filling with the broth. The broth is filled into the cans mechanically at a temperature of 180°–190°F., after which the cans are closed and processed.

Processing.—Processes which have been reported as satisfactory for thin chicken broth are 30 min. at 240° F. for 307 × 409 (No. 2) cans or smaller, and 45 min. at 240° F. for 603 × 700 (No. 10) cans. The cans should be thoroughly water cooled after processing.

Boned Chicken and Turkey

Continental Can Co. (Anon. 1965B) suggests the following procedure for boning canned chicken:

Approximately 50 fowl ranging from 4 to 5 lb. are pre-cooked by simmering in water or broth for about 90 min., or in a retort for either 90 min. at 220°F. or 60 min. at 250°F. Generally, cooking by either of these methods results in a shrink of approximately 30%.

Boning is done by hand with care being taken to remove the meat in large pieces and to remove all cartilage and bone. Generally 12–15 lb. of chicken meat or 25–30 lb. of turkey meat can be removed by an experienced operator in 1 hr.

In the case of turkey, meat from meaty parts of the carcass may be removed for canning before cooking. Then the remainder of the carcass can be cooked before boning. Generally the meat is packed in cans in the proportion of 84% boneless meat, 10% ground skins, and 6% poultry fat. About 10% of the whole can contents should be broth which contains 1–2% salt by weight. The skin is sometimes ground through an 8-in. plate and the chicken fat may be rendered. These ingredients are then mixed together by hand and placed into the empty cans. After filling, the cans are closed and processed.

Chicken Fricassee

Chicken fricassee consists of pieces of chicken in gravy. The chicken can be either uncooked or cooked before canning. A typical gravy formula supplied by Continental Can Co. consists of the following:

Chicken broth	10 gal.
Wheat flour	5 lb.
Salt	3 lb.
Ground white pepper	1 oz.

Chicken pieces generally make up 50–65% of the weight of the can contents.

Defects occurring in boned chicken with gravy are classified in Table 11.2.

Chicken and Noodle Dinner

Risch (1963) reported that two varieties are now being packed; a chicken and noodle dinner containing small pieces of boned chicken and the other containing only giblets, broth, and noodles.

Broth is made by first concentrating the water used in cooking. To each 10 gal. of broth about 8 oz. of salt, 1–2 oz. of white pepper, and monosodium glutamate are added for seasoning. The broth is generally strained through a flannel drip cloth. Fat is added after the stock is concentrated.

Noodles containing at least $5^1/_2$% egg solids and blanched at least 5–20 min. to remove air are mixed with the chicken meat and weighed directly into washed glass containers. Hot broth (135°F.) is measured into the containers automatically to provide a 90–94% fill and the jars are then sealed and tumbled. Generally a 16-oz. container requires a processing time of 75–90 min. at 240°F., depending upon the contents. After partial cooling in the retort, the jars of chickens and noodles are cooled below 110°F. and then rinsed with a hot water detergent solution before labeling and packing.

Chicken A-La-King

Chicken a-la-king usually contains green peppers, pimientos, and sometimes mushrooms. The following recipe was reported in The Canning Trade (Anon. 1958B).

To 100 lb. of properly prepared chicken, add lukewarm water to cover and cook until tender. Add from two to three pounds of salt a few minutes before removing the chicken from the kettle. Take the chicken from the kettle and remove the skin and bones. About one pound of fresh mushrooms, which should be cooked separately and cut into small slices. A half pound of pimientos should be sliced and cut into the desired size. Next prepare the sauce as follows:

The sauce is made from the chicken stock, which is the concentrated water left in the kettle after the chickens have been cooked. Some formulas call for the addition of milk. The butter is melted by heat, and flour is added to the melted butter and stirred to smooth consistency. The cooled chicken stock is added to the flour and butter mixture and cooked until it is of creamy consistency; then add the chicken, peppers, pimientos, and mushrooms. Mix and heat thoroughly and fill into the cans.

No. 1 cans should be processed 55 min. at 250°F.

TABLE 11.2

CLASSIFICATION OF DEFECTS OCCURRING IN BONED CHICKEN WITH GRAVY*

Examine	Defect	Major A	Major B	Minor
	External Defects			
Can				
Type, style, or size	Not as specified		X	
Condition	Severe dent		X	
	Moderate dent			X
	Sharp ridge, gnarl, or side buckle		X	
	Improper seam or cable cut		X	
	Buckled		X	
	Rusty[1]		X	
	Not clean and bright[2]			X
	Leaker, sweller, springer, or flipper	X		
Exterior coating	Coating not present		X	
	Not type specified[3]		X	
	Uneven coating[3]		X	
	Interior Defects			
Vacuum	Less than 2 in.		X	
	Less than 5 in. but not less than 2 in.			X
Interior of can	Rusted		X	
	Enamel absent		X	
	Blistered areas which cannot be peeled by fingertip abrasion			X
	Denuded areas (other than scratches)		X	
	Blistered or softened areas which can be peeled by fingertip abrasion		X	
	Scratches through enamel			X
	Product adheres to sides of can			X
	Weight Tolerances[4]			
1 lb. 13 oz.	More than $^3/_4$ ounce under contract net weight		X	
	More than $^3/_8$ ounce but not more than $^3/_4$ ounce under contract net weight			X
	Product Defects[5]			
Condition	Presence of large piece (in excess of $1^1/_2$ in. in any dimension)			X
	Meat shredded			X
	Gravy not smooth			X
	Appearance not appetizing		X	
	Objectionable or not appetizing odor or flavor		X	
	Texture of chicken pieces other than tender		X	
	Component missing (chicken or gravy)		X	
Presence of prohibited material	A piece of skin			X
	Each piece of bone in excess of 1, which is greater than $^1/_4$ in. in any dimension			X
	Whole or partial heart, gizzard, liver, or kidney			X
	A piece of blood vessel, tendon or cartilage, greater than $^1/_8$ in. in any dimension			X

[1] Cans from which rust can be removed by wiping with a soft cloth shall not be considered rusty or rusted. Rust not removable in this manner shall be considered pitted rust or corrosion.
[2] Cans showing a very thin film of grease which is discernible to the touch but not readily discernible visually are considered to be clean.
[3] Breaks in the coating film incurred in good commercial double seaming, such as narrow ruptures, will be permitted, but coarse flakes will be classfied as uneven coating.
[4] Sample average net weight shall be not less than contract net weight per can.
[5] Presence of foreign material, e.g, wood, paper, insects or insect parts, glass or metal particles, dirt or other extraneous materials, shall be the basis for rejection of the lot.
*Mil. Spec. C-3528A and Amend 1, 1958.

Chicken Sandwich Spread

Campbell, Isker, and Maclinn (1950) developed the following formula for preparing chicken sandwich spread:

80 lb. chicken meat and skins	1 oz. ground cloves
2 lb. onions	1 oz. ground mace
2 lb. salt	1 gal. chicken broth
1 oz. ground white pepper	4 lb. flour (if desired)

Generally the meat is finely ground in a silent cutter and the remaining ingredients added during this operation. The mixture should be preheated to 160°F. before filling.

Canned Chicken and Vegetables

The Armed Forces (Anon. 1951B) require that canned chicken and vegetables be prepared using the following formula:

	Lb.	Oz.
Chicken meat (white and dark meat in the same proportions as in the carcass)	36	
Chicken skin	4	8
Chicken fat	5	12
Potatoes	14	
Carrots	11	8
Peas	7	8
Peppers	2	12
Salt	1	4
Broth—sufficient to give a moisture content of not over 75%		

Potted Chicken

The following formula for preparing chicken sandwich spread was reported in The Canning Trade (Anon. 1958B):

90 lb. chicken	1 lb. parsely
10 lb. salt pork	1/2 lb. ground white pepper
5 lb. onions sliced	1/4 lb. ground whole cloves
4 lb. salt	2 oz. mace
	1 oz. bay leaves

Cook and skin the pork, draw and clean the chickens, cut into pieces; place in kettle with 2 lb. of salt, the onions, parsley, cloves, mace, and bay leaves; cover with cold water; bring to a boil; simmer until tender; take from kettle and remove skin and bone; grind to a fine paste; mix the remainder of the salt and the pepper with it; place in cans; seal and process as potted beef.

Use the liquor in which the chickens are cooked for chicken soup, or concentrate it to one-half its bulk; place in 1-gal. cans; seal and process 70 min. at 250°F. and sell as concentrated chicken soup.

Chicken Soup

The following formula for preparing chicken soup was reported in The Canning Trade (Anon. 1958B).

400 lb. chicken	2 lb. parsley
75 lb. water	$1/8$ lb. white pepper
20–25 lb. onions, finely chopped	35 lb. rice

Chicken Gumbo Soup

Campbell *et al.* (1950) suggest the following directions for making chicken gumbo soup:

20 gal. of chicken soup stock	3 lb. of butter
10 lb. of ham	1 oz. of white pepper
12 lb. of minced chicken	1 lb. of salt
2 lb. of onions	2 lb. of wheat flour

Cut the ham into cubes; mince the chicken; chop the onions very fine. Cook the ham in the soup stock about 1 hr. Make a thin paste of flour, add this, with the salt, pepper, butter, chicken, and onions to the soup stock, bring it to a boil, and add 10 oz. of Louisiana gumbo file, or powdered okra mixed with 2 qt. of water. The flour can be browned in butter and then added as this makes a richer product. Exhaust 3 min., process 40 min. at 250°F. for No. 1 cans.

DEHYDRATED SOUPS

During the past few years dehydrated soups have become popular in America. Binsted and Devey (1960) reported the following formula for a cream of chicken soup mix:

Cream of Chicken Soup Mix

	%
Dehydrated chicken meat	28.25
Wheat flour*	24.60
Skim milk powder*	22.70
Chicken fat*	18.20
Salt	3.55
M.S.G.	1.13
Onion Powder*	0.57
Protex C.S.C. powder*[1]	0.55
Sugar	0.38
Saromex white pepper (on salt)[2]	0.04
Saromex celery (on salt)[2]	0.03
	100.00

[1] A hydrolyzed protein product manufactured by Frederick Boehm Ltd., London, England.

[2] Manufactured by Stafford Allen & Sons, Ltd., London, England.

Method.—Mix all the ingredients thoroughly. If desired, the ingredients marked with an asterisk may be pre-dried together to lower the final moisture content.

Packaging.—Fill 91 gm. of the mix into each 4-ply laminated soup packet and seal.

Reconstitution.—Mix the contents of a packet with 1 pint of cold water, bring to boil, and simmer for 10–15 min.

Chicken Noodle Soup Mix

These same authors listed the following formula for a chicken noodle soup mix:

	%
Salt	37.86
Monosodium glutamate	21.70
Chicken fat	16.30
Dehydrated chicken	14.08
Wheaten base	3.26
Onion powder	2.72
Sugar	1.74
Protex No. 5 powder	1.36
Dried parsley	0.54
Ground white pepper	0.22
Ground turmeric	0.22
	100.00

Method.—Mix all the ingredients thoroughly.

Packaging.—Fill 17 gm. of the soup mix and 40 gm. of noodles into each 4-ply laminated soup packet and heat seal.

Reconstitution.—Add the contents of a packet to one pint of boiling water and simmer until the noodles are tender, about 5–7 min.

FROZEN SOUPS

Hulse (1962) reported that "delicately flavored" soups lose some of their savor when canned at sterilizing temperatures. For this reason they should be processed, frozen, and merchandised in frozen form. Losses in flavor of soups processed for freezing can be minimized by filling containers rapidly with the soup while still at the boiling point, by keeping head space to a minimum and by rapid cooling and freezing.

Soups for freezing are generally packaged in a 10-oz. can treated with a sulfur-resistant enamel. The canned soups are then frozen by immersion freezing which reduces the temperature of a 10-oz. can from 190°F. to below freezing in 30 min.

BIBLIOGRAPHY

ANON. 1951A. Recommended specifications for standard packs, containers and packaging materials for poultry and poultry products. U.S. Dept. Agr. Prod. Mktg. Admin. Agr. Handbook 25.

ANON. 1951B. Chicken and vegetables canned. Military Specification C-673A, U.S. Government Printing Office, Washington, D.C.

ANON. 1958A. The canning of boned, disjointed and whole chickens; chicken a-la-king; chicken broth. Tech. Serv. Div. Mem. American Can Co.

ANON. 1958B. A Complete Course in Canning, 8th Edition. The Canning Trade, Baltimore.

ANON. 1962. The canning of chicken fricassee. Continental Can Co., Canning Memo. 3 (revised).

ANON. 1965A. The canning of whole chicken. Continental Can Co., Canning Memo. 6 (revised).

ANON. 1965B. The canning of boned chicken or turkey. Continental Can Co., Canning Memo. 1 (revised).

BINSTED, R., and DEVEY, J. D. 1960. Soup Manufacture, Canning, Dehydration and Quick-freezing, 2nd Edition. Food Trade Press, London, England.

CAMPBELL, C. H., ISKER, R. A., and MACLINN, W. A. 1950. Campbell's Book, A Manual on Canning, Pickling, and Preserving, 3rd Edition. Vance Publishing, Chicago.

HULSE, J. H. 1962. Pre-cooked frozen foods. In Recent Advances in Food Science, Vol. II. J. Hawthorn, and J. M. Leitch (Editors). Love & Malcomson. Redhill, Surrey, England.

LOPEZ, A. 1969. A Complete Course in Canning, 9th Edition. The Canning Trade, Baltimore.

MARION, J. E., BOGGESS, T. S., JR., and WOODROOF, J. G. 1964. Pre-treatment and processing methods for canned whole chickens. Poultry Sci. 43, 1097–1101.

MILLEVILLE, H. P. 1964. Swift and Trenton foods revolutionary canning process. Food Process. 25, No. 3, 76–83.

RISCH, W. 1963. Canning chicken and chicken products in glass. Anchor Hocking Glass Co., Lancaster, Ohio. (Mimeo)

STRANDINE, E. J. 1963. Poultry production and processing. In Food Processing Operations, Vol. 2. J. L. Heid, and M. A. Joslyn (Editors). Avi Publishing Co., Westport, Conn.

CHAPTER 12

Dehydrating

INTRODUCTION

Moisture can be removed from poultry meat by freeze-dehydration, drum drying on heated rollers, spray drying, oven drying, or by dehydration at 212° F. in edible oil (Figs. 12.1, 12.2 and 12.3). In general, costs and special characteristics required for the intended use and quality determine the method of drying.

FREEZE-DRYING

Freeze-drying poultry meat consists of quick-freezing a product, placing it in a chamber under vacuum, and then raising the temperature so that the material is kept near the triple point of water during dehydration. The triple point of water is that point where theoretically the conditions of temperature and pressure are such that water can exist as a solid, liquid, or gas. At this point the meat is still frozen and a minimum amount of energy is required to remove moisture. The moisture changes directly from the solid ice state to the gaseous state. It is because of this phenomenon, called sublimation, that freeze-dried products possess several unique properties different from food dehydrated unfrozen. The process is based on Le Chatelier's second principle which states that a given mass of a substance occupies a larger volume as a gas than as a solid, and, if the outside pressure is below the vapor pressure, the equilibrium will shift from the solid state to the gaseous state, or shift to the right.

Advantages of Freeze-Drying

According to Flosdorf (1949), the freeze-drying process has a number of advantages compared with other methods, particularly drying with hot air. They are:

(1) Because only low temperatures are required for processing there is a minimum change in labile constituents; (2) the loss of volatile compounds is small. The flavor of the product returns upon rehydration; (3) because the product is frozen no foaming occurs; (4) because the moisture is removed from the tissues while in a solid state, the product retains its original structure; (5) coagulation is reduced to a minimum; (6) no case hardening occurs; (7) in the frozen state bacterial growth and enzyme changes are retarded; and (8) because the process occurs in a vacuum little oxygen is present.

Courtesy Ohio Agr. Ext. Service

FIG. 12.1.   COOKED DARK (LEFT) AND LIGHT (RIGHT) FREEZE-DRIED
CHICKEN MEAT

Courtesy Ohio Agr. Ext. Service

FIG. 12.2.   CHUNK STYLE, DEHYDRATED, COOKED, CHICKEN

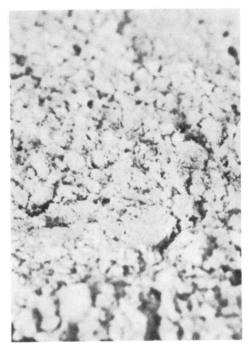

Courtesy Ohio Agr. Ext. Service

FIG. 12.3. POWDERED, DEHYDRATED, COOKED, CHICKEN MEAT

Freeze-dried products possess a number of desirable characteristics. They can be stored without refrigeration, they are light in weight, and they have a better appearance and acceptability than conventionally dehydrated products. Such products are similar in size and shape to the fresh counterpart. Bird (1964) reported that 29 lb. of freeze-dehydrated, raw deboned, chicken meat requires 100 lb. of frozen, raw chicken. Tappel *et al.* (1955) reported that ". . . freeze-drying appears to be the only practical method for the production of high quality serving-size pieces of dehydrated meat, fish, and poultry."

Processing by Freeze-Drying

In preparation for freeze-drying, poultry meat is first quick frozen. Tappel *et al.* (1957) reported that slow freezing produces a coarse, spongy structure with a large number of spaces occupied by ice crystals arranged longitudinally to the muscle fibers. Quick frozen meats, on the other hand, have a fine porous structure because the ice crystals do not form longitudinally and the interstitial spaces are not as large as those in slow frozen meat. Large interstitial areas in tissues have a tendency to col-

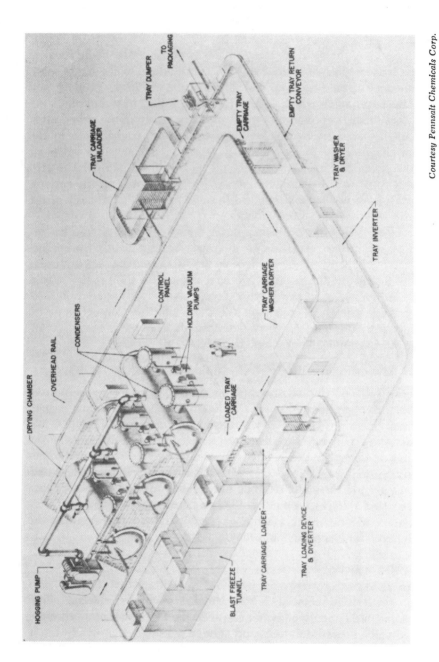

Courtesy Pennsalt Chemicals Corp.

Fig. 12.4. An "In-Line" Automated Freeze-Drying Plant

lapse. This retards rehydration. Freeze-dried meat which has been quick frozen before drying is more tender but not as juicy as slow frozen tissues.

After freezing, the meat is placed in a vacuum chamber where removal of water is accomplished in three steps. Heat is added to accelerate sublimation, water is removed from the subliming ice within the product, and finally the water vapor which reaches the surface must be removed.

Flosdorf (1949) reported that moisture extracted from the dehydrating food can be removed by condensation on a refrigerated plate in the vacuum chamber, by desiccants or by pumping the moisture laden air from the chamber with an ejector or oil sealed rotary pump. The efficiency of refrigerated plates declines as frost condenses on the surface. Desiccants have not proved practical because of the original costs of the chemicals and the costs of recharging.

To accelerate the drying process during freeze-drying, heat can be furnished by conduction, radiation, or dielectric heating. Heat by conduction is most commonly used. In the final drying stages, the temperature is raised to just below the point where heat damage to the product would occur. An "in-line" automated freeze-drying plant is illustrated in Fig. 12.4.

To prevent growth of microorganisms the moisture content must be below ten per cent, but to prevent deterioration from other causes during storage the moisture content should not be over one per cent.

Factors Influencing the Rate of Dehydration and Quality

Yao et al. (1956) studied a number of factors which influence the rate of chicken meat dehydration under vacuum including temperatures both above and below freezing. They observed that increases in temperature increased the drying rate and decreased the drying time. Frozen samples had a faster drying rate than unfrozen ones, possibly because the water formed outside the cells as ice crystals. Pre-cooking, initial moisture content, and sample thickness did not have great effects on drying rates. They reported a drying time of 12–13 hr. was required for samples $5/8$ in. in thickness. Tappel et al. (1957), on the other hand, reported that the time required for freeze drying is mainly a function of thickness. In taste tests with chicken, red meats and seafood (Fig. 12.5), it was observed that freeze-dried chicken had some of the best organoleptic properties. Chicken meat had good storage stability for six months at 100° F. and below. The stability of turkey meat was not as good as for chicken. Both chicken and turkey received better flavor scores as a result of a browning reaction which occurred during short storage periods.

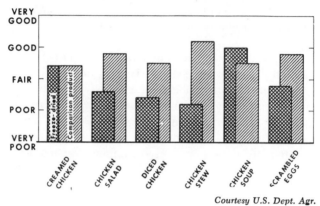

Courtesy U.S. Dept. Agr.

Fig. 12.5. Flavor Ratings of Freeze-Dried Foods, Poultry
Products

Taste tests performed at Agricultural Research Center, Beltsville,
Summer 1962.

Preparation and Handling Poultry for Freeze-Drying.—The Quartermaster Corps Interim Purchase Description (Anon. 1961) for pre-cooked
dehydrated chicken pieces and the instructions contained therein serve
as a good description of the freeze-drying process applied to chicken meat.

Preparation.—The carcass or parts shall be skinned and boned. The head,
feet, metacarpus-phalanges section of wings, giblets, viscera, bones, bone slivers,
cartilage, coarse connective tissue, blood clots, skin, and bruised meat shall be
excluded. When necessary, sufficient fat shall be removed to insure compliance
with fat requirement of the finished product. The meat shall be mixed so that
the light and dark portions are evenly distributed. Any processing or holding of
the meat prior to cooking shall be done where the room temperature or the temperature of the meat is maintained at 45°F. or lower. After draining and cooling, the cooked meat shall be diced by machine into pieces approximately 1 in. x
1 in. x ³/₈ in. The diced meat shall be placed in a wind tunnel or sharp freezer
with circulating air at a temperature of −10°F. or lower within 12 hr. after completion of cooking. Infrequent and requisite rise of room temperature to not
higher than 15°F. is permissible provided surface temperature of product, after
once being thoroughly frozen, does not exceed −10°F.

Dehydration.—The product shall be freeze-dehydrated (i.e., conversion of
the water directly from solid to vapor phase, omitting the liquid phase entirely),
at an absolute pressure not to exceed 1.5 mm. of mercury, except that momentary
increases in pressure for short periods of time due to introducing additional
chambers into the system or other operation factors, may be permitted provided
that no thawing of the product or moisture drip in the product shall occur.
After dehydration is completed, the pressure shall be equalized to atmospheric
level with nitrogen, and product shall be immediately packaged as specified

in 5.1. In no case shall more than 8 hr. elapse between time chamber is opened and time product is completely packaged. During the interim, the product shall be adequately protected from oxygen and moisture.

Flexible Package.—Eight ounces of the product shall be filled into a heat-sealable laminated bag. The bag shall be constructed from not less than 0.002-in. food grade vinyl, laminated to 0.00035-in. aluminum foil, laminated to 0.0005-in. polyester. The laminate shall be an odorless and permanently plastic water-resistant material other than wax. The combined sheet shall show no evidence of delamination when made into bags or heat sealed. Prior to sealing the bag, the air in the bag shall be replaced with nitrogen in such a manner that the oxygen content of the sealed package shall not exceed two per cent after at least one week from the time of sealing the bag, when tested in accordance with 4.6.2. All seals and closures shall be made with heat seals having a minimum width of 1/4 in. The sealed bag shall be free from leaks when tested in accordance with 4.6.3.

Instructions for Rehydrating Chicken Pieces, Pre-cooked, Dehydrated.— Bring salted water to a boil (Allow 3 qt. water and 1/2 tablespoons salt per pound of dehydrated chicken). Add chicken and stir to separate pieces. Remove from heat, cover, and allow to soak for 10–15 min. Drain. (Chicken is ready to use in the same manner as fresh, cooked, and boned chicken.) When chicken stock is required in a recipe, substitute 1 oz. (2 1/2 tablespoons) chicken soup base for the salt in each quart of water. Caution: The salt content of chicken soup base is high. When using chicken stock made with this base, reduce by approximately one-half the amount of salt specified in a recipe and omit salt in water.

Packaging

Taylor (1961) lists the following requirements for packaging materials used for freeze-dried foods: The material must keep out water vapor and oxygen, protect the product from crushing, resist puncturing, be light in weight, and modest in cost. The oxygen level must be maintained at less than two per cent inside the package and the moisture content below three per cent. Cans and plastic pouches most nearly meet these requirements.

Cans have several advantages. They can be filled and hermetically sealed easier, the stability is good during long storage periods, there is good physical protection, and they can be filled under vacuum at high speeds.

Cans also have several disadvantages. They are not as light in weight as pouches and shifting of the contents can cause the contents to become powdery.

Pouches are light in weight and have a number of different shapes and are less expensive than cans. By the use of aluminum foil laminates, pouches can be made impervious to moisture. A pouch developed by the Quartermaster Food and Container Institute which will keep freeze-dried foods in good condition for two years is made from a heat-sealable

TABLE 12.1

AMINO ACID CONTENT OF PROCESSED CHICKEN PRODUCTS

State of Sample	Cystine	Histidine	Isoleucine	Leucine	Lysine	Methionine	Phenylalanine	Threonine	Tryptophan	Tyrosine	Valine
				mg./gm. Nitrogen							
Chicken											
Frozen, raw	72	180	338	502	586	178	234	281	86	218	322
Processed											
Dehydrated, raw	66	191	352	520	608	170	248	290	80	199	329
Dehydrated, pre-cooked	74	195	366	563	636	175	268	298	85	221	357
Irradiated, enzyme-inactivated	64	164	327	501	569	159	247	279	74	259	322
Irradiated, pre-cooked	90	240	474	725	824	242	361	402	101	232	458
Canned	78	188	360	518	614	181	262	298	98	265	354
Percentage of Above as Free Amino Acids after *in Vitro* Pepsin Digestion[1]											
Chicken											
Frozen, raw	10	8	55	63	7	24	31	68	36	23	25
Processed											
Dehydrated, raw	10	6	54	63	4	24	27	65	38	22	20
Dehydrated, pre-cooked	9	4	52	56	3	19	22	64	31	14	16
Irradiated, enzyme-inactivated	8	3	45	54	4	19	21	57	28	13	17
Irradiated, pre-cooked	5	2	32	43	2	12	14	41	23	13	12
Canned	4	4	34	44	3	13	15	44	15	11	13

From Thomas and Calloway (1961).
[1] Acid or alkaline hydrolysis.

3-mil vinyl, 1/3-mil foil, and 1/2-mil polyester film. However, it is too expensive for commercial use. (See QMC Interim Purchase Description for pre-cooked dehydrated chicken pieces, above.)

One problem in the use of pouches is that of the product puncturing the wrapper. To prevent this a cushioning layer can be added to the laminate or it may be necessary to use paperboard sleeves.

One commercial firm is using a nitrogen flushed pouch of saran-coated cellophane laminated to foil which is coated on both sides with two-mil polyethylene. To prevent crushing the pouches are packed in paperboard containers.

Nutritive Value

Thomas and Calloway (1961) have compiled tables showing the nutrient values of frozen and dehydrated raw poultry meat; pre-cooked, dehydrated, irradiated, and canned poultry meat; and meat irradiated after enzyme inactivation. These values are shown in Tables 12.1, 12.2 and 12.3.

TABLE 12.2

POLYUNSATURATED FATTY ACIDS IN PROCESSED CHICKEN PRODUCTS

State of Sample	Hexaene	Pentaene	Tetraene	Triene	Diene	Total
			Chicken			
			gm./100 gm. crude fat			
Frozen, raw	0.34	0.36	2.06	1.47	21.77	26.00
Processed						
Dehydrated, raw	0.26	0.27	1.17	1.46	18.35	21.51
Dehydrated, pre-cooked	0.25	0.28	1.33	1.42	16.58	19.86
Irradiated after enzyme inactivation	0.26	0.21	0.78	1.16	16.22	18.63
Irradiated, pre-cooked	0.25	0.25	0.77	1.26	14.94	17.47
Canned	0.21	0.21	1.04	1.42	14.72	17.60

From Thomas and Calloway (1961).

Problems in Freeze-Drying Poultry Meat

A number of problems still remain to be solved in the freeze-drying process and in handling freeze-dried products. Seltzer (1961) indicated that in order to compete with conventionally dehydrated foods the resulting product must (1) be better than those dehydrated by conventional methods and (2) the value of the solids content must be great enough so that the dehydration process is only a small portion of the sale price.

Goldblith *et al.* (1963), in a discussion of problems associated with freeze-dehydrated foods, reported that lipid oxidation is a major problem because of the large surface areas associated with such foods. Packaging

TABLE 12.3

PROXIMATE COMPOSITION AND VITAMIN CONTENT OF PROCESSED CHICKEN PRODUCTS

State of Sample	Moisture	Protein (N × 6.25)	Fat	Thia-mine	Ribo-flavin	Niacin	Pyri-doxine	Panto-thenic Acid	Folic Acid	Alpha-toco-pherol
		gm./100 gm.		mcg./100 gm.		mg./100 gm.		mcg./100 gm.		mg./100 gm.
Chicken										
Frozen, raw	77	18.8	2.7	57	175	6.90	500	960	4	0.42
Processed										
Dehydrated, raw	1.5	84.0	13.6	198	665	30.80	260	3960	26	1.15
Dehydrated, pre-cooked	1.2	88.2	10.5	122	518	18.40	140	1980	14	1.16
Irradiated after enzyme in-activation	66	28.4	4.2	2	169	6.10	180	980	4	0.30
Irradiated, pre-cooked	66	28.7	3.9	5	202	8.25	300	1220	4	0.28
Canned	71	24.3	3.9	9	187	6.90	420	850	5	0.26
As eaten, simmered										
Dehydrated, raw	71.4	22.4	2.4	27	86	4.22	...	...	...	...
Dehydrated, pre-cooked	69.4	24.5	2.6	33	76	3.40	...	...	...	...
Irradiated after enzyme in-activation	64.7	28.0	5.1	5	150	4.21	...	...	...	...
Irradiated, pre-cooked	59.0	30.7	6.8	5	102	8.35	...	...	...	...
Canned	67.5	24.2	3.9	5	276	6.66	...	...	...	...

From Thomas and Calloway (1961).

in opaque packages to prevent light retards but does not prevent oxidation. Antioxidants only retard rancidity on the surface. Excluding oxygen is the most effective means of retarding oxidation. These authors reported that changes in the protein structure also occur as a result of drying. At the same time tissues toughen and waterholding capacity declines. The microflora of freeze-dehydrated foods and the effect of dehydration on the microbiological population need further study.

Seltzer (1961), in a discussion of problems associated with freeze-dried chicken, observed that ease of rehydration and toughness are problems with poultry meat. These two problems can be reduced by grinding the meat but shelf-life then becomes more of a problem because of the increased surface exposure. Dried chicken meat deteriorates rapidly above a three per cent moisture content. The dark meat, which is higher in heme pigments, oxidizes to form a deep brown color. In addition, the induction period leading to fat rancidity tends to be completed during freezing and drying, accelerating later rancidity development. Sosebee *et al.* (1964) in a study of the effect of papain and Rhozyme P-11 on the tenderness of freeze-dried poultry reported that papain had the most effect in tenderizing but that the problem of adequate penetration of the enzyme into the tissue before processing still remained.

The fragile nature of freeze-dried foods means that shattering is a problem. Proper packaging helps prevent this problem.

Costs of Freeze-Drying

Bird (1964) set up four hypothetical but representative freeze-dehydration plants. He concluded that the cost factors in dehydration depend upon plant size, duration of the drying cycle, and continuity of operation. The food dehydrated, wage rates, and utility rates are other factors influencing costs.

In a plant with a daily capacity for removing four tons of water, labor accounts for 31% of the processing costs (not including costs of raw materials and packaging); equipment depreciation, 37%; utility costs, 18–21%; fixed expenses, 16–19%; and salaries of workers, 3–5%.

Chicken meat freeze-dried in a plant with a four-ton daily capacity was estimated to cost eight cents for each pound of water removed. The author predicted that chicken meat will be the largest quantity of any meat freeze-dried.

Markets for Freeze-Dehydrated Foods

Bird (1964) lists the following potential sources for marketing freeze-dried foods:

A large demand for freeze-dehydrated foods can be expected from the armed forces. Two characteristics, lightweight and no refrigeration requirements make such products ideal for meals in combat areas.

A large demand can also be expected for chicken meat for combining with other ingredients to make soups, stews, and other prepared dishes.

Freeze-dehydrated products lend themselves to constant portion control, thus they are convenient to prepare and serve, and are in demand by institutions.

Camping, although a small outlet at present, offers a good potential for growth. Some demand for freeze-dried foods can also be expected from retail grocery stores.

OTHER METHODS USED FOR DEHYDRATING POULTRY MEAT

A recent development in processing poultry meat has been a method where finely comminuted chicken meat is spray dried. Generally, whole, boned-out, cooked fowl are used. The product is used in soup mixes and convenience foods which lend themselves to the use of fine particles of poultry meat. Poultry meat can also be dried by oven heating and by using ground cooked poultry spread in thin layers in pans or trays. By using a vacuum, moisture can be removed at lower temperatures than when no vacuum is used and less damage to the meat results. Chunk-size dehydrated poultry meat which has been dried by conventional air drying methods is also available commercially.

Other methods which have been used for drying are the use of drum driers on heated rollers and the heating of meat above 212°F. in edible oil. The latter method results in a product which contains some of the oil.

PROCESSING POULTRY FAT

Poultry fat, if properly handled and processed, makes an ideal ingredient for further processed poultry products including dehydrated soup mixes. Strandine (1963) reported that the fat is washed and then recovered by settling, filtering, skimming, or centrifuging. Length of storage, temperature, cooking, and care given during storage and handling all influence the quality of the resultant product. After processing the fats can be stored at 0° to −20°F. until used.

Poultry fats contain a large proportion of polyunsaturated fat and the natural odors and flavors are considered pleasant and desirable.

The U.S. Department of Agriculture's Poultry Inspector's Handbook (Anon. 1964) gives the following information concerning the treatment and processing of poultry fat.

Water or moisture may be removed from poultry fat by heating at temperatures slightly above water boiling point (212° F.). However, for more complete removal of moisture, higher temperatures must be reached. Temperatures in excess of 220° F. result in rendered fat that has darkened color, altered odors and flavors, and poor keeping quality. Excess heating may be completely avoided by removal of moisture by centrifuging the liquid fat. Equipment is available for operation at various speeds and temperatures.

There is no objection to the addition of suitable antioxidants or mixtures of such antioxidants for the purpose of improving stability or keeping quality of the finished product. It is the inspector's responsibility to see that only the kinds and amounts of antioxidants are permitted that are specifically indicated as part of label approval for the finished product. The total combined weight of the antioxidants shall not exceed 0.02% of the weight of the rendered fat in any case.

Recovery of edible mesenteric poultry fat for rendering or marketing in raw form or use in poultry products has not proved satisfactory. Undesirable odors cannot be completely removed and/or there seems to be no practicable method of removing the fat under conditions that do not result in contamination with intestinal contents materials.

Nair (1964), in suggesting specifications important for products used in dry soup mixes, reported that strict standards are necessary for purchasing poultry fats. Only rendered leaf fat should be used that has been processed in stainless steel equipment at temperatures not exceeding 220°-230° F. Peroxide values should not exceed 2%, free-fatty acids should amount to less than 1%, and moisture should be less than 0.25%.

BIBLIOGRAPHY

ANON. 1961. Quartermaster Corps Interim Purchase Description for Chicken Pieces, Precooked, Dehydrated. IP-DES CS-5-1. Quartermaster Corps, Quartermaster Food and Container Institute for the Armed Forces.

ANON. 1964. Poultry Inspector's Handbook. Agr. Mktg. Serv. Poultry Div., Inspection Branch, U.S. Dept. Agr.

BALLANTYNE, R. M., BRYNKO, C., DUCKER, A. J., and SMITHIES, W. R. 1958. Rehydrated cooked meat products. Food Technol. *12*, 398–402.

BIRD, K. 1964. Freeze-drying of foods: Cost projections. U.S. Dept. Agr., Mktg. Res. Rept. *639*.

BIRD, K. 1964. Selected writings on freeze-drying of foods. U.S. Dept. Agr., Econ. Res. Serv. ERS-*147*.

BURKE, R. F., and DECAREAU, R. V. 1964. Recent advances in the freeze-drying of food products. *In* Advances in Food Research. C. O. Chichester, and E. M. Mrak (Editors). Academic Press, New York.

CHARM, S. E. 1963. Fundamentals of Food Engineering. Avi Publishing Co., Westport, Conn.

COPSON, D. A. 1958. Microwave sublimation of foods. Food Technol. *12*, 270–272.

COPSON, D. A. 1962. Microwave Heating in Freeze-Drying, Electronic Ovens, and Other Applications. Avi Publishing Co., Westport, Conn.

CORRIDON, G. A. 1963. Freeze-drying, a list of selected references. Natl. Agr. Library, U.S. Dept. Agr., Library List 77.

DOTY, D. M., WANG, H., and AUERBACH, E. 1953. Chemical and histological properties of dehydrated meat. J. Agr. Food Chem. *1*, 664–668.

FLOSDORF, E. W. 1949. Freeze-Drying. Reinhold Publishing Corp., New York.

GOLDBLITH, S. A., KAREL, M., and LUSK, G. 1963. Freeze dehydration of foods. Food Technol. *17*, 21–26.

HARPER, J. C., and TAPPEL, A. L. 1957. Freeze-drying of food products. Advan. Food Res. *7*, 171–234.

KING, C. J., LAM, W. K., and SANDALL, O. C. 1968. Physical properties important for freeze-drying poultry meat. Food Technol. *22*, 1302–1308.

KLOSE, A. A., and OLCOTT, H. S. 1964. Meat, poultry, and sea foods. *In* Food Dehydration, Vol. II. W. B. Van Arsdel, and M. J. Copley (Editors). Avi Publishing Co., Westport, Conn.

NAIR, J. H. 1964. Dry soups and other dry mixes. *In* Food Dehydration, Vol. II. W. B. Van Arsdel, and M. J. Copley, (Editors). Avi Publishing Col, Westport, Conn.

SELTZER, E. 1961. Importance of selection and processing method for successful freeze-drying of chicken. Food Technol. *15*, 18, 20, 22.

SHOCKLEY, R. T. 1962. Picking pouch for freeze-dries. Food Eng. *34*, No. 12, 100–101.

SOSEBEE, M. E. , MAY, K. N., and POWERS, J. J. 1964. The effects of enzyme addition on the quality of freeze-dehydrated chicken meat. Food Technol. *18*, 551–554.

STRANDINE, E. J. 1963. Poultry production and processing. *In* Food Processing Operations, Vol. II. J. L. Heid, and M. A. Joslyn (Editors). Avi Publishing Co., Westport, Conn.

TAPPEL, A. L. *et al.* 1955. Freeze-dried meat. I. Preparation and properties. Food Technol. *9*, 401–405.

TAPPEL, A. L., MARTIN, R., and PLOCHER, E. 1957. Freeze-dried meat. V. Preparation, properties, and storage stability of precooked freeze-dried meats, poultry, and seafoods. Food Technol. *11*, 599–603.

TAYLOR, T. C. 1961. Packaging of freeze-dried foods. Food Eng. *33*, No. 9, 41–44.

THOMAS, M. H., and CALLOWAY, D. H. 1961. Nutritional value of dehydrated foods. J. Am. Dietet. Assoc. *39*, No. 2, 105–116.

WELLS, G. H., and DAWSON, L. E. 1966. Tenderness and juiciness of freeze-dried chicken meat as related to maturity of birds. Poultry Sci. *45*, 1004–1007.

WELLS, G. H., MAY, K. N., and POWERS, J. J. 1962. Taste-panel and shear press evaluation of tenderness of freeze-dried chickens as affected by age and preslaughter feeding. Food Technol. *16*, 137–139.

YAO, A., NELSON, A I., and STEINBERG, M. P. 1956. Factors affecting the rate of chicken meat dehydration under vacuum. Food Technol. *10*, 145–150.

CHAPTER 13

Curing and Smoking

INTRODUCTION

The opportunities for merchandising smoked poultry as specialty items are good. Smoked poultry is a unique taste treat for banquets, gifts, and as a gourmet item. To fill this demand a number of methods and formulations for curing poultry have been developed. Generally each processor develops his own formula or improves a standard formulation by the addition of spices and herbs. In some instances locker plants or individuals have, through promotion and advertising of smoked turkey as a gourmet item, merchandised as many as 5,000 smoked turkeys a year. Unfortunately, many of the cures used in the past were the same ones used for curing hams and other meats. As a result the salt and spice content were so high that the delicate flavor of turkey meat was masked and the turkey products were almost indistinguishable from ham. The general practices of smoking large turkeys, the large losses in weight from smoking, and a high profit margin have resulted in smoked turkeys which sell for eight to ten dollars or more a bird and a product which tasted almost like ham (Table 13.1). The secret of merchandising smoked poultry is to use mild cures, in units which are convenient for the consumer to purchase and handle.

The estimated building and equipment requirements and costs for a plant to manufacture smoked poultry are shown in Table 13.2.

EFFECTS OF SMOKING

Smoke helps to preserve meat by acting as an antioxidant, a bactericidal agent, a bacteriostatic agent, and by providing a protective film on the product's surface. Phenols appear to be the most active antioxidant compounds and formaldehyde the principal bactericidal agent. Jensen (1949) reported that the greatest reduction in non-spore forming bacteria occurred one half to two hours after smoking and that the more resistant forms were eliminated after three hours.

A number of different compounds result from the slow burning of wood. According to a literature review by Draudt (1963) typical compounds in smoke from oak wood contain formaldehyde, higher aldehydes, ketones, formic acid, acetic and higher acids, methyl alcohol, tar, and water. Jensen (1949) reported that analysis of smudges on the sides of a commercial smoke house yielded 25–40 p.p.m. of formaldehyde, 140–180 p.p.m. of

TABLE 13.1

RETAIL PRICES OF SELECTED SMOKED POULTRY PRODUCTS IN PENNSYLVANIA IN 1965

Whole smoked turkey (this price will frequently vary 50¢ either way)	$ 1.50 per lb.
Canned smoked breast meat	$ 2.50 per lb.
Smoked turkey roll	$ 2.25–2.50 per lb.
Smoked goose (approx. 5 lb.)	$ 9.50
Smoked Cornish game hens (brace 3–4 lb.)	$ 8.95
Smoked turkey sausage	$ 1.75 per lb.
Smoked pheasant (brace)	$13.95
Smoked Mallard duck (brace)	$12.95
Smoked chicken	$ 0.95 per lb.
Sliced smoked chicken	$ 1.75 per lb.
Smoked chicken sausage	$ 1.02 per lb.
Smoked chicken spread (8-oz. cup)	$ 0.50

Bauermann (1965).

TABLE 13.2

ESTIMATED BUILDING AND EQUIPMENT REQUIREMENTS FOR MANUFACTURING SMOKED POULTRY

	Costs, $	
Item	Poultry Processing Plant	New Plant
Land and building		
Plant area	. . .	4,000
Office	. . .	1,000
Land	. . .	1,000
Plant equipment[1]		
Freezer	. . .	10,000
Smoker	4,800	4,800
Brine tanks	260	260
Work table	. . .	150
Packaging table and equipment	. . .	500
Cages for smoker	170	170
Overhead track	70	70
Steam generator	. . .	400
Delivery truck, insulated body	. . .	5,000
Total		27,350

From Marshall (1963).
[1] Approximate list price f.o.b. factory, midwestern United States, September 1962.

higher aldehydes, 90–125 p.p.m. of formic acid, 460–500 p.p.m. of acetic and higher acids, 20–30 p.p.m. of phenols, 190–200 p.p.m. of ketones, and over 1,000 p.p.m. of resins.

Smoke imparts a specific flavor to meats. Although a number of compounds undoubtedly are involved, phenolic compounds are one of the principal flavor constituents. The type of wood also influences the flavor of smoked meat. It is generally accepted that the best smoked products come from using smoke from hardwoods.

Smoke also influences the color of the cured product. The time, temperature, and density of smoking are important factors. The type of wood used may also have some influence on color. Humidity should be controlled. Low humidity during smoking can cause excessive drying and shrinkage. No specific data are available on the specific humidity or conditions to use.

Snyder and Orr (1964) reported that smoking poultry imparts an aroma and flavor of hardwood smoke to the product, it produces meat of a firm, smooth, uniform texture with a light pink to mahogany color and increases storage life.

The chemical analysis of cured turkey meat is shown in Table 13.3.

TABLE 13.3

CHEMICAL ANALYSIS OF CURED TURKEY MEAT[1]

	Moisture, %	NaCl, %	Nitrites, p.p.m.
Light meat	68	2.8	30
Dark meat	62	3.3	42

S. C. Agr. Expt. Sta. Bull. 506.
From Hindman, Wheeler and Mitchell (1963).
[1] Processed according to the formula and methods of Hindman, Wheeler and Mitchell (1963).

SMOKING POULTRY

For smoking, only high quality, well-fleshed, well-bled, clean carcasses with a good covering of fat should be used. If the carcasses are too fat a high shrinkage results during smoking; if the carcasses are not well-fleshed with some fat the smoked meat will be dry, tough, and stringy. Carcasses with excessive tears or scalded above 128°F. do not make good material for smoking. Removing the tendons in the drumsticks helps the curing mixture to penetrate into the meat. Generally, giblets are not cured and smoked. Some processors trim off the neck skin and a few remove the first joint of the wings before curing. Others prefer to overlap the flap from the neck skin to close the front of the body cavity after curing. This overlapping prevents the loss of fats during smoking.

Chicken fryers over 3 lb. in weight are suitable for smoking (Fig. 13.3). Light and heavy fowl can also be used but meat from such carcasses is not as tender as from younger birds, there is a great loss in moisture, and the yield is lower. Turkeys used for smoking should be under two years of age.

Curing and Smoking

A number of different curing formulations are available. Poultry meat is mild flavored. As a result cures which contain large amounts of salt or spices will mask the flavor of the meat.

Courtesy Ohio Agr. Ext. Service

FIG. 13.1. A MODERN SMOKEHOUSE

The main ingredients of most curing solutions are salt, sugar, and nitrite. Salt influences the flavor and texture of the meat and acts as a preservative. Sugar adds to the flavor and counteracts the drying and toughening process which is characteristic of salt alone. It may also influence color fixation. Nitrites are responsible for the pink color of the meat. The nitrite reacts with the hemoglobin found in the meat to form nitrosohemoglobin.

Curing solutions can be applied by immersion, stitching, or pumping. The entire carcass is often immersed in the curing solution until the "cure" draws through the meat. To ensure faster and more even distribution the solution can be pumped under pressure throughout the tissues or "stitched." Stitching is the name given to the process where a

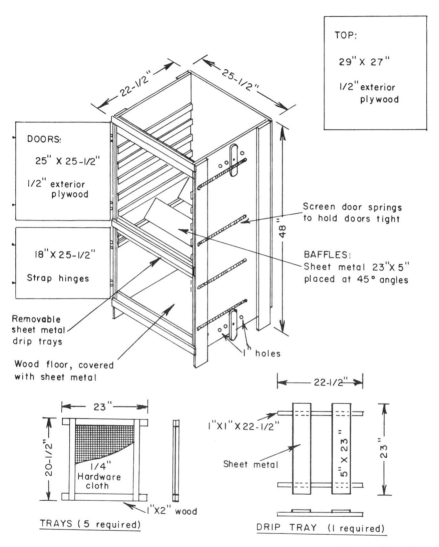

TOP:

29" X 27"

1/2" exterior
plywood

DOORS:

25" X 25-1/2"

1/2" exterior
plywood

18" X 25-1/2"

Strap hinges

Removable
sheet metal
drip trays

Wood floor, covered
with sheet metal

Screen door springs
to hold doors tight

BAFFLES:
Sheet metal 23"X 5"
placed at 45° angles

1" holes

TRAYS (5 required)

23"

20-1/2"

1/4"
Hardware
cloth

1"X2" wood

DRIP TRAY (1 required)

22-1/2"

1"X1" X 22-1/2"

Sheet metal

5" X 23"

23"

*Courtesy Oregon Agr.
Ext. Service*

FIG. 13.2. A SMOKE-HOUSE DESIGNED FOR THE SPORTSMAN AND
HOBBYIST

bank of hollow needles connected to a pump is forced into the meat so the curing solution can be distributed under pressure throughout the tissue.

Smith *et al.* (1941) developed a salt curing solution which contains the following ingredients:

Salt	6 lb.
Sugar	3 lb.
Saltpeter	2 oz.

Hiner and Marsden (1961) used the same formulation except that they substituted brown sugar for the sugar.

A more complicated formulation was reported by Highlands and Burns (1941). Their formulation is as follows:

Water	5 gal.	Oil of thyme	5 cc.
Salt	4 lb.	Oil of marjoram	5 cc.
Sugar	30 oz.	Oil of bay leaves	6 cc.
Oil of celery	8 cc.	Oil of sweet basil	6 cc.
Oil of black pepper	8 cc.	Oil of coriander	5 cc.
Oil of parsley leaves	8 cc.	Oil of cardamom	5 cc.
Oil of sage	5 cc.		

To make the curing solution dissolve the oils in 20 cc. of ethyl alcohol. Add 22 cc. to a small amount of sugar and 1 gm. of gum tragacanth and mix thoroughly with mortar and pestle.

Dissolve 4 lb. of salt and 30 oz. of the sugar and spice mixture in 5 gal. of water with constant stirring. Pickle $1\frac{1}{2}$ days per pound of dressed weight. Smoke 6–9 hr. at 110°–115°F.

Marshall (1963) reported the following process for chickens:

Salt	12 lb.
Light brown sugar	6 lb.
Sodium nitrite	80 gm.
Water	9 gal.

Stir until dissolved, cook to 34°-36° F. This formulation should be sufficient for about 25 fryers. Soak for 48 hr. in solution, then in cold water for 1 hr. to remove excess salt.

Smoke with legs up at 180°F. for 1 hr. then at 130°F. for 5–12 additional hours. Yields of 85% were reported by this method. After smoking, cook the carcasses at either 5 lb. pressure for 10 min. or in steam for about 25 min. or until the internal temperature of the meat reaches 165°F. After cooking and cooling package the carcasses.

A number of other factors should be considered in curing poultry. Frozen poultry should be thawed before immersion in the curing solution. Carcasses should be kept around 35°-40° F. during curing. To ensure that the curing solution comes in contact with all carcasses it is a good idea to remove and then repack the carcasses in the solution.

Courtesy Ohio Agr. Ext. Service

FIG. 13.3. SMOKED CHICKEN

The carcasses should be weighted on top to make sure that all parts are immersed during curing. To reduce curing time the legs, wings, and breast can be pumped with curing solution.

As soon as carcasses are removed from the curing solution they should be thoroughly washed or soaked in cold water for 4-6 hr. and then drained. When reasonably dry they can be placed in stockinettes for smoking or hung by the wings in the smoker. Stockinettes hold the legs and wings against the sides of the body so that areas under these parts are not as brown after smoking as the remainder of the carcass.

To produce a ready-to-eat product, a smokehouse temperature of 170°F. for 6–8 hr. and then 185°F. should be used until the internal temperature of the meat reaches 160°F. Poultry smoked below this time-temperature range requires cooking before eating. Low smokehouse temperatures of about 100°–120°F. keep shrinkage at a minimum. To produce the minimum amount of smoke the fire should be small and smothered. Allow room in the smoker for good distribution of the heat and smoke. The average weight yields of cured smoked turkey are shown in Table 13.4.

After smoking, the carcasses can be removed from the stockinette, wrapped, and refrigerated. If carcasses are to be held longer than two weeks they should be frozen. Hindman *et al.* (1963) reported "a decrease in acceptance scores of a taste panel tasting smoked turkey white

TABLE 13.4

AVERAGE WEIGHT YIELDS[1] OF CURED SMOKED TURKEY[2]

	Lb.	% of Body Weight
Body[3]	9.6	...
Cured	9.9	101
Smoked	8.4	87
Roasted	7.2	74

S.C. Agr. Expt. Sta. Bull. 506.
[1] Average of 12 turkey halves weighing from 8.7 to 10.7 lb.
[2] Processed according to the formula and methods of Hindman, Wheeler, and Mitchell (1963).
[3] Weight of dressed birds after giblets and neck are removed.

meat after 22 weeks in frozen storage and for the dark meat after 34 weeks." Maximum storage time at 0° F. for smoked meats is 2-4 months.

The following information relative to curing and smoking poultry meat is taken from the U.S. Department of Agriculture Poultry Inspector's Handbook (Anon. 1964).

Poultry food products that are heat processed by smoking or barbecuring may be frozen or canned following customary procedures for manufacture of these products. They may be directly packaged after processing and are considered to be perishable foods requiring the usual precautions in handling, storing, and transporting.

Curing processes that usually precede actual smoking may be permitted by immersion of the entire carcass in a cure solution containing salt, approved levels of flavorings, and sodium nitrate. Curing may also be accomplished by injecting the thick muscle tissue with the cure solution or a combination of injection and immersion in cure solution may be used. It is the inspector's responsibility to see that only approved amounts of the above mentioned nitrites and nitrates are used in cure solutions. Two pounds or less of the pure chemical per 100 gal. of cure (or "pickle") is a practical rule to go by. When cure mixtures containing several ingredients are used to prepare the solution, the inspector must restrict the weight of the mixture to the amount specified with the label approval for the finished product, since the exact composition of the mixture may not be available to the inspector. Different brands of cure mixture may not be used interchangeably. The curing process shall be carried out in sanitary non-corrosive type containers (preferably stainless steel) at temperatures approximately 35°-40° F. Curing solutions may not be reused.

Cure mixtures containing sodium nitrite or potassium nitrite, and sodium nitrate or potassium nitrate, must be clearly marked and kept under the care of a responsible plant employee. Since the specific nitrite content is usually marked on the containers of such supplies, the inspector should make checks to ensure that nitrites are not used in excess of the following limits:

(1) 2 lb. to 100 gal. liquid cure
(2) 1 oz. to each 100 lb. of poultry in a dry cure procedure
(3) $1/4$ oz. in 100 lb. of chopped poultry meat

Smoking may be carried out by heat and smoke from a common source or from separate sources. After carcasses have been removed from cure solutions, washed, and drained, the smoking is continued until a minimum internal temperature of 155°F. is reached. The time and temperatures maintained during smoking may vary depending on the tolerances for cooking loss and degree of coloration desired in the final product.

Further Processed Smoked Turkey Products

Turkey livers, gizzards, and necks which amount to about 5.4% of the dressed weight of turkeys are generally not smoked. Hindman *et al.* (1963) give the following formulation for utilizing these parts as turkey liverwurst.

8 lb. neck meat[1]	3 lb. giblet fat
4 lb. gizzards	11 gm. custom cure[2]
5 lb. livers	4 drops liverwurst seasoning[3]

Cook necks and gizzards under pressure (10 lb. pressure, 15 min.); simmer livers and fat 15 min. Discard the neck bone and the outer skin of the gizzard. Mix and grind together.

Stuff into permeable cellulose casings[4] and smoke at 180° F., to 150° F. internal temperature, or stuff into fibrous casing[4] and process in 165° F.-175° F. water bath to an internal temperature of 150°F.

---

[1] The necks and giblets of six large turkeys yield approximately 20 lb. of cooked meat.

[2] Hellers Custom Cure, B. Heller and Co., Chicago 15, Ill.

[3] Liverwurst Viandarome Seasoning, Fritzche Brothers, Inc., Port Authority Building, 78 Ninth Avenue, New York 11, N.Y.

[4] Union Carbide Co. Food Products Division, 6733 W. 65th Street, Chicago 38, Ill.

They also give the following formulation for cured turkey roll.

(1) Cure and smoke turkeys.

(2) Bone turkeys. (At this stage the birds bone very easily.) Preserve the skin and fat.

(3) Chop two-thirds of the meat into approximately $1/_2$-in. cubes.

(4) Grind (using very fine blade or blender) the other one-third of the meat including the skin and fat.

(5) Mix chopped meat with ground meat.

(6) Sprinkle on gelatin (use one per cent of meat by weight) and blend.

(7) Cured turkey rolls may be (1) stuffed in permeable cellulose casings and hung in 180°F. smokehouse or (2) stuffed in fibrous casings and processed in 165°–175°F. water bath until internal temperature of roll reaches 150°F.

(8) Chill.

Cooking

It is best to cook smoked turkey on a rack to prevent the salt in the drippings from being reabsorbed. Some cooks soak the carcasses in water overnight to remove more of the salt. The bird can be basted with a mixture of brown sugar and vinegar. Other spices can be added if desired.

The exact times and temperatures for cooking smoked poultry depend upon the smoking time and temperature as well as other factors. Warm turkeys direct from smoking can be cooked about 2 hr. at 300°F. Other turkeys can be cooked at about 350°F. for the first 15–30 min. Then the temperature is lowered to 250°–300°F. for 3–4 hr. depending on the size of the turkey. When an internal temperature of 165°F. is reached or when leg joints move easily and the flesh on the legs is soft and pliable the turkey is finished cooking. Because of its salt content smoked turkey goes well with bland foods. It can be served hot or cold.

Turkey Salami[1]

Raw Material

Turkey dark meat trim.

Formulation

Turkey dark meat trim	90 lbs.
Turkey hearts	10 lbs.
Water	5 lbs.
Salt	2.5 lbs.
Salami seasoning	1 lb.
Phosphate	0.5 lbs.
Cure agent	4 ozs.
Hydrolyzed vegetable protein	4 ozs.

Preparation of Emulsion

Place meat into mixer, dissolve phosphate in small amount of water and add to meat. Then add salt, water, and other spices and mix until emulsion becomes tacky (minimum of five minutes). After mixing, emulsion is removed from mixer and passed through a grinder with a coarse plate ($3/16$ in. to $1/4$ in. plate). Emulsion is then transferred to a suitable stuffing machine.

Stuffing

The product is stuffed into a suitable size UCC Fibrous casing to a desired length.

Processing Schedule

The product is smoked and processed using a cycle of 140° F. to 180° F. in one hour with 40% relative humidity. Product is processed to an internal temperature of 155° F. and then cold showered. After showering, product is stored at 40° F.

---

[1] Courtesy of Union Carbide Corp., Films-Packaging Division (1973).

Turkey Ham[1]

Raw Material

Boneless, skinless turkey thigh meat.

Formulation

Boneless, skinless turkey thigh meat	100 lbs.
Water	5 lbs.
Salt	2.5 lbs.
Ham seasoning	12 ozs.
Phosphate	8 ozs.
Curing agent	4 ozs.

Preparation of Emulsion

Place meat into mixer. Dissolve phosphate in water and add to meat. Water, spices, and all other additives are then added and mixed until emulsion becomes tacky (minimum of five minutes). After mixing, emulsion is transferred to the sausage stuffer.

Stuffing

The product is stuffed into a suitable size Union Carbide Fibrous casing to desired length.

Processing Schedule

Product is placed into smokehouse, smoked, and processed using a cycle of 140° F. to 180° F. in one hour with 40% relative humidity added. Product is processed to an internal temperature of 155° F. Product is then cold showered and stored at 40° F.

[1] Courtesy of Union Carbide Corp., Films-Packaging Division (1973).

Chicken or Turkey Bologna
and/or
Pickle Pimento Loaf

Raw Material

Mechanically deboned chicken or turkey meat.

Formulation

Mechanically deboned chicken or turkey meat	100 lbs.
Water (Amount will vary according to moisture content of the mechanically deboned meat)	15 lbs.
Turkey bologna seasoning (cure agents included)	4 lbs.
Extender (milk powder, soy protein, rice, flour, wheat flour, etc.)	3 lbs.
Phosphate	8 ozs.

NOTE: When making Pickle Pimento Loaf, diced sweet pickles and pimentos are added to the formulation in amounts of 5 lbs. and 4 lbs., respectively.

NOTE: Fat content of turkey meat will determine if fat should be added to emulsion.

Preparation of Emulsion

Place mechanically deboned meat into chopper. Dissolve phosphate in water and add to emulsion. Water, spices, and all other additives are also added to the cutter and chopped to 35°–38° F. When frozen meat is used, hot water should be added instead of cold water to help raise the temperature. Maximum chopping time should be five minutes. The chopped product is then emulsified and transferred to the sausage stuffer.

Stuffing

The product is stuffed into a suitable size UCC Fibrous casing.

Processing Schedule

The smoke cycle used is 140° to 180° F. in one hour with 40% relative humidity added. After an internal temperature of 155° to 160° F. is reached, product should be cold showered for 15 min. and then stored in a 40° F. cooler.

---

[1] Courtesy of Union Carbide Corp., Films-Packaging Division (1973).

BIBLIOGRAPHY

ANON. 1964. Poultry Inspector's Handbook. U.S. Dept. Agr., Agr. Mktg. Serv., Poultry Div., Inspection Branch.

BAUERMANN, J. F. 1965. Personal Communication.

BEANBLOSSOM, F. Z. 1948. Merchandising turkeys. Texas Agr. Ext. Bull. B-163.

BEASLEY, A. K., and MARSDEN, S. J. 1941. A study of turkey curing and smoking. Poultry Sci. 20, 496–506.

DRAUDT, H. W. 1963. The meat smoking process, a review. Food Technol. 17, 85–90.

HIGHLANDS, H. E., and BURNS, J. W. 1941. Poultry smoking tests indicate successful methods. Food Ind. 13, No. 7, 46–49.

HINDMAN, M. S., WHEELER, H. O., and MITCHELL, J. H., JR. 1963. Preparing cured smoked turkey. S. Carolina Agr. Expt. Sta. Bull. 506.

HINER, R. L., and MARSDEN, S. J. 1961. Curing and smoking turkeys. U.S. Dept. Agr., Agr. Res. Serv. Mimeo.

HUBER, M. G., ONSDORFF, T., and LONG, J. B. 1963. A smokehouse for the sportsman and hobbyist. Oregon State Univ. Ext. Bull. 788.

JENSEN, L. B. 1949. Meat and Meat Foods. Ronald Press Co., New York.

MARSHALL, J. H. 1963. New marketable poultry and egg products. Cornell Univ. Agr. Expt. Sta., A. E. Res. 110.

SMITH, E.Y., SCHOLES, J. C., and HALL, G. O.   1941.   Smoke flavoring turkey
    and poultry meats.   Cornell Ext. Bull. *446.*
SNYDER, E. S., and ORR, H. L.   1964.   Poultry Meat.   Ontario Agr. Dept. Publ.
    9.
ZIEGLER, P. T.   1962.   The Meat We Eat.   Interstate Publishing Co., Danville,
    Illinois.

CHAPTER 14

Preservation by Radiation

INTRODUCTION

The possibility of sterilization of foods by radiation has been recognized since 1895. However, it was not until the discovery of the fission process and the subsequent developments brought about by the impetus of World War II that a concentrated effort to preserve food by radiation was made.

At the present time, all of the possibilities and potentials of radiation preservation still have not been fully explored. However, it appears that there will be a place for the practical use of radiation in the preservation of some foods and that radiation preservation will supplement rather than replace other methods of preservation.

ADVANTAGES AND DISADVANTAGES OF RADIATION PRESERVATION

Coleby (1959) gave the following advantages for radiation preservation of meats. Meat can be preserved by means of radiation for long periods, under conditions of continuous processing and sufficient penetration can be achieved to treat large pieces of meat. It might also be possible to use plastic film packaging materials.

The chief handicap of irradiated foods lies in the undesirable side reactions which occur as a result of the radiation. These include changes in flavor, color, odor, texture, and destruction of some nutrients.

SOURCES OF RADIATION FOR FOOD PRESERVATION

Goldblith (1963) lists the following types of radiation as being suitable for food preservation.

Beta Particles.—Negatively charged particles ejected from the nucleii of radioactive atoms during their disintegration process. Identical to electrons with the single exception of origin.

Cathode Rays (or Electrons).—Streams of negatively charged electrons generated by "boiling off" the electrons from a cathode in an evacuated tube and accelerating them down the tube by applying a potential difference between the cathode and the anode.

Gamma Rays.—Short wavelength electromagnetic radiation of high energy emitted from the nucleii of radioactive atoms during their decay process.

X-rays.—Identical with gamma rays except in their origin. X-rays are produced in man-made machines by bombardment of heavy metal targets (at anode) with cathode rays.

220

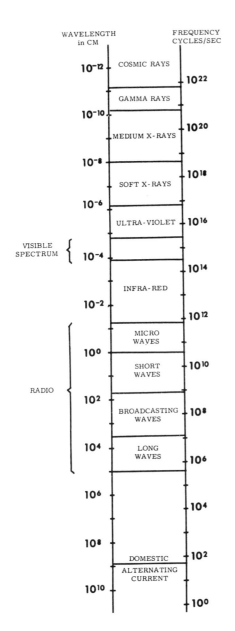

WAVELENGTH in CM

FREQUENCY CYCLES/SEC

10^{-12} — COSMIC RAYS — 10^{22}

GAMMA RAYS

10^{-10} — 10^{20}

MEDIUM X-RAYS

10^{-8} — 10^{18}

SOFT X-RAYS

10^{-6} — ULTRA-VIOLET — 10^{16}

VISIBLE SPECTRUM { 10^{-4} — 10^{14}

INFRA-RED

10^{-2} — 10^{12}

MICRO WAVES

10^{0} — SHORT WAVES — 10^{10}

RADIO { 10^{2} — BROADCASTING WAVES — 10^{8}

10^{4} — LONG WAVES — 10^{6}

10^{6} — 10^{4}

10^{8} — DOMESTIC — 10^{2}

ALTERNATING CURRENT

10^{10} — 10^{0}

From Robert Taft Sanitary Engineering Center

FIG. 14.1. THE ELECTRO-MAGNETIC SPECTRUM

Neutrons.—Heavy, electrically neutral, particles produced in immense quantities in nuclear piles.

The bactericidal effect of different wavelengths of radiant energy are shown in Table 14.1.

TABLE 14.1

BACTERICIDAL EFFECTS OF DIFFERENT WAVELENGTHS OF RADIANT ENERGY

Classification	Wavelength Angstroms	Germicidal Effects
A. Invisible long		
Radio	Very long	None
Infrared heat	8,000 and longer	Temperature may be raised
B. Visible		
Red, orange, yellow, green, blue, violet	4,000–8,000	Little or none
C. Invisible short		
Ultraviolet total range	136 to 4,000	
	3,200–4,000	Photographic and fluorescent range
	2,800–3,200	Human skin tanning antirachitic-vitamin D
	2,000–2,800	Maximum germicidal power
	1,500–2,000	Shuman region
	1,000	Ozone forming germicidal in proper concentration
X-rays	1,000–1,500	
Alpha, beta, and gamma rays	Less than 1,000	Germicidal
Cosmic rays	Very short	Probably germicidal

From Weiser, Mountney, and Gould (1971).

Robinson and Urbain (1960) reported that both gamma rays and electron beams destroy spoilage microorganisms. They differ in their manner of penetrating food and in absorption. Josephson (1963) reported that electrons can penetrate water or material of similar density approximately 1/10 in. per million electron volts.

Josephson (1963) cites the advantages and disadvantages for both gamma and beta irradiation. The costs for construction and installation of high energy radiation are expensive, highly trained personnel are required, maintenance is expensive, and measurable induced radioactivity from electron beams occurs with energies in excess of 12 mev.

Advantages of electron irradiation are: (1) the machine can be turned on and off; (2) it can deliver large doses of radiation in seconds; and (3) it has a high efficiency of utilization.

When isotopes are used, little expert attention is required once operational and safety procedures have been established. However, problems do occur because the radio isotopes disintegrate constantly making it difficult to work in the area, new isotopes must be moved in from the point of production, and replenishment must be made at relatively frequent intervals.

Units of Measurement

Goldblith (1963) has defined the units of measurement used for measuring radiation doses as follows:

Roentgen (r).—That quantity of X or gamma radiations producing one e.s.u. of charge of either sign per cc. of air under standard conditions of temperature and pressure.

Equivalents: 2.08×10^9 ion pairs/cc. of air (dry); 1.61×10^{12} ion pairs/gm. of air (dry); 5.24×10^7 mev. absorbed/gm. air (dry); 83.8 erg absorbed/gm. air (dry).

Rad.—Quantity of ionizing radiation which results in the absorption of 100 ergs per gram of irradiated material.

Erg.—A unit of energy expended when a force of one dyne acts through a distance of one centimeter.

$$1 \text{ erg} = 10^{-7} \text{ joules}$$

Watt.—Unit of power (P).

$$1 \text{ w.} = 10^7 \text{ ergs per sec.} = 1 \text{ joule per sec.}$$

Joule.—Amount of work $(W) = 10^7$ ergs.

$$P = \frac{W \text{ (joules)}}{\text{(watts) } t \text{ (sec.)}}$$

Curie.—That quantity of radioactive isotope which results in 3.700×10^{10} disintegrations per second.

Electron Volts (ev.).—Energy acquired by any charged particle carrying unit electronic charge when it falls through a potential difference of 1 v. ($1 \text{ ev.} = 1.60207 \times 10^{-12}$ erg).

Since the electron volt represents such a minute amount of energy, it is customary to calculate in units of million electron volts (mev.), where 10^6 ev. $= 1$ mev.

RADIATION PRESERVATION

Methods of Preservation

To be successful, radiation preservation of foods should kill or markedly reduce all microorganisms and parasites, produce food that is wholesome and safe with no undesirable change in color, flavor, or texture and at a reasonable cost. Four general criteria are used to measure the wholesomeness of irradiated food. They are the effects on nutritive value, the

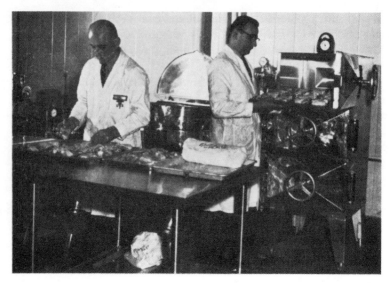

Courtesy U.S. Army Natick Laboratories

Fig. 14.2. Modern Food Preparation Area in U.S. Army Radiation Laboratory

Here, food technologists put preliminary touches on chicken portions which will later be preservation processed by ionizing radiation source.

Courtesy U.S. Army Natick Laboratories

Fig. 14.3. Overhead Conveyor System which Moves Foods for Processing Through the Cobalt 60 Radiation Area at the U.S. Army Laboratories. Foods Packed in Cans are Stacked in the Racks which Transport them to the Processing Chambers

possibility that toxic substances can be produced, the possibility that carcinogens might be produced and the possibility that the product itself might become radioactive.

Food can be preserved by radiation doses which kill all organisms (sterilization) or by pasteurization where large numbers but not all organisms are killed. Radiation can also be used as a component in combination with other methods of preservation such as chemical additives or with heat.

Figures 14.2 to 14.8 illustrate the various steps required for preparing and irradiating poultry meat.

Courtesy U.S. Army Natick Laboratories

FIG. 14.4.   CLOSED-CIRCUIT TV IS USED TO MONITOR EXPERIMENTAL
FOOD PROCESSING IN THE COBALT 60 SOURCE

To counteract the undesirable effects caused by radiation some products may need additional treatments. Goldblith (1963) reported that to prevent undesirable reactions from radiation, the products, depending upon their individual characteristics, can also be irradiated (1) while frozen, (2) in a vacuum or inert atmosphere, (3) with free radical scavengers, (4) after off-flavor precursors in the product have been removed by distillation, (5) after some moisture has been removed from the product, and (6) by pretreatment of the product to reduce the microbial load or make microorganisms more sensitive to radiation.

FIG. 14.5.　COBALT-60 SOURCE USED IN PRESERVATION PROCESSING OF FOODS

Products to be processed pass through cobalt pile, which is raised from this 25-foot-deep, water-filled storage pool, via an overhead conveyor system.　Tubes containing the cobalt may be seen rising from the pool.　All movement is monitored or "tracked" on a panel by remote control.

Effects of Radiation on Bacteria

Several possible explanations of the lethal effect of radiation on cells have been made (Fig. 14.9).　They are: (1) that the lethal properties of irradiation are caused by both direct and indirect hits; (2) radiation causes a change in the material of the nucleus; (3) mutation of the genes in the cell; or (4) inactivation of the enzyme system; or (5) a combination of these factors.

To determine the effects of radiation on bacteria, Kempe *et al.* (1954)

Courtesy U.S. Army Natick Laboratories

FIG. 14.6. WORLD'S LARGEST COBALT-60 RADIATION SOURCE USED IN EXPERIMENTAL PROCESSING OF MEATS, FISH, VEGETABLES, FRUITS AND OTHER FOODS AT NATICK, MASS., LABORATORIES OF U.S. ARMY MATERIAL COMMAND

inoculated two strains of *Cl. botulinum* and a heat resistant spore former into the center of cans of ground beef after sterilization but while still hot. The cans were sealed immediately after inoculation and irradiated in stacks of two with a dosage of 85,500 rep per hr. in the center of the can by rotating the cans in a field of Co^{60} gamma radiation. The central axes of the cans were $2\frac{1}{2}$ in. from the shield. The amount of gamma radiation required to sterilize meat varied linearly with the log of the spore concentration. Toxins were produced. The sterility dosage for canned beef increased from 2,500,000 to 4,000,000 rep of Co^{60} gamma radiation as the concentration of spores of *Cl. botulinum,* strain 62A increased from 0.4 to 40,000 per gm. of meat.

Proctor *et al.* (1956), in a study of the use of cathode ray irradiation of

Courtesy U.S. Army Natick Laboratories

FIG. 14.7. AN 18 KILOWATT, 24 MILLION ELECTRON VOLT (MEV) LINEAR
ACCELERATOR, USED FOR THE PRESERVATION OF FOOD BY IONIZING ENERGY

Courtesy U.S. Army Natick Laboratories

FIG. 14.8. FOOD CONTAINER CARRIER BEING LOADED ONTO CON-
VEYOR SYSTEM OF THE LINEAR ACCELERATOR AT U.S. ARMY NATICK
LABORATORIES

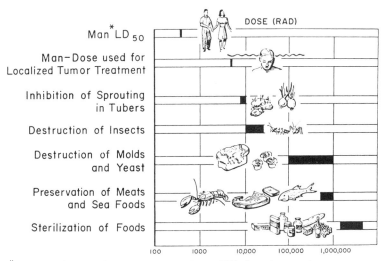

From Goldblith (1963)

FIG. 14.9. APPROXIMATE DOSAGES OF IONIZING RADIATIONS REQUIRED FOR SPECIFIC EFFECTS

chicken for extending shelf-life, reported that in four out of six trials chicken irradiated with levels of 2×10^6 high-voltage cathode rays and no pretreatment were not significantly different from control groups but in six trials where the dose was 2.5×10^6 rep there were significant differences. In three additional tests at the same levels they observed that vacuum packed chicken, frozen chicken, and chickens treated with free radical acceptors were not significantly different from control groups.

Cain et al. (1958), in a study of the effects of radiation and antibiotics on the shelf-life of meats, reported that after radiation at low levels antibiotics retained sufficient activity to protect meats during storage but that at 4.65 megarads, the level required for sterilization, the antibiotics were almost completely destroyed. Carcasses with antibiotics applied by injection and then irradiated at pasteurization levels had more than a threefold extension of shelf-life at 50°F. They concluded that the radiation level required for certain preservative effects could be lower if antibiotics were used, and, as a result, fewer adverse organoleptic changes would occur.

Coleby (1959) observed that there is general agreement that meat held at 32°–41°F. after irradiation at levels of 50,000 to 1,000,000 rads has a shelf-life five to ten times as long as non-irradiated meat. About 4.8 Mrads are required for sterilization doses for chicken meat.

Effect of Radiation on Organoleptic Qualities

Several workers have studied the effects of radiation and cooking on the organoleptic qualities of poultry meat. Coleby (1959), in a review of the effects of irradiation on the quality of meat and poultry reported that it is possible to detect organoleptic changes after irradiation with doses as low as 50,000 rads. After cooking, it is difficult if not impossible to detect such changes. In one experiment, after light cooking a dose

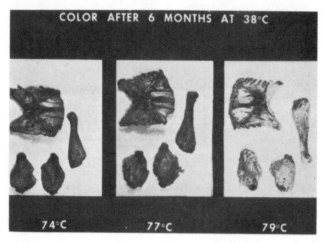

Courtesy U.S. Dept. Agr.

FIG. 14.10. EFFECT OF ENZYME INACTIVATION TEMPERATURES BEFORE IRRADIATION ON THE COLOR OF POULTRY MEAT STORED SIX MONTHS AT 100°F

of 250,000 rads was required before changes in minced chicken meat caused by irradiation could be detected. When chickens were roasted changes were only scarcely detectable at 800,000 rads. The shelf-life of chickens treated at this level was increased from 10–12 days to 60 days at 34°F.

Hanson *et al.* (1964) reported that taste panels could readily detect the odor and flavor in chicken meat caused by 0.1 Mrad if irradiated at ambient temperature. Deep fat frying reduced unpleasant odors and flavors more than other cooking methods. Almost no irradiation odor occurred when chicken was irradiated below −20°F. Upon storage at elevated temperatures irradiation odors and flavor decreased so that the differences between those irradiated at ambient temperatures and below freezing declined. Activated charcoal reduced adverse flavors. These workers concluded that the best combination of treatments appears to be enzyme inactivation prior to irradiation, irradiation at subfreezing temperature, packing with dry charcoal and then deep fat frying.

Oxygen present at the time of radiation tends to cause browning; in its absence a pink coloration occurs. Irradiation also hastens the onset of oxidative deterioration. Hanson *et al.* (1963) reported that chicken meat irradiated at 4.5-4.6 Mrads developed an objectionable red color after storage at elevated temperatures in the absence of oxygen. Heating the chicken to 176°F. before irradiation markedly reduced this condition (Fig. 14.10). Irradiated chicken meat stored at elevated temperatures also had liquids exuding from the meat and after cooking had a soft disintegrated texture and dryness.

The problem of flavor deterioration is as important as inhibition of microbial growth. Coleby (1959) found that although chickens irradiated with 800,000 rads at 34°F. will not spoil because of bacteria for more than eight weeks, the meat becomes insipid after three weeks.

Groninger *et al.* (1956) reported that the carotenoid pigments of chicken fat (mainly lutein depalmitate) are relatively labile to irradiation. As a result, the yellow skin and fat pigment are bleached during radiation treatment.

Lineweaver (1959) summarizing the status of radiation preservation of poultry meat made the following conclusions.

Shelf-life measured by microbial inhibition can be extended considerably. The spoilage pattern is altered and could be more hazardous than normal spoilage. Inert gas packing would probably be required to control rancidity. Antibiotics can supplement radiation. Neither, of course, is a substitute for sanitation.

Safety.—Extensive toxicity and nutritional studies make it appear thus far that no danger exists from chemical changes due to growth of pathogens resulting from accidental exposure to temperatures above 41°F.

Acceptability.—A half to one megarad, which is a pasteurizing dose, causes changes in flavor of cooked poultry that expert tasters can detect. The odor of uncooked birds is considered objectionable. The color of cooked birds (pinkness) is possibly objectionable.

Costs.—It is generally considered that a pasteurizing dose would cost only a few tenths of a cent per pound for machine-produced beta rays. At present the cost for gamma rays would be significantly higher. These costs do not include product handling charges but do include radiation power, equipment, operation, and overhead.

BIBLIOGRAPHY

ANON. 1964. Commercial radiation processes. Food Process. 25, 67-76.

CAIN, R. F., ANDERSON, A. W., and MALASPINA, A. S. 1958. Effect of radiation on antibiotic-treated meats. Food Technol. 12, 582-584.

COLEBY, R. 1958. Processing of foods with ionizing radiations. Nature 181, 877.

COLEBY, R. 1959. The effects of irradiation on the quality of meat and poultry. Intern. J. Appl. Radiation Isotopes 6, 115-121.

GOLDBLITH, S. A. 1963. Radiation processing of foods and drugs. In Food Processing Operations, Vol. I. M. A. Joslyn and J. L. Heid (Editors). Avi Publishing Co., Westport, Conn.

GRONINGER, H. S., TAPPEL, A. L., and KNAPP, F. W. 1956. Some chemical and organoleptic changes in gamma irradiated meats. Food Res. 21, 555-563.

HANSON, L. L., BRUSHWAY, M. J., and LINEWEAVER, H. 1964. Flavor studies of irradiation-sterilized chicken. Food Technol. 18, 141-146.

HANSON, H. L., BRUSHWAY, M. J., POOL, M. F., and LINEWEAVER, H. 1963. Factors causing color and texture differences in radiation-sterilized chicken. Food Technol. 17, 188-194.

JOSEPHSON, E. S. 1963. Radiation preservation of foods. In Eastern Experiment Station Collaborator's Conference on Food Processing Techniques. Eastern Util. Develop. Div., Agr. Res. Serv., U.S. Dept. Agr.

KEMPE, L. L., GRAILOSKI, J. T., and GILLIES, R. A. 1954. Gamma ray sterilization of canned meat previously inoculated with anaerobic bacterial spores. Appl. Microbiol. 2, 330-332.

LINEWEAVER, H. 1959. Use of high energy radiation to pasteurize poultry. Proc. Conf. Eggs Poultry, U.S. Dept. Agr., Agr. Res. Serv., Albany, Calif.

MCGILL, J. N., NELSON, A. I., STEINBERG, M. I., and KEMPE, L. L. 1959. Gamma ray pasteurization of whole eviscerated chicken. Food Technol. 13, 75-80.

PIZER, V. 1970. Preserving Food with Atomic Energy. United States Atomic Energy Commission, Division of Technical Information, Oak Ridge, Tenn.

PROCTOR, B. E. NICKERSON, J. T. R., and LICCIARDELLO, J. J. 1956. Cathode ray irradiation of chicken meat for the extension of shelf life. Food Res. 21, 11-20.

ROBINSON, H. E., and URBAIN, W. M. 1960. Radiation preservation of foods. J. Am. Med. Assoc., 174, 1310-1311.

SHEFFNER, L. A., ADACHI, R., and SPECTOR, H. 1957. The effect of radiation processing upon the in vitro digestibility and nutritional quality of proteins. Food Res. 22, 455-461.

WEISER, H. H., MOUNTNEY, G. J., and GOULD, W. A. 1971 Practical Food Microbiology and Technology, 2nd Edition. Avi Publishing Co., Westport, Conn.

CHAPTER 15

Other Processed Products

INTRODUCTION

A number of factors have contributed to the rapid development of a variety of new further processed convenience items made from poultry meats. Among them are: the surpluses of poultry meat, particularly lightweight fowl which in some cases are sold at a low price; the resulting small price of poultry meat relative to other meats; better quality poultry; development of deboning machines; improvements in processing, storing, and marketing further processed items to prevent decline in quality; and the increase in demand for convenient heat-and-serve poultry items.

Bauermann (1962) reported that of 35 Pennsylvania plants manufacturing 108 different items made from eggs and poultry meat over half contained chicken meat in some form and slightly over a third contained turkey meat. Chicken products included part of a dinner such as barbecued chicken meat, chicken roll, or chicken steak. A second area was in the combination with other ingredients to manufacture products such as chicken pie, chicken a-la-king, chicken croquettes, and chicken soup. Preparations such as chicken stew and chicken noodle dinners constituted the third category. Examples of turkey products included turkey pies, turkey rolls, turkey croquettes, and turkey steaks. Other products included specialty items such as smoked goose, duck, game hen, and pheasants. Seventeen brands and sizes of frozen chicken pies alone were observed.

Harp and Dunham (1963) in a comparison of costs of convenience foods and home-prepared foods found that eight out of twelve poultry convenience foods in which comparisons were made were more expensive than the home-prepared counterpart (Figs. 15.1, 15.2, 15.3). In general, canned poultry products sold for less than the housewife could prepare them, but frozen foods were considerably higher than those prepared at home. In a few cases where frozen foods were low in price, it was because they did not contain as much meat as their canned counterpart. Cut-up chickens for frying cost 5% more than whole chickens. Frozen batter-dipped chicken cost 50% more than the home-prepared forms and frozen pre-fried chicken 100%. Frozen chicken and turkey dinners cost $2^1/_2$ times as much as the home-prepared form.

BONING POULTRY MEAT

Marshall (1964) working at Cornell University reported that the cost of meat from chickens must be comparable in price and/or more desirable than competing products if demand is to be increased. Cutter-canner cow meat is the chief competitor with poultry meat, particularly fowl. In the period July 1961–July 1962 he reported that the delivered price of frozen hand-boned, raw chicken meat in large quantities ranged from 41 to 53 cents a pound with an average price of about 46 cents, which is about the same price as boned cow meat. Meat boned with a machine should sell for even less. If the price of uncooked poultry meat, particularly from fowl, can be reduced further, then poultry meat should be in a position to compete with comminuted products made from red meats.

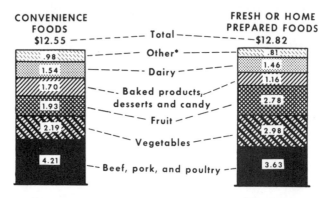

Courtesy U.S. Dept. Agr.

FIG. 15.1. COST OF CONVENIENCE FOODS VS. FRESH OR HOME PREPARED FOODS

Amounts normally spent on convenience foods processed from U.S. farm commodities per $100 spent for all food in grocery stores and cost of duplicating these amounts with fresh or home prepared foods. ° Includes berries, potatoes, rice, pizza, spaghetti and baby food.

MECHANICALLY DEBONED POULTRY MEAT (MDPM)[1]

The rapid development of further processed poultry products and the ever-increasing demand for animal source protein have heightened the interest in and the demand for mechanically deboned poultry meat (MDPM). MDPM is a comminuted product commonly obtained from turkey frames, poultry backs and necks, or the entire carcass of spent fowl which have been processed through an automatic deboner.

Mechanical deboned meat products are believed to have originated with the Japanese who have used forms of mechanical deboning for generations in the production of boneless fish meat. Mechanical

---

[1] This section prepared by Dr. Morris Mast, Pennsylvania State University.

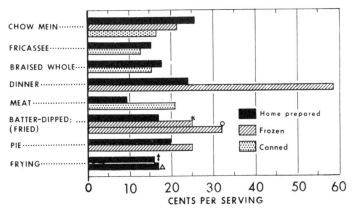

Courtesy U.S. Dept. Agr.

FIG. 15.2. RETAIL COST PER SERVING OF CHICKEN

° Raw, breaded; ○, prefried; ‡, purchased whole; Δ, purchased cut-up.

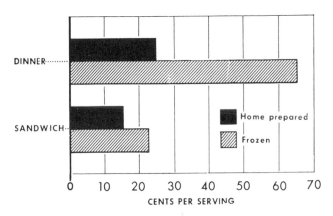

Courtesy U.S. Dept. Agr.

FIG. 15.3. RETAIL COST PER SERVING OF TURKEY

deboners were first used on a limited basis in the poultry industry in this country in the late 1950's. However, it was not until the mid-1960's that the machines were accepted and used on a larger scale by the poultry industry. Currently, several manufacturers market mechanical deboners which have been approved by the USDA Animal and Plant Health Inspection Service. These approved machines are listed in the publication "Accepted Meat and Poultry Equipment" (Anon. 1975A).

Waskiewicz (1962) described a machine developed for deboning cooked, whole poultry and poultry parts. The machine mechanically loosens meat on the bone with an extractor and impact plate which presses the meat through a grill. Then the bones and meat are separated by means of brine flotation. The meat floats and the heavier bone sinks. The machine can process an average volume of 2000 lb. per hour of fowl, 2400 lb. of roosters, 3400 lb. of turkeys, 1000 lb. of fowl necks, or 1500 lb. of turkey necks. The yields are reported to be better than those obtained by hand.

Most of the currently used automatic deboners, however, do not use brine flotation in their operation. Instead, a two-step procedure is generally used where the meat/bone is initially chopped or cut-up and then passed through a separator device. Separation of meat (soft

Courtesy Stephen Paoli Manufacturing Co.

Fig. 15.4.   A Deboning Machine for Raw Poultry Meat

material) from the bone (hard material) is achieved by forcing the material through a screen or seive device, normally under high pressure. This results in a finely chopped deboned meat coming out of the separator in one stream and tendons, bones, gristle, and sinews in another.

In addition to using USDA approved equipment, processors preparing MDPM must also adhere to the following rules specified by USDA (Anon. 1975B):

1. Process each species or kind of poultry separately.

2. Use equipment and raw materials that will eliminate or reduce collagenous material (skin, tendons, etc.) to the extent that the finished product will meet the nutritional requirements shown in Table 15.1. Raw materials may be either chilled, cooked, or warmed parts and/or carcasses.

TABLE 15.1

PROPOSED PROTEIN QUALITY[1] AND FAT STANDARDS FOR MECHANICALLY DEBONED POULTRY MEAT

	Minimum Protein (%)	Minimum PER	Minimum Amino Acids (%)	Maximum Fat (%)
Raw chicken meat	15	2.5	33.0	30
Cooked chicken	21	2.5	33.0	30
Raw turkey meat	16	2.5	33.0	30
Cooked turkey meat	22	2.5	33.0	30

Source: Anon. (1975B).
[1]Minimum protein quality shall be on the basis of either protein efficiency ratio (PER) or the percentage of the following amino acids expressed as a percentage of the total protein: phenylalanin, isoleucine, leucine, lysine, methionine, tryptophan, valine, and threonine. PER if used, should be adjusted to 2.50 for casein.

3. Raw bones and adhering meat from chilled carcasses must be held at temperatures no higher than 40°F., and processed or frozen within 72 hours after boning.

4. Raw bones and adhering meat from warm carcasses of freshly slaughtered poultry or cooked bones and adhering meat must either be machine processed within 4 hours, or held in storage at 40°F. or less for not more than 72 hours. If not processed within 72 hours, it must be placed in storage facilities maintained at 0°F. or less.

5. Mechanically deboned poultry meat must be used immediately in formulating other meat or poultry food products, or chilled to 40°F. within one hour. If not used within 72 hours, it must be placed directly into storage facilities maintained at 0°F. or less and held at that temperature until used.

The percentage of bone solids (PBS) in the final MDPM must be below 1% (Code of Federal Regulations 1971). This is determined by measuring the amount of calcium present in the meat and subsequently converting this value to PBS. Grunden and MacNeil (1973) noted that the deboned meat from the more mature types of poultry, such as mature female turkey racks and spent layer carcasses, had higher bone solids than their younger counterparts, i.e., young male turkey racks and broiler parts. This reflects the higher degree of calcification in the bones of older birds, causing more fragmentation when passing through the deboner, and thereby resulting in an increased level of bone particles.

The composition of MDPM varies considerably depending upon the raw material, the type of deboning equipment, and the processing procedure used. Although the protein requirements proposed by USDA for MDPM prepared from raw chicken meat and raw turkey meat, as presented in Table 15.1, are 15% and 16% respectively, a review of the current literature (Table 15.2) shows many of the reported protein

TABLE 15.2

PROXIMATE DATA OF MECHANICALLY DEBONED POULTRY MEAT

Deboned Material	Protein (%)	Moisture (%)	Fat (%)
Broiler necks and backs[5]	9.3	63.3	27.2
Chicken necks and backs[3]	14.5	66.6	17.6
Chicken backs[7]	12.5	65.5	11.2
Chicken backs[3]	13.2	62.8	21.2
Turkey, male, entire carcass[6]	16.2	61.5	19.5
Turkey, male, carcass, dark meat[2]	13.3	67.6	15.0
Turkey, male, carcass, light meat[2]	11.8	70.8	12.4
Turkey frame[3]	13.5	73.1	11.5
Turkey, male, racks, 24 wk[5]	12.8	73.7	12.7
Turkey, female, racks, 52 wk[5]	11.7	63.4	22.5
Turkey, frame, no skin[4]	13.1	68.4	17.2
Turkey, breast bone[7]	14.7	72.4	10.0
Spent hens, carcass[5]	14.2	60.1	26.2
Spent hens, carcass[1]	16.5	65.2	16.6

[1] Cunningham and Mugler (1974).
[2] Essary and Ritchey (1968).
[3] Froning (1970).
[4] Froning et al. (1971).
[5] Grunden et al. (1972).
[6] Johnson et al. (1974).
[7] Pauly (1967).

levels below these standards. In addition, only a few of the fat values shown in Table 15.2 approach the 30% maximum allowable.

Protein quality standards for MDPM (see Table 15.1) propose that this product possess a minimum protein efficiency ratio (PER) of 2.5, or that 33% of the total protein be composed of the eight essential amino acids. Essary and Ritchey (1968) examined the amino acid composition of mechanically deboned raw dark and light turkey meat. They found this meat to have a satisfactory amino acid content quite similar to that of regular turkey meat.

Due to the comminuted nature of mechanically deboned meat, this material readily lends itself for use in emulsified products such as frankfurters. At the present time, 15% poultry meat may be added into frankfurter formulations without changing the name of the finished product. In addition, all-poultry frankfurters have been successfully formulated using MDPM as the meat source. Such products are currently on the market.

Schnell et al. (1973) prepared all-chicken frankfurters from hand-deboned meat and also MDPM. The flavor and acceptability of the products were not significantly different; however, the hand-deboned product was firmer. Maurer (1973) reported that mechanically deboned broiler backs and necks had similar emulsifying characteristics as their hand-deboned counterparts. By removing the skin from these parts prior to mechanical deboning, thereby lowering the fat content, the emulsifying and water-holding capacities were increased. Froning *et al.* (1971) reported that if frankfurters were prepared using 15% fresh deboned poultry meat, the end product was comparable to an all red meat frankfurter in flavor stability. However, they also noted that if MDPM which had undergone 90 days of frozen storage, was used in the preparation of the frankfurters, an inferior product resulted as indicated by flavor scores and thiobarbituric acid (TBA) values.

Decrease in the quality of the lipid portion of mechanically deboned meat is a problem when the product is held under frozen conditions for prolonged periods of time. This deterioration is frequently monitored by using the TBA test to detect oxidative rancidity.

Freshly processed MDPM will usually have a TBA value below 2. However, during storage the TBA values generally increase. When Moerck and Ball (1974) stored mechanically deboned chicken meat at 4°C. for 15 days, the TBA value increased to 22. Froning *et al.* (1971) and Johnson *et al.* (1974) reported TBA values of 16.8 and 13, respectively, for mechanically deboned turkey meat stored under frozen conditions (−24°C. and −26°C.) for 90 days.

Materials such as polyphosphates, butylated hydroxyanisole (BHA) plus citric acid, and rosemary spice extractive (RSE) have been experimentally added to MDPM in an attempt to control oxidative rancidity. In one such study, MacNeil *et al.* (1973) demonstrated that MDPM containing these additives maintained lower TBA values and reduced bacterial levels, as compared to untreated MDPM, when stored at 3°C. Moerck and Ball (1974) were also able to effectively control the TBA value of mechanically deboned chicken meat, during storage at 4°C., by adding 0.01% Tenox II (BHA, propyl gallate, and citric acid). Mast (1975) reported that the TBA values of MDPM could be stabilized during frozen storage (−18°C.) by initially subjecting the product to heat pasteurization (e.g., 59°C. for 4 min.).

Mechanically deboned poultry meat, which is stored untreated at temperatures above freezing has a relatively short shelf-life. Spoilage of most poultry, including MDPM, is usually evidenced by off-odor as the total number of microorganisms approaches 10^7 cells per gram. When Ostovar *et al.* (1971) investigated the microbiological quality of mechanically deboned broiler necks and backs, whole fowl, and turkey racks, they found the average microbial count of these products to be 4.6×10^5 per gram. This increased to more than 1.0×10^8 per gram when stored at 3°C. for 12 days. The predominant psychrotolerant bacteria which they isolated were species of *Pseudomonas*, *Flavobacterium*, and *Achromobacter*. Maxcy *et al.* (1973) reported similar results on the microbial quality of both hand-deboned and

MDPM. The products had an initial microbial level of approximately 1.0 × 10⁵ and this increased within 4 days of storage at 5°C. to approximately 1.0×10^8 per gram. *Bacillus* species and Gram negative rods accounted for most of the microflora isolated.

By adding 1% aureomycin to MDPM prior to storage at 4°C., Moerck and Ball (1974) effectively reduced the microbial load to less than 1,000 cells per gram and maintained this level throughout the 15-day storage period. However, the TBA of this product increased to 50 during this period.

Young and Lyon (1973), in an effort to lower the bacterial load of mechanically deboned meat, heated the product to an internal temperature of 65°C. before incorporating it into frankfurters. Frankfurters which they produced were satisfactory when they contained no more than 30% MDPM. The problem with heating MDPM before incorporating it into a product is that some physical and functional properties are destroyed as the protein is denatured. This is particularly critical if an emulsion type product is desired. Mast and MacNeil (1975) were successful in extending the shelf-life of mechanically deboned meat by reducing the initial level of bacteria through heat pasteurization. However, the rate of bacterial growth in the pasteurized MDPM was equivalent to that of the nonpasteurized MDPM. Mast (1975) demonstrated that certain functional properties of MDPM, such as emulsifying capacity and water-holding capacity, were impaired through the heat pasteurization process.

In the past, many of the poultry backs, hand-deboned carcasses, etc., were sold at low prices by the processor to pet food and fertilizer manufacturers. By processing these materials through mechanical deboners, yields of 40–75% edible bone-free meat of good protein quality can be economically obtained. The wholesale price of MDPM is approximately $0.25 per lb.; however, prices have flucuated from $0.15 per lb. to more than $0.60 per lb., depending on current supplies and demands.

In addition to its use in frankfurters, MDPM is suitable for use in most products where conventional ground meat is used. Such products may include poultry rolls, soups, salads, chicken a la king, etc. As advancements are made in controlling the shelf-life of both non-frozen and frozen MDPM, its acceptance will improve and additional markets, such as direct sale to the consumer, will be expanded.

QUALITY CONTROL PROCEDURES FOR COOKING AND DEBONING

The United States Department of Agriculture Poultry Inspector's Handbook (Anon. 1964A) has listed the following policy statements concerning processing, cooking, and deboning of poultry meat:

Open kettle cooking of thawed ready-to-cook poultry is the most common acceptable method of cooking and may be carried out in steam jacketed or direct heat kettles of various sizes and designs. Poultry carcasses of approximately the same size are placed into kettles and covered with water or broth. Cooking at boiling temperatures shall be continued until the meat can be readily removed from the bone without falling from the bone. Good commercial practice permits two to four batches of raw poultry to be cooked in the same broth. Skimming of fat and replacing moisture loss due to evaporation is usually carried out as conditions warrant.

Cooked whole carcass poultry may be cooled in air, in flowing water, in broth, or in contact with chipped ice. Contact with ice or cooling liquids (ice and water), shall not exceed 30 minutes. Even dispersion of product is essential to assure uniform chilling.

Pressure kettle cooking is satisfactory and permits reduction in cooking time and exposure to water.

Precautions to be observed with open kettle cooking also apply to pressure type cooking procedures.

Deboning cooked poultry by hand, by mechanical means, or a combination of the two methods is acceptable providing bone is thus actually all removed. During the boning process bones shall not be changed in size or form to the extent the visual identification is impossible at normal production rates. The use of laboratory procedures in lieu of complete visual inspection to ensure freedom from bone is not acceptable.

In order to reduce contamination introduced by deboning, the following practices shall be permitted and receive attention by the inspector: (1) Use of knives and plastic or hard rubber cutting boards; (2) frequent sanitizing of operator's hands during deboning and following interruption of work and sanitizing knife handles, aprons, etc., are essential; (3) use of stainless steel tables and deboning pans; (4) complete rinsing of tables, floors, etc., during work interruption, at lunch breaks, and when practical at rest period, and thorough cleanup during scheduled change of work shifts; (5) frequent dismantling and cleaning of dicing equipment, grinders, etc. (at mid-shift and at end of each work shift, or more frequently when deemed necessary by the inspector-in-charge); and (6) rapid cooling of deboned product. Cooked and/or deboned product should be placed under refrigeration or further processed by cooking within 2 hr. from the time of exposure to room temperature.

Mechanical deboning of cooked poultry carcasses or parts is satisfactory provided the design, construction, and efficiency of the equipment have received prior approval from the Inspection Branch, Washington Offices, and plant blueprints have been officially modified. Approval must also be obtained concerning the water, salt, etc., that may be introduced to the deboned end product through use of the equipment.

Brine Flotation Systems used in deboning have been approved. However, there are certain requirements necessary to maintain the sanitation of the brine and equipment: (1) unless otherwise provided (approved), all brine tanks shall be drained and sanitized after 4 hr. operation; (2) the reserve brine tank shall be drained and sanitized after every 2 hr. operation; and (3) a continuous overflow of brine shall be maintained during the operation. The overflow shall be sufficient to maintain a solution which is acceptable from the viewpoint of wholesome appearance.

Special procedures in handling deboned poultry and poultry products shall not be permitted unless the procedure is outlined in the approved formula for the product or products being further processed.

CONVENIENCE POULTRY PRODUCTS

Harp and Dunham (1963) defined convenience foods as those which have services added to the basic ingredients to reduce the amount of preparation required in the home.

Pre-Cooked Frozen Diced Poultry Meat

J. D. Jewell, Inc. (Anon. 1964B) merchandised cooked diced chicken meat packaged in waxed cardboard cartons which contain two 5-oz poly bags of diced chicken meat in the natural proportions of white to dark. The packages also contain a number of recipes for using the meat. The product is used in salads, creamed dishes, and exotic recipes.

Frozen Poultry Pot Pies

An article in *Food Engineering* (Anon. 1956A), describes the production of frozen poultry pot pies (Fig. 15.5A–15.5H). The first step involves thawing the carcasses in a defrosting tank and then cooking them 15 min. at 15 lb. pressure or for about 4 hr. in steam vats. Next the carcasses are cooled in tanks and filtered. The carcasses are then deboned with the skin and meat sorted into separate batches. The meat and skin are then chilled at around 36°F. for 3–4 hr. at which time the meat is run through a dicer. The skins are run through a meat grinder and then a comminuter. Precooked vegetables, separately prepared and blended, are then mixed with gravy. The gravy is prepared from skin-paste broth, spices, seasonings, stabilizers, etc., in a jacketed kettle fitted with an agitator. After mixing vegetables and gravy, the material is ready for cooling and filling.

Aluminum foil pie plates are dispensed onto chain-driven metal plate holders for transfer to the pie-making machine where an automatic divider cuts out dough balls. The dough balls eventually are dropped into dusting flour where they are picked up and then rolled twice. The crust is then deposited and tamped around the bottom and sides of the plates. Then the gravy mix is automatically measured into the pies in 5-oz. portions. Next girls add diced poultry meat to the pies, the top is placed on, crimped, and sealed. Finally the pies are cartoned, quick frozen, and then overwrapped.

One of the main problems in merchandising poultry pies has been the tendency to add more and more filler and less meat. As a result the U.S.

Department of Agriculture has set up standards which require all plants operating under government inspection to have at least 14% cooked chicken by weight or $1^1/_8$ oz. for each 8-oz. pie.

Complete Prepared Frozen Dinners

Fried chicken and sliced chicken and turkey are used extensively as the meat portion of complete "heat and serve" dinners. The first such dinners used poultry as the meat item.

Frozen Fried Chicken

In the past it has not been possible to produce a satisfactory frozen fried chicken product. Such products were dry, stringy, soggy, and had a distinct warmed-over flavor. Although more progress has been made, these problems have never been solved satisfactorily. Because of the cooking loss, the price in relation to fresh chicken is high. Another problem has been to get a breading mixture which sticks after frying and freezing.

By adding antioxidants, the development of rancidity has been reduced and some of the other problems have been modified by quick freezing. Monosodium glutamate can be used to enhance the flavor which is lost on prolonged storage. Several companies have attempted to market frozen fried chicken but at present only a few brands are on the market (Fig. 15.6).

The following information relative to producing fried poultry products is taken from the U.S. Department of Agriculture poultry division, Poultry Inspector's Handbook (1964).

Heat processing by deep-fat frying may be performed in continuous frying machines with endless belt type equipment or in batch type open kettles. Poultry products that are pre-cooked with moist heat followed by battering

FIG. 15.5.   MANUFACTURING POULTRY PIES

(A) Bones are sorted from cooked chicken which has been broken into smaller pieces by machine for use in prepared poultry products. (B) A U.S. Dept. Agr. poultry inspector examines dough to be used in poultry pies. (C) Dough for making poultry pies is placed in the rolling machine, which rolls it thin for crusts. (D) The machine shown here places a measured amount of sauce in each poultry pie prepared at the processing plant. (E) The turkey filling and top-crust operation is accomplished as turkey pies move in groups of four along the conveyor line. (F) As the pies move to the right under this machine, each set of four automatically receives a top crust. (G) A machine crimps the edge of the crust on poultry pies to form a seal between the upper and lower layers. It then trims away extra dough around the edges of the tins. (H) The finished poultry pies are packaged and sealed in this operation. $\longrightarrow$

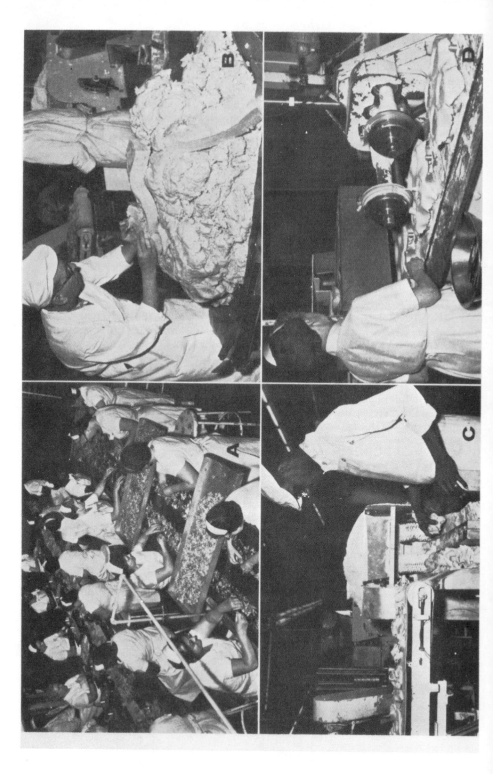

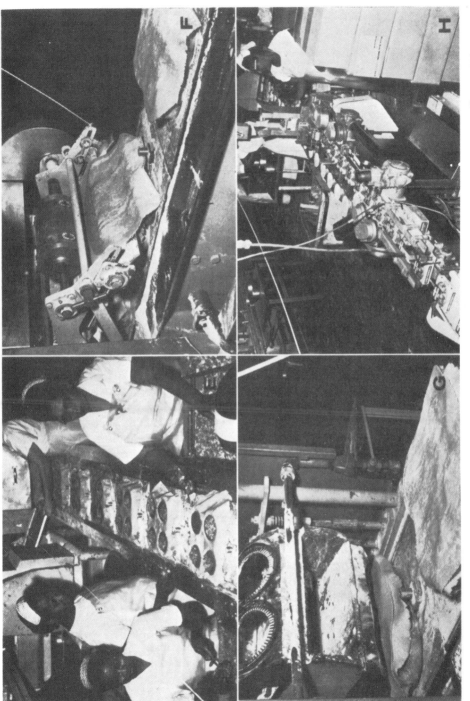

Courtesy U.S. Dept. Agr.

FIG. 15.6. FRIED CHICKEN PARTS COMING OFF THE END OF THE CONVEYOR IN A
PROCESSING PLANT. THE PARTS WILL BE FROZEN FOR USE IN POULTRY CONVENIENCE
FOODS

and breading to render them ready-to-fry are not considered fried products
of the ready-to-eat variety.

Reinspection of poultry products prior to battering, breading, and frying
is necessary to determine that they are sound and free from pin feathers,
bone fragments, etc., and are in ready-to-cook condition. Subsequent processing may obscure unwholesome conditions of the original product.

Battering and breading may be performed in a single operation or may
be carried out in separate operations. Mixtures for battering or breading may
be prepared from individual components or they may be purchased ready-mixed.
Where commercial mixtures are used, the inspector shall limit the use to
the particular brand specified in the label approval. Those mixed at the
official plant shall be strictly limited to the approved formula. Components
in these mixtures must be properly listed in the ingredient statement on the
approved label for the finished product.

The amount of batter and breading permitted on fried poultry parts will
vary, depending on the amount of water used to reconstitute the mixtures,
as well as with the particular poultry part to be fried. The inspector shall
limit the amount of batter-breading on the finished product to less than 30%
of the total product weight. Where necessary, during inspection sampling,
the inspector shall remove batter-breading by washing or other satisfactory
method in order to weigh the exact amount on the product.

Time and temperature required to completely fry poultry parts depends on the type and weight of product being fried as well as the equipment. Acceptable frying operations should be carried out at approximately 275°F. or higher from 10 to 13 min. when there has been no pre-cooking of the parts.

Frying fats especially adapted to frying poultry are commercially available. These commercially prepared fats may contain antioxidants or antifoaming agents for the purpose of retarding breakdown of the fat into free-fatty acids and other noxious materials. There is no objection to these agents. Such materials do not require separate declaration in the label ingredient on the finished product. If the poultry processor himself adds any of these agents to the frying fat, it must be noted in the approved product formula of the poultry product although it need not be listed in the ingredient statement.

The inspector must determine the acceptability of fat that has been previously used, and to reject as unwholesome fat that is not free of impurities. Used fat may at times be rendered satisfactory by filtering, adding additional fresh fat, and thorough regular adequate cleaning of the equipment. Large amounts of sediment and free-fatty acid content in excess of two per cent are the usual indications that frying fats are unwholesome and require reconditioning or replacement. Sediment is usually removed by filtering and the addition of fresh or new fat automatically reduces the free-fatty acid to acceptable levels. Some types of frying equipment are designed to continuously filter the fat during operation periods while in other types, the fat must be filtered following the end of processing. The filter medium through which the fat is filtered must not contaminate the fat. Maintaining frying fat in satisfactory condition is governed by the amount of use, the type of product being fried, and the frequency and thoroughness of cleaning. Fat used for frying marine products (fish, including shell fish) is not satisfactory for purposes of frying poultry although there is no objection to the use of fat for frying poultry which has been used for the frying of potatoes. It is satisfactory to keep frying fat warm in liquid form when not in use, since this practice avoids localized excess heating and breakdown of the fat that may occur during melting of the fat providing that the holding temperature is not permitted to fall below 180°F.

Cleaning of frying equipment is required at regular intervals. Continuous filtering or flushing with clean fat is satisfactory for limited periods of time. Complete draining, however, followed by dismantling and scouring or otherwise thorough cleaning of the equipment is necessary to accomplish acceptable sanitizing. Traces of water and detergents increase the rate of fat breakdown, and must be completely removed from pipelines, valves, pumps, etc., prior to refilling the deep fat fryer with clean fat. All connecting pipelines, valves, filters, pumps, etc., must be of sanitary construction, readily accessible to cleaning, and preferably constructed of stainless steel. Rubber and some types of plastic connecting lines are not acceptable.

Frozen Stuffed Poultry

Problems regarding bacterial contamination and growth and variations in housewives preferences for different recipes, are involved in the production of frozen stuffed poultry.

Bacterial growth can result both from the materials used in most stuffings which are also good bacteriological media and from possible mishandling of the carcass by leaving it at room temperature after thawing or by not cooking the carcass sufficiently so that the heat can penetrate and sterilize the stuffing. Strict quality control methods are used to control these problems during production and to ensure low bacterial counts. The ingredients used are of the type which do not support the growth of microorganisms. Because the body cavity is filled, particular attention must be given to make sure the entire carcass and stuffing are frozen rapidly.

The U.S. Department of Agriculture Poultry Inspector's Handbook (Anon. 1964A) lists the following precautions to be observed in preparing such stuffing:

(1) Bread to be used in preparation of stuffing should not be damaged or contaminated in any way, and shall be delivered and held in sanitary containers. Fresh commercially prepared bread, as well as day-old bread, is satisfactory. (2) Stuffing by hand or mechanical equipment is satisfactory. The filling of the carcasses with stuffing must be accomplished as rapidly as possible to avoid time lags which invite objectionable bacterial growth. (3) The prepared stuffing should be used within a short time after preparation and should be chilled to approximately 35°F. prior to use. (4) Stuffing operations should be carried on at room temperature of less than 70°F. while birds are kept chilled. (5) Stuffed poultry carcasses should be placed in freezer immediately after stuffing and bagging and should be solidly frozen within 24 hr.

Stuffing for commercial use generally contains dry bread, shortening, salt, chopped peeled onions, chopped celery, seasoning, and monosodium glutamate, Generally no moisture is added to prevent the bread from becoming soggy.

Courtesy Cornell University

Fig. 15.7.   Chicken Sticks

Chicken Sticks

Tressler *et al.* (1968) reported that chicken sticks were first introduced in 1954. They contain prepared rice, small pieces of cooked chicken, a purée of chicken meats, and seasonings. Marshall (1963), working in the Poultry Dept. at Cornell University, used the following ingredients and processes (Fig. 15.7).

Ingredient	Amount	
Ground raw chicken	90	lb.
Cereal binder[1]	1.8	lb.
Non-fat dry milk	4.5	lb.
Seasonings[2]	10.5	oz.
Salt	21	oz.
Water	3.75	qt.
Vinegar (4–5% acidity)	28	oz.
Batter mix		
Flour	4	lb.
Fresh or frozen whole eggs	3	lb.
or dried whole eggs	0.75	lb.
Seasoning[3]	4	oz.
Water to make	2	gal. batter
Cornflake crumbs[4]	13	lb.

[1] Cereal binder = a mixture of corn, wheat, oats, rye, and barley.

[2] Seasonings = that used in chicken loaf, containing approximately 52% salt. This can be adjusted according to preference.

[3] Seasoning in batter mix = a poultry seasoning blend originally developed for flavoring a chicken barbecue sauce.

[4] Cornflakes crumbs were used in preference to other types of crumb coatings because they made the product look attractive before cooking as well as after cooking. Since the chicken sticks were sold uncooked and could be seen through the window in the package, this was important.

Procedure.—The partially thawed, boned chicken was first ground, using a 1/2-in. plate, and then reground with 1/8-in. plate. The dry ingredients were blended first and then all ingredients were well mixed in a mixer. Two methods were used to form the chilled mixture into sticks of 3/4 in. × 3/4 in.: (1) It was fed into a machine designed to shape pork sausage sticks and other related items. The sticks were then frozen, and later dipped in the batter and cornflake crumbs. (2) The mixture was frozen in pans 3/4 in. deep and cut into sticks with a meat saw. These were then dipped in batter and cornflake crumbs. The final product was packaged and stored in the freezer at −10°F. until market-tested.

Steaks

To manufacture chicken and turkey steaks and patties, raw breast and thigh meat are cut from the bones and then the skin is removed. Several chunks of meat, usually 4 oz., are run through a steak tenderizer which kneads the pieces into a patty about 3 in. in diameter. These are seasoned and fried. Steaks can be made from mixed white or dark meat. They are quick and easy to prepare and have a rather delicate flavor.

A number of problems are involved in the production of turkey steaks. Among them are finding a use for the backs, wings, necks, and giblets, the expense of deboning turkey meat by hand, dehydrating, and rancidity.

Patties

Skin, fat, and miscellaneous pieces of raw, deboned poultry meat can be ground, mixed, made into patties, and frozen. In some ways these have a better texture and flavor than steaks. With fat incorporated in the patty, rancidity becomes a problem. Antioxidants must be used. Turkey fat in

Courtesy Cornell University

FIG. 15.8.   CHICKEN FRANKS

Courtesy Cornell University

FIG. 15.9.   TWO TYPES OF BOLOGNA MADE FROM CHICKEN MEAT

particular is very unstable because it does not have the natural antioxidants contained in chicken fat. Both steaks and patties can be placed in the frying pan while frozen. Generally the meat is seasoned, floured, or dipped in batter before frying.

Sausage

Sausage preparations can be made from poultry meat. Essary and Goff (1951) give the following directions for making chicken sausage.

Sausage is made from poultry meat free from skin, bones, and tendons. The meat should be coarsely ground, mixed with seasoning, and reground. The product may be prepared as bulk sausage or as link sausage. (Additional fat should be incorporated in this product.)

6 lb. ground poultry meat
3 tbsp salt $^1/_4$ tbsp red pepper
1 $^1/_2$ tbsp black pepper $^1/_4$ lb. dried milk

Chicken Franks

Marshall (1961) working in the Poultry Department at Cornell University reported the following formulation and procedure for making chicken franks (Fig. 15.8).

Ingredients	Amount
Raw chicken	86 lb.
Chicken fat, cubed	14 lb.
Ice	38 lb.
Non-fat dry milk	4 lb. 10 oz.
Stange cream of spice	
Chicken loaf seasoning	3 lb. 5 oz.
Salt	1 lb. 10 oz.
Monosodium glutamate	2 oz.
Paprika	2 oz.
Cure mixture[1]	1 qt.
Sodium isoascorbate[2]	12 fl. oz.

Grind partially frozen chicken through $^1/_2$-in. plate. Place chicken, cure and salt, and $^1/_3$ of ice in cutter bowl and start chopping. Add rest of ice and non-fat dry milk and seasonings alternately. When chop is nearly fine enough, add cubed chicken fat (45°F.). Add sodium isoascorbate 1 min. before end of chop (56°F.). Remove emulsion from chopper at 58–60°F. Smoke immediately and cook to internal temperature of 156°F.

---

[1] Cure mixture: 3 lb. 7 oz. sodium nitrate, 5 oz. sodium nitrite, 10 lb. dextrose. Add water to equal 5 gal. of cure mixture.
[2] Sodium isoascorbate: 1$^1/_4$ oz. sodium isoascorbate, add water to equal 1 pint of sodium isoascorbate mixture.

Chicken Bologna Preparations

Marshall (1962) working in the Poultry Department at Cornell University reported the following formulations and procedures for making chicken bologna (Fig. 15.9).

Chickalone Formula

Ingredients	Amount
Raw boned chicken	83 lb.
Chicken fat	17 lb.
Phosphate (sodium tripolyphosphate and sodium hexametaphosphate)	5 oz.
Ice	28 lb.
Non-fat dry milk	4¹/₂ lb.
Seasoning (salt included)	4 lb.
Sodium erythorbate (dissolved in 1 pint of water)	³/₄ oz.

Chicken Bologna Formula

Use the above ingredients plus:

Paprika	5 oz.
Cure mixture (3 lb. 7 oz. sodium nitrate, 5 oz. sodium nitrite, 10 lb. dextrose. Add water to equal 5 gal. of cure mixture)	1 qt.

Manufacturing Procedure.—The meat was partially thawed, then ground through a ¹/₈-in. plate. This size plate was preferred to a larger one because, if the meat should accidentally contain a small bone, it would be either finely ground or caught behind the grinder plate.

Fat was ground through a ¹/₂-in. plate. Chicken, phosphate, and cure (when used) were chopped in a silent cutter. Ice and dry ingredients (non-fat dry milk, seasoning, and paprika) were added alternately and chopped to about 40°F. Fat was added and the cutting continued until the emulsion reached 50°F. The sodium erythorbate solution was added about 1 min. before the cutting was completed.

Chicken Loaf

Marshall (1964) gives the following formulations and procedure for making chicken loaves.

Ingredients	Amount
Cooked boned chicken	26 lb.
Chicken broth	25 lb.
Raw chicken, ground	22 lb. 8 oz.
Chicken fat, ground	8 lb.
Sodium erythorbate[1]	¹/₂ oz.
Phosphate[2]	4 ¹/₂ oz.
Oatmeal (quick cooking type)	12 lb. 8 oz.

Ingredients	Amount
Salt	6 oz.
Seasonings[3]	2 lb. 4 oz.
Powdered onion	4 oz.
Hydrolyzed plant protein[4]	11 oz.
Frozen eggs	6 lb.

---

[1] Sodium isoascorbate.

[2] Blend of sodium tripolyphosphate and sodium hexametaphosphate. The sodium erythorbate (sodium isoascorbate) and phosphates act as antioxidants to help prevent a stale taste in the cooked chicken. It is important to incorporate them with the cooked chicken as early as possible, preferably by boning the chicken when warm and grinding it promptly into the broth-antioxidant mixture.

[3] The seasoning used was a commercially blended seasoning for chicken loaves, which contained 44% salt in addition to spices and other seasonings. Any good blend of spices made for seasoning chicken loaves may be used by adjusting the salt level to give the same salt: spice ratio used in this formula.

[4] The hydrolyzed plant protein used was the fully decolorized type manufactured for use with chicken.

In the manufacturing process, it was found desirable to cook and bone the chicken to be added as cooked chicken on the day before blending it with the other ingredients for the final product. The skins were kept separate and ground twice through a $1/_8$-in. plate before being added to the cooked meat. This blend was then weighed and ground (through a $1/_8$-in. plate) directly into the broth fat that had been weighed and mixed with the sodium erythorbate and phosphate. This cooked meat and broth mixture was blended and refrigerated for use in the final product the next day. The chicken fat derived from the cooked fowl was re-added to meet the fat requirement.

On the day of making the final product, the raw chicken and raw fat were ground separately through a $1/_8$-in. plate and weighed. The mixer was of a commercial size commonly used for this type of operation. The oatmeal, salt, and seasoning were blended together, as were also the yolks and whites of eggs, before being added to the chicken in the mixer. The product was then weighed into aluminum pans, covered, and immediately put into a freezer at $-15°F$. The author reports that after market testing it was found that chicken loaf possesses only a limited market potential.

Chicken Hash

Darfler and Jack (1964) reported a formulation for chicken hash developed at Cornell University (Fig. 15.10). It contains chicken, chicken broth, potatoes, seasoning, eggs, and flour. It may be canned in No. 303 cans for home use and No. 10 cans for institutions using commercial processing and canning equipment.

Jellied Chicken Loaf

Union Carbide Co., Food Products Division (Anon. 1958) developed the following formulation and instructions for making jellied chicken loaves.

Courtesy Cornell University

FIG. 15.10.   CHICKEN HASH

To prepare 200 lb. of jellied chicken loaf:

300 lb. Dressed stewing hens   7.0 oz. Pepper
20 lb. Carrots   7.0 oz. Onion powder
17 lb. Celery   3.5 oz. Monosodium glutamate
9 lb. Salt   8.0 lb. Gelatin per 100 lb. chicken broth
5 lb. Pimiento

Dismember chickens. Place in pot with necks. Cover with water. Add salt, pepper, onion powder, and monosodium glutamate. Place carrots and celery in stockinettes and then into pot. Cook at boiling temperature for $3^1/_2$–4 hr.

Strain broth through clean cheese cloth. Cool broth and chicken in cooler and remove surface layer of chicken fat that forms. Heat chicken broth to 160° F. in steam kettle. Dissolve gelatin and allow to cool to temperature suitable for handling.

Remove meat from bones. Discard bones, skin, and neck. Anticipate 30% yield (including cooking losses). Dice the chicken meat and mix with diced pimiento. Add chicken and pimiento to cooled gelatin-broth solution (1/1 ratio). Pour mixture through a wide mouth funnel into suitably prepared 80 MP fibrous casings manufactured by Food Products Division. Tie casings, wash with hot water or vinegar solution. Transfer to cooler immediately.

Poultry Rolls

Poultry rolls are made in both raw and cooked forms, and in a number of shapes. They can be made in cylindrical form; in tied rolls where the skin is used as the casing; in formed rolls where a plastic casing is used; in rectangular molded shapes; and in oblong tied shapes. Generally they are seasoned with salt, pepper, and sometimes monosodium glutamate is added. To bind pre-cooked rolls, gelatin or other binders, such as wheat gluten, are added and the rolls are molded under pressure.

The military specifications (Anon. 1954), covering the amounts of meat and skin permitted in frozen cooked boneless turkey state the following:

	% by weight
1 Large piece of (raw) whitemeat (one-half breast)	35–38
1 Large piece of (raw) dark meat (one leg and thigh section)	32–25
1 Skin piece (from one side of bird backbone to breast-bone)	10–12
Cooked meat pieces	18–20

The following information relative to producing cooked turkey rolls is taken from the U.S. Department of Agriculture Poultry Inspector's Handbook (Anon. 1964A).

(1) If the cooking or roasting of the rolls is not to begin within 30 min. after the roll is fabricated, the rolls shall be placed in shallow pans or on wire racks to speed cooling and immediately placed under refrigeration at 40°F. or lower until such time as they can be placed in the oven for immediate cooking.

(2) The cooking operation shall be continuous and should be timed so that the cooking cycle is completed during the approved work schedule of the plant. This is necessary in order that the inspector may make temperature checks, and to eliminate charging firms overtime.

(3) In operations where the cookout juices from the cooking operations are recovered for later use in the product, the following precautions shall be taken: (a) The juices shall be kept in a kettle at a temperature of at least 160°F. until used. Alternatively, juices, which are to be carried over for the next day shall be put in containers of a size which will facilitate cooling and placed under refrigeration at a temperature of 40°F. or lower. (b) The natural juices may not be held in excess of 48 hr. unless frozen.

(4) Any time lags which permit the product to attain temperatures suitable to the growth of microorganisms must be kept to a minimum.

The following processed poultry products formulas are published through the courtesy of the Films-Packaging Division of Union Carbide Corporation.

Turkey Roll

Raw materials: boneless, skinless turkey white meat, turkey dark meat, turkey skin.

Formulation

Turkey meat (boneless, skinless white or dark meat)	90 lb.
Emulsion (see below)	10 lb.
Salt	1½ lb.
Prepared seasoning	1½ lb.
Phosphate (Kena, Poultry FOS, etc.)	½ lb.

Emulsion Preparation.—Emulsion made from body skins, wing meat and wing skin, can be omitted if desired. A binder such as soy protein concentrate, sodium caseinate, etc., may be mixed with the skin emulsion at a maximum level of 3½% of the meat and skin weight. Grind skins and/or wing meat and wing skin through a ³/₈ in. grinder plate. The ground skins and/or meat are then put through a 1.7 mm plate of a Mincemaster or chopped to a fine emulsion. If an all-dark meat roll is made, automatically deboned turkey meat or emulsified dark meat can be used as the emulsion. This will prevent a grainy appearance from occurring in the finished product as would occur if emulsified skins were used in dark meat emulsion type rolls.

Trimming and Mixing.—Trim meat of tendons, blood vessels, etc., and cut into desired size pieces. Place meat in mixer, add phosphate slurry made of 1 part phosphate to 3 parts water and begin mixing. Add salt and continue mixing until the meat surfaces become tacky or sticky (mixing time depends on efficiency of mixer). The skin emulsion, seasoning, and binder, if desired, are then added and mixing continued for an additional 1–2 min.

Stuffing and Closing.—The mixture is stuffed into Union Carbide MP or EP-PS Fibrous casings of suitable size using a conventional pneumatic stuffer or other suitable stuffing equipment, and pressure packed on conventional closing equipment.

A combination white and dark meat turkey roll can be made by preparing the dark meat similarly to the white and layering the two types of meat so that each slice of the finished product will contain both white and dark meat portions. Pressure packing and closing procedures are similar to that used for all-white emulsion type rolls.

Processing.—*Water Cooking.*—The rolls are cooked in 180°F. water until an internal temperature of at least 160°F. is obtained in the center of the product. Cooking time is about 2½ hours when a No. 6 MP Fibrous casing is used. The product is chilled in cold running water (50°–55°F.) for approximately 15 min. and placed in slush ice overnight and frozen the following day.

***Dry Roasting.*—**The rolls are stuffed into Union Carbide EP-PS Fibrous casing and cooked at 300°F. in a rotary oven or smokehouse until the internal temperature reaches 160°F. To ensure complete browning on all sides, the rolls should be rotated 1 or 2 times during the cooking period. The rolls may be chilled similarly to the water-cooked product.

Chicken or Turkey Liver Sausage

Raw material: Chicken or turkey livers and chicken or turkey mechanically deboned meat.

Formulation

Chicken or turkey livers	50 lb.
Mechanically deboned chicken or turkey meat	50 lb.
Extender (milk powder, sodium caseinate, etc.)	4 lb.
Salt	2 lb.
Liver sausage seasoning	³/₄ lb
Dehydrated onions (onions should be rehydrated)	7½ oz.
Curing agents	4 oz.

Preparation of Emulsion.—Place livers into chopper, add curing agents, and chop until bubbles start to form on the surface of the mixture. Add mechanically deboned meat and chop a maximum of five minutes with remaining ingredients. Chopped product is then emulsified and transferred to the sausage stuffer.

Stuffing.—The product is stuffed into a suitable size Union Carbide Moistureproof Fibrous casing.

Processing Schedule.—Product is water cooked at 180°F. until an internal temperature of 155°-160°F. is reached. Product is then cold showered for 15 min. and stored at 40°F.

Turkey Style Pork Sausage and/or Turkey Style Brown-and-Serve

Raw material: (Turkey dark meat trim, turkey white meat trim, raw chicken fat and regular pork trim.

Formulations

	I	II	III
Turkey Dark Meat Trim	80 lb.	80 lb.	
Turkey White Meat Trim	—	—	50 lb.
Raw Chicken Fat	20 lb.	—	—
Regular Pork Trim	—	20 lb.	50 lb.
Salt	1 lb.	1 lb.	1 lb.
Pork Sausage Seasoning	6 oz.	6 oz.	6 oz.
Sage	3 oz.	3 oz.	3 oz.
Ginger	1 oz.	1 oz.	1 oz.
Nutmeg	1 oz.	1 oz.	1 oz.

Preparation of Emulsion.—Place meats in chopper and chop for 30 seconds with salt and seasonings. Emulsion is then transferred to sausage stuffer.

Stuffing and Linking.—The product is then stuffed into Union Carbide Tendrjax collagen casing and linked to a desired length.

Processing Schedule.—Product is then placed into steam cabinet and steam cooked to an internal temperature of 160°F. Product is then stored at 40°F.

Product may just be frozen without any processing and sold as a frozen product.

Other Convenience Poultry Items

The opportunities for developing and manufacturing new products from poultry products are numerous. As progress is made in controlling rancidity, more economical boning, and in other ways to control the quality of the resultant products more new products will be made and tested. Examples of other poultry products already developed are fried chicken skins, frozen chicken and gravy packed in a pouch, turkey and waffles, scrapple, pressed chicken loaves, and casseroles.

BIBLIOGRAPHY

ANON. 1954. Turkey, boneless, frozen (cooked). Mil. Spec. MIL-T-35006.

ANON. 1955. Poultrymen pinpoint quality, handling costs. Food Eng. 27, 112–115.

ANON. 1956A. Frozen pot-pies produced in 5-step operation. Food Eng. 28, 162, 165–166.

ANON. 1956B. Turkey, prefabricated, frozen (raw). Mil. Spec. MIL-T-16660B.

ANON. 1958. Visking service manual. Union Carbide Co., Food Products Division, Chicago.

ANON. 1962. Profit making opportunities with eggs—four-page supplement. Poultry and Egg National Board, Chicago, Ill.

ANON. 1964A. Poultry Inspector's Handbook. U.S. Dept. Agr., Agr. Mktg. Serv. Poultry Div., Inspection Branch.

ANON. 1964B. Quality Controlled Frozen Foods. J. D. Jewell, Gainesville, Georgia.

ANON. 1975A. Accepted Meat and Poultry Equipment. U.S. Dept. Agr. Animal Plant Health Inspection Serv. *MPI-2.*

ANON. 1975B. Mechanically deboned poultry and poultry meat. U.S. Dept. Agr. Animal Plant Health Inspection Serv. MPI Bull. *75-30.*

BAUERMANN, J. F. 1962. Poultry products in Pennsylvania—a status report. Farm Economics. Penn. State Univ. Ext. Serv.

CODE OF FEDERAL REGULATIONS. 1971. Title 7. Parts 53 to 209. Office Federal Register, Natl. Archives Records Serv., General Services Admin., U.S. Govt. Printing Office, Washington, D.C.

CUNNINGHAM, F. E., and MUGLER, D. J. 1974. Deboned fowl meat opportunities. Poultry Meat 25, 47–48, 50.

DARFLER, J., and JACK, J. W. 1964. New marketable poultry and egg products. 14. Chicken hash. Cornell Univ. Agr. Expt. Sta., Agr. Econ. Res. *151.*

ESSARY, E. O., and GOFF, O. E. 1951. Poultry specialities. Univ. Tenn. Inform. Circ. *88.*

ESSARY, E. O., and RITCHEY, S. J. 1968. Amino acid composition of meat removed from boned turkey carcasses by use of commercial boning machine. Poultry Sci. 47, 1953–1955.

FRONING, G. W. 1970. Poultry meat sources and their emulsifying characteristics as related to processing variables. Poultry Sci. 49, 1625–1631.

FRONING, G. W. *et al.* 1971. Quality and storage stability of frankfurters containing 15% mechanically deboned turkey meat. J. Food Sci. 36, 974–978.

GRUNDEN, L. P., MacNEIL, J. H., and DIMICK, P. S. 1972. Poultry product quality: chemical and physical characteristics of mechanically deboned poultry meat. J. Food Sci. 37, 274–249.

GRUNDEN, L. P., and MacNEIL, J. H. 1973. Examination of bone content in mechanically deboned poultry meat by EDTA and atomic absorption spectrophotometric methods. J. Food Sci. 38, 712–713.

HARP, H. H., and DUNHAM, D. F. 1963. Comparative costs to consumers of convenience foods and home-prepared foods. U.S. Dept. Agr., Econ. Res. Serv. Mktg. Res. Rept. *609.*

HUBER, L. J. 1964. Deboning poultry meat. U.S. Pat. 3,129,455, April 21.

JOHNSON, P. G., CUNNINGHAM, F. E., and BOWERS, J. A. 1974. Quality of mechanically deboned turkey meat: Effect of storage time and temperature. Poultry Sci. 53, 732-736.

JOULE, T. L. 1959. How to make turkey rolls. Univ. Missouri Agr. Ext. Serv. Folder 70.

MACDOUGALL, D. B. 1961. The formulation and development of composite precooked dehydrated foods. Food Process. Pkg. 30, No. 352, 3-10.

MACNEIL, J. H., DIMICK, P. S., and MAST, M. G. 1973. Use of chemical compounds and a rosemary spice extract in quality maintenance of deboned poultry meat. J. Food Sci. 38, 1080-1081.

MARSHALL, J. H. 1961. New marketable poultry and egg products. 6. Chicken franks. Cornell Univ. Agr. Expt. Sta. Agr. Econ. Res. 57.

MARSHALL, J. H. 1962. New marketable poultry and egg products. 9. Chicken bologna and chickalona. Cornell Univ. Agr. Expt. Sta. Agr. Econ. Res. 83.

MARSHALL, J. H. 1963. New marketable poultry and eggs products. 12. Chicken sticks. Cornell Univ. Agr. Expt. Sta. Agr. Econ. Res. 111.

MARSHALL, J. H. 1964. Expanding the market for fowl through new products. Cornell Univ. Agr. Expt. Sta. Bull. 998.

MAST, M. G. 1976. Physical and functional properties of heat pasteurized mechanically deboned poultry meat. Poultry Sci. (in press).

MAST, M. G., and MACNEIL, J. H. 1975. Heat pasteurization of mechanically deboned poultry meat. Poultry Sci. 54, 1024-1030.

MAURER, A. J. 1973. Emulsifying characteristics of mechanically and hand-deboned poultry meat mixtures. Poultry Sci. 52, 2061.

MAXCY, R. B., FRONING, G. W., and HARTUNG, T. E. 1973. Microbial quality of ground poultry meat. Poultry Sci. 52, 486-491.

MOERCK, K. E., and BALL, H. R. JR., 1974. Lipid autoxidation in mechanically deboned chicken meat. J. Food Sci. 39, 876-879.

OSTOVAR, K., MACNEIL, J. H., and O'DONNELL, K. 1971. Poultry product quality. 5. Microbiological evaluation of mechanically deboned poultry meat. J. Food Sci. 36, 1005-1007.

PAULY, M. R. 1967. Machine deboned poultry and what to do with the meat. Proc. Poultry Egg Further Process. Conf., Ohio State Univ., Columbus, June 16-17.

SCHNELL, P. G. et al. 1973. Physical and functional properties of mechanically deboned poultry meat used in the manufacture of frankfurters. Poultry Sci. 52, 1363-1369.

SWEET, M. C. 1964. A mechanical bone separator that works. Poultry Meat 70, No. 9, 30-31.

TRESSLER, D. K., VAN ARSDEL, W. B., and COPLEY, M. J. 1968. The Freezing Preservation of Foods, 4th Edition, Vol. 4. Avi Publishing Co., Westport, Conn.

WASKIEWICZ, S. F. 1962. Mechanizing poultry boning. Food Process. 23, No. 3, 63-65.

YOUNG, L. L., and LYON, B. G. 1973. The use of heat-treated meat in chicken frankfurters. Poultry Sci. 52, 1868-1875.

CHAPTER 16

Cooking and Barbecuing Poultry

INTRODUCTION

The sweet delicate flavor and tender juicy texture of poultry meat can be brought to perfection by broiling, roasting, frying, barbecuing, or simmering. Chicken is adaptable. It has no intensely individual flavor of its own and accommodates itself to every method of cookery and every possible sauce. The number of different poultry dishes which can be cooked from poultry meat are limited only by the ingenuity of the cook.

Unfortunately, much of the enjoyment derived from eating such meat can be lost if the carcasses are not carefully stored, prepared, and cooked. Serving partially cooked poultry with bloody joints or overcooked, dry, tough, stringy poultry will do more to discourage poultry consumption than all the promotion used by the industry can do to increase sales.

PHYSICAL AND CHEMICAL CHANGES CAUSED BY COOKING

Dawson (1959) describes the effects of heat on meats as follows:

"Heat causes the coagulation of proteins, melting of the fat, and change in color of red meat to pink and finally brown or gray. In the presence of water or moisture naturally present in meat, collagen hydrolyzes to gelatin when heated.

Heat affects tenderness of meat. The coagulation of proteins causes a toughening of the meat and the hydrolysis of collagen to gelatin makes it tender. The total effect of heat depends on which reaction predominates. The changes in flavor caused by heat are due partly to the loss of volatile matter, caramelization of carbohydrates, decomposition of proteins and fats and coagulation of protein. More and more changes in flavor take place the longer the meat is cooked.

The shrinkage of meat during cooking is due mainly to the loss of water, which escapes as steam, and to the loss of the water and fat, which are released from the meat and collect at the bottom of the cooking pan."

Alexander (1941) suggests two general rules to be used in cooking poultry. First, cook at a moderate heat so the meat will cook evenly throughout all the way to the bone and will be tender and juicy. Poultry cooked under an intense heat has a high cooking shrinkage, the muscle shrinks more, it is less juicy, loses flavor, and has harder and tougher flesh than poultry cooked with moderate heat.

A second rule is to let the age and fatness of the bird be the criteria to determine which cooking method will be used. Broiling, frying, and oven pan roasting are best for young, tender birds with a good covering of fat. For carcasses that are lean or past the roasting stage braising in a covered roaster or casserole produces tender, flavorful meat. Carcasses from older birds, on the other hand, need long slow cooking in water or steam to make them tender.

PREPARATION OF CARCASSES FOR COOKING

Chicken is available either chilled or frozen. Although frozen poultry has a much longer shelf-life, the added expense of holding it in a frozen state and the inconvenience of thawing tend to offset somewhat the benefits of a longer shelf-life.

Chilled Poultry

Chilled poultry should be kept uncooked, loosely wrapped, unfrozen, in the coldest part of the refrigerator. Although the shelf-life of chilled poultry purchased at a supermarket is generally more than three days, to prevent spoilage and allow a margin of safety, it is a good rule not to hold it in the refrigerator, unfrozen, more than this length of time.

Most poultry is marketed ready-to-cook, but it is still good practice to wash the carcass and giblets to remove bloody water which has drained from the body cavity. After washing, blot the carcass dry.

Frozen Poultry

A common practice among homemakers is to freeze chilled poultry, which has not been properly wrapped for freezing, in the frozen food compartment of the refrigerator. Poultry handled in this manner soon begins to dehydrate and lose flavor.

For freezing, poultry should be tightly wrapped in a moisture-vapor-proof film, foil, or paper and then frozen at 0°F. or lower as soon as possible and then it should be held at 0°F. or lower. Although no abrupt changes in quality occur during the first few months of poultry storage, it is good practice always to use those chickens first which have been in storage longest and those with torn wrappers.

It is possible, but not considered desirable, to re-freeze poultry a second time. Freezing and thawing release fluids, generally called drip, and the chances for bacterial spoilage are increased.

Thawing Poultry.—Two conditions are important during thawing. First it is generally accepted that slow thawing gives tissues a better chance to rehydrate and, second, bacterial growth will start during thawing and continue even after thawing. To prevent rapid bacterial growth the carcass should either be cooked immediately upon thawing or be held refrigerated. Sufficient time should be allowed for thawing so that the carcass is ready for cooking when needed.

The Poultry and Egg National Board (1955A) gives the following instructions for thawing chicken.

"Frozen: Thaw before cooking. Prompt cooking after thawing is preferable. Follow package directions or thaw by one of the following methods: (1) place chicken in refrigerator or in its original wrap, 12–24 hr.; or, (2) place chicken in pan under running cool water in its original wrap, $1/2$–1 hr."

For thawing turkey:

"All frozen turkeys should be thawed slowly and never at room temperature or in warm water. In thawing, follow package directions, or thaw by one or a combination of these methods: (1) place bird, still in its original body wrap, under running cold water. Allow 2–6 hr. for thawing; (2) leave bird in its original body wrap. Place on tray in refrigerator. Allow 1 to 3 days for thawing.

Prompt cooking of a fresh or thawed turkey is preferable. A thawed, ready-to-cook or fresh turkey can be kept for two to three days in a refrigerator at 38°F. or less. Wrap bird loosely in foil or moisture-proof paper for refrigerator storage. It is not advisable to refreeze poultry."

POULTRY COOKING

Frying

Only young, tender, plump poultry carcasses should be cooked by frying. They can be fried by four general methods: deep fat frying, pan frying, and oven frying. They can also be deep fat fried under pressure.

Generally carcasses are cut up for frying into portions suitable for serving and then seasoned with salt, pepper, and other condiments as desired. Then the chicken is rolled in flour or dipped in a batter, generally eggs, milk, flour, and seasoning. Another method sometimes used is to dip the parts in an egg-milk batter and then in flour. The coating or batter retards dehydration, aids browning, and helps to impart a crispness to the fried parts.

To deep fat fry poultry meat, the coated parts are dropped in fat heated to 350°F. with all parts covered. Generally the temperature of the fat is held between 300° and 325°F. during frying. When the meat is pressure fried, the parts are first deep fat fried for a short period to ensure browning and then cooked under pressure for about 8 min.

For pan frying, Alexander (1941) reported that a thick frying pan should be used which contains a half inch or more of hot but not smoking fat. Add the coated parts to the fat, the largest pieces first, and then cover the pan with a lid. Use moderate heat and turn the pieces when they become brown. Generally broiler-fryer chickens cooked by this method require 20–25 min. After frying, the pieces can be placed on absorbent paper.

When chicken is to be oven-fried the coated parts are first browned lightly, the same as with pan-fried chicken. Then the chicken is placed in a baking pan and a mixture of melted butter and milk poured over it.

The parts are then cooked slowly in the oven at 350°F. until "fork tender." The meat should be turned once or twice during cooking.

Broiling

Young chickens, turkeys, squabs, guineas, and ducklings, whole, cut in halves, or quarters can be cooked in a broiler at 400°F. (Fig. 16.1). Before cooking, the meat is wiped dry, brushed with fat and seasoned with salt and pepper. Some cooks prefer to use special sauces as lemon barbecue sauce, wine sauce, or other gourmet sauces instead of fat. Then the carcass is placed in a shallow pan with the skin side down and so the chicken fills the pan one layer deep with no pan area exposed. Aluminum foil can be used to line the pan if desired. Next the pan of meat is placed in the pre-heated broiler. After cooking for approximately 30 min., the pieces are turned and basted with fat or sauces. For best results the surface of the chicken should be about 7–9 in. from the source of heat. The meat is considered done when the drumstick or wing twists out of joint.

Roast Chicken

Young broiler-fryers of any weight may be roasted. A plump chicken of at least $2^1/_2$ lb. is particularly desirable. It may be stuffed or unstuffed.

Wash chicken; drain and pat dry. Rub cavity lightly with salt, if desired. Do not salt if stuffed.

Fill wishbone area (neck) with stuffing,[1] if used. Fasten neck skin to back with skewer. Shape wings "akimbo" style; bring wing tips onto back. Fill body cavity lightly if stuffing is used. Tie drumsticks together, then tie to tail.

Place chicken on rack in a shallow open pan, breast up. Brush skin with melted butter or margarine.

Roast in 400° or 375°F. oven (see time-table below) depending on size of bird. Follow time-table for approximate total cooking time. Chicken is done when meaty portions are fork tender, and drumstick feels soft when pressed with protected fingers.

TIME-TABLE FOR CHICKEN

Ready-to-Cook Weight, Lb.	Oven Temperature, °F.	Approximate Total Time, Hr.
$1^1/_2$–2	400	$^3/_4$–1
2–$2^1/_2$	400	1–$1^1/_4$
$2^1/_2$–3	375	$1^1/_4$–$1^3/_4$
3–4	375	$1^3/_4$–$2^1/_4$

[1] Spoon favorite stuffing into cavities just before roasting—not ahead of time. Allow an extra 15 min. roasting time when chicken is stuffed. One and a half cups stuffing is adequate for a three-lb. broiler-fryer.

Roast Turkey

The following table showing the number of servings for different size turkeys and time-tables for roasting turkeys was also compiled by the Poultry and Egg National Board (1962) and the National Turkey Federation (1963).

RATIO OF SERVINGS TO WEIGHT OF TURKEY

Ready-to-Cook Turkey, Lb.	Number of Servings
6–8	6–10
8–12	10–20
12–16	20–32
16–20	32–40
20–24	40–50

Courtesy National Turkey Federation

FIG. 16.1.   BASTING A YOUNG TURKEY HALF BEFORE BROILING IN
THE OVEN

When using the time-table, sufficient time, usually 20–30 min. should be allowed to avoid delay in serving if the turkey takes longer to cook than originally planned.   The following tables are for cooking turkeys in an open pan.

Turkey can also be cooked by wrapping it in aluminum foil.   By using this method, cooking temperatures can be increased and cooking times de-

Courtesy National Turkey Federation

FIG. 16.2.   BASTING A TURKEY BEFORE ROASTING IN THE OVEN

TIME-TABLE FOR TURKEY ROASTED IN A PAN

Purchased Ready-to-Cook Weight, Lb.	Oven Temperature, °F.	Interior Temperature, °F.	Approximate Total Time for Thawed Stuffed Turkey, Hr.
6 to 8	325	185	$2 - 2^1/_2$
8 to 12	325	185	$2^1/_2 - 3$
12 to 16	325	185	$3 - 3^3/_4$
16 to 20	325	185	$3^3/_4 - 4^1/_2$
20 to 24	325	185	$4^1/_2 - 5^1/_2$

creased without undue dehydration or toughening of the meat.   Spattering from the cooking juices is contained within the foil.

Before cooking, the carcass is wrapped in foil with a drugstore fold. About 30–40 min. before the carcass is cooked the foil should be opened and folded back so the skin will brown.   The following table compiled by Poultry and Egg National Board (1962) and National Turkey Federation (1963) is for cooking turkeys wrapped in aluminum foil.

Time-Table for Turkey Roasted in Foil

Purchased Ready-to-Cook Weight, Lb.	Oven Temperature, °F.	Interior Temperature, °F.	Guide to Total Roasting Time, Hr.
6–8	450	185	$1^1/_2$–2
8–12	450	185	2–$2^1/_2$
12–16	450	185	$2^1/_2$–3
16–20	450	185	3–$3^1/_2$
20–24	450	185	$3^1/_2$–4

Turkeys can also be cooked in covered pans. Dawson (1959) reported that when carcasses are cooked in covered pans:

"...Steam is held around the bird and the collagen is solubilized to gelatin faster than by roasting in dry heat. The roasted turkeys have less splitting, the skin is less blistered and shriveled, and the browning is richer and more even."

Roast Duck and Goose

Generally duck and goose are roasted the same as other poultry meat but with a few modifications. They yield less cooked edible meat and contain more fat than other classes of poultry; therefore, they do not require basting during roasting. If the carcasses are excessively fat the skin can be punctured to permit some of the fat to drain out. Some fat can be spooned or siphoned off during roasting and saved for other uses.

Schlosser and Gilpin (1959) give the following times and temperatures for roasting duck and goose.

Time-Table for Duck and Goose

	Ready-to-Cook Weight, Lb.	Oven Temperature, °F.	Approximate Roasting Time for Stuffed, Chilled Bird, Hr.
Duck	3–5	325	$2^1/_2$–3
Goose	4–8	325	$2^3/_4$–$3^1/_2$
Goose	8–14	325	$3^1/_2$–5

Cooking Giblets

Giblets can be washed, salted, wrapped in aluminum foil, and cooked with the remainder of the carcass if desired or simmered in salted water until tender.

Stuffing

Stuffing should be packed lightly in the body and crop cavities. If packed too tight, expansion during cooking and absorption of juices will cause it to become soggy. If the opening by the tail is unusually large, a slice of bread will prevent stuffing from leaking out.

Courtesy National Turkey Federation

FIG. 16.3.   CARVING TURKEY

When cooking stuffed poultry, care should be taken to make sure that the heat penetrates to the center of the stuffing and cooks it enough to kill microorganisms.   When frozen commercially stuffed poultry, which is cooked directly from the frozen state is used, care should be taken to see that extra time is allowed for the thawing and cooking.   Electronic cooking of frozen stuffed turkey is not considered to be a good practice.

Gravy

Alexander (1941) reported that a 4-lb. chicken yields about 1 to $1\frac{1}{2}$ cups of gravy and a 10-lb. turkey 3 to 4 cups.   Finely ground cooked giblets can be added to the gravy if desired.

Cooking with Chicken Fat

Stevenson and Miller (1960) reported that chicken fat can be used as an all purpose fat for home cooking.   Products cooked with chicken fat are similar to those cooked with lard. Excess fat from stewing hens can be used in cookies, cream sauces, and similar preparations.

Meyer (1960) reported that chicken fat has a specific gravity of 15° at 59°F. —0.924, an acid value of 1.2; a saponification value of 193–204.6; an iodine value of 66–71.5; and a Reichert Meissel value of 1.4.

Lowe (1958) reported on a study of the breaking and crushing strengths of different pastries made under standardized conditions. It required 233 gm. to break pastries made from chicken oil or fat and 375 gm. for crushing it. In general fats containing the highest proportions of unsaturated glycerides also produce the shortest pastries. Corn oil, cottonseed oil, and chicken fat produced the most tender pastries.

Carving Poultry Meat

There are several methods of carving meat (Fig. 16.3). Joule (1956) describes how to carve turkey by the so called "standard method" as follows.

"(1) Remove leg; hold firmly, pull away from body, cut skin between leg and body. (2) Continue pulling leg away from body. Cut through thigh joint joining to body. Hold leg on serving platter, separate thigh, and drumstick. (3) Slice drumstick meat, holding at convenient angle; cut down, turning drumstick to get even slices. (4) Slice thigh meat, hold with fork, cut slices parallel to bone. (5) Cut into breast meat, above wing joint, and parallel to wing. Cut through to body frame. (6) Slice breast meat. Start at front, halfway up breast. Cut slices down to cut made in step 5."

He also gives the following helpful suggestions for carving:

"Cool bird out of oven 30 min. or longer before carving. Leave bird in pan 15–30 min. out of oven to absorb juice. Remove trusses and skewers in kitchen. Carve enough meat at one time to serve everyone at table. Use platter large enough for garnish and space for sliced meat. Use very sharp—long thin bladed knife."

Meat on the breast of waterfowl is too shallow to carve in the same manner as other poultry. Ducks and geese are generally carved by first releasing the meat from the keel bone with the point of the knife and then carving at right angles to the grain of the meat.

Cooking Mature Poultry

Older, less tender, poultry is generally stewed or fricasseed. Stewing requires simmering in water with seasoning for an extended period. Fricasseed chicken is prepared by first coating with flour and then slow browning in a small amount of hot fat or salad oil. The fat is then drained and water is added. It is then cooked, covered, at around 325°F. in the oven or simmered on top of the stove until "fork tender."

For pressure cooking place cut-up poultry in the cooker with water and seasoning and cook for 25–35 min. at 15-lb. pressure or according to manufacturer's instructions. Release pressure slowly or let cool before releasing the pressure.

BARBECUING

Barbecuing can be done in a number of ways and with a number of different types of equipment. This method of cooking lends itself to large-scale cooking and mass feeding. Poultry barbecues can be held indoors using the kitchen stove or on grills over charcoal outside. Not only chickens, but turkeys, (Fig. 16.4) ducks, and even geese can be barbecued.

Barbecuing in the Kitchen

The Poultry and Egg National Board gives the following procedure for barbecuing on a rotisserie.

Young chickens of any weight may be used. Two or more chickens may be cooked at one time if length of spit permits. It is not advisable to stuff a chicken for rotisserie cooking.

Wash chicken; drain and pat dry. Rub cavity lightly with salt. Fasten neck skin to back with skewer. Flatten wings over breast, then tie cord around breast to hold wings securely. Tie drumsticks securely to tail.

Insert spit rod through center of bird from tail end toward front. Insert skewers firmly in place in bird and screw tightly. Test the balance. *Bird must balance on spit so it will rotate smoothly throughout the cooking period.* Place spit in rotisserie. Brush chicken with melted butter or margarine. Follow manufacturer's direction for temperature setting and cook until done. Barbecue sauce may be used, if desired, the last 15 to 25 minutes of cooking period.

Timetable

Ready-to-cook Weight	Approximate Total Cooking Time
$1^1/_2$–2 lb.	$^3/_4$–$1^1/_4$ hr.
2–$2^1/_2$ lb.	$1^1/_4$–$1^1/_2$ hr.
$2^1/_2$–3 lb.	$1^1/_2$–$1^3/_4$ hr.

For oven barbecue:
2 broiler-fryers, $1^1/_2$–3 lb. each, halved
1 recipe Robin-red Sauce

Add $^1/_2$ cup water to the sauce. Place chicken halves, skin side up, in roasting pan and pour sauce over them. Bake in a 350°F. (moderate) oven uncovered until chicken is fork-tender, 1–$1^1/_4$ hr., depending on size. Baste frequently and add water if sauce thickens too much before chicken is done.

To make Robin-red sauce:
1 tbsp onion salt
1 tbsp dry powdered mustard
$3/4$ tsp ground pepper
1 tsp Tabasco

$1/2$ bottle Worcestershire sauce
2 cups tomato paste
1 cup water
1 cup vinegar
$1/3$ cup butter, margarine, or salad oil

Combine ingredients in saucepan and heat to boiling. Keep hot for basting chicken. 5 cups—enough to barbecue and serve with 2–4 chickens.

Outdoor Barbecuing

For most people barbecuing holds the image of recreation, outdoors, and picnics. Equipment can vary from four bricks and a grill from the oven of the kitchen stove all the way up to a 100-ft. pit capable of handling several thousand chicken halves at a time. Backyard fireplaces and portable outdoor grills have become quite popular as well as the permanent type grills found in roadside picnic areas and parks. An ideal pit can be made from a half grease drum or a 55-gal. metal drum (Fig. 16.5). For larger operations a pit made from a framework of steel rods and sheet metal designed so the chicken is about 20–24 in. above the coals makes a good portable arrangement. A more permanent pit can be made from 8 by 8 by 16-in. cinder blocks.

Hicks (1958) reported that grids can be made from $3/8$-in. barstock with 1×2-in. welded wire. A deluxe set of racks can be made from

Courtesy National Turkey Federation

Fig. 16.4. Young Turkeys Being Barbecued

Courtesy Ohio Poultry Association

FIG. 16.5. A SIMPLE TYPE OF RACK MADE FROM DISCARDED OIL
DRUMS

welded stainless steel bars with a hinged cover. Such a rack holds 35 chicken halves which all can be turned at one time.

Do not make grills from galvanized hardware cloth or use discarded refrigerator shelves. The metallic coatings on these materials can react with the acids in the barbecue sauce to form salts which are toxic and can cause food poisoning. At least one case of food poisoning has been reported from this source.

Grids can be cleaned after use by soaking them in hot water with trisodium phosphate, then stiff brushing and finally a rinse.

Hicks (1958) lists the following equipment in addition to the food supplies for a small barbecue: chef's hat and apron; 2 pairs white canvas gloves; 2 two-qt. sauce pans; dish mop; rake; shovel; charcoal ($3/4$ lb. per chicken half); work table; and starter fuel.

Organizing a Barbecue

A well-planned, organized barbecue can serve a surprisingly large number of diners in a short time. Members of the Ohio Poultry Association and the Ohio State University Poultry Department each year prepare over 6,500 barbecued chicken halves in a 6-hr. period for an annual dinner held on the Ohio State University Campus. Each summer at the Ohio State Fair in past years, with the cooperation of poultry industry personnel, members of the Ohio Poultry Association Barbecue serve 15,000–20,000 chicken dinners in an eight-day period. With a little planning, any church, fraternal organization, PTA, business club, or similar organization can conduct a barbecue.

Food and Supplies.—The food and supplies required for holding barbecues for different groups of from 4 to 500 have been worked out by the Poultry and Egg National Board and the needed pit materials and utensils are given in Table 16.1.

In addition to the number of chickens required, the Poultry and Egg National Board has also arranged a table listing other food and beverages which can be served with barbecued poultry and which are easy to prepare and serve. A menu can be selected from these items (Table 16.2).

TABLE 16.1

PIT MATERIALS AND UTENSILS

You can easily figure from this list the amount of materials and utensils needed for a barbecue of any size

	Number of Persons				
	4	10	50	100	500
Sectional plates, paper	5	12	60	125	600
Pie plates, paper	5	12	60	125	600
Coffee cups, paper	4	20	100	150	700
Spoons, wood or paper	10	25	100	200	1000
Forks, wood or paper	5	12	60	125	600
Paper napkins	12	24	100	250	1200
Salt and pepper shakers	1 pr.	1 pr.	3 pr.	5 pr.	25pr.
Fine kindling, bushels	$1/8$	$1/4$	1	2	10
Charcoal briquets (20-lb. bags)	$1/2$	1	3	5	25
Wire, $1/2$ in. sq. mesh 3 ft. wide	*	4 ft.	11 ft.	18 ft.	74ft.
Pit—width blocks	*	$2^1/2$	$3^1/2$	$3^1/2$	$3^1/2$
Pit—length blocks	*	3	$6^1/2$	$11^1/2$	$53^1/2$
Pit—number blocks 8 x 8 x 16	*	18	54	84	333
Pipe 1 in. x 4 ft. 6 in. long	*	2	9	12	40
8-qt. pail for sauce	1	1	1	2	8
Brushes for sauce	1	1	1	2	8
Forks to turn chicken	1	2	4	6	30
Persons to turn chicken	1	1	2	3	15
Persons to serve	1	1	2	3	15

From Poultry and Egg National Board (1955B).
° Use fireplace or home barbecue grill.

Barbecuing Suggestions.—To start the fire in a barbecue pit, pile the briquets in the middle of the pit, pour kerosene or commercial charcoal lighter fluid on the charcoal, and light the pile or piles with paper. As soon as a white ash covers the briquets spread the charcoal over the entire pit. Let the charcoal burn until all kerosene odors burn off. This takes about 20 min. *Do not pour fuel on the burning coals.*

Cooking over a charcoal fire is not as dependable as on a kitchen range so allow plenty of extra time for the meat to cook. The fire may become too hot or not hot enough to supply sufficient heat, depending on wind and weather conditions. The secret of tender, juicy, succulent, cooked poultry is slow cooking at a moderate temperature.

When the charcoal has ignited and gives off a steady heat place the racks containing the chickens over on the fire. Baste the chickens with barbecue sauce and turn them every 4–8 min. For small barbecues a dish rag mop or a brush is good for applying sauce. Stainless steel or glass sprayers are better when large numbers of chicken are barbecued. Watch for "hot spots" or areas where one or two racks are cooking too fast, causing the skin to blister. Birds in these areas will need more turning and

TABLE 16.2

ALL-AMERICAN MENU

Make up your menu from this list

	Number of Persons				
	4	10	50	100	500
Number of chickens	2	5	25	50	250
$1^3/_4$–$2^1/_2$ lb. ready-to-cook					
Cranberry sauce	1 pt.	1 qt.	5 qt.	10 qt.	50 qt.
Cole slaw	1 pt.	1 qt.	5 qt.	10 qt.	50 qt.
Potato chips	$1/_2$ lb.	1 lb.	3 lb.	6 lb.	30 lb.
Pickled or deviled eggs					
(Allow $1/_2$–1 per person)					
Pickles	$1/_2$ pt.	1 pt.	2 qt.	1 gal.	5 gal.
Rolls	$2/_3$ doz.	$1^1/_2$ doz.	5 doz.	10 doz.	50 doz.
Bread, loaves (sliced)	$1/_2$	1	5	10	50
Butter or margarine	$1/_8$ lb.	$1/_4$ lb.	1 lb.	2 lb.	10 lb.
Coffee	$1^1/_2$ qt.	3 qt.	3 gal.	6 gal.	30 gal.
Iced tea	2 qt.	1 gal.	5 gal.	10 gal.	50 gal.
Coffee cream	$1/_2$ pt.	1 pt.	2 qt.	3 qt.	15 qt.
Sugar	$1/_8$ lb.	$1/_4$ lb.	1 lb.	$1^1/_2$ lb.	$7^1/_2$ lb.
Ice cream cups	5	10	50	100	500
Pies (9–10 in.)	1	2	5	10	50
Milk, $1/_2$ pints	$1^1/_2$	3	12	25	125
Bottled cold drinks	5	12	60	120	600

From Poultry and Egg National Board (1955B).

basting than those on other areas of the pit. Racks where carcasses are cooking too slowly can be moved to hotter areas of the pit when the first racks of chicken are done. The birds are tested for "doneness" by twisting the thigh or wing joints. When they break loose on gentle twisting they are considered cooked.

Portion control is important. Poultry meat is purchased by the pound but chicken is served by the piece regardless of weight. Several hundred carcasses each an ounce or more overweight can increase the cost of raw materials considerably. Halves without neck, back, wing tips, and giblets which weigh three-quarters to one pound make ideal portions for adults.

The Ohio Poultry Association (1960) offers the following additional suggestions for barbecuing:

"(1) Be sure the chicken is done before you serve it—when it is not done —ugh—your reputation is shot. (2) Be sure all the kerosene has burned out of the charcoal before you put the chicken on (stir the coals and you can smell the kerosene). (3) If chicken blisters, your fire is too hot—turn and baste. (4) If fire gets too hot or too cool, you can raise or lower the grill; or (5) you can control fire by raking coal around, or putting more on (which cools it for a few minutes). (6) When using small pits with only a few chickens, it will take slightly longer because so much heat escapes. (7) Keep your sauce recipe simple. When chicken has excess fat, cut down on oil or butter. (9) Sauce recipe can be expanded by multiplying all ingredients by 2, 4, 6, etc., depending on number of halves you want to barbecue. (10) You can use glass or stainless steel sprayer for putting on sauce in place of brush, it's quicker."

Recipes.—A quick easy-to-prepare sauce for ten chicken halves which is recommended by the Ohio Poultry Association consists of a pint of vinegar, a pint of water, a half pint of cooking oil or a half pound of butter, and two tablespoons of salt. For 100 halves use one quart of water, one quart of vinegar, one cup of cooking oil, and one cup of salt.

TABLE 16.3

ALL-PURPOSE BARBECUE SAUCE

Number of Persons →	6	24	50	250	500
Number of Chickens →	3	12	25	125	250
Ingredients					
Salt	$3/4$ tsp[1]	1 tbsp[1]	2 tbsp	$1/2$ cup & 2 tbsp	$1^1/4$ cups
Pepper	$1/2$ tsp	$1^3/4$ tsp	$2^1/2$ tsp	$1/4$ cup	$1/2$ cup & 1 tbsp
Paprika	$3/4$ tsp	1 tbsp	2 tbsp	$1/2$ cup & 2 tbsp	$1^1/4$ cups
Sugar	2 tsp	3 tbsp	$1/3$ cup	$1^3/4$ cup	$3^1/2$ cups
Garlic salt	$1/4$ tsp	1 tsp	2 tsp	$1/4$ cup	$1/2$ cup
Catsup	$1/3$ cup	$1^1/3$ cups	$2^2/3$ cups	14 cups	$2^1/3$ No. 10 cans (28 cups)
Tomato juice	$1/3$ cup	$1^1/3$ cups	$2^2/3$ cups	14 cups	$2^1/3$ No. 10 cans (28 cups)
Onions, chopped fine	1 small	3 med.	$1^1/4$ lb.	$6^1/4$ lb.	$12^1/2$ lb.
Water	$2/3$ cup	$2^2/3$ cups	$5^1/2$ cups	$1^3/4$ gal.	$3^1/2$ gal.
Vinegar or lemon juice	$1/4$ cup	1 cup	$1^3/4$ cup	2 qt. & 1 cup	1 gal. & 1 pt.
Worcestershire	$1/2$ tsp	2 tsp	$1^1/2$ tbsp	$2/3$ cup	$1^1/4$ cups
Butter, margarine or salad oil	2 tbsp	$1/4$ lb. or $1/2$ cup	$1/2$ lb. or 1 cup	2 lb. or 4 cups	$4^1/2$ lb. or 9 cups

Method: Measure all ingredients in pan or kettle. Heat to boiling. Keep hot for basting on grill. Oven barbecuing: pour sauce over halved birds in roasting pan to about 1 in. deep. If sauce becomes too thick, add a little hot water.

From Poultry and Egg National Board (1955B).
[1] tsp means teaspoon; tbsp means tablespoon.

More complicated sauces are the "All-Purpose Barbecue Sauce" (Table 16.3) and the "Southern Style Sauce" (Table 16.4) suggested by Poultry and Egg National Board.

Serving.—Portions generally consist of half a chicken for each adult and quarters for children. Beverages can include bottled cold drinks, milk in half-pint cartons, iced tea, and hot coffee. Remember that the spices and salt on barbecued chicken make diners thirsty, particularly on a hot summer day. Celery or carrots go well with barbecued meat.

TABLE 16.4

SOUTHERN STYLE SAUCE[1]

Onion, grated	1 large	1$^1/_2$ lbs.	3 lb.
Brown sugar	1$^1/_2$ tsp[2]	2 tbsp[2]	$^1/_4$ cup
Dry mustard	1 tbsp	$^1/_4$ cup	$^1/_2$ cup
Salt	1 tbsp	$^1/_4$ cup	$^1/_2$ cup
Black pepper	$^3/_4$ tsp	1 tbsp	2 tbsp
Tabasco or cayenne	$^1/_4$ tsp	1$^1/_2$ tsp	1 tbsp
Worcestershire	$^1/_2$ 5-oz. bot.[2]	2 5-oz. bot.	4 5-oz. bot.
Tomato juice	3 cups	1 No. 10 can (12 cups)	2 No. 10 cans (24 cups)
Vinegar ·	1 cup	1 qt. and $^3/_4$ cup	2 qt. and 1$^1/_2$ cups
Butter, margarine or salad oil	$^1/_3$ cup	$^3/_4$ lb. or 1$^1/_2$ cup	1$^1/_2$ lb. or 3 cups
Note: For oven barbecuing, use same ingredients and add water	1 cup	4 cups	8 cups

Method: Measure all ingredients in pan or kettle. Heat to boiling. Keep hot for basting poultry on grill. Oven barbecuing: Use same method described above.

From Poultry and Egg National Board (1955B).
[1] For 3, 12 and 25 chickens respectively.
[2] tsp means teaspoon; tbsp means tablespoon; bot. means bottle.

Generally food is served cafeteria style. Guests pick up their napkins, spoons, sugar, etc., and then pass the serving area where a plate containing chicken and main items on the menu is passed to them. Cellophane envelopes containing a plastic fork and spoon, sugar, salt, and a napkin can be purchased. The fewer decisions people have to make, the faster the line moves. Drinks and desserts can be placed at the end of the line away from the main serving area so they can be picked up after the meal and will not slow down the main serving line.

Left-over food can usually be sold to guests to take home. The fact that food is available for sale to take home should be announced as early as possible. Emphasizing that it will be wrapped and that it will keep in the refrigerator will help sales. Soft drinks, potato chips, and other semiperishable supplies which are left over can often be returned to the supplier if prior arrangements are made.

BIBLIOGRAPHY

ALEXANDER, L. M. 1941. Poultry cooking. U.S. Dept. Agr. Farmer's Bull. *1888*.

DAWSON, E. H. 1959. When you cook. *In* U.S. Dept. Agr., Yearbook of Food.

HICKS, F. 1958. Charcoal-broiled chicken. Mich. State Univ., Coop. Ext. Serv. Bull. *355*.

JOULE, T. 1956. Carving turkey. Univ. Missouri Ext. Serv. Folder *45*.

LOWE, B. 1958. Experimental Cookery. John Wiley & Sons, New York.

McHENRY, S. L. 1963. Chicken barbecues. Univ. Hawaii Ext. Serv. Circ. *393*.

MEYER, L. H. 1960. Food Chemistry. Reinhold Publishing Co., New York.

NATIONAL BROILER COUNCIL. 1964. Hooray for chicken. Richmond, Virginia.

NATIONAL TURKEY FEDERATION. 1963. Turkey Handbook. Mount Morris, Illinois.

OHIO POULTRY ASSOCIATION. 1960. So you are going to have a chicken barbecue. Columbus.

ORR, H. L., and INGRAM, R. H. 1964. The outdoor barbecue. Ontario Dept. Agr. Publ. *84*.

POULTRY AND EGG NATIONAL BOARD. 1954. Goose. Leaflet. Chicago, Ill.

POULTRY AND EGG NATIONAL BOARD. 1955A. The miraculous broiler-fryer chicken. Pamphlet. Chicago.

POULTRY AND EGG NATIONAL BOARD. 1955B. Let's have a barbecue with chicken, turkey, duck, goose. Pamphlet. Chicago.

POULTRY AND EGG NATIONAL BOARD. 1962. Cooking the big and small turkey. Leaflet. Chicago.

POULTRY AND EGG NATIONAL BOARD. 1964. Let's barbecue turkey. Leaflet. Chicago.

POULTRY AND EGG NATIONAL BOARD. 1965. Broiler-fryer the all-purpose chicken. Leaflet. Chicago.

RINGROSE, A. T., and THOMPSON, M. L. 1963. Chick-n-que. Virginia Polytechnic Inst., Agr. Ext. Serv. Circ. *924*.

SCHLOSSER, G. G., and GILPIN, G. 1959. What and how to cook. *In* U.S. Dept. Agr. Yearbook of Food.

STEVENSON, G. T., and MILLER, C. 1960. Introduction to Foods and Nutrition. John Wiley & Sons, New York.

CHAPTER 17

Inedible By-products

INTRODUCTION

Inedible by-products in the poultry industry consist of water, manure, dead birds, feathers, blood, offal, and eggs, including cracked eggs, those with blood spots, rots, and those which did not hatch. Although many of these materials are still wasted and dumped as refuse, considerable progress has been made in utilizing them. In the past, the chief problem in utilizing by-products has been assembling enough material in one place to make the operation profitable. In those areas where there was not a sufficient amount of raw material to establish a poultry by-product processing plant, it was generally utilized along with cattle and hog by-products.

POULTRY MANURE

At the present time, disposal of poultry manure is probably the most inefficient and costly operation in the production and marketing of poultry. The need to find practical, economical methods for the disposal of poultry manure is more urgent now than it was ten years ago, despite many attempts and different approaches to find uses which will at least help defray the costs of disposal.

The following statistics help to illustrate the magnitude of the problem. White *et al.* (1944) estimated that it would require 1,750 acres of land to use profitably the annual production of manure from a 100,000-bird-cage-enterprise. Ostrander (1963) estimated that a flock of 100,000 layers produces 25,000 lb. or over 12 tons of manure daily, 365 days a year. Over 278,000,000 lb. of poultry manure are produced daily in the United States. The situation has become so acute that some large operators must figure the cost of manure disposal as one of their operating expenses rather than as a by-product with some value.

A number of investigators have attempted to develop new uses for poultry manure. Fertilizer has been traditionally and still is the most important use. Other uses which have been proposed are re-use as poultry litter, for livestock feed, briquettes for fuel, and for production of gas.

Fertilizer

Several properties of poultry manure have made it a particularly difficult material to handle and process. Modern methods for rearing poultry have complicated the problem further. Much of the manure now produced contains no litter. Litter is not used when birds are reared in cages or slots. When poultry litter is used it absorbs moisture and helps keep the manure friable so a large surface area is exposed to the air. Manure free of litter on the other hand contains 70–80% moisture and has the consistency of a wet concrete mix. Spreaders cannot distribute such material easily.

Dyal (1963) reported other limitations on the use of poultry manure as fertilizer. Because it is a low analysis fertilizer, handling costs in relation to the nutrients distributed are high. There is considerable variation in the composition of poultry manure. Manure must be distributed throughout the year even if it is not convenient to do so. If stored, nutrient losses occur and handling costs increase. Another problem peculiar to poultry manure is that the nitrogen is too quickly available so that, if care is not taken in applying it, burning occurs.

The characteristics of poultry manure produced under several conditions are shown in Table 17.1.

TABLE 17.1

CHARACTERISTICS OF POULTRY MANURE PRODUCED UNDER SEVERAL CONDITIONS

Source of Manure	Treatment	Moisture Content as Sampled, %	Analysis Dry Basis, %			Organic Matter Dry Basis
			N	P	K	
Broiler	Fresh	76	5.66	1.50	2.06	...
Hen	Fresh	76	6.18	1.74	1.64	79.17
Turkey	Fresh	74	5.04	1.19	1.58	77.82
Broiler litter	Accumulated (Ark.)	29	4.09	1.46	2.00	...
Broiler litter	Accumulated (Ga.)	25	2.27	1.07	1.70	...
Hen litter	Accumulated (Ga.)	37	2.00	1.91	1.88	...
Hen	Accumulated (Pa.)	68	3.64	2.64	2.29	64.13
Turkey	Accumulated (Pa.)	63	3.15	2.14	2.62	62.18

From data compiled by Dyal (1963).

Crops Fertilized with Poultry Manure

The fertilizing value of poultry manure has been recognized for years. Kroontje et al. (1958) tested the effects of poultry manure on yields of corn and wheat. Papanos and Brown (1956) reported the results of tests with 14 different crops over a three-year period. Among the crops tested were mixed grasses, corn, sweet corn, tomatoes, lettuce, cabbage, potatoes, onions, beets, carrots, and squash. With some crops it was necessary to supplement the manure with other fertilizer nutrients to provide a balanced formula. Poultry manure was particularly effective in improving the yields of hay from mixed grasses.

Rahn (1949) reported that poultry manure needed no supplement when applied to tomatoes, cantaloups, watermelons, and lima beans. Hitz (1955) reported that five tons of poultry floor litter applied to strawberries was equivalent to 600 lb., of 5-10-10 or 5-10-5 inorganic fertilizer if applied in the fall so as to prevent plant damage. Fischer *et al.* (1961) observed that a soybean-manure system used with apple trees gave higher average cumulative yields of U.S. Fancy apples than other systems tested. The acceptable rates and times of application for poultry manure when used on various crops are shown in Table 17.2.

TABLE 17.2

POULTRY MANURE, ACCEPTABLE RATES AND TIMES OF APPLICATION FOR VARIOUS CROPS

Crop	Condition of Manure	Rate	Time
Corn, sorghum Sudangrass	Dry-dusty Moist-crumbly	2 tons/A 4 tons/A	Spring-before plowing or late fall on cover crop
Grass pasture	Dry-dusty Moist-crumbly	1 ton/A 2 tons/A	Late fall or early spring
Small grains	Do not use		
Potatoes	Dry-dusty Moist-crumbly	2 tons/A 4 tons/A	Fall on cover crops
Sweet corn, celery, cabbage, broccoli	Dry-dusty Moist-crumbly	2 tons/A or 1 bu./500 sq. ft. 4 tons/A or 2 bu./500 sq. ft.	Spring before plowing or late fall on cover crops
Tomatoes, beans, peppers, egg plants	Dry-dusty Moist-crumbly	$1/2$ ton/A or $1/2$ bu./1000 sq. ft. 1 ton/A or 1 bu./1000 sq. ft.	Fall on cover crop or Spring before plowing
Vine crops—cucumbers, melons, squash, pumpkins	Dry-dusty Moist-crumbly	$3/4$ ton/A or 1 bu./800 sq. ft. $1^1/2$ ton/A or 2 bu./800 sq. ft.	Fall on cover crop
Apples, cherries, grapes, raspberries	Dry-dusty Moist-crumbly	$1/2$ ton/A 1 ton/A	Do not apply from June to mid-November
Strawberries	Dry-dusty Moist-crumbly	$1/2$ ton/A 1 ton/A	Apply year prior to planting

If excess vine or foliage growth has occurred on vegetable crops in the last season, poultry manure should not be used.

Compiled by Hinish and Jordan (1963).

Another use for poultry manure is as a fertilizer for lawns, shrubs, and suburban gardens. Poultry manure not only is a good fertilizer for use when starting lawns and flower beds but it also helps to improve the physical structure of the soil, especially where the topsoil has been removed.

In experiments comparing chemical fertilizers and manure on soils where the top layer was removed, yields were higher than when chemical fertilizer was used even several years after the manure was applied.

Burtner (1959) conducted comparative tests on the fertilizing values of dried cow, sheep, and poultry manure applied at rates of 12.5, 25, and 50 lb. per 100 sq. ft. on the growth and color of lawn grasses (Fig. 17.1). Not only was the grass on plots treated with poultry manure higher at the time of cutting but the color of the blades was a deeper green than on the plots treated with cow and sheep manure. In one series of trials, where prolonged dry weather followed application of the poultry manure and no watering was practiced, burning resulted.

Courtesy Ohio Agr. Research and Development Center

FIG. 17.1.   EFFECTS OF SHEEP, COW, AND POULTRY MANURES RESPECTIVELY FROM FRONT TO BACK ON GROWTH OF GRASS

Nutrient Value as a Fertilizer.—Nutrient values of poultry manure vary considerably depending upon the conditions under which it is produced and handled. The ratio of litter to manure and the moisture content cause considerable variation among manures from different pens or houses.

Besides nitrogen, phosphorus, and potassium, poultry manures contain small amounts of boron, calcium, copper, iron, magnesium, manganese, molybdenum, sulfur, and zinc.

In addition to supplying nutrients to the soil, poultry manure also improves soil structure with its organic content. When large quantities of poultry manure are used, it is a good plan to have an analysis of the nitrogen, phosphorus, and potassium content made before application.

Other Uses

Use of Poultry Manure as Litter.—Because of the cost of litter and the labor required to remove manure from poultry houses, some producers use the same litter and manure for several lots of chickens. With good litter management, the manure remains dry and absorbs moisture the same as the litter. Wet manure areas are removed and new litter is frequently spread over the top of the old litter. However, the practice of re-using old litter is not considered a good one because of the danger of infecting new broods of chicks with diseases from the previous brood.

Use of Poultry Manure for Feed.—Several experiments have been conducted to determine the value of poultry manure as feed for livestock. Both the poultry manure and litter have some nutrient value.

Noland and Ray (1956) reported the results of feeding trials with ewes and lambs fed litter containing shredded cane stalks and peanut hulls. The litter contained 25–30% crude protein and amounted to 25–30% of the total weight of the ration. Ewes and lambs did as well on the poultry manure-litter ration as they did on a similar ration where soybean meal replaced the poultry litter. In other trials with fattening steers, the animals had to eat 15% more poultry litter to obtain the same results achieved when fed a cottonseed meal ration. These workers estimated the cost of the ration containing poultry litter to be $2.35 per 100 lb. compared with $3.00 for the cottonseed ration.

Camp (1956) tested rations utilizing up to 40% composted poultry litter for feeding dairy cattle. The cost of the entire ration was $1.45 per 100 lb. Davis (1956) reported that it is possible to produce pork for six cents a pound when shoats receive 50% of their feed from poultry litter. The use of poultry litter reduced the costs of the ration by 60%.

Use of Poultry Manure for Gas Production and Fuel.—In European countries manure gas generators have been used on individual farms as a source of heat. The low quality of the gas and the large amounts of labor required for adding and removing the manure from the generator have prevented adoption of this practice in the United States. Gas produced from manures is toxic and explosions are also a problem.

Taiganides (1963) reported that when sufficiently high rates of digestion of manure can be maintained, combustible gases can be produced which have commercial value. Hart (1960) as reported by Taiganides reported that under laboratory conditions poultry manure held at 95°F. without mixing yielded 10.7 cu. ft. of gas per pound of volatile material destroyed. In a commercial process about a third of the gas produced would have to be used to maintain the temperature of the process.

FEATHERS

Feathers are used for livestock feed, bedding, ornaments, some sporting equipment, fertilizer, and as a filler for chemical fertilizer. Feathers can also be hydrolyzed and made into cloth. Other possibilities for the utilization of feathers which have been considered and either found uneconomical or which have not been perfected reported by Davis et al. (1961) are as paint brush bristles; phenol-formaldehyde resin extenders; foaming agents for use in extinguishing fires; sizing agents; and set-retarding agents for plaster, for adhesives, and in insulating boards.

Types of Feathers

The characteristics of feathers vary according to the age, sex, species, and the area of the body from which the feathers are removed. Hardy and Hardy (1949) have classified feathers into the following groups:

(1) Hard feathers—those with stiff quills, heavy vanes, and a very small amount of fluff; (2) saddle feathers—long narrow, vaned feathers from the saddle and back of the rooster only; (3) half fluff—vane feathers with fluff along the lower half of the quill; (4) three-quarters fluff-vaned feathers with fluff along the lower three-quarters of the quill; (5) fluff—body feathers with firm shafts bearing only fluff, or the soft part of a feather; (6) plumules—small down feathers with soft shafts, bearing only fluff; and (7) down—feathers without a shaft, composed of only a tuft of fluff.

Feathers from waterfowl have considerably more "bulking value" than those from land birds. This characteristic makes them particularly valuable as a filling material for use in bedding.

Processing Feathers

When feathers are to be saved from carcasses, the wing and tail feathers are generally removed immediately after slaughter before the carcass is scalded. "Fancy feathers" such as rooster neck hackles and tails and feathers from turkey hips, necks, backs, wings, and tails are also removed before scalding and separated from other feathers. The remainder of the feathers must be collected from under the pickers and, to prevent deterioration, processed as soon as possible after scalding. Lundgren et al. (1950–1951) described processing feathers. They reported that feathers

can be held overnight in a solution of 30 gal. of water, 15 lb. of salt, and a
pint of muriatic acid to prevent deterioration. Then they can be washed
with a mild soap solution to remove blood and dirt and dried and fluffed
by aeration. In some cases they are sprayed lightly with mineral oil to replace some of the natural oils. If the feathers have a bad odor a preliminary cleaning in Stoddard's solvent (a high-flash-point gasoline) may be
used. The feathers may also be bleached with potassium permanganate,
hydrogen peroxide, or chlorine solutions. Care should be taken to see that
the feathers are thoroughly rinsed after bleaching.

After cleaning the feathers are sorted by blowing them into a tower or
tunnel where the small feathers and down are separated from the larger,
heavier feathers. A variable speed blower is used to blow the feathers up
and out of the tower or through outlets at various heights in the tower.
Steam must sometimes be used to overcome static electricity. Color,
cleanliness, source, and size then determine the values of the feathers.
For some uses different types of feathers are blended together; for certain
other uses feathers are crushed.

Bedding

Bedding includes pillows, comforts, sleeping bags, mattresses, and
upholstery. With the development of synthetic fibers and plastic foams
the market for feathers used in this manner has declined. Only body
feathers are used for bedding and these are generally from waterfowl.
Weiner (1956) reported that the basic requirements for feathers used for
bedding are that they possess maximum bulk or volume when in use and
occupy a minimum of space for handling and storage when not in use.
Other criteria for materials used as bedding are resilience or the ability to
return to original volume, fluffability, low absorption, softness,
drapability, warmth, cleanliness, fire resistance, launderability, and
durability. Feathers, especially down from waterfowl, come about
as close as any natural or synthetic material yet developed to meeting
these requirements. Down is three-dimensional, therefore, it does not
have as much of a tendency to pack as other types of fibers and the
fiber length is longer than that of feathers. Down does not have
the high proportion of shaft weight which contributes more to weight
than bulking capacity.

Ornaments

Shape, color, size, and plumage patterns are particularly important
when feathers are used for decorative purposes. Because of their bright
plumage certain feathers from wild fowl such as cock pheasants are in demand. Such feathers are used for millinery, plume pens, toys, artificial

flowers, Christmas decorations, and other similar uses. In many cases the feathers are dyed, bent, and trimmed to meet specific needs.

Sporting Equipment

Only carefully selected feathers from specific parts of the body of the bird, in some cases from specific species, can be used for sporting equipment. Turkey feathers used for fletching arrows must come from birds with feathers sufficiently mature so that they will not bend when the arrow is shot. Feathers on an individual arrow must all come from either the right or left wing because the spin of the arrow depends upon whether feathers from the right or left wing are used. One large bow and arrow manufacturer requires the wing feathers from over six million turkeys annually. Stiff feathers are also needed for shuttlecocks. A small number of carefully selected feathers are used in making artificial lures for fishing.

Fertilizer

Feathers make good fertilizer and mulch. They decompose and release nitrogen slowly. Unfortunately, when dry they blow easily which limits their use to rural areas or to those conditions where they can be plowed under.

Artificial Fibers

Cloth and paint brush bristles can be made from artificial fibers made from poultry feathers. The feathers are first ground and broken down in a hot concentrated chemical solution, redispersed in water, and then extruded through a spinneret into a chemical bath which precipitates the fibers. They are then washed, stretched, dried, and the detergent extracted. Because other fibers with similar characteristics can be manufactured at lower prices, the fiber has never been mass produced.

BLOOD AND OFFAL

Offal consists of heads, feet, and inedible viscera. Inedible viscera consist of the intestinal tract, lungs, spleen, windpipe, preen gland, and the reproductive organs.

Blood can be utilized for fish bait, fertilizer, rendered for blood meal, or discarded. In many cases it is donated to renderers for the hauling.

Offal is used for domestically grown fur-bearing animals such as mink, for pet food, for fish hatcheries, for hog food, and for meat scrap for poultry and other livestock. Because of the danger of transmitting pathogenic organisms, all offal should be cooked. When saving offal for these purposes, care should be taken to see that all leg bands, wing bands, and other pieces of metal, glass, and extraneous material are removed.

Poultry offal can replace horsemeat as feed for fur bearing animals, particularly mink. According to Schiable (1963), mink in their wild state feed on a diet of fish, frogs, small mammals, and birds. Meat from poultry offal is quite palatable for mink and produces early growth. When used for mink feeding, it is generally prepared by washing, grinding, and freezing. It is then held frozen until just before feeding. A typical mink ration consists of 25% of a high-quality protein source such as horsemeat, eggs, cheese, rabbit, whalemeat, etc., 20% poultry by-products, 20% supplemented cereal, 15% tripe, 15% whole fish, and 5% liver.

Poultry offal also makes good pet food. For preparation, the offal is first washed and ground and then mixed with meal or pellets. An increasing amount of poultry offal is being canned for pet food.

The yields of processed by-products from broilers, fowl, and turkeys are shown in Table 17.3 and the composition in Table 17.4.

TABLE 17.3

YIELDS OF PROCESSED BY-PRODUCTS FROM BROILERS, FOWL AND TURKEYS

	Feather Meal	By-product Meal	Blood Meal	Grease
	% of Live Wt.			
Broiler	5.50	5.16	0.78	0.64
Fowl	5.50	4.27	0.67	3.17
Turkey	5.90	4.17	0.78	0.84

From data compiled by Lortscher et al. (1957).

TABLE 17.4

COMPOSITIONS OF POULTRY BY-PRODUCTS, %

	Feather Meal		Dried Blood		By-product Meal		Tankage	
	Range	Avg.	Range	Avg.	Range	Avg.	Range	Avg.
Protein	75–90	85	75–85	80	50–60	55	45–55	50
Moisture	5–15	8	5–15	8	5–15	8	5–12	8
Fat	2–4	3	0.8–1.2	1.0	6–15	10	16–25	20
Fiber and ash	2–7	4	8–14	11	25–30	27	20–25	22

From data compiled by Lortscher et al. (1957).

RENDERING

Lortscher et al. (1957) reported that the following practices are generally used in processing poultry by-products. First, a large proportion of the water is evaporated in a dry-rendering cooker and then the material is reduced to about 8% moisture either in the same cooker or in a separate drier. The dehydrated material is then pressed to remove excess fat so the rendered material has a fat content of about 10%. Finally, the product is

Courtesy Big Dutchman/Barker

FIG. 17.2.   A BY-PRODUCT OFFAL SEPARATOR

ground to a size small enough to pass through 8- to 12-mesh screens.

Kahle and Gray (1956) compiled the following list of recommendations made by renderers for increasing the value of by-products:

(1) Use a rotary screen or some other method to keep the water content of offal to a minimum [Fig. 17.2]; (2) keep feathers out of offal; (3) keep crop and gizzard contents separate; (4) clean viscera to remove impurities (grit, wood, fiber, etc.); (5) bale feathers to reduce moisture content and reduce cooking time; (6) fill drums properly and provide a more uniform daily volume; (7) use bulk handling methods and increase mechanization if volume is great enough; (8) provide elevators and loading devices; (9) use a chemical in drums to help keep down obnoxious odor in summer; (10) install hoppers so that material from one or more small plants can be held longer and a pickup truck can get a full load at a single stop; and (11) operate poultry plants more regularly.

Rendered Poultry By-products

Poultry by-products processed by rendering can be divided into five general categories depending upon the composition of the raw materials.

They are: (1) Blood meal which consists of ground dry blood. (2) Poultry by-product meal which contains only clean, dry-rendered, wholesome parts such as the heads, feet, undeveloped egg, gizzards, and intestines, but not feathers except as a few might be included in the normal processing and collection practice. (3) Hydrolyzed feathers which are the product resulting from the treatment of clean, undecomposed feathers free of additives. (4) Mixed poultry by-product meal which contains blood, offal, and feathers, generally in their natural proportions. Mixed poultry by-products produce a more balanced product nutritionally than the other formulations, but it takes longer to process mixed by-products because feathers are harder to decompose than offal. (5) In some cases fat is extracted from the resulting product.

Grease

Kahle and Gray (1956) reported that grease extracted from the offal is stored in tanks or drums. Grease extracted from poultry offal is generally darker in color and lower in grade than that extracted from beef, mutton, and pork.

BY-PRODUCTS FROM EGGS

Eggs for hatching and for culinary purposes utilize the majority of the eggs produced. Eggs are also used for virus culture, vaccines, tissue cultures, toxicity studies, embryology work, as adhesives, in tanning, in medicines and cosmetics, and in culture media. They are also used as semen diluters, fibers, for mosaics, in art work, as Easter eggs, and for animal feed, and finally for fertilizer. Despite all of the above uses, only a small proportion of the entire production is utilized in forms other than for hatching eggs and for culinary purposes. Romanoff and Romanoff (1949) have described the inedible uses for eggs in detail.

Uses in the Laboratory

Eggs make ideal laboratory material for virus culture, production of vaccines, tissue culture, toxicity studies, and for embryology studies. They can be obtained throughout the year in large quantities with good fertility and hatchability at a relatively low cost. Fertile eggs can be shipped long distances without reducing hatchability and, because of their short incubation period, it is possible to complete a set of experiments in three weeks or less.

Developing chick embryos are an excellent material for the propagation of viruses. Viruses require living tissue in order to grow. Bacteria and protozoa which will not grow on culture media can sometimes be propagated on developing embryos. Malignant tumor cells can also be propagated in developing embryos under some conditions.

Vaccines used for the control of encephalomyelitis, laryngotracheitis, lymphogranuloma venereum, measles, and pox have been extracted from the organisms grown on chick embryos.

Germicides and other toxic or inhibitory substances can also be assayed or tested by the use of developing chick embryos. Different concentrations of the substance are injected into the egg before incubation or during embryo development. After a short incubation period, the eggs are opened and the number of dead or deformed embryos are determined. The effects of specific compounds, for example, thalidomide, on the development of malformations can be measured by examining the embryos and determining the specific malformations.

Manufacturing Uses

Romanoff and Romanoff (1949) reported that eggs have been used in artist's paints, cosmetics, photographic supplies, printer's ink, tanner's yolk, mordants, soaps, and in a number of synthetic products. Some of these uses for eggs have been discontinued with the development of new and better chemical compounds.

Oil in egg yolk and protein in the albumen make egg a desirable material for tanning leather. The oils help to produce a leather with a soft texture and the albumen and yolk together help to stabilize the emulsion of the mixture used in tanning. Egg yolk also increases the tensile strength and the tear strength of the leather. In a few cases eggs can also be used in the finishing of leather and to produce a luster and gloss on the surface of furs.

Technical albumen, a dehydrated egg albumen produced by centrifuging crushed egg shells to remove the albumen left in the eggs after breaking, is used as an adhesive for cementing cork gaskets to the crown of soft drink bottle caps.

Artificial fibers can also be manufactured from egg albumen.

Cosmetic and Medicinal Uses

The emulsification properties and the oil content of egg yolks make them a valuable ingredient in cosmetics and some medicines. Oil from yolks helps to impart a sheen to hair after shampooing and the emulsifying action of the yolk aids in removing soil. Yolks have been used in ointments for their oil and raw egg white is a common household antidote for poison.

Animal Feeds

A common use for inedible eggs has been for hog feed. To prevent the spread of disease, eggs should be cooked before feeding to animals. One deterrent to the widespread use of inedible eggs for feed is the high proportion of calcium contained in eggs in relation to the other nutrients. Egg shells, whose main ingredient is calcium carbonate, constitute about 10% of the total weight of the egg. Not only is the ratio of calcium to other nutrients high but the hard gritty texture of the shell makes whole eggs unpalatable.

Some eggs used for animal foods are broken and the shells discarded. The liquid egg is then mixed with other ingredients and partially cooked or canned and sterilized.

Egg Shells

A number of attempts have been made to find uses for egg shells. Since the major ingredient in shells, calcium carbonate, can be obtained from other sources at much lower cost, little progress has been made. When egg shells are to be used as a mineral supplement in animal or human food, they must be sterilized. Sterilization adds an additional cost to the shells. Lundgren et al. (1950-1951) reported results of tests by U.S. Department of Agriculture in which ground eggs shells were used as calcium supplements in foods. Grittiness was partially eliminated by grinding the shells fine enough to pass through a No. 400 sieve. Ground egg shell at a level of 0.4% in baked custards, ice cream, foundation cake, muffins, yeast rolls, popovers, and mayonnaise did not affect palatability or cooking quality.

At the present time, most egg shells are discarded and used for fertilizer for liming soil. In 1950, it was estimated that shells were worth $2-$5 a ton when used for this purpose.

BIBLIOGRAPHY

BURTNER, R. H. 1959. Processing poultry manure for fertilizer and mulch. M.S. Thesis, Ohio State University, Columbus.

CAMP, A. P. 1956. Poultry litter fed to cattle. Poultry Dig. 15, No. 8, 504.

DAVIS, D. 1956. Feeding poultry litter. Poultry Tribune 62, No. 8, 10.

DAVIS, J. G., MECCHI, E. P., and LINEWEAVER, H. 1961. Processing of poultry by-products and their utilization in feeds. Part I. Processing of poultry by-products. U.S. Dept. Agr. Util. Res. Rept. 3.

DYAL, R. S. 1963. Agricultural value of poultry manure. Proc. of Natl. Symp. Poultry Ind. Waste Management, Univ. Nebraska, Lincoln.

FISCHER, U. J., RALPH, E. H., and WILLIAMS, D. B. 1961. Effect of apple soil management practices upon growth, fruitfulness and fruit quality. Delaware Agr. Expt. Sta. Tech. Bull. 336.

FLAMM, W. 1963. Good news is offal. Proc. Natl. Symp. Poultry Ind. Waste Management, Univ. Nebraska, Lincoln.

HARDY, J. J., and HARDY, T. M. P. 1949. Feathers from domestic and wild fowl. U.S. Dept. Agr. Circ. *803*.

HART, S. A. 1960. Sludge digestion tests for livestock manures. Mimeo. Calif. Agr. Engr. Dept., Univ. Calif. as cited by Taiganides (1963) in Proc. Natl. Symp. Poultry Ind. Waste Management. Univ. Nebraska, Lincoln.

HINISH, W. W., and JORDAN, H. C. 1963. Using poultry manure. Penn. State Univ., Coll. Agr. Ext. Serv. Leaflet *255*.

HITZ, C. W. 1955. Utilization of poultry manure in strawberry production. Delaware Agr. Expt. Sta. Bull. *312*.

KAHLE, H. S., and GRAY, L. R. 1956. Utilization and disposal of poultry by-products and wastes. U.S. Dept. Agr. Mktg. Res. Rept. *143*.

KROONTJE, W., GISH, P. T., and STIVERS, R. K. 1958. Nutrient value of poultry manure compared with that of mineral fertilizer. Virginia Agr. Expt. Sta. Bull. *468*.

LORTSCHER, L. L., SACHSEL, G. F., WILHELMY, O. JR., and FILBERT, R. B. JR. 1957. Processing poultry by-products in poultry slaughtering plants. U.S. Dept. Agr. Mktg. Res. Rept. *181*.

LUNDGREN, H. P., LINEWEAVER, H., and MCNALLY, E. H. 1950–1951. Utilization of poultry wastes. U.S. Dept. Agr. Yearbook of Crops.

NOLAND, P. H., and RAY, L. M. 1956. Poultry litter found useful in cattle feeds. Broiler Grower *7, 56*.

OSTRANDER, C. E. 1963. Waste management problems on the farm. Proc. Natl. Symp. Poultry Ind. Waste Management, Univ. Nebraska, Lincoln.

PAPANOS, S., and BROWN, B. A. 1950. Poultry manure: its nature, care, and use. Univ. Conn. (Storrs) Agr. Expt. Sta. Bull. *272*.

PAPANOS, S., and BROWN, B. A. 1956. Care and use of poultry manure. Conn. Agr. Expt. Sta. Prog. Rept. *12*.

RAHN, E. M. 1949. Poultry manure as a fertilizer for vegetable crops. Delaware Agr. Expt. Sta. Bull. *281*.

ROMANOFF, A. L., and ROMANOFF, A. J. 1949. The Avian Egg. John Wiley & Sons, New York.

SCHIABLE, P. J. 1963. The fur industry and its use of animal feedstuffs. Merck Agr. Memo Winter, 1962–63.

TAIGANIDES, E. P. 1963. Digestion of farm poultry wastes. Proc. Natl. Symp. Poultry Ind. Waste Management, Univ. Nebraska, Lincoln.

WEINER, L. J. 1956. Physical properties of feathers and down with particular reference to their use as filling materials in sleeping bags. Proc. Conf. Util. Chicken Feathers as Filling Materials, U.S. Army Quartermaster Corps.

WHITE, J. W., HOLBEN, F. J., and RICHER, A. C. 1944. Production, composition and value of poultry manure. Penn Agr. Expt. Sta. Bull. *469*.

WISMAN, E. L., HOLMES, C. E., and ENGEL, R. W. 1958. Utilization of poultry by-products in poultry rations. Poultry Sci. *37*, 834.

CHAPTER 18

Egg Quality
Identification

INTRODUCTION

Egg quality standards are based on shell cleanliness, soundness, texture, and shape; relative viscosity of the white and freedom from foreign matter; and the shape, firmness and freedom from defects of the yolk. Since deterioration in quality can occur because of conditions happening before a hen lays an egg or during handling between production and consumption, it is helpful if one is familiar with the parts of an egg and the physiology of egg formation.

FORMATION OF AN EGG YOLK

Egg formation begins when visible red rays from sun or electric light strike the hen's eye. The light rays cause the pituitary gland to secrete a follicle stimulating hormone (FSH) which is carried through the bloodstream to the ovaries located under the backbone. When one small selected ovum, pinpoint in size, from among a thousand or more present in the ovary is stimulated by FSH it suddenly begins growing at a rapid rate until it outgrows the thin transparent cellophane-like sac enclosing the developing yolk. At that time the yolk sac ruptures along the suture line, a whitish ridge or line around the yolk sac. The yolk sac itself contains many blood vessels to carry nutrient material to the developing yolk. If one of these blood vessels ruptures at the time the yolk sac splits a small blood spot may be included in the egg. Although a normal hen usually has from 3,600 to 4,000 ova, there appears to be no relationship between the number of ova a hen carries and the number of eggs a hen lays.

SECRETION OF EGG WHITE AND SHELL IN THE OVIDUCT

The infundibulum, magnum, isthmus, uterus, and vagina make up the oviduct. When a completed yolk is shed from a ruptured yolk sac it drops down into the infundibulum, so called because it is shaped like a funnel, where it remains for about 15 min. Fertilization takes place in this area. Then the yolk moves by peristaltic action into the magnum. Peristaltic action is caused by a series of coordinated, synchronized, involuntary muscle expansions and contractions.

In the magnum the yolk is surrounded by the thick egg white most of which is thick white. About half the volume of egg white is secreted here. The albumen quality of the egg is also largely determined by

291

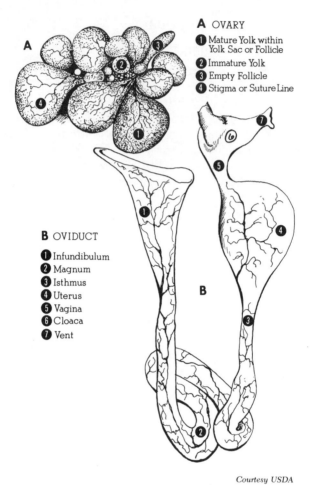

A OVARY
❶ Mature Yolk within Yolk Sac or Follicle
❷ Immature Yolk
❸ Empty Follicle
❹ Stigma or Suture Line

B OVIDUCT
❶ Infundibulum
❷ Magnum
❸ Isthmus
❹ Uterus
❺ Vagina
❻ Cloaca
❼ Vent

Courtesy USDA

FIG. 18.1.   ENLARGED DRAWINGS OF OVARY (A) AND OVIDUCT (B)

the amount of ovomucin secreted in this area.   After remaining in the magnum for about three hours the egg passes into the isthmus.

In the isthmus, so called because it is a narrow area in the oviduct, water, some salts and the shell membranes are added.   An egg removed from the isthmus at this point is wrinkled because the thin white has not been added.   The egg remains in the isthmus about 1¼ hr.

As the egg moves down the oviduct it spirals similar to a bullet passing through a rifle barrel.   This spiraling action causes the white at the ends of the yolk to twist and form chalazae cords.   In the same area, a change in the colloidal structure of the white also occurs

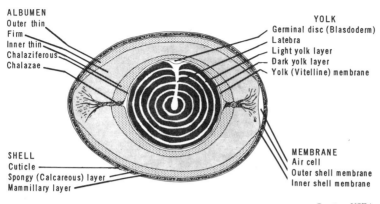

ALBUMEN
Outer thin
Firm
Inner thin
Chalaziferous
Chalazae

YOLK
Germinal disc (Blasdoderm)
Latebra
Light yolk layer
Dark yolk layer
Yolk (Vitelline) membrane

SHELL
Cuticle
Spongy (Calcareous) layer
Mammillary layer

MEMBRANE
Air cell
Outer shell membrane
Inner shell membrane

Courtesy USDA

FIG. 18.2.   THE PARTS OF AN EGG

which contributes to the formation of the chalazae.

The uterus also secretes thin white and salts which pass through the egg shell membrane by osmosis. The calciferous layer of the shell is formed in the uterus. The egg can be detected at this stage by feeling or palpitating the abdomen of a hen almost ready to lay. The egg remains in this area from 10 to 21 hr.

The completed egg then moves through the vagina, cloaca, and finally out the vent. The complete laying cycle which takes from 24 to 48 hr can start over again as early as 30 min after an egg is laid.

PARTS OF AN EGG

The extreme outer coating of an egg shell, consisting of an invisible mucous coating deposited on the surface of the shell while the hen is in the process of laying, is called the cuticle or bloom. It is a keratin-like protein of the same general structure as feathers, hair and fingernails. Because the cuticle fills the shell pores in the calcium part of the shell and deteriorates with age causing the pore to enlarge, it controls the passage of molds, bacteria, moisture, and gases through the shell.

The spongy calciferous layer, although made up mainly of calcium, is so named because of its spongy appearance after the protein has been removed. The protein is removed by soaking the shell in acid, which leaves only the calcium portion of the shell. It consists of calcium crystals set at right angles to the surface of the shell.

The mammillary or inner layer consists of knobs of calcium perpendicular to the surface of the shell. The cuticle, spongy layer, and

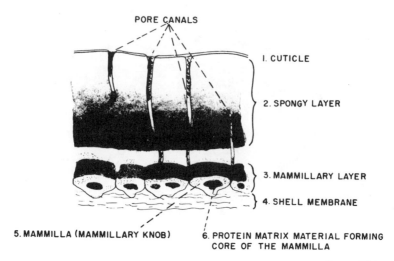

PORE CANALS

1. CUTICLE

2. SPONGY LAYER

3. MAMMILLARY LAYER

4. SHELL MEMBRANE

5. MAMMILLA (MAMMILLARY KNOB)

6. PROTEIN MATRIX MATERIAL FORMING CORE OF THE MAMMILLA

Courtesy USDA

FIG. 18.3.   MAGNIFIED CROSS SECTION OF THE SHELL OF AN EGG

mamillary layer can only be observed under a microscope.

Underneath and attached to the calcium part of the shell are the inner and outer shell membranes. These are also made of keratin. Immediately after laying, the warm egg cools and loses gases and moisture through the shell, causing the contents to contract. At that time the two shell membranes separate at the large blunt end of the shell to form an air cell.

The shell consists of about 94 to 97 percent calcium carbonate. The other three to six percent are organic matter and shell pigment. Blue and brown pigments give eggs their characteristic color.

Shell pores, which may amount to as many as 8,000 per shell, vary greatly in number and size. Many of them do not go completely through the shell.

The watery gelatinous material around the yolk is the white or albumen. It is divided into four layers. Around the edge of the broken out egg is a thin watery layer of white. This is called the outer thin white. Next to this layer is a more gelatinous material called the outer thick white. If the outer thick white is cut carefully with a knife the next layer or inner thin white will run out. The thick layer immediately surrounding the yolk is called the inner thick or chalaziferous layer. It has two whitish cords, one on each end of the yolk, called the chalazae cords.

The yolk consists of concentric layers of light and dark yolk enclosed by the vitelline membrane, the latebra, which is part of the concentric layers, and the germinal disc.

The small white disc found on the surface of the yolk is the germinal disc or blastoderm and is the spot where embryo development begins if the egg is fertile. However, the germinal disc is always present, whether the egg is fertilized or not.

A thin membrane called the vitelline membrane holds the yolk together and gives the yolk its shape. The high concentration of yolk fluids causes the yolk to absorb water from the white over time. In so doing, the yolk becomes large and flabby.

The concentric layers of light and dark yolk are visible white and yellow bands of color resulting from secretion of different amounts of pigment by the hen during yolk formation. Light layers of yolk indicate periods when less pigment was available. The latebra keeps the germinal disc floating upright.

Carotenoid pigments give egg yolks their characteristic yellow color. They are made up mostly of cryptoxanthin, alcohol soluble xanthopylls, and carotenes. Vitamin A is included in this group.

Egg shell quality is influenced by the color, shape, and structure of the shell. Colors range from white, through tints to brown. One breed, the Araucana, lays eggs with bluish green shells. Egg shape can vary from long and narrow to short and round with most eggs between these extremes. Normal shells are smooth, about 15 thousandths of an inch thick, and withstand normal handling during marketing.

A number of abnormal conditions can occur in eggs. These are described in the USDA Egg Grading Manual (1972) as follows:

Double-yolked eggs result when two yolks are released about the same time or when one yolk is lost into the body cavity for a day and is picked up by the funnel when the next day's yolk is released.

Yolkless eggs are usually formed about a bit of tissue that is sloughed off the ovary or oviduct. This tissue stimulates the secreting glands of the oviduct and a yolkless egg results.

The abnormality of an **egg within an egg** is due to reversal of direction of the egg by the wall of the oviduct. One day's egg is added to the next day's egg and shell is formed around both.

Bloodspots are caused by a rupture of one or more small blood vessels in the yolk follicle at the time of ovulation.

Meat spots have been demonstrated to be either blood spots which have changed in color, due to chemical action, or tissue sloughed off from the reproductive organs of the hen.

Soft-shelled eggs generally occur when an egg is prematurely laid, and insufficient time in the uterus prevents the deposit of the shell.

Thin-shelled eggs may be caused by dietary deficiencies, heredity, or disease.

Glassy- and chalky-shelled eggs are caused by malfunction of the uterus of the laying bird. Glassy eggs are less porous and will not hatch but may retain their quality.

Off-colored yolks are due to substances in feed that cause off-color.

Off-flavored eggs may be due to disease or to certain feed flavors.

EGG QUALITY CHARACTERISTICS

For marketing, eggs are sorted into uniform classifications of shell size, color, shape and degree of severity of blemishes. The official terms used by the USDA to describe shell conditions, air cells, white, and yolk are as follows:

Check

An individual egg that has a broken shell or crack in the shell but with its shell membranes intact and it's contents do not leak. A "check" is considered to be lower in quality than a dirty.

Terms Descriptive of the Shell

Clean.—A shell that is free from foreign material and from stains or discolorations that are readily visible. An egg may be considered clean if it has only very small specks or stains, if such specks or stains are not of sufficient number or intensity to detract from the generally clean appearance of the egg. Eggs that show traces of processing oil on the shell are considered clean unless soiled.

Dirty.—A shell which has dirt or foreign material adhering to its surface, which has prominent stains, or has moderate stains covering more than one-fourth of the shell surface.

Practically Normal (AA or A Quality).—A shell that approximates the usual shape and that is of good even texture and strength and is free of rough areas or thin spots. Slight ridges and rough areas that do not materially affect the shape, texture and strength of the shell are permitted.

Slightly Abnormal (B Quality).—A shell that may be somewhat unusual in shape or that may be slightly faulty in texture or strength. It may show definite ridges but no pronounced thin spots or rough areas.

Abnormal (C Quality).—A shell that may be decidedly misshapen or faulty in texture or strength or that may show pronounced ridges, thin spots or rough areas.

Terms Descriptive of the Air Cell

Depth of Air Cell (Air Space Between Shell Membranes, Normally in the Large End of the Egg).—The depth of the air cell is the distance from its top to its bottom when the egg is held air cell upward.

Practically Regular (AA or A Quality).—An air cell that maintains a practically fixed position in the egg and shows a fairly even outline with not more than 2/8-in. movement in any direction as the egg is rotated.

Free Air Cell (B or C Quality).—An air cell that moves freely toward the uppermost point in the egg as the egg is rotated slowly.

Bubbly Air Cell (B or C Quality).—A ruptured air cell resulting in one or more small separate air bubbles usually floating beneath the main air cell.

Terms Descriptive of the White

Clear.—A white that is free from discolorations or from any foreign bodies floating in it. (Prominent chalazaes should not be confused with foreign bodies such as spots or blood clots.

Firm (AA Quality).—A white that is sufficiently thick or viscous to prevent the yolk outline from being more than slightly defined or indistinctly indicated when the egg is twirled under a candling light. With respect to a broken-out egg, a firm white has a Haugh unit value of 72 or higher when measured at a temperature between 45° and 60°F.

Reasonably Firm (A Quality).—A white that is somewhat less thick or viscous than a firm white. A reasonably firm white permits the yolk to approach the shell more closely which results in a fairly well defined yolk outline when the egg is twirled. With respect to a broken-out egg, a reasonably firm white has a Haugh unit value of 60 to 72 when measured at a temperature between 45° and 60°F.

Slightly Weak (B Quality).—A white that is lacking in thickness or viscosity to an extent that causes the yolk outline to appear well defined when the egg is twirled. With respect to a broken-out egg, a slightly weak white has a Haugh unit value of 31 to 60 when measured at a temperature between 45° and 60°F.

Weak and Watery (C Quality).—A white that is thin and generally lacking in viscosity. A weak and watery white permits the yolk to approach the shell closely, thus causing the yolk outline to appear plainly visible and dark when the egg is twirled. With respect to a broken-out egg, a weak and watery white has a Haugh unit value lower than 31 when measured at a temperature between 45° and 60°F.

Blood Clots and Spots (Not Due to Germ Development).—Blood clots or spots on the surface of the yolk or floating in the white. These blood clots may have lost their characteristic red color and appear as small spots or foreign material commonly referred to as meat spots. If they are small (aggregating not more than ⅛-in. in diameter) the egg may be classed as "C Quality." If larger, or showing diffusion of blood in the white surrounding them, the egg shall be classified as loss.

Terms Descriptive of the Yolk

Outline Slightly Defined (AA Quality).—A yolk outline that is indistinctly indicated and appears to blend into the surrounding white as the egg is twirled.

Outline Fairly Well Defined (A Quality).—A yolk outline that is quite definite and distinct as the egg is twirled.

Outline Well Defined (B Quality).—A yolk outline that is quite definite and distinct as the egg is twirled.

Outline Plainly Visible (C Quality).—A yolk outline that is clearly visible as a dark shadow when the egg is twirled.

Slightly Enlarged and Slightly Flattened (B Quality).—A yolk in which the yolk membranes and tissues have weakened somewhat causing it to appear slightly enlarged and slightly flattened.

Enlarged and Flattened (C Quality).—A yolk in which the yolk membranes and tissues have weakened and moisture has been absorbed from the white to such an extent that it appears definitely enlarged and flat.

Practically Free from Defects (AA or A Quality).—A yolk that shows no germ development but may show other very slight defects on its surface.

Definite But Not Serious Defects (B Quality).—A yolk that may show definite spots or areas on its surface but with only slight indications of germ development or other pronounced or serious defects.

Other Serious Defects (C Quality).—A yolk that shows well developed spots or areas and other serious defects, such as olive yolks which do not render the egg inedible.

Clearly Visible Germ Development (C Quality).—A development of the germ spot on the yolk of a fertile egg that has progressed to a point where it is plainly visible as a definite circular area or spot with no blood in evidence.

Blood Due to Germ Development.—Blood caused by development of the germ in a fertile egg to the point where it is visible as definite lines or as a blood ring. Such an egg is classified as inedible.

General Terms

The following general terms are also used to characterize eggs:

Loss.—An egg that is inedible, smashed or broken so that contents are leaking, cooked, frozen, contaminated, or containing bloody whites, large bloodspots, large unsightly meat spots, or other foreign material.

Inedible Eggs.—Eggs of the following descriptions are classed as inedible: black rots, yellow rots, white rots, mixed rots (addled eggs), sour eggs, eggs with green whites, eggs with stuck yolks, moldy eggs, musty eggs, eggs showing blood rings, eggs containing embryo chicks (at or beyond the blood ring stage), and any eggs that are adulterated as such term is defined pursuant to the Federal Food, Drug, and Cosmetic Act.

Leaker.—An individual egg that has a crack or break in the shell and shell membranes to the extent that the egg contents are exuding or free to exude through the shell.

In addition to the above official classifications there are a number of terms used to characterize certain conditions found in eggs. Generally, these are observed and removed during candling. They are:

Stuck Yolks occur when the yolk membrane becomes attached to the shell membrane. It generally occurs in older eggs that have been left in a fixed position for a long time. When the thick white becomes thin, the yolk floats close to the shell and becomes attached to the shell membrane.

Mixed rot (addled egg) occurs when the vitelline membrane of the yolk breaks and the yolk mixes with the white, resulting in a murkiness throughout the interior of the egg when viewed before the candling light.

Sour eggs are often difficult to detect by standard candling methods. Generally, eggs in this condition show a weak white and murky shadow around an off-center swollen yolk. The bacteria causing sour eggs belong to a group named *Pseudomonas.* These organisms produce a material which fluoresces under ultraviolet light giving off a green sheen. The adoption of ultraviolet light in candling (black light) has made the detection of this type of loss easier.

Green whites are caused by *Pseudomonas* bacteria and will fluoresce under an ultraviolet light. Frequently they also have a sour odor.

White rots appear as threadlike shadows in the thin white. In later stages the yolk appears severely blemished when viewed before the candling light. Frequently there is a fishy odor.

Musty eggs do not show up in front of a candling light but can be detected by their musty odor. They can be caused by absorption of odors, molds, and bacteria.

TABLE 18.1

OFF-ODORS AND -FLAVORS IN EGGS

Material Used	Effect on Eggs	Remarks
Insecticides		
BHC	Taste and smell like BHC	*Do not use*
Malathion (liquid)	Taste and smell like cat urine	If needed, use at night—chemical carrier used may influence
Ronnel (Korlon)	Bad chemical taste and smell	*Do not use*
Sevin (wettable)	Slight bitter taste, especially in albumen	Do not spray on eggs
Packing material		
Moldy, dirty, damp filler-flats	Musty, cardboard smell and taste	Definitely will cause trouble. Oil keeps filler-flats damp for mold growth
Petroleum products		
Oil not fully refined	Chemical smell and flavor	Make sure that egg oil is odorless, tasteless, and colorless (approved)
Kerosene	Taste and smell like kerosene	Avoid kerosene fumes
Gasoline	Taste and smell like gasoline	Avoid gasoline fumes
Sanitizer-detergents		
Chlorine products (concentrated)	Slight bitter taste and chemical smell of chlorine gas trapped in	Follow directions of manufacturers
Products used in rinse		
Chlorine products similar to Clorox (concentrated)	Bitter taste and chemical smell	Follow directions of manufacturer; be sure the product is being dispensed properly
Destainers		
Citric acid	Slight off-flavor if held in destainer too long	Follow direction of manufacturer
Apples		
All varieties (some worse than others)	Bad bitter, cardboard flavor and odor	*Do not allow eggs to be stored near apples*
Vegetables and citrus fruits		
Most vegetables and citrus fruits	Most vegetables and citrus fruits will impart flavor and odor to eggs	Do not store eggs with citrus fruit or vegetables
Hen house odors		
Fumes of chicken manure	Possible to pick up odors and flavor if fumes strong and eggs are not gathered frequently	If odors are bad, should gather eggs three times a day
Odors in egg room	Musty odors, etc., will be picked up by eggs	Keep egg rooms clean and free of odors

Source: Anonymous mimeograph report; no date or source available.

TABLE 18.2

U.S. WEIGHT CLASSES FOR CONSUMER GRADES FOR SHELL EGGS

Size or Weight Class	Minimum Net Weight per Dozen (Oz.)	Minimum Net Weight per 30 Dozen (Lb.)	Minimum Weight for Individual Eggs at Rate per Dozen (Oz.)
Jumbo	30	56	29
Extra large	27	50½	26
Large	24	45	23
Medium	21	39½	20
Small	18	34	17
Peewee	15	28	—

Courtesy USDA

Moldy eggs show up as mold spots on the shell or by mold growth in checked areas of the shell or by actual growth inside the shell itself. In advanced cases the egg appears completely black before the candler with the exception of the air cell.

Black rots are generally opaque (with the exception of the air cell) when viewed before the candling light.

Cooked eggs are eggs which have been subjected to heat resulting in coagulation of the contents. They usually have threadlike shadows in the albumen or a dark opaque appearance when completely coagulated.

Blood rings and embryo chicks are caused by germ development in fertile eggs held at incubation temperatures.

No grade eggs include eggs of possible edible qualities that have been contaminated by smoke, chemicals, or other foreign material which has seriously affected the character, appearance, or flavor of the eggs.

Off-flavored eggs come from a variety of causes. Table 18.1 lists some of the more common sources of off-flavor contamination.

EGG SIZE

Eggs, in addition to being segregated on the basis of quality, are also sorted into weight classes for uniformity. Table 18.2 shows the weight classes for U.S. Consumer Grades for Shell Eggs.

U.S. CONSUMER GRADES

Consumer grades are determined by inspection of all eggs individually under a candling light. The grades are AA, A, B, and C quality. Table 18.3 shows the minimum requirements for the several grades.

AA Quality eggs have clean, unbroken, practically normal shells

TABLE 18.3

SUMMARY OF U.S. STANDARDS FOR QUALITY OF INDIVIDUAL SHELL EGGS

Specifications for Each Quality Factor

Quality Factor	AA Quality	A Quality	B Quality	C Quality
Shell	Clean. Unbroken. Practically normal.	Clean. Unbroken. Practically normal.	Clean; to very slightly stained. Unbroken. May be slightly abnormal.	Clean; to moderately stained. Unbroken. May be abnormal
Air cell	1/8 in. or less in depth. Practically regular.	3/16 in. or less in depth. Practically regular.	3/8 in. or less in depth. May be free or bubbly.	May be over 3/8 in. in depth. May be free or bubbly.
White	Clear. Firm. (72 Haugh units or higher.)	Clear. May be reasonably firm. (60 to 72 Haugh units.)	Clear. May be slightly weak. (31 to 60 Haugh units.)	May be weak and watery. Small blood clots or spots may be present.[1] (Less than 31 Haugh units.)
Yolk	Outline slightly defined. Practically free from defects.	Outline may be fairly well defined. Practically free from defects.	Outline may be well defined. May be slightly enlarged and flattened. May show definite but not serious defects.	Outline may be plainly visible. May be enlarged and flattened. May show clearly visible germ development but no blood. May show other serious defects.

For Eggs with Dirty or Broken Shells, the Standards of Quality Provide Three Additional Qualities. These are:

Dirty	Check	Leaker
Unbroken. May be dirty	Checked or cracked but not leaking.	Broken so contents are leaking.

[1]If they are small (aggregating not more than 1/8 inch in diameter)

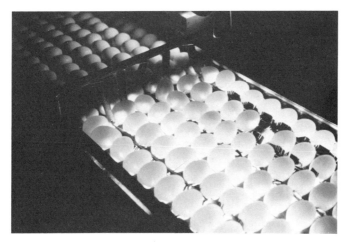

Courtesy U.S. Dept. of Agr.

FIG. 18.4.   EGGS ARE "FLASH CANDLED" WHILE ON A MOVING CONVEYOR

with air cells less than ⅛-in. in depth and clear, firm whites with the yolk practically free from apparent defects.

A Quality eggs also have clean, unbroken, practically normal shells but the air cell can be up to ³/₁₆-in. in depth.   The white must be clear and reasonably firm and the yolk must be practically free from apparent defects.

B Quality eggs can have slightly abnormal shells with slight stains but no adhering dirt as long as the shell is unbroken.   The air cell must not exceed ⅜-in. in depth, may show unlimited movement, and may be free or bubbly.   The white must be clear but may be slightly weak so that the yolk outline is well defined when the egg is twirled before a candling light.   The yolk may be slightly flattened and may have definite, but not serious defects.

C Quality eggs must have unbroken shells and be edible.

CONTROLLED QUALITY PROGRAMS

Studies of egg quality produced by a number of different flocks in a number of areas over a period of years have demonstrated that a small sample of eggs selected from a flock weekly is quite accurate in representing the average quality of the entire lot.   Because of this observation and the high labor requirements for hand candling a USDA controlled quality (CQ) program was established.   Eggs marketed under this program can carry the Fresh Fancy or AA label or Grade A label.

Some general provisions for qualifying for this program are:

(1) Eggs must come from a flock not varying in age over 60 days with eggs from separate flocks packed separately.

(2) Eggs are gathered twice and preferably three times a day.

(3) Washing and oil treatments must be in compliance with sanitary regulations.

(4) Eggs shall be cooled and held at 60°F. and approximately 70% relative humidity.

(5) Eggs shall be handled in such a manner to prevent sweating.

(6) Periodic checks of farm and distribution programs will be made by government graders.

(7) Weekly samples of 25 eggs drawn at random must average 74 Haugh units or better.

To be packed under the U.S. Grade A mark the requirements are not as strict. The main differences are that the flock may remain on the program as long as a moving average of 62 Haugh units or higher is maintained and a tolerance of 5 percent is permitted of shell, meat, or bloodspots, and checks in any combination which results in C or better quality.

BIBLIOGRAPHY

ANON. 1972. Egg Grading Manual. U.S. Dept. Agr., Agr. Mktg. Serv. Agr. Handbook 75.

BROOKS, J., and TAYLOR, D. J. 1955. Eggs and egg products. Food Invest. Spec. Rept. 60, Dept. Sci. Ind. Res. HM Stationery Office, London, England.

CARD, L. E., and NESHEIM, M. C. 1972. Poultry Production. Lea & Febiger, Philadelphia.

DAWSON, E. H., MILLER, C., and REDSTROM, R. A. 1956. Cooking Quality and Flavor of Eggs as Related to Candled Quality, Storage Conditions, and Other Factors. U.S. Dept. of Agr., Agr. Inform. Bull. 164.

ROMANOFF, A. L., and ROMANOFF, A. J. 1949. The Avian Egg. John Wiley & Sons, New York.

SNYDER, E. S. 1961. Eggs, the production, identification, and retention of quality in eggs. Ontario Dept. Agr. Toronto, Canada, Publ. 446.

STADELMAN, W. J., and COTTERILL, O. J. (Editors) 1973. Egg Science and Technology. Avi Publishing Co., Westport, Conn.

CHAPTER 19

Measuring Egg Quality

Several measurements of egg quality are used by poultry products technologists and breeders. Some of the more important and common ones deal with the interior quality of eggs, often referred to as IQ, and the porosity and thickness of the shell.

Most measurements of interior quality are either direct or indirect measurements of the viscosity of the albumen or yolk. Viscosity is the resistance of a liquid against flow. The surface tension is also important. It is defined as the resistance of a liquid to the formation of additional surface.

Despite many limitations, hand candling is probably still the most widely used measurement in research to measure egg quality where treatments bring about wide differences. The chief advantage of using candling to determine interior quality is that it is a quick, non-destructive way of testing.

The following excerpts from the USDA Egg Grading Manual (1972) describe the techniques of hand candling.

Hand candling is used very little in the present commercial grading operations. Automated equipment and mass scanning devices have practically replaced these manual operations. However, hand candling is still an excellent method for teaching and demonstrating quality determination and is used for spot checking and determining accuracy in grading.

In determining interior quality by hand candling it is customary to hold two eggs in each hand, supporting one egg by the tips of the thumb and index finger and holding the other against the palm with the other fingers. The small ends of the eggs should point toward the palm of the hand. After one egg in the hand has been candled, it is shifted back in a rotating motion to the palm of the hand and the second egg is brought into candling position. The eggs are viewed alternately before the light.

The ability to quickly rotate two eggs in each hand make for more rapid work and should be practiced until reasonable dexterity is acquired. In manipulating eggs before the candling light it is important that the rotation of eggs in each hand and the twirling motion before the light become mechanical.

Some of the more common methods used to measure interior quality are given below.

TABLE 19.1

INFLUENCE OF TIME, TEMPERATURE AND HUMIDITY ON EGG QUALITY

Storage Period (Days)	Percentage Moisture Loss	Change in Air Cell Size	Dye Porosity Score	Albumen (mm)	Haugh Units	USDA Score	Grade	Van Waggenen Score	Grade
Fresh egg	0	0	3.5	6.5	77.0	5.3 avg.	A	2.1 avg.	A
Stored at 55°F. 2	0.08	0	5.9	6.4	77.0	4.6 avg.	A	2.3 avg.	A
7	0.13	1/16	6.75	5.7	73.2	5.6 low	A	2.7 low	A
14	0.53	1/16	7.8	4.6	64.7	6.6 high	B	2.9 high	B
Stored at 100°F. 2	1.05	1/16	7.9	5.1	66.1	6.0 low	A	2.9 high	B
7	2.94	3/16	8.7	4.3	55.7	8.4 avg.	B	3.7 low	B
14	5.20	3/16	9.6	3.2	48.3	8.8 low	B	4.3 avg.	C

From Mountney (1961).

TABLE 19.2

EFFECT OF OILING AND THERMOSTABILIZATION ON EGG QUALITY

Treatment	Albumen Ht. (mm)	Avg. Haugh Units	U.S. Grade
No storage	7.7	88.8	AA
2 weeks at 100°F.	2.9	47.1	B
Thermostabilized (2 weeks at 100°F.)	3.8	65.2	A
Oil Treated (2 weeks at 100°F.)	3.6	59.1	A

From Mountney (1961).

ALBUMEN QUALITY

Albumen index is computed by dividing the height of the thick albumen by the width.

The Haugh unit, which is the logarithm of height of thick albumen multiplied by 100 adjusted by egg weight to the equivalent of a standard 2-oz. egg, has become the most commonly used method to measure the quality of broken-out eggs. Figure 19.1 shows how to measure albumen height for calculating Haugh units.

The Van Waggenen Chart uses a set of photographic standards, each with a numerical value from 1 to 5 for broken-out eggs.

When the United States Department of Agriculture Chart (Fig. 19.2) is used, eggs are compared with pictures of broken-out eggs corresponding to high, medium, and low AA, A, B, or C quality. The pictures are given numbers from 1 to 12. The broken-out egg is given the number of the picture which most nearly corresponds with it.

YOLK QUALITY

The yolk index, which is an indirect measurement of the spherical shape of the yolk and the strength of the yolk membrane, is calculated by dividing the average width by the height of the yolk and multiplying the result by 100.

SHELL THICKNESS

Specific gravity has been used quite extensively to measure shell quality. With this method, eggs are dipped in a solution of a selected specific gravity. When an egg floats in a particular solution it is considered to have that specific gravity. All eggs must be treated and stored alike when this method is used or they cannot be compared. As an egg ages and loses weight the specific gravity also changes because of the loss of moisture.

FIG. 19.1.   THE MICROMETER OR HEIGHT GUAGE FOR MEASURING THE HEIGHT OF THE THICK
WHITE

Gauge is shown here in position over a broken-out egg.

Shell thickness measurements are easier to perform than measurements of specific gravity. A paper thickness guage with the end filed round is used to measure the actual thickness of the shell, generally in three areas of the shell. A shell with a thickness below 0.013 in. is considered to be too thin to send through ordinary market channels without the risk of breaking. Figure 19.3 illustrates how to measure shell thickness.

A close correlation exists between specific gravity and shell thickness. With specific gravity, the egg can be marketed or hatched after it is measured. With a thickness gauge, the egg must be opened but the shells can be held indefinitely before measuring. Close correlations also exist between the percentage of the egg which is shell and the above measurements.

SHELL POROSITY

Weight loss is a common measurement of shell porosity. Shell porosity is closely related to the loss in weight of an egg during storage.

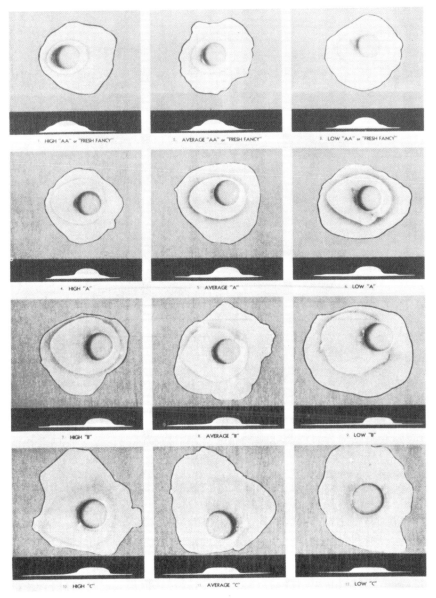

FIG. 19.2.   THE PICTURES OF THIS CHART SHOW THE INTERIOR QUALITY OF EGGS THAT MEET THE SPECIFICATIONS OF THE U.S. STANDARDS FOR QUALITY OF INDIVIDUAL SHELL EGGS WITH RESPECT TO ALBUMEN AND YOLK QUALITY

Quality factors dealing with the shell, air cell, and defects are not included. Scores 1, 2, and 3 represent the appearance of broken-out eggs of high, average, and low AA Quality or Fresh Fancy Quality; 4, 5 and 6 represent high, average, and low A Quality; 7, 8, and 9 represent high, average, and low B Quality; and 10, 11, and 12 represent high, average, and low C Quality.

Courtesy U.S. Dept. Agr.

FIG. 19.3. MEASURING SHELL THICKNESS WITH A PAPER THICKNESS GUAGE

The general procedure is to determine the loss in weight of eggs held two weeks at 100°F.

The "dye method" is a visual measurement of egg shell porosity and, as such, is a somewhat subjective measurement. Porosity is determined by dying the egg shell in an alcoholic solution of methylene blue or crystal violet (3 gm. per liter) and then breaking the egg open. The number of pores penetrated by the dye is compared with a group of photographic standards and a score between 1 and 10 is given to each shell. The dye score is closely related to the amount of weight lost by an egg.

MEASURING YOLK COLOR

There are a number of ways to measure yolk color. For measuring whole yolk of individual broken-out eggs, a set of concave aluminum discs ranging in color from light yellow to deep orange can be used as a basis of comparison with the yolk. Other variations include comparison with concave colored glass discs or colored fans.

Two other methods of measuring yolk color are used in the commercial egg-breaking and egg-drying industry. The Egg Products Association (formerly NEPA) devised a method in which comparisons were made

Courtesy U.S. Dept. Agr.

FIG. 19.4. A FEDERAL INSPECTOR AT AN EGG PROCESSING PLANT DRILLS INTO A CONTAINER
OF FROZEN EGGS TO CHECK THE CONDITION OF THE PRODUCT

by use of a colorimeter of extracted yolk color and a series of potassium
dichromate standards.   Prices of some egg products are still based
partially on these standards which range from 1 to 5.

A newer and more accurate method uses β-carotene as a standard
of comparison with egg yolk pigment.

EXAMINATION OF EGG PRODUCTS

Eggs are examined by the United States Department of Agriculture, the Armed Forces, and other commercial and private laboratories to determine such characteristics as total solids content, yolk color, salt or sugar content, functional properties, palatability, overall bacterial count, and the presence of specific types of organisms such as coliforms and salmonella. The USDA laboratory methods used for these analyses are given in Chap. 23. Figure 19.4 shows a Federal inspector collecting a sample of frozen egg meats for laboratory analysis.

BIBLIOGRAPHY

ANON. 1968. Shell Egg Graders Handbook. U.S. Dept. Agr., Consumer Mktg. Serv., Poultry Div.

ANON. 1972. Egg Grading Manual. U.S. Dept. Agr. Agr. Mktg. Serv. Agri. Handbook 75.

DAM, R., FRONING, G. W., and SKALA, J. H. 1970. Recommended methods for the analysis of eggs and poultry meat. Univ. Nebraska North Central Regional Res. Publ. 205.

FRANCIS, F. J., and CLYDESDALE, F. M. 1972. Color measurement of food. XXXV. Miscellaneous: Part V—egg yolks. Food Prod. Develop. 6, No. 5, 47, 50, 55.

LOWE, B. 1955. Experimental Cookery, 4th Edition. John Wiley & Sons, New York.

MOUNTNEY, G. J. 1961. What causes a decline in egg quality? Ohio Agr. Expt. Sta. Mimeo Ser. 62.

STADELMAN, W. J., and COTTERILL, O. J. (Editors) 1973. Egg Science and Technology. Avi Publishing Co., Westport, Conn.

STILES, P. G., FRONING, G. W., and KILPATRICK, L. 1965. Quality control of poultry products. Univ. Conn. Coll. Agr. Coop. Ext. Serv.

CHAPTER 20

Egg Quality
Maintenance

Low temperature preservation, shell treatment, thermostabilization, carton overwraps, controlled humidity, sealed bucket egg gathering, and combinations of these are all methods which have been used to help maintain egg quality. All of the above methods of preservation depend on a few basic principles.

PHYSICAL-CHEMICAL BREAKDOWN OF EGG QUALITY

As soon as an egg is laid its quality starts to decline. With present knowledge of the physical and chemical structure of the egg, all that can be done is to delay this decline in quality. As the warm egg cools, its contents contract and the air cell is formed. At the same time the mucous-like coating on the shell, commonly called the cuticle or bloom, dries on the surface and begins to dry in the calcium pores of the shell. The cuticle acts as a series of plugs in the shell pores which retard the passage of gases and microorganisms through the shell. As the cuticle dries it shrinks, the size of the pores increase, and it becomes easier for gases and microorganisms to pass in and out of the shell.

The white or albumen gives off carbon dioxide which passes through the pores of the shell. During the first few hours after an egg is laid the rate of carbon dioxide loss is rapid. Additional carbon dioxide is held in the white as a weak solution of carbonic acid. As carbon dioxide escapes, the carbonic acid breaks down and supplies more carbon dioxide and water.

The breakdown of carbonic acid in the white causes the egg to change from an almost neutral media (about pH 7.6) to one of the most alkaline biological fluids known (pH 9.7). As the white loses carbon dioxide and pH changes, the mucin fibers which give egg white its gel texture lose their structure and the white becomes watery.

The yolk absorbs water from the albumen. Although the vitelline membrane surrounding the yolk separates it from the albumen, water moves through the vitelline membrane from the albumen into the yolk in an attempt to equalize the difference in concentration between the two fluids. As the yolk absorbs water, it swells and exerts pressure on the vitelline membrane. This pressure eventually causes the yolk to change from a spherical shape to a round flabby mass.

While the yolk is absorbing water from the albumen, water is also evaporating from the albumen through the shell pores. Eventually as deterioration progresses, the concentration of water in the albumen becomes greater than the yolk and begins to move back into the albumen from the yolk. The egg becomes an inedible product when either the yolk settles to the bottom or side of the shell and becomes attached, in which case it is rejected as a stuck yolk, or the vitelline membrane breaks and the egg becomes a mixed rot.

RETARDING THE DECLINE IN QUALITY

All methods of preservation depend on retarding one or more of the above series of events. The use of any method of preserving eggs requires a compromise. Eggs held at 35°F. may retain quality longer than when held at 60°F., but the retention in quality may not be great enough to justify the expense of extra refrigeration. Or, the difference in temperature and humidity between the cooler and the outside may be great enough to cause the eggs to sweat when removed from the cooler. Theoretically a relative humidity close to 100 percent would be optimum for storing eggs, but because of the increased rate of mold growth above 70% RH such a humidity is not practical.

Low temperature, especially below 60°F., is the most important single treatment which can be used for preserving eggs. However, since humidity depends upon the amount of moisture the air can hold at a given temperature, temperature and humidity cannot be considered separately.

Since gases are more soluble in cold liquids than warm ones, low temperatures retard the loss of carbon dioxide through the shell. Less carbon dioxide is released at 55°F. than at 90°F.

Less evaporation takes place at low storage temperatures. At the same relative humidities, less moisture is lost from the albumen at 55°F. than at 90°F. The rate at which shell porosity increases is also reduced because the cuticle does not dry out.

The flow of water from the albumen through the vitelline membrane to the yolk is also retarded at low temperatures. These factors, in turn, help prevent an increase in pH, which in itself helps prevent egg white thinning.

Although temperature is the most important single factor in maintaining egg quality, other treatments can be used to supplement preservation. If the amount of carbon dioxide surrounding the outside of the shell is the same as inside the egg, an equilibrium is formed and carbon dioxide losses from inside the egg are retarded, but not stopped completely. Sealed bucket egg gathering and carton overwrapping all depend on reducing the loss of carbon dioxide from the egg white.

Shell treatments such as oiling depend upon closing the pores of the shells to prevent the release of carbon dioxide and the evaporation of moisture. To be successful, these treatments must be applied before the white has lost most of its carbon dioxide. In some cases, such treatments work too well. If the pores are sealed soon after laying so the carbon dioxide cannot escape, the white will be cloudy and the pH will remain near 7.6. At this pH the mucin fibers will begin to squeeze water from the albumen so that there is an increase in the outer thin white and the egg will not peel when hard cooked. As the egg loses carbon dioxide, these conditions disappear.

Thermostabilization by holding eggs in an oil bath at 60°C. for 10 min. seals the pores of the shell with a thin layer of coagulated albumen and retards the passage of gases and fluids through the shell.

In summary, eggs should be cooled as soon as possible, held at 55°-60°F. and 70 percent relative humidity. If additional protection can be justified, then some of the other methods just discussed can be used to supplement these basic treatments.

EGG CLEANING

Most eggs are now cleaned by washing with a detergent sanitizer solution in an egg washer at the assembly point. By washing in the plant rather than at the farm, abuse of egg washing can be controlled.

Porous egg shells and expansion and contraction of egg contents during washing can cause problems. Cold eggs subjected to hot water will expand too fast and crack the shell (expansion checks). On the other hand, the interior contents of eggs washed in hot water and then rinsed by immersion in cool water contract and aspirate bacteria through the shell. The organisms multiply and the eggs spoil.

Modern egg washers are designed to minimize the above conditions by spraying the eggs with water rather than immersing them, using a sanitizer in the water along with a detergent for cleaning them, using rinse water warmer than the wash water, and finally drying the eggs with hot air. Scrubbing action by the washers is provided by rotating the eggs during washing and using pressure sprays and oscillating brushes.

The U.S. Department of Agriculture compiled the following recommendations for egg washing: Wash eggs promptly after gathering. Do not try to clean excessively dirty eggs. Water with an iron content in excess of 2 ppm should not be used. Do not immerse eggs in wash water for more than 5 min. Do not reuse wash water except when used in a continuous type washer. Wash water temperature should be 90°F. or higher. Maintain wash water at a temperature 20°F. to 40°F. warmer than the eggs. Spray rinse washed eggs with warm potable water containing an approved sanitizing compound. Eggs should be reasonably dry before casing or breaking.

HANDLING EGGS

The effects of duration of lay and mechanized handling were studied at 24 mechanized cage operations in seven Northeastern States. The following were some of the observations made in the course of the study.

Duration of lay had the greatest influence on egg shell damage.

Shell damage at point of lay averaged lower in stair step than in flat deck systems.

Damage which could not be attributed to horizontal straight line travel was not significant.

The amount of shell damage that could be attributed to such factors as right angle transfer, vertical travel and orienting varied with the operator's ability to manage egg flow and keep equipment properly adjusted. Poorly adjusted equipment and situations which permitted eggs to become crowded resulted in serious breakage.

Washing was not an important factor in causing shell breakage.

In some instances, damage attributable to the packing operation, i.e., after the eggs had been washed, was found to be as great as that which occurred in all the other handling operations combined.

Shupe *et al* (1972) reported that "In typical egg-grading and packing plants in California, 2.32 to 11.76 percent of the eggs handled were either cracked or smashed while they were enroute from the nest (or were either cracked or smashed while they were enroute from the nest (or cage) to the carton. Seventy-one percent of the breakage took place while the eggs were being transported between the nest and the packing plant, and 29 percent took place during the grading and packing operations—13 percent during the machine-loading and the washing and drying procedures, and 16 percent during the weighing and packing procedures."

PACKAGING

Mellor and Gardner (1970) studied the effects of egg cartons on interior quality and breakage of shell eggs. When egg cases were subjected to rough handling during shipment over the normal distribution route of a supermarket chain, molded pulp tray cartoned eggs and center fold plastic foam cartons offered better protection against breakage than the other cartons.

FACTORS AFFECTING QUALITY DURING PRODUCTION

Numerous factors can cause low or unacceptable egg quality. With new drugs and supplements being administered to chickens and the increased chances for accidents from unintentional additives, this number will probably continue to increase. Even old contaminants still appear, such as an excess of cottonseed meal in rations developed for chickens by organic food faddists which causes discolored yolks.

The problem of identifying the source of trouble is in some ways even more difficult than disease diagnosis. Often the condition terminates without the cause ever being identified. The economic and aesthetic effects in market channels can be illustrated by the following actual case history. One lot of improperly washed eggs was sent into a grading station. The eggs were graded and sorted into different lots and dispersed throughout the plant. Complaints on eggs with the same spoilage characteristics were received simultaneously from two supermarkets, a hospital, a school cafeteria, and a local store. Further investigation made it possible to isolate the cause as simply rinsing the hot eggs after washing in contaminated cold water. The costs of settling all claims amounted to several hundred dollars, in addition to the loss in good will and confidence.

In diagnosing egg quality problems the biggest difficulty is obtaining good case histories. By the time a complaint is received the eggs are generally 3-4 weeks old and the eggs cannot be traced back to the individual flock. The following information is of value in determining case histories: (1) A specific and accurate description of the complaint. (2) Who first observed the condition; where; and in how many eggs? (3) Suggestions as to the possible cause: (4) Name and address of the possible farm. (5) Were the eggs washed? In the plant? On the farm? (6) Estimated age of the eggs. (7) Any known disease out-breaks in the flock? (8) Recent vaccinations? (9) Recent medication? (10) Changes in feeding or management practices? (11) Age of birds? (12) Egg production pattern. (13) Other pertinent comments or observations.

The following routine tests on samples of eggs from lots containing the defect can sometimes supply additional information: (1) Examination of shells. (2) Candling with both incandescent and ultraviolet lights of eggs in the shell and broken out. (3) Break-out and examination of the interior quality including checking for off-odors and -color. Cooking often amplifies certain defects. (4) Incubate samples of egg for three weeks to see if rots occur. (5) Occasionally run bacteria counts on individual eggs or lots of eggs.

OTHER ABNORMAL CONDITIONS

The following abnormal conditions are found in eggs.

Egg size is influenced by strain, age, and drugs, (for example, nicarbazin causes mottling). The largest chicken egg on record weighed ³/₄ lb. and the smallest slightly over ¹/₂₈ oz.

Egg shape is a characteristic of the individual hen and also of specific breeds or strains. Respiratory diseases, and especially Newcastle disease, cause abnormally-shaped shells. Arasan and exposure to X-rays also cause hens to lay abnormally-shaped eggs.

Shell texture is to some extent hereditary. Newcastle disease can cause temporary rough shells. Bronchitis causes permanent shell damage. In some cases vaccination for the above diseases is believed to cause poor shell quality. Porous shells have been reported to come from areas with high relative humidity. Soft shells can be caused by estrogens and avian pest disease as well as lack of calcium or vitamin D.

Shell color can be affected by nicarbazin which causes hens who normally lay brown shelled eggs to lay white shelled ones. Aureomycin can cause yellow shells. Eggs washed in excessively high chlorine concentrations sometimes have a brownish cast.

Albumen quality can be influenced by breeding. It is possible to develop lines with high and low albumen quality. The process becomes self-terminating when the albumen becomes too thin because chicks will not hatch from the eggs. Age, heat, and possibly excessive vibration also cause thinning of white. Riboflavin in the albumen gives it a greenish cast. Pink albumen can be caused by cottonseed and soybean meal.

Bloodspots are a breed characteristic and so can be inherited. Incidence in flocks can be as low as two percent and as high as 24 percent. Warfarin, vitamin K, other ingredients, and frightening the birds apparently have no effects on the incidence of bloodspots.

Abnormal yolks include mottling which can be caused by nicarbazin, tannic acid, gallic acid, and inheritance. Cottonseed meal can cause a brownish discoloration. Platinum colored yolks can be caused by vitamin A or xanthophyll deficiency, bacteria, or heavy infestations of round worms.

A number of conditions can cause off-flavored eggs: Undesirable flavors caused by bacteria have a moldy, earthy, sour, cabbage, fruity, or putrid odor. Fish meal, garlic, and rancid fat odors can be absorbed from these substances through the intestinal wall. Eggs buried in litter have also shown off-flavors. Pesticides can cause off-odors in eggs. Absorption of odors is not as easy as one might expect. Odors can be lost almost as easily as they are gained.

Cooking can cause a green ring around the yolk, green scrambled eggs, brown or tough albumen, and a bubbly white. Aluminum and stainless steel cooking pans can also cause a condition described as rusty albumen.

BIBLIOGRAPHY

COTTERILL, O. J., GARDNER, F. A., FUNK, E. M., and CUNNINGHAM, F. E. 1958. Relationship between temperature and carbon dioxide loss from shell eggs. Poultry Sci. *37*, 479-483.

JOHNDREW, O. F., and BEZPA, J. 1972. Field studies on eggshell damage and bloodspot detection. Northeast Regional Publ. Coop. Ext. Serv., Rutgers Univ.

LOWE, B. 1955. Experimental Cookery. John Wiley & Sons, New York.

MELLOR, D. B., and GARDNER, F. A. 1970. The effect of egg cartons on interior quality and breakage of shell eggs. Poultry Sci. *49*, 793-798.

MOUNTNEY, G. J. 1961. What causes a decline in egg quality? Ohio Agr. Expt. Sta. Mimeo Ser. *62*.

MUELLER, W. J. 1958. Shell porosity of chicken eggs. 1. CO_2 loss and CO_2 content infertile eggs during storage. Poultry Sci. *37*, 437-444.

PAUL, P. C., and PALMER, H. H. 1972. Food Theory and Applications. John Wiley & Sons, New York.

STADELMAN, W. J., and COTTERILL, O. J. (Editors) 1973. Egg Science and Technology. Avi Publishing Co., Westport, Conn.

SHUPE, W. L., SPANGLER, E. W., HAMANN, J. A., and BRANT, A. W. 1972. Reducing egg breakage in mechanized egg-grading and packing lines. U.S. Dept. Agr., Agr. Res. Serv. Bull. *52-73*.

CHAPTER 21

Eggs—
Physical, Chemical, Nutritional
and Functional Characteristics

Eggs are economical; they are quick, convenient, and easy to prepare; they are easily digestible; appetizing; and they have a high satiety value. The mild flavor of eggs and some of the natural compounds in the white and yolk supply functional properties such as leavening, binding, thickening, retardation of sugar crystallization, emulsification, clarification, coating, coloring, and high nutritive value and make them an ideal ingredient to combine with other foods.

PHYSICAL CHARACTERISTICS OF EGGS

A "large" egg weighs about 2 oz. or 58 gm. of which approximately 11 percent is shell, 58 percent white, and 31 percent yolk. When calculated on the basis of interior contents, 65 percent is white and 35 percent yolk. Under commercial breaking conditions, the yields are generally 55 to 57 percent white and 43 to 45 percent yolk because some of the white stays with the yolk on separation. A whole egg contains about 65.5 percent water, the white 88 percent and the yolk 48 percent.

The viscosity of egg albumen at pH 9 begins to change at 134°-135°F. Coagulation occurs rapidly at 140°F. Addition of sugar, salt or other additives increases the temperature required for coagulation. Egg yolk coagulates at about 149°F.

CHEMICAL COMPOSITION

The chemical composition of shell eggs and raw liquid egg products are shown in Tables 21.1 and 21.2.

NUTRIENT COMPOSITION

An egg contains from six to seven grams of protein. Egg protein is one of the highest quality proteins known for human food. Egg proteins contain all of the essential amino acids, those amino acids required in the diet of man, and are of such high quality that nutritionists use the egg as a standard of reference against which other protein foods are evaluated. An egg also contains five to six grams of fat which is readily digestible and includes both saturated and unsaturated fatty acids. The amounts of desirable unsaturated fatty acids are more

320

TABLE 21.1

CHEMICAL COMPOSITION OF EGGS

	%	Water (%)	Protein (%)	Fat (%)	Ash (%)
Whole egg	100	65.5	11.8	11.0	11.7
White	58	88.0	11.0	0.2	0.8
Yolk	31	48.0	17.5	32.5	2.0
	%	Calcium Carbonate (%)	Magnesium Carbonate (%)	Calcium Phosphate (%)	Organic Matter (%)
Shell	11	94.0	1.0	1.0	4.0

From U.S. Dept. of Agr.

Table 21.2

CHEMICAL COMPOSITION OF EGG PRODUCTS

	Whole Liquid	Whites	Yolks	Yolks (Commercially Separated)
Water (%)	73.7	87.6	51.1	55.5
Protein (%)	12.9	10.9	16.0	15.4
Fat (%)	11.5	Tr	30.6	26.9
Carbohydrate (%)	1.1	1.1	1.0	1.0
Free carbohydrate (%)	0.3	0.4	0.2	0.2
Ash (%)	1.0	0.7	1.7	1.6

From U.S. Dept. of Agr.

than are found in most other animal products.

An egg contains less than 0.4 gm. of carbohydrates. Eggs are also low in calories, which means that one can use eggs in a low calorie diet that is still nutritionally balanced.

Eggs contain generous quantities of all the essential vitamins, except vitamin C. The fat-soluble vitamins (A, D, E, and K,) and water-soluble vitamins (the B-complex; thiamin, riboflavin, pantothenic acid, niacin, folic acid and vitamin B_{12}) and other related growth factors are present.

Egg yolk is high in cholesterol, a fat-like material found in blood, nerve tissues, and other parts of the body. At the present stage of knowledge, the exact functions of cholesterol are not fully understood except that it plays an important physiological role in the body.

Tables 21.3, 21.4, and 21.5 show the nutrient contents of eggs.

BIOCHEMICAL CHARACTERISTICS

Egg white, unlike most animal tissues, has a low concentration of enzymes. Lysozyme is considered to be enzymatic. Tributyrinase,

TABLE 21.3

U.S. RDA IN RELATION TO NUTRIENT CONTENT OF LARGE EGGS

Nutrient	U.S.[1] RDA	Amount From One Whole Egg	% U.S. RDA From One Whole Egg (%)
Protein[2]	45 gm.	6.5 gm.	13.3
Vitamins			
A	5000 IU	590 IU	11.8
D[3]	400 IU	25 IU	6.3
E	30 IU	1 IU	3.3
C	60.0 mg.	—	—
Folacin[4]	0.4 mg.	2.5 ug.	0.625
Thiamin	1.5 mg.	0.055 mg.	3.7
Riboflavin	1.7 mg.	0.15 mg.	8.8
Niacin	20.0 mg.	0.05 mg.	0.3
B_6	2.0 mg.	0.13 mg.	6.5
B_{12}	6.0 ug.	0.14 ug.	2.3
Biotin[3]	0.3 mg.	10.0 ug.	3.7
Pantothenic acid	10.0 mg.	0.81 mg.	8.0
Minerals			
Calcium	1.0 gm.	0.027 gm.	2.7
Phosphorus[5]	1.0 gm.	0.1 gm.	10.0
Iodine	150.0 ug.	6.0 ug.	4.0
Iron	18.0 mg.	1.15 mg.	5.8
Magnesium	400.0 mg.	5.5 mg.	1.4
Copper[3]	2.0 mg.	0.08 mg.	4.0
Zinc[3]	15.0 mg.	0.7 mg.	4.7
Sodium	Not determined	66.0 mg.	Not determined
Chloride	Not determined	74.0 mg.	Not determined
Potassium	Not determined	76.0 mg.	Not determined
Sulphur	Not determined	67.0 mg.	Not determined
Molybdenum	Not determined	Present	Not determined
Cobalt	Not determined	Present	Not determined

From American Egg Board (1974).
[1] Adults and children 4 or more years of age.
[2] Protein with nutritive value equal to or greater than that of casein.
[3] Optional for adaults and children 4 or more years of age.
[4] Optional for liquid products.
[5] Optional for pregnant or lactating women.

peptidase, and catalase also have been observed in low concentrations in the white. The enzymes tributyrase, peptidase, catalase, amylase, and phosphatidase have been demonstrated in yolk.

A number of components of egg white have biological properties. Lysozyme has been observed to lyse the cell walls of some bacteria, cause flocculation of bacterial cells, and hydrolysis of B-1-4-glycosidic bonds. Conalbumin is responsible for chelation of iron, zinc, and copper while ovomucoid acts as a trypsin inhibitor. Avidin combines with biotin and inactivates its vitamin activity and riboflavin is responsible for chelation of cations. Other uncharacterized proteins are responsible for inhibition of trypsin and chemotrypsin, inhibition of fungal proteinase, combination with riboflavin, combination with vitamin B_6, and chelation of calcium.

TABLE 21.4

NUTRITIVE VALUE OF LARGE EGGS WITHOUT SHELL (FRESH AND HARD-COOKED)

Composition	Whole	Fresh Raw Egg Albumen	Yolk	Whole Hard-Cooked
Weight (gm.)	50.0	33.0	17.0	50.0
Water (%)	73.7	87.6	51.1	73.7
Energy (Cal)	79.9	15.7	63.7	79.9
Protein (gm.)	6.45	3.6	2.72	6.45
Fat—total lipid (gm.)	5.75	Tr	5.75	5.75
Total saturated fatty acids	1.65	—	1.65	1.65
Total unsaturated fatty acids	3.30	—	3.30	3.30
Oleic (gm.)	2.2	—	2.20	2.2
Linoleic (gm.)	0.5	—	0.5	0.5
Cholesterol (mg.)[1]	230.0	0	230.0	230.0
Carbohydrate (gm.)	0.36	0.264	0.1	0.36
Fiber (gm.)	0	0	0	0
Ash (gm.)	0.5	0.231	0.289	0.5
Calcium (mg.)	27.0	2.97	23.97	27.0
Iron (mg.)	1.15	0.033	1.117	1.15
Magnesium (mg.)	5.5	2.97	2.72	—
Phosphorous (mg.)	102.5	4.95	96.73	102.5
Potassium (mg.)	64.5	45.87	16.66	64.5
Sodium (mg.)	61.0	48.18	8.84	61.0
Vitamin A (IU)	590	0	590	590
Ascorbic acid (mg.)	0	0	0	0
Choline (mg.)	253.0	0.4	253.0	—
Inositol (mg.)	16.5	—	—	—
Niacin (mg.)	0.05	0.033	0.017	0.05
Riboflavin (mg.)	0.15	0.089	0.076	0.14
Thiamine (mg.)	0.055	—	0.037	0.045

From American Egg Board (1974).
Note: Raw yolk includes a portion of egg albumen.
[1] For a 17-gram egg yolk.

TABLE 21.5

FATTY ACID COMPOSITION OF SELECTED FOODS

	Weight Gm	Total Saturated Fatty Acids Gm	Total Unsaturated Fatty Acids Gm	Linoleic Acid Gm
Bacon, 2 slices	16	2.93	5.43	0.76
Beef, round	120	5.22	7.32	0.20
Butter, 1 teaspoon	5	2.36	1.54	0.14
Chicken, leg	120	0.98	2.06	0.95
Eggs, 2 medium	108	3.42	6.46	1.26
Milk, skim, 1 cup	246	0.11	0.08	0.01
Milk, whole, 1 cup	244	5.24	3.79	0.55
Oil, corn, 1 tablespoon	14	1.56	11.74	5.63
Turkey, dark meat	120	0.98	2.06	0.95

From American Egg Board (1974).

FUNCTIONAL PROPERTIES

In addition to their nutritive value, eggs have eight important functional properties.

(1) Eggs act as a leavening agent in baked goods. They are partially responsible for the textures of breads, cakes, and other bakery products. One of the measures of the functional performance of egg white is to bake angel food cakes and measure the volume, texture, moistness, and other characteristics of the cake to determine the qualities of the egg white.

(2) Eggs also act as a binding agent to hold other ingredients together. The liquid egg is mixed with the ingredients and, when heated, the albumen is denatured or coagulated and forms a network which helps bind the other ingredients together.

(3) A third function is that of a thickening agent, particularly in custards, puddings, and cream fillings. Eggs also combine with milk, sugar, flavoring, and other ingredients which when heated form a gel. The quality of the gel is determined to a large extent by the amount and quality of the egg white and the combinations of the various ingredients, such as sugars and other stabilizers.

(4) Eggs retard crystallization and prevent a gritty texture in cake icings and candies. Smooth, moist, sweet icings result to a large extent from the addition of egg white to give it a pleasing desirable texture.

(5) Egg yolk contains natural emulsifiers. Lecithin, for example, keeps fats and other ingredients in a uniform suspension until the other ingredients are cooked or bound together permanently by heat.

(6) Eggs are also used as a clarifying agent. They are used to remove extraneous materials from beverages, coffee, soup stock, wines, and other food ingredients.

(7) Eggs are an excellent coating for cakes, rolls, cookies, breads, and other bakery foods. They not only help to prevent dehydration, but give a firm, glistening coating over the surface of the baked foods.

(8) Eggs add color and richness to foods. Some frozen eggs are sold on the basis of the color of the mixture. Mixtures with very dark colors bring the highest prices because they will impart the darkest, rich, yellow color to the resulting baked foods.

BIBLIOGRAPHY

ANON. 1974. A Scientist Speaks About Eggs. American Egg Board, Chicago.
CARTER, T. C. 1968. Egg Quality, A Study of the Hen's Egg. British Marketing Board, Vol. 4. Oliver & Boyd, Edinburgh, Scotland.
MOUNTNEY, G. J. 1959A. The eggs in your diet. Am. Egg Poultry Rev. Aug. 26-28.

MOUNTNEY, G. J. 1966. Eggs Your Hidden Profit. Bakers Weekly, Aug. 29, 31-36.

ROMANOFF, A. L., and ROMANOFF, A. J. 1949. The Avian Egg. John Wiley & Sons, New York.

STADELMAN, W. J., and COTTERILL, O. J. (Editors) 1973. Egg Science and Technology. Avi Publishing Co., Westport, Conn.

VADEHRA, D. V., and NATH, K. R. 1973. Eggs as a source of protein. Critical Rev. Food Technol. 4, No. 2, 193-309.

WARNER, R. C. 1954. The proteins. In Egg Proteins. Academic Press, New York.

CHAPTER 22

Processing Eggs

Eggs can be purchased as shell eggs; chilled liquid white, yolk or whole egg; and frozen white, whole egg, whole egg with yolk added, plain yolk, fortified whole egg with corn syrup, sugared egg yolk, salted egg yolk, and salted whole egg. They are also available in dried egg form as spray-dried white, flake albumen, as plain whole egg and yolk in the form of standard whole egg solids, stabilized (glucose free) whole egg solids, standard egg yolk solids, stabilized egg yolk solids, free flowing whole egg solids, free flowing yolk solids, and blends of whole egg and yolk with carbohydrates, sugar, and corn syrup. Table 22.1 shows some of the shell egg equivalents for frozen and dried eggs.

LIQUID EGGS

The sequence of operations for producing liquid eggs is as follows: Eggs are candled to remove leakers and inedibles; washed; broken (Fig. 22.1); then churned and/or milled (Fig. 22.2); followed by pressure filtration after which they are clarified or filtered and pasteurized. Then they are cooled to 40°F; packaged and delivered chilled, or frozen for storage, delivery, or freezing.

Automatic egg breaking machines open the shell eggs and separate yolks and whites at rates up to 40 cases per hour. To operate efficiently, eggs to be machine broken must be of uniform high quality and sound shelled. Malfunctioning of the breaker can cause yolks to break and contaminate the whites, which reduces their functional properties. If eggs are too warm at the time of breaking, yolks break. If they are too cold the whites do not separate satisfactorily from the yolks.

PACKAGING

In some cases chilled, liquid eggs are pumped directly into refrigerated truck tankers and delivered to the user. There they are pumped into refrigerated storage tanks for holding. Most frozen eggs are packaged in either 30-lb. tins or 8-lb. cardboard, plastic coated cartons. The eggs are frozen in a blast freezer at −10 to −40°F and then held at 0°F.

FUNCTIONAL ADDITIVES

A number of chemical additives can be used to preserve or enhance functional properties of liquid and dried eggs. Liquid eggs are often

TABLE 22.1

SHELL EGG EQUIVALENTS OF FROZEN AND DRIED EGGS

Product	Shell Egg (Large Size) Equivalent
	No. Per Pound
Frozen	
Whole	9 whole eggs
Yolks	26 yolks
Whites	14 whites
Dried	
Whole	32 whole eggs
Yolks	54 yolks
Whites	100 whites

Frozen Eggs

Amount of Product to Use		Shell Egg Equivalent (Large Size)
Weights	Measures (Approx.)	
Whole		No.
1 lb.	2 cups less 2 tbsp.	9
1 lb. 1³/₄ oz.	2 cups	10
Yolks		
1 lb.	2 cups less 2 tbsp.	26
6¹/₄ oz.	³/₄ cup	10
Whites		
1 lb.	2 cups less 2 tbsp.	14
11¹/₂ oz.	1¹/₄ cups, 2 tbsp.	10

Dried Eggs

Amount of Product of Use		Amount of Water to Add	Shell Egg Equivalent (Large Size)
Weights	Measures (Approx.)	Measures	
Whole[1]			No.
1 lb	1 qt. 1¹/₃ cups	1 qt. 1¹/₃ cups	32
5 oz.	1²/₃ cups	1²/₃ cups	10
Yolks			
1 lb.	1 qt. 2³/₄ cups	2¹/₄ cups	54
3 oz.	1¹/₄ cups	6²/₃ tbsp.	10
Whites			
1 lb.	1 qt. ¹/₄ cup	3 qt. ¹/₂ cup	100
1¹/₂ oz.	6²/₃ tbsp.	1¹/₄ cups	10

From U.S. Dept. of Agr.
[1] Quantities are for dried whole eggs. For blends and specialty egg products, use equivalent on package label.

sold as salted eggs with up to 10 percent salt, or sugared eggs with up to 10 percent sugar. Generally, in the case of frozen egg yolk one of these materials or some other additive must be included in the mixture to prevent a condition known as "gelation." This condition is brought about by freezing and causes the yolk to become sticky and gummy upon thawing. The reaction is irreversible and prevents a uniform dispersion of the yolks throughout the rest of the ingredients

Courtesy U.S. Dept. Agr.

FIG. 22.1.   A USDA EGG PRODUCTS INSPECTOR EXAMINES A BROKEN-OUT EGG TO ENSURE
THAT IT IS WHOLESOME AND SUITABLE FOR CONSUMPTION

when used.   In some cases, corn syrup is added to the mixture instead
of sugar.

Other commercial egg products have various additives to improve
certain of the functional properties.   For example, certain acids such
as lactic and citric are sometimes added to adjust pH and to act as
a sequestering agent.   The acid ties up any metal which may be present
as a result of being handled in metal containers.   Another group of
additives influence whipping characteristics and foam stability.
Among these additives are the general groups of bile acids and salts
and certain detergent-type materials.   Triethyl citrate repairs heat-in-
duced damage to egg white.   Other additives used for specific pasteurizing processes include lactic acid, aluminum sulfate, hydrogen
peroxide, and catalase.   Silicoaluminate is used as an anticaking agent
in egg solids.

EGG SOLIDS

Dried eggs or egg solids (as they are now called) are being used
in increasing amounts in the baking industry.   The biggest advantage

Courtesy U.S. Dept. Agr.

FIG. 22.2. A FEDERAL INSPECTOR WATCHES AS LIQUID EGGS AND OTHER INGREDIENTS ARE MIXED IN THIS 1,000-LB. BLENDER INTO ONE OF THE MANY SPECIAL BLENDS IN DEMAND BY COMMERCIAL FOOD PROCESSORS

in using egg solids is that they can be stored in cool areas and keep for a fairly long time, providing they are well packaged and the packages are not opened so that the materials are exposed to air. Egg solids absorb moisture readily.

The following steps are employed in drying liquid whole eggs. After storing eggs which are held in a holding vat at 40°F. up to 48 hr., they are pumped to a dryer by a high pressure pump at about 3,000 lb. pressure where spray nozzles reduce the liquid eggs to a fine spray and force the particles into a chamber heated to 340°F. The powdered eggs are collected at the bottom of the sprayer and passed through a system of cooling coils. The powder is then cooled around 90°F. or less. The whole egg powder is then collected and packed in barrels or 14-lb. cartons and stored at 50°F. Figure 22.3 shows the steps involved in processing egg solids. Egg whites are sometimes dried in pans in heated ovens at 125°F. or higher to produce flake albumen. Foam-mat drying and freeze drying of eggs have been tried but are too costly.

Albumen in egg shells recovered from breaking operations can be dried and used for non-food purposes, such as adhesive. It is called technical albumen.

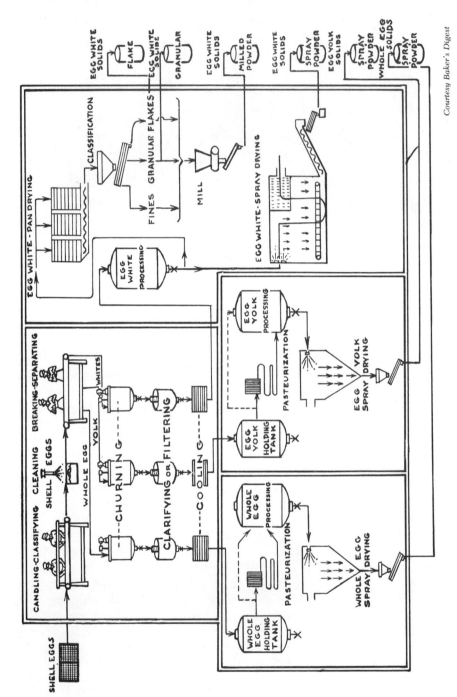

Courtesy Baker's Digest

Fig. 22.3. Schematic Outline Showing the Various Processing Steps Involved in the Production of Whole Egg, Egg Yolk, and Egg White Solids

FERMENTING EGG WHITE

Egg whites, and sometimes yolk and whole egg containing products, are fermented before drying to prevent a browning or Maillard reaction caused by the aldehyde groups of the carbohydrates reacting with the amino group of the proteins to form an insoluble brown, off-odor compound. The reaction can be prevented by removing the glucose in the egg by fermentation. Fermentation can be accomplished by using bacteria such as *Aerobacter aerogenes*, or the enzyme glucose oxidase.

PASTEURIZING LIQUID EGG PRODUCTS

Eggs are pasteurized primarily to destroy bacteria pathogenic to humans, especially *Salmonella*. One problem in pasteurizing liquid eggs is that the temperature at which egg white proteins are denatured is very close to that required to kill *Salmonella*. For the above reason accurate temperature regulation is essential to prevent the loss of functional properties in the white. To help solve this problem several different methods of pasteurization have been developed. Table 22.2

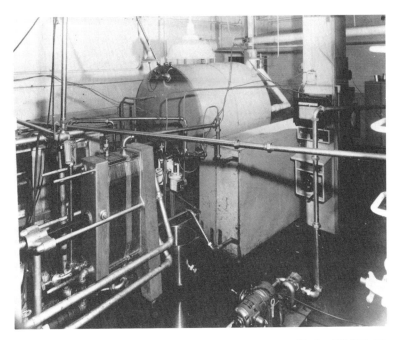

Courtesy U.S. Dept. Agr.

FIG. 22.4.   EGG PASTEURIZING EQUIPMENT

TABLE 22.2

PASTEURIZATION REQUIREMENTS [1]

Liquid Egg Product	Minimum Temperature Requirements	Minimum Holding Time Requirements
	°F.	Min.
Albumen (without use of chemicals)	134	3.5
	132	6.2
Whole egg	140	3.5
Whole egg blends (less than 2 percent added nonegg ingredients)	142	3.5
Fortified whole egg and blends	140	6.2
(24–38 percent egg solids, 2–12 percent added nonegg ingredients)	144	3.5
	142	6.2
Salt whole egg (with 2 percent or more salt added)	146	3.5
	144	6.2
Sugar whole egg (2–12 percent sugar added)	142	3.5
	140	6.2
Plain yolk	142	3.5
	140	6.2
Sugar yolk (2 percent or more sugar added)	146	3.5
	144	6.2
Salt yolk (2–12 percent salt added)	146	3.5
	144	6.2

From U.S. Dept. of Agr.
[1] Pasteurization of egg products not listed in this table shall be in accordance with USDA requirements.

lists the pasteurization requirements for different types of liquid eggs.

When using the pasteurizing process developed by the USDA Western Regional Research Laboratory, egg whites are acidulated with lactic acid to pH 6.8–7.3, and then aluminum sulfate is added to prevent damage by heat to the egg whites. After this treatment the eggs can be pasteurized at 140°F for the usual 3.5 min.

In a process patented by Armour & Co., egg whites are heated to 125°F for 1.5 min. to inactivate the enzyme catalase. Then hydrogen peroxide is added and the pasteurization process continues at 125°F for two more minutes. After cooling, the enzyme catalase is again added to remove the hydrogen peroxide.

A process where the white can be heated to 134°F for 3.5 min. under vacuum has been developed by the Ballas Egg Products Co.

BIBLIOGRAPHY

Anon. 1969. Egg pasteurization manual. U.S. Dept. Agr., Agr. Res. Serv., Western Util. Res. Develop. Div., Albany, Calif.

Anon. 1972. Regulations governing the inspection of eggs and egg products. U.S. Dept. Agr., Agr. Mktg. Serv., Poultry Div.

Forsythe, R. H. 1964. Recent advances in egg processing technology and products. Baker's Dig. 38, No. 5, 52–59.

FORSYTHE, R. H.   1969.   Current practice in further processed eggs.   Proc. 56th Ann. Meeting Intern. Assoc. Milk, Food, Environ. Sanitarians, Louisville, Kentucky.

KAHLENBERG, O. J.   1967.   Recent developments in the egg industry.   Baker's Dig. *41*, No. 5, 100–102, 113.

MOUNTNEY, G. J. 1966. Eggs . . . your hidden profit.   Baker's Weekly, Aug. 29, 31–36.

STADELMAN, W. J., and COTTERILL, O. J. (Editors)   1973.   Egg Science and Technology.   Avi Publishing Co., Westport, Conn.

WEISER, H. A., MOUNTNEY, G. J., and GOULD, W. A.   1971.   Practical Food Microbiology and Technology, 2nd Edition.   Avi Publishing Co., Westport, Conn.

CHAPTER 23

Methods of Analyses
of Eggs and Egg Products[1]

STORAGE AND PREPARATION OF SAMPLES FOR ANALYSIS

A. Microbiological Analysis

1. Liquid Samples

Liquid samples may be sent to a laboratory for examination if the plant is close enough so the sample may be drawn, sent to the laboratory, and analyzed the same day. The analyst must be satisfied that the sample has not been exposed to elevated temperatures. Samples so exposed are not to be analyzed.

2. Frozen Samples

If frozen samples arrive at the laboratory in a thawed condition, they shall not be analyzed. The chemist-in-charge is to contact the supervisor and request another sample.

If the frozen sample arrives at the laboratory too late for analysis, it may be stored in a freezer until analysis is to be started. Frozen samples that are to be analyzed the next day may be held in a refrigerator until the next day. This will permit tempering of the frozen samples.

In no case should samples be refrozen prior to the initial analysis. They may be refrozen after analysis.

To prepare frozen samples for analysis, thaw the contents of the container as rapidly as possible. They may be set in a water bath at 40°–50°C. (104°–122°F.) until at the slush ice stage. The container is to be removed occasionally from the water bath and shaken. This will keep the temperature of the contents low enough to prevent bacterial growth.

The time of the sample container in the water bath should not exceed 30 min.

3. Dried Samples

If a dried egg sample arrives at the laboratory in a condition which might cause unreliable results, it is not to be analyzed. The chemist-in-

---

[1]Reprinted from *USDA Laboratory Methods for Egg Products*, courtesy of U.S. Department of Agriculture, Agricultural Marketing Service, Poultry Division, Grading Branch, Washington, D.C.

charge is to contact the supervisor and request another sample.

Dried egg samples should be analyzed upon arrival. They may be held over-night at 21°C. (69.8°F.), or less. If they are to be held longer than overnight, the samples are to be held in a cooler.

B. Chemical Analysis

1. Liquid Samples

Unless specifically instructed, liquid samples may be frozen until they are analyzed. Decomposed samples are not to be analyzed.

2. Frozen Samples

If frozen samples arrive at the laboratory in a thawed condition, they may be analyzed if they contain some ice crystals. Otherwise, the chemist-in-charge is to contact the supervisor and request another sample.

Frozen samples may be thawed as described under the foregoing section A, Microbiological Analysis, or tempered to room temperature for ease in weighing, handling, etc.

3. Dried Samples

Dried egg samples are to be analyzed upon arrival if possible. If the sample is not immediately analyzed, it is to be held in a cooler until it can be analyzed.

STANDARD PLATE COUNT

References: *A.O.A.C.*, 11th Edition; and *Standard Methods for the Examination of Dairy Products*, 13th Edition.

1. From a thoroughly mixed sample of liquid or dried eggs, aseptically prepare a 1:10 dilution by weighing 11 gm. of eggs into a sterile dilution bottle containing 99 ml. of sterile phosphate buffer water, sterile physiological salt (NaCl) solution, or 0.1% sterile peptone water.

2. Thoroughly agitate the bottle by shaking rapidly 25 times in a 1-ft. arc within 7 sec.

3. Prepare subsequent dilutions as shown in Fig. 23.1

4. Transfer 1 ml. from the appropriate dilutions, (see Fig. 23.1) to petri plates (15 × 100 mm.). Duplicate plates are to be made for each dilution used for plating.

5. Add 15 gm. of prepared plate count agar (tryptone glucose yeast agar) to the petri dishes.

6. Mix by gently swirling the petri dishes on a flat surface.

7. After the agar has solidified, invert the plates and incubate at 35°C. (95°F.) for 48 ± 2 hr.

Dilution Ratio

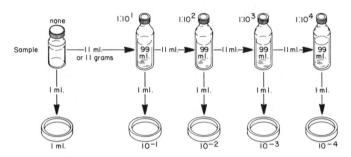

FIG. 23.1. METHOD OF EMPLOYING ELEVEN MILLILITERS OF SAMPLE

8. Count the colonies on the plates using a Quebec colony counter.

9. Report the result as standard plate count per gram.

Notes:

(A) Prepare a series of dilutions so that one or both plates in a given set of duplicates will contain from 30 to 300 colonies.

(B) Pasteurized egg products, if plated at 1:10 and 1:100 dilutions, should provide one or both plates that will contain from 30 to 300 colonies per plate. However, if the history of the product is not known, a 1:1000 and a 1:10000 dilution may be needed.

(C) The melted agar is to cool to 42°-45°C. (107.6°-113°F.) before pouring. Temperatures in excess of this will inactivate or destroy some of the bacteria. Do not use a thermometer to determine the temperature of the agar. Hold melted agar in water bath set at the proper temperature.

(D) Pour all plates within 15 min. after preparation of the first dilution to prevent growth or death of the microorganisms.

(E) Do not blow out the material in the pipette when making the transfer for preparing a dilution or adding material to a petri dish.

(F) Petri plates are inverted during incubation to prevent the formation of spreaders on the agar surface.

(G) Yolks and whole eggs, particularly in the dried form, may mask colonies on petri plates made at the 1:10 dilution.

(H) Refer to *Standard Methods for the Examination of Dairy Products,* Chap. 5, "Standard Plate Count Method" for additional methodology.

(I) Use the sections "Counting Colonies and Recording" and "Computing and Recording Counts" in Chap. 5, for counting, interpreting, calculating, and reporting the results of the duplicate plates. Do not report the counts as "Estimated."

(J) When colonies on duplicate plates and/or consecutive dilutions are counted and the results are averaged prior to reporting, round off counts to one significant figure when average is 1000, or less (e.g., 100, 500, and 1000). When the average count is more than 1000, round off to two significant figures (e.g., 1100, 2200, 25,000, etc).

When rounding off, raise the first digit (for counts of 1000 or less) to the next highest number when the second digit is 5, 6, 7, 8, or 9 (580 would be 600). For counts over 1000, raise the second digit to the next highest when the third digit from the left is 5, 6, 7, 8, or 9; if the third digit is 1, 2, 3, or 4, the second digit is unchanged. Use zeroes for each successive digit toward the right of the second digit.

(K) Check the sterility of dilution water, media, petri dishes, and pipettes by pouring control plates for each sterilization lot of dilution blanks, media, pipettes, etc.

(L) A dried phosphate buffer adjusted to pH 7.2 is available commercially.

Reagents Used:

1. **Phosphate buffer water** (a) Stock solution: Dissolve 34 gm. of monopotassium phosphate (KH_2PO_4) in 500 ml. distilled water. Then adjust to pH 7.2 with 1N sodium hydroxide (NaOH). This will require about 175 ml. Dilute to 1 liter. Keeps indefinitely. (b) Use solution: Dilute 1.25 ml. of stock solution to 1 liter.

2. **Physiological saline (NaCl) solution.** Dissolve 8.5 gm. of chemically pure sodium chloride (NaCl) in 1 liter of distilled water.

3. **0.1% peptone water.** Dissolve 1 gm. of peptone in 1 liter of water.

COLIFORM DETERMINATION:
MOST PROBABLE NUMBER METHOD
PLATE COUNT METHOD

References: *A.O.A.C.*, 11th Edition; *Bacteriological Analytical Manual for Foods*

A. Most Probable Number Method

1. Prepare dilutions as described in Fig. 23.1 using sterile phosphate buffered water, physiological saline solution or 0.1% peptone water.

2. Prepare sterile test tubes containing 10 ml. of lauryl sulfate tryptose broth with an inverted fermentation tube.

TABLE 23.1

MOST PROBABLE NUMBERS (MPN)

MPN per gram of sample using 3 tubes with each of 1.0, 0.1, and 0.01 ml. portions

No. of Positive Tubes			MPN Per Gram	No. of Positive Tubes			MPN Per Gram
1.0 (Gm.)	0.1 (Gm.)	0.01 (Gm.)		1.0 (Gm.)	0.1 (Gm.)	0.01 (Gm.)	
0	0	0	0.3	2	0	0	0.91
0	0	1	0.3	2	0	1	1.4
0	0	2	0.6	2	0	2	2.0
0	0	3	0.9	2	0	3	2.6
0	1	0	0.3	2	1	0	1.5
0	1	1	0.61	2	1	1	2.0
0	1	2	0.92	2	1	2	2.7
0	1	3	1.2	2	1	3	3.4
0	2	0	0.62	2	2	0	2.1
0	2	1	0.93	2	2	1	2.8
0	2	2	1.2	2	2	2	3.5
0	2	3	1.6	2	2	3	4.2
0	3	0	0.94	2	3	0	2.9
0	3	1	1.3	2	3	1	3.6
0	3	2	1.6	2	3	2	4.4
0	3	3	1.9	2	3	3	5.3
1	0	0	0.36	3	0	0	2.3
1	0	1	0.72	3	0	1	3.9
1	0	2	1.1	3	0	2	6.4
1	0	3	1.5	3	0	3	9.5
1	1	0	0.73	3	1	0	4.3
1	1	1	1.1	3	1	1	7.5
1	1	2	1.5	3	1	2	12.0
1	1	3	1.9	3	1	3	16.0
1	2	0	1.1	3	2	0	9.3
1	2	1	1.5	3	2	1	15.0
1	2	2	2.0	3	2	2	21.0
1	2	3	2.4	3	2	3	29.0
1	3	0	1.6	3	3	0	24.0
1	3	1	2.0	3	3	1	46.0
1	3	2	2.4	3	3	2	110.0
1	3	3	2.9	3	3	3	>110.0

3. Inoculate each of three lauryl sulfate tryptose broth tubes with 1 gm. or 1 ml. of undiluted egg product. Inoculate three additional tubes using 1 ml. of a 1:10 diluted egg sample and inoculate three additional tubes using 1 ml. of a 1:100 dilution.

Hold transfer pipette at an angle so that the sample will go into the lauryl tryptose broth. Allow the pipette to drain for 2–3 sec. Do not blow the contents out of the pipette.

4. Incubate 48 ± 2 hr. at 35°C. (95°F.), but examine in 24 hr. for gas production.

5. Using the Most Probable Number, Table 23.1, compute the MPN

TABLE 23.2

MOST PROBABLE NUMBERS (MPN)

MPN per gram of sample using 3 tubes with each of 0.1, 0.01, and 0.001 ml. portions

No. of Positive Tubes			MPN Per Gram	No. of Positive Tubes			MPN Per Gram
0.1 (Gm.)	0.01 (Gm.)	0.001 (Gm.)		0.1 (Gm.)	0.01 (Gm.)	0.001 (Gm.)	
0	0	0	3.0	2	0	0	9.1
0	0	1	3.0	2	0	1	14.0
0	0	2	6.0	2	0	2	20.0
0	0	3	9.0	2	0	3	26.0
0	1	0	3.0	2	1	0	15.0
0	1	1	6.1	2	1	1	20.0
0	1	2	9.2	2	1	2	27.0
0	1	3	12.0	2	1	3	34.0
0	2	0	6.2	2	2	0	21.0
0	2	1	9.3	2	2	1	28.0
0	2	2	12.0	2	2	2	35.0
0	2	3	16.0	2	2	3	42.0
0	3	0	9.4	2	3	0	29.0
0	3	1	13.0	2	3	1	36.0
0	3	2	16.0	2	3	2	44.0
0	3	3	19.0	2	3	3	53.0
1	0	0	3.6	3	0	0	23.0
1	0	1	7.2	3	0	1	39.0
1	0	2	11.0	3	0	2	64.0
1	0	3	15.0	3	0	3	95.0
1	1	0	7.3	3	1	0	43.0
1	1	1	11.0	3	1	1	75.0
1	1	2	15.0	3	1	2	120.0
1	1	3	19.0	3	1	3	160.0
1	2	0	11.0	3	2	0	93.0
1	2	1	15.0	3	2	1	150.0
1	2	2	20.0	3	2	2	210.0
1	2	3	24.0	3	2	3	290.0
1	3	0	16.0	3	3	0	240.0
1	3	1	20.0	3	3	1	460.0
1	3	2	24.0	3	3	2	1,100.0
1	3	3	29.0	3	3	3	>1,100.0

of coliforms on the basis of the tubes of lauryl sulfate tryptose broth with gas production.

The above test is to be used when the MPN is not expected to exceed 110 coliforms per gram. For all samples where the coliform count is expected to exceed 110 organisms per gram, use the plate count method in addition to the above tube method.

B. Plate Count Method

1. Prepare additional dilutions beyond the 1:100 dilution, as needed.

2. Prepare duplicate petri dishes at each dilution, using 1 ml. of diluted egg product.

3. Add about 15 gm. of violet red bile agar into each petri dish. Mix and cool.

4. When agar has solidified, pour a cover over the cooled agar, using about 3–4 gm. of violet red bile agar.

5. When cool, invert and incubate 24 ± hr. at 35°C.

6. Count as coliform only those dark red colonies that are at least 0.5 mm. in diameter.

7. Report as coliforms per gram of product.

E. coli DETERMINATION

Reference: *A.O.A.C.,* 11th Edition.

1. Determine the coliform as described in Steps 1, 2, 3, and 4 of "COLIFORM DETERMINATION: MOST PROBABLE NUMBER METHOD."

2. From each tube of lauryl sulfate broth showing gas, inoculate a tube of EC broth by transferring a 3-mm. loopful of lauryl sulfate broth to the EC broth.

3. Incubate in a covered water bath 48 ± 2 hr. at 45.5° ± 0.05°C. (113.9° ± 0.09°F.), examining in 24 hr. for gas production.

4. Using the Most Probable Number, Table 23.1, compute the MPN of *E. coli* on basis of EC broth tubes producing gas.

Notes:

(A) The temperature of the water bath is critical to the test.

(B) A covered water bath must be used.

(C) Eight milliliter amounts of EC broth are to be used in each tube.

YEAST AND MOLD

References: *Recommended Methods for the Microbiological Examination of Foods, 2nd Edition; Standard Methods for the Examination of Dairy Products,* 13th Edition.

1. Prepare a 1:10 dilution as described in Fig. 23.1.

2. Divide 10 ml. of the 1:10 dilution equally into five petri plates.

3. Add about 20 gm. of potato dextrose agar, acidified to pH 3.5, into each petri plate.

4. Incubate the plates at 32°C. (89.6°F.) for 3 days.

5. Determine and report separately the total number of yeast and the total number of molds per gram.

Notes:

(A) Potato dextrose agar without the added acid may be autoclaved and held refrigerated.

(B) Acidify the agar just before pouring with the amount of sterile acid as required.

(C) The amount of acid required may vary in each shipment of dried agar. The manufacturer's label will give the exact amount required.

(D) Any unused acidified agar is to be discarded.

(E) If more than 100 yeast and/or 100 molds are expected per gram: (1) Make in addition, a 1:100 dilution using Fig. 23.1. (2) Proceed as in steps 2, 3, 4, and 5 but multiply results by 10.

COAGULASE-POSITIVE STAPHYLOCOCCI

Reference: *A.O.A.C.*, 11th Edition, and as revised in *Journal of AOAC*, Vol. 54, No. 2, 1971, pp. 495–496.

1. Weigh aseptically 50 gm. of the egg sample into a sterile blender or jar.

2. Add 450 ml. of sterile 0.85% saline solution or buffered dilution water. Mix or blend. This is a 1:10 dilution.

3. Prepare subsequent dilutions of 1:100, 1:1000, etc., as shown in Fig. 23.1, dilution Ratio.

4. Inoculate three tubes containing 10 ml. of previously prepared trypticase soy broth with 10% sodium chloride at each test dilution with 1 ml. aliquots of decimal dilutions of sample. The maximum dilution of the sample must be high enough to yield at least one tube showing a negative end point.

In addition, prepare three tubes of trypticase soy broth with 10% sodium chloride with 1 gm. of the undiluted sample.

5. Incubate the tubes for 48 ± 2 hr. at 35°–37°C. (95°–98.6°F.).

6. Using a 3-mm. loop, transfer one loopful from each inoculated tube to previously prepared Baird-Parker agar plates. Streak the plates to give well-isolated colonies.

7. Incubate the plates 48 ± 2 hr. at 35°–37°C. (95°–98.6°F.).

Suspect colonies on Baird-Parker medium are:

(A) Convex, shiny black, with or without narrow gray-white margins, surrounded by a clear zone extending into the opaque medium.

(B) Convex, shiny black, with or without narrow gray-white margin, surrounded by a clear zone with an inner opaque zone.

(C) Or, convex, shiny black with or without a gray-white margin, 1.0 to 1.5 mm. in diameter.

8. Pick a small amount of growth from at least one suspect colony from each test tube dilution with growth, to 13 × 100 mm. tubes containing 0.2 ml. brain heart infusion broth (BHI).

9. Incubate the tubes 18 to 24 hr. at 35°–37°C. (95°–98.6°F.).

10. Add 0.5 ml. reconstituted coagulase plasm (rabbit) with EDTA to the BHI tube. Mix thoroughly.

11. Incubate 35°–37°C. (95°–98.6°F.), and examine at hourly intervals from 1 to 6 hr. for clot formation. Any degree of coagulation, even a fibrin strand, is considered positive. See Fig. 23.2, Types of Coagulase Test Reactions.

12. Doubtful coagulase results may be rechecked by additional testing of colonies by steps 8, 9, 10, and incubate the BHI at 35°–37°C. (95°–98.6°F.) for more than 18 hr. but for less than 48 hr.

13. Report number of coagulase-positive staphylococci as based on Most Probable Number (MPN) from Table 23.1.

Notes:

(A) The poured Baird-Parker plated medium is to be aged, and the surfaces very dry before use. Refer to *A.O.A.C.* for details.

TYPES OF COAGULASE TEST REACTIONS

NEGATIVE	
1+POSITIVE	SMALL UNORGANIZED CLOTS
2+POSITIVE	SMALL ORGANIZED CLOT
3+POSITIVE	LARGE ORGANIZED CLOT
4+POSITIVE	ENTIRE CONTENT OF TUBE COAGULATES AND IS NOT DISPLACED WHEN TUBE IS INVERTED

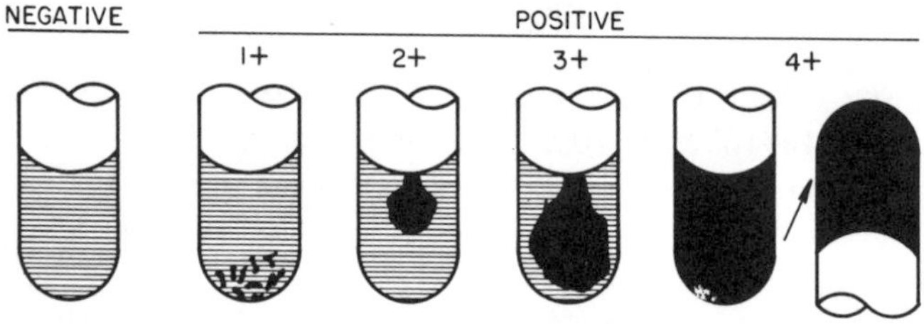

NEGATIVE — NO EVIDENCE OF FIBRIN FORMATION

FIG. 23.2. TYPES OF COAGULASE TEST REACTIONS

"The clot produced varies from one which is solid and immovable when the tube is inverted, to a loose clot or occasionally only a trace of fibrin. Any degree of clotting is regarded as a positive reaction"—As stated by J. E. Blair *in* Dubois' *Bacterial and Mycotic Infections of Man* published by J. B. Lippincott Co., Philadephia (1952), p. 372.

From *The Use of a Lyophilized Human Plasma, Standardized for Blood Clotting Factors* presented by F. J. Turner and B. S. Schwartz before the Society of American Bacteriologists, Houston, May 3, 1956.

(B) The Baird-Parker base medium without the tellurite enrichment may be stored for 1 month in a refrigerator. Reheat by melting in boiling water. Do not autoclave to melt the sterile agar.

(C) Temper the base media at 45°-50°C. (113°-122°F.) in a water bath. The tellurite medium must also be tempered before adding to the base medium. If not tempered, the tellurite will solidify the base medium.

(D) The unused portions of the complete medium (Baird-Parker plus tellurite) are to be discarded and not remelted for reuse.

SALMONELLA DETECTION

Reference: This method is from *A.O.A.C.*, 11th Edition, except not all of the biochemical tests in *A.O.A.C.* are required. Only the biochemical tests described are needed. Additional biochemical tests may be used to supplement this method. This method emphasizes some of the main points of the A.O.A.C. method.

Prepare, sterilize, and handle culture media, biochemical, agar plates, tubes (slant and butt), etc., as outlined in *A.O.A.C.*

A. Preparation of Liquid, Frozen, Cooked or Dried Egg Samples

1. Open sample container aseptically.
2. Mix contents with a sterile spoon or spatula.
3. Aseptically weigh 25, 50, 75, 100, or 125 gm. of egg sample into a sterile container containing 225, 450, 675, 900, or 1125 ml. of sterile lactose broth, respectively. The ratio of egg sample to lactose broth is 1:10.
4. Mix well by shaking.
5. Aseptically determine the pH of mixture by use of narrow range pH papers or pH machine. If below pH 6.5 or above pH 7.5, adjust to pH 6.8 ± 0.2 with sterile 1N NaOH or 1N HCl.
6. Loosen the cap to permit gas to escape. Incubate 24 ± 2 hr. at 35°C. (95°F).

B. Isolation of Cultures

1. Gently shake incubated mixture and transfer 1 ml. of it to 10 ml. of selenite cystine broth, and an additional 1 ml. to 10 ml. of tetrathionate broth. The tubes must not have tight caps.
2. Incubate 24 ± 2 hr. at 35°C. (95°F.).
3. Streak a 3-mm. loopful selenite cystine broth onto differential plates of brilliant green agar, *Salmonella-Shigella* agar and bismuth sulfite agar. Streak an additional set of differential agar plates from

the incubated tetrathionate broth. Streaking must be such as to get well isolated colonies after incubation.

4. Incubate plates 24 ± 2 hr. at 35°C. (95°F.). If bismuth sulfite plates do not have typical or suspicious colonies, or do not contain growth, incubate an additional 24 ± 2 hr.

5. Examination of plated material.

(A) Brilliant green agar. Suspect *salmonella* colonies are colorless, pink to fuschia, translucent to opaque, with surrounding medium pink to red. Some salmonellae appear as transparent green colonies if surrounded by lactose—or sucrose—fermenting organisms which produce colonies that are yellow-green or green.

(B) *Salmonella-Shigella* agar. Suspect *salmonella* colonies are uncolored to pale pink, opaque, transparent or translucent; some strains produce black-centered colonies.

(C) Bismuth sulfite agar. Suspect *salmonella* colonies are brown or black, sometimes with a metallic sheen. Surrounding medium is usually brown at first, turning black with increasing incubation time. Some strains produce green colonies with little or no darkening of surrounding medium.

6. AT THIS POINT, THE TEST IS CALLED THE "DIFFERENTIAL AGAR TEST." IF NO GROWTH APPEARS ON ANY OF THESE AGAR PLATES, OR IF DEFINITE NONSALMONELLA COLONIES APPEAR AFTER INCUBATION, THE TEST IS CONCLUDED, AND THE SAMPLE IS NEGATIVE FOR *SALMONELLA*.

C. Treatment of Typical or Suspect Colonies

1. Pick suspect *salmonella* colonies and inoculate triple sugar iron (TSI) agar tubes and lysine iron (LIA) agar tubes. Streak the slants and stab the butts. If possible, pick at least two typical or suspicious looking *salmonella* colonies from each of the differential agar plates. When a suspect colony is picked from any of the six differential agar plates, the transfer must be from the colony to TSI and then to LIA, without reflaming the needle and repicking the colony between inoculating the TSI and LIA.

2. Incubate TSI and LIA 24 ± 2 hr. at 35°C. (95°F.)

3. Presumptive positive *salmonella* LIA cultures are alkaline (purple) throughout the medium. The color may be darker than the original purple color of the medium. Hydrogen sulfite may or may not be present.

Negative LIA cultures have red or purple slants *and* yellow butts.

Presumptive positive *salmonella* TSI cultures have alkaline (red) slants and acid (yellow) butts with or without hydrogen sulfide.

Negative TSI cultures may be all red or all yellow. However, lactose or sucrose fermenting salmonellae have been reported and would produce TSI tubes which are all yellow, or a slight red slant with balance of tube yellow. The tube may or may not have gas.

4. AT THIS POINT, THE TEST IS CALLED THE "PRESUMP-TIVE POSITIVE TEST." A PARTICULAR CULTURE IS NEGA-TIVE IF THERE IS DEFINITE ATYPICAL GROWTH IN BOTH THE TSI AND THE LIA TUBES.

IF ALL COLONIES PICKED TO TSI AND LIA IN STEP C-1 ARE ATYPICAL, OR IF THE LIA IS ATYPICAL, THEN THE SAMPLE OF EGG IS NEGATIVE FOR SALMONELLAE AND THE TEST IS CONCLUDED. THE SAMPLE IS REGARDED AS "PRE-SUMPTIVE POSITIVE" WHEN BOTH THE TSI AND LIA ARE TYPICAL, OR WHEN THE LIA IS TYPICAL AND THE TSI IS ALL YELLOW OR A SMALL AREA OF SLANT IS RED AND BALANCE OF TUBE IS YELLOW. ANY LYSINE IRON AGAR CULTURE WHICH GIVES A TYPICAL *SALMONELLA* REAC-TION, WHETHER CONFIRMED WITH A CORRESPONDING TYPICAL *SALMONELLA* REACTION IN THE TRIPLE SUGAR IRON AGR CULTURE OR NOT, SHOULD ALERT THE ANALYST THAT THE CULTURE IS QUITE POSSIBLY A *SALMONELLA*.

5. All presumptive positive cultures from TSI and LIA are to be confirmed by biochemical and serological tests until one or more give a typical *salmonella* reaction.

D. Culture Testing

1. Polyvalent somatic (0) test.

(A) Using a wax pencil, mark off two sections about 1 × 2 cm. on the inside of a glass or plastic petri dish or a glass slide.

(B) Place 1/2 of a 3-mm. loopful of the culture from a 24 to 48-hr. TSI or LIA agar slant on the dish in the upper part of each marked section.

(C) Add one drop of a saline solution to the lower part of each section.

(D) Emulsify the culture in the saline solution with a clean, sterile transfer loop or needle in both of the sections.

(E) Add one drop of a *salmonella* polyvalent somatic (0) antiserum to one section only.

(F) Mix the antiserum and culture with a clean, sterile transfer loop or needle.

(G) Tilt the mixtures back and forth for 1 min. and observe them against a dark background in good illumination.

Any degree of agglutination is a positive reaction.

(H) Classify polyvalent somatic (0) test: (1) *Positive*—Agglutination in the test mixture; no agglutination in the saline control. (2) *Negative*—No agglutination in the test mixture; no agglutination in the saline control. (3) *Nonspecific*—Agglutination in both the test and the control mixtures. Repurify cultures on MacConkey's agar or differential agars and repeat TSI, LIA, and agglutination tests.

The individual group somatic (0) antisera including Vi, may be used instead of the *salmonella* polyvalent somatic (0) antiserum. Follow steps (A) through (H).

2. Polyvalent flagellar (H) screening test.

(A) Transfer one loopful (approximately 3 mm.) of growth from a urease negative TSI or LIA agar slant to:

(1) BHI broth—incubate 4-6 hr. at 35°C. (95°F.) until visible growth occurs (tested on same day) or overnight.

(2) Trypticase or tryptose soy broth—incubate 24 ± 2 hr. at 35°C. (tested the following day).

(B) To 5 ml. of each broth culture, add 2.5 ml. formalized physiological saline solution. Mix.

(C) Test the formalized broth culture with *salmonella* polyvalent flagellar (H) antiserum.

(1) Place 0.5 ml. of an appropriately diluted *salmonella* polyvalent flagellar (H) antiserum, in a 10 × 75 or 13 × 100 mm. serological test tube.

(2) Add 0.5 ml. of the antigen to the formalized broth culture.

(3) Prepare a saline control by mixing 0.5 ml. of the formalized saline with 0.5 ml. of antigen.

(4) Incubate the mixtures 1 hr. in a water bath at 50°C. (122°F.).

(5) Observe at 15-min. intervals, and read the results in 1 hr. (a) *Positive*—Agglutination in the test sample; no agglutination in control. (b) *Negative*—No agglutination in test sample; no agglutination in control. (c) *Nonspecific*—Both test and control mixtures agglutinate. Repurify such cultures on MacConkey's agar or differential agars and repeat TSI, LIA and agglutination test.

(The "Spicer-Edwards" flagellar (H) test tube test using the seven "Spicer-Edwards" flagellar (H) antisera as in (1) through (5) may be used in place of the polyvalent antiserum.)

3. Biochemical tests

(A) Urease test.

(1) Subculture two 3-mm. loopfuls of a presumptive positive TSI

or LIA culture to a tube containing 1.5 to 3 ml. of urea broth and incubate 24 ± 2 hr. at 35°C. (95°F.) or 1.5 to 3 ml. of rapid urea broth and incubate 2 hr. in a water bath at 37°C. (98.6°F.).

(2) Discard as *salmonella* negative all cultures that are urease positive (purple-red color). Salmonellae are urease negative (no change in the orange color of medium).

(B) Phenol red dulcitol broth (or purple broth base with dulcitol.)

(1) Inoculate broth with a loopful of a presumptive positive culture.

(2) Incubate 24 ± 2 hr. at 35°C. (95°F.).

(3) If necessary, incubate an additional 24 hr. (a) Most salmonellae give a positive test: gas and acid reaction (yellow color). (b) A negative test has no gas and an alkaline reaction (red color).

(C) Phenol red lactose broth (or purple lactose broth).

(1) Inoculate broth with a loopful of a presumptive positive culture.

(2) Incubate 24 ± 2 hr. at 35°C. (95°F.).

(3) If necessary, incubate an additional 24 hr. (a) Most salmonellae give a negative test: no gas formation and an alkaline reaction (red). (b) Organisms not *salmonella* give a positive reaction: gas and an acid reaction (yellow color). (c) Any urease negative culture that agglutinates in the somatic "O" and flagellar "H" test is a *salmonella*, even though the lactose (or sucrose) is fermented.

(D) Phenol red sucrose broth (or purple sucrose broth).

(1) Same as in 3C(1), (2), and (3).

(E) Malonate broth.

(1) Inoculate malonate broth with a loopful of a presumptive positive culture.

(2) Incubate 48 ± 2 hr. at 35°C. (95°F.).

(3) Examine at least every 24 hr. (a) Salmonellae give a negative test. The green color remains unchanged. (b) Nonsalmonella organisms give a positive test and will change the green color to a blue color.

AT THIS POINT, THE TEST IS CALLED THE "CONFIRMA-TORY TEST." IF ANY SINGLE CULTURE GIVES A TYPICAL REACTION, THE EGG SAMPLE WILL BE REPORTED AS *SAL-MONELLA* POSITIVE.

The following will serve as a guide for clarification of results:

A—Both antisera agglutinate and the biochemicals are typical: The culture is a *salmonella*.

B—The "H" Antiserum agglutinates, but not the "O", and the biochemicals are typical: The culture is a *salmonella*.

C—The "O" agglutinates, but not the "H", and the biochemicals appear typical: This culture may be a nonmotile *salmonella*. Test the culture for motility.

D—Both antisera do not agglutinate, and the biochemicals are not typical: The culture is not a *salmonella*.

Notes:

(A) Pint widemouth screwcap jars are recommended for the lactose broth in the first enrichment step.

(B) Glass beads are an aid in getting dried eggs into solution. One tablespoon per pint jar can be used. It will be necessary to dissolve pan-dried egg albumen by mixing with a sterile rod, spoon, or spatula. Depending on the nature of the egg albumen solids, it may be advantageous to add it in five 5-gm. amounts. The analyst may use other aseptic means to put the dried eggs into solution.

(C) The depth of the selenite cystine broth and tetrathionate broth with the lactose egg mixture must be at least 2 in. Larger amounts, if in the same proportion, may be transferred, e.g., 10 ml. of the incubated sample to 100 ml. of either selenite cystine or tetrathionate.

(D) Selenite cystine broth is not to be autoclaved. It is heated to dissolve the medium, but not to boiling. It is then dispensed into sterile tubes, and heated in flowing steam for 10 min. It is to be used the same day as prepared.

An alternate procedure in preparation is to weigh the selenite cystine powder on sterile paper, then add the powder to sterile cool water. Mix. Then dispense into sterile test tubes. Use the same day as prepared.

(E) The tetrathionate broth base is not to be autoclaved. It is heated to boiling. The precipitate will not dissolve completely. Prepared broth may be refrigerated and held.

(F) Immediately prior to use, add I-KI solution and brilliant green dye solution to the tetrathionate broth. Do not heat the medium after the addition of either the I-KI and/or dye solution. Dispense in sterile tubes.

The order of preparation of the I-KI solution as described in the AOAC must be followed; otherwise, it will not be a complete solution.

(G) The brilliant green agar is autoclaved for 12 min. at 121°C., not 15 min. *Salmonella-Shigella* agar and bismuth sulfite agar are heated to boiling; they are not to be autoclaved.

After the agars have been heated or autoclaved, cool to 45°-50°C. Then pour 20 gm. into a 15 × 100 mm. petri dish. Let dry for about 2 hr. with covers partially removed; then close plates.

(H) The TSI and LIA media are to be autoclaved for 12 min. at 121°C., not 15 min. Before the tubed media solidifies, place the tubes in a slanted position.

Deep butts, 1½-in., are needed in the LIA agar to provide anaerobic conditions. A short slant, 1-in., is satisfactory.

A 2-in. slant is needed with the TSI to provide an adequate growth of bacteria for subsequent tests. A short butt, 1¼-in., is satisfactory.

(I) As the urease test is a chemical test, the amount of urea broth, 1.5–3 ml., must not be exceeded. A generous amount of the suspect culture must be used.

(J) The serological and biochemical tests require the use of a pure culture. Any mixed culture may be streaked on MacConkey's agar or BG agar. (1) Typical *salmonella* colonies on MacConkey's agar are transparent or colorless. (2) Typical *salmonella* colonies on BG agar are pink to red, with similar coloring in surrounding media.

(K) No order for testing is specified in the section "Culture Testing." The scheduling is up to the analyst.

(L) Each new lot of medium supplied by the manufacturer is to be checked with known bacteria cultures to determine that the medium is satisfactory.

(M) Uninoculated controls are to be made on each batch of prepared medium to determine sterility.

(N) An additional reference for the analyst as an aid in this test is *Identification of Enterobacteriaceae* by Edwards and Ewing. This is available from Burgess Publishing Company, 426 South Sixth Street, Minneapolis, Minnesota 55415.

COLOR—NEPA METHOD

Reference: O. J. Kahlenberg "Now—A Quick Reliable Gauge of Yolk Color" *Food Industries 21*, 1949, pp. 467–470.

A. Preparation of Sample

1. Liquid whole egg.

(A) Weigh exactly 5.0 gm. of a well-mixed sample into a clean tared 150-ml. beaker.

(B) Slowly add 2.5 ml. of chemically pure (C.P.) acetone.

(C) Mix gently with a glass rod until lumps are removed, and stir until smooth.

(D) Slowly add 92.5 ml. additional acetone in small portions, mixing between addition of the acetone.

(E) Mix thoroughly.

(F) Filter through a Whatman No. 4 filter paper into a glass-stoppered bottle. As soon as sufficient clear filtrate has been collected to make the colorimetric test, stopper the bottle immediately, or transfer the filtrate to a clean absorption cell and proceed to "C."

2. Liquid sugared whole eggs.

(A) Weigh exactly 5.5 gm. of a well-mixed sample into a clean tared 150-ml. beaker. Then follow the same procedure as for liquid whole eggs except use a Whatman No. 12 fluted filter paper.

3. Liquid salted whole eggs.

(A) Weigh exactly 5.5 gm. of a well-mixed sample into a clean tared 150-ml. beaker.

(B) Add 2.25 ml. of distilled water.

(C) Mix gently with a glass rod, and stir until smooth.

(D) Add 2.5 ml. acetone and continue the same procedure as for liquid whole eggs except use 90 ml. of acetone rather than 92.5 ml. of additional acetone.

4. Liquid egg yolk.

Weigh exactly 2.5 gm. of a well-mixed egg sample into a clean, tared 150-ml. beaker. Then follow the same procedures as for A.1., liquid whole eggs, except use 95 rather than 92.5 ml. of additional acetone.

5. Liquid sugar egg yolks (7–12% sugar).

Weigh exactly 2.75 gm. of a well-mixed sample into a clean tared 150-ml. beaker. Then follow the same procedures as for A.4., liquid egg yolk; except use a Whatman No. 12 fluted filter paper.

6. Liquid salted egg yolks (7–12% salt).

(A) Weigh accurately 2.75 grams of a well mixed sample into a clean, tared 150-ml. beaker.

(B) Add 2.25 ml. of distilled water.

(C) Mix gently with a glass rod and stir until smooth.

(D) Slowly add 2.5 ml. acetone. Then follow the same procedures as for A.5., Liquid sugar egg yolks; except use 92.5 ml. of additional acetone, and a Whatman No. 4 filter paper.

7. Dried whole eggs.

(A) Weigh exactly 1.35 grams of a well mixed sample into a clean tared 150-ml. beaker.

(B). Add 3.6 ml. of distilled water.

(C) Stir with a glass rod until mixture is smooth. Then follow the same procedures as for A.1., liquid whole egg.

8. Dried egg yolks.

(A) Weigh exactly 1.15 grams of a well mixed sample into a clean tared 150-ml. beaker.

(B) Add 1.3 ml. of distilled water.

(C) Stir with a glass rod until mixture is smooth. Then follow the procedures for A.4., liquid egg yolk.

B. Calibration of Curve

1. Using semilogarithmic graph paper, mark on the horizontal log scale transmittancy-percent readings, using 0, 15, 20, 25, 30, 40, 50, 60, 70, 80, 90, and 100.

2. On the same graph paper, mark on the vertical arithmetic scale full NEPA values of 0, 1, 2, 3, 4, 5, 6, 7, 8, 9, and 10.

3. Prepare solutions of 0.005, 0.01, 0.015, 0.02, 0.025, 0.03, 0.035, 0.04, 0.045, and 0.05 percent potassium dichromate, (K_2CrO_7). These solutions are equivalent to NEPA colors of 1, 2, 3, 4, 5, 6, 7, 8, 9, and 10, respectively.

4. Use a Cenco-Sheard-Sanford Photelometer, industrial type B-2 with a blue filter, and standardize the photelometer to the 100% reading using acetone in the tubular absorption cell.

5. Transfer portions of potassium dichromate solution into a tubular absorption cell, and place in the Cenco-Sheard-Sanford Photelometer.

6. Measure transmittances of each dilution with photelometer and record meter reading. Restandardize the photelometer between each reading of potassium dichromate solution.

7. On the semilogarithmic paper, plot each potassium dichromate solution reading against the transmittancy percent scale and against its corresponding NEPA value.

8. Draw a calibration curve using each plotted reading from 7, above.

C. Determination of NEPA color

1. Measure the transmittance of acetone extraction of egg sample. Record meter reading.

2. Locate the reading on the calibration curve, and read the corresponding NEPA value. Report results to nearest 0.1 NEPA unit.

3. Report the result as NEPA color based on the respective weight of the sample, e.g., Color (NEPA) 1.8 using 5.0-gm. sample.

Notes:

(A) Because the glass wall of the tubular absorption cell is not of uniform thickness, there can be a large difference in the transmittancy between the individual tubular absorption cells. The same tubular absorption cell, or two cells of similar transmittancy, must be used when standardizing the photelometer and when taking a reading of the sample.

(B) Dust particles in the light path or on the cell and scratches on the cell will reduce transmittancy.

(C) The photelometer must be standardized with acetone before any testing.

(D) Since the amount of acetone remaining after filtering is not standardized to a given amount, it is necessary to take precautions in reducing the evaporation of the acetone.

(E) The tubular cells need to be rinsed with the solution to be tested prior to filling the tube. The rinse solution is to be discarded.

(F) A torsion balance will not give the accuracy required for this test. Use an analytical balance. The color value is based on an accurately weighed sample and the given volume of acetone.

(G) Mount the color machine on a sponge rubber pad to reduce vibrations.

(H) If there is a possibility of electric current fluctuations, a constant voltage regulator must be used.

(I) Periodically check the photelometer against known concentrations of potassium dichromate standards. The machine is to be restandardized if the readings vary more than 5%.

(J) This test is specific and requires the use of a Cenco-Sheard-Sanford Photelometer, industrial type B-2, with a blue filter (approximately maximum transmission is 410 mμ).

(K) The filtrate of the acetone extraction is to be clear. If not, refilter using a new filter paper and fresh clean funnel.

(L) The total amount of eggs weighed, water if used, and both amounts of acetone will equal 100 ± 0.5.

EGG FAT TEST—ACID HYDROLYSIS
Reference: *A.O.A.C.*, 11th Edition.

1. (a) Weigh accurately about 5 gm. of liquid whole eggs or liquid egg yolks, or 1 gm. of dried whole eggs or egg yolks, into a Mojonnier fat extraction tube.

(b) Weigh accurately about 20 gm. of liquid egg whites or 4 gm. of dried egg whites. Equally divide the sample into four Mojonnier fat extraction tubes.

2. While vigorously shaking the Mojonnier tube, add slowly 10 ml. of concentrated hydrochloric acid (HCl) to the tube with the liquid egg sample, or 10 ml. of diluted hydrochloric acid (4 parts acid, 1 part distilled water) to the tube with the dried egg sample.

3. Set the tubes in a water bath at 70°C. (158°F.) and bring the water in the bath to boiling. Boil for 30 min.

4. During the boiling period, carefully shake the tubes at 5-min. intervals.

5. Remove the tubes from the bath, and add water to nearly fill the lower bulb of the tube so that the ethers added later may be completely poured off.

6. Cool to room temperature.

7. Add 25 ml. of ethyl ether, stopper the tube, and shake vigorously. Loosen stopper carefully to release the pressure inside the tube.

8. Add 25 ml. petroleum ether [boiling point 30°-60°C. (80°-140°F.)], stopper the tube, and shake vigorously. Loosen stopper carefully to release the pressure inside the tube.

9. Let stand until the solvent layer separates from the water, about 20 min., or centrifuge the tube for about 20 min. at 600 rpm.

10. Decant the solvent into a conditioned, weighed 100- to 250-ml. aluminum dish, glass beaker, or flask. Combine tubes of Step 1(b), when applicable.

11. Evaporate the ethers to dryness very slowly in a hood on a hot plate.

12. Repeat steps 7, 8, 9, 10, and 11 for a second extraction.

13. Repeat steps 7, 8, 9, 10, and 11 for a third extraction.

14. Transfer the dish to a vacuum oven at 100°C. (212°F.) for about 10 min., or a Mojonnier oven at 135°C. (275°F.) for about 5 min.

15. Cool the dish to room temperature.

16. Weigh, calculate, and report as percentage of fat.

Notes:

(A) The ethers used are highly inflammable.

(B) The evaporation must be done in a ventilated hood.

(C) Prior to decanting the solvent from the tube, it may be necessary to add a few milliliters of water to raise the water level so that the ether layer may be completely poured off.

(D) It is important that none of the water layer be allowed to run into the weighing dish.

(E) Stoppers for the Mojonnier flask may be cork, neoprene, or other synthetic rubber. Do not use natural rubber stoppers since ether, fats, and oils are solvents for natural rubber. Also, do not use wax-impregnated corks.

(F) The dish used for evaporation is to be conditioned as follows: Before any weighing, heat dish as described in step 14. It may be cooled in a desiccator or at room temperature. If cooled in a desiccator, remove the cooled dish and let it stand in room air until a constant weight is obtained. Dishes, beakers, or flasks that contain fat or oil do not lose heat quickly. Bring such equipment to room temperature to avoid errors in weighing.

SUCROSE ADDED TO EGG PRODUCTS

Reference: *A.O.A.C.*, 11th Edition, Lane-Eynon Method.

A. Sucrose Standard

1. Weigh exactly 0.7500 gm. of chemically pure (C.P.) sucrose and transfer into a 250-ml. volumetric flask using about 100 ml. of warm distilled water.

2. Add 10 ml. of a 1 to 1 dilution of concentrated hydrochloric acid (HCl).

3. Invert the sugar solution by placing the flask in a 70°C. (158°F.) water bath for exactly 13 min.

4. Cool.

5. Neutralize with a 25% sodium hydroxide solution (NaOH). This will require at least 7.4 ml. of solution. Determine the neutrality with red litmus paper, phenolphthalein, or pH machine.

6. Bring to volume in the 250-ml. volumetric flask.

B. Preparation of Egg Sample

1. Weigh exactly 7.5000 gm. of liquid sugared egg product into a 100-ml. beaker.

2. Transfer egg sample to a 250-ml. volumetric flask using about 100 ml. of warm distilled water, and continue as in A. 2. to and including A.6.

3. Make slightly acid with a 1 to 1 dilution of concentrated hydrochloric acid to assure a complete precipitation of the protein and the fat.

4. Test for completeness of the precipitate by adding 5–10 ml. of saturated phosphotungstic acid solution.

5. Bring to volume in the 250-ml. volumetric flask.

6. Filter.

C. Reagents to be used

Soxhlet modification of Fehling solution. Prepare by mixing equal volumes of 1. and 2., below, immediately before use.

1. Copper sulfate solution: Dissolve 34.639 gm. of copper sulfate ($CuSo_{4.5}H_2O$) in water, dilute to 500 ml. and filter.

2. Alkaline tartrate solution: Dissolve 173 gm. Rochelle salt ($KNaC_4H_4O_6.4H_2O$) and 50 gm. sodium hydroxide (NaOH) in water. Dilute to 500 ml., allow to stand 2 days and filter.

3. Methylene blue, 0.2% aqueous solution.

D. Determination of Sucrose Standard

1. Pipette 5 ml. each of the copper sulfate and alkaline tartrate solutions (C-1 and C-2) into a 250-ml. Erlenmeyer flask.

2. Add 20 ml. of distilled water.

3. From a burette, add the inverted sucrose solution from step A6, within about 2 ml. of the amount required to reduce all the copper in the copper sulfate-alkaline tartrate solution. This will be about 15.5 ml. for a 10% added sucrose egg product.

4. Add 3 or 4 glass beads or other inert material to prevent bumping of solution during boiling.

5. Heat the cold mixture in the flask to boiling within 2 min.

6. Continue the boiling for about 15 sec. more.

7. While still boiling, rapidly add further quantities of the standard inverted sucrose solution, A.6., until only the faintest perceptible blue color remains.

8. While still boiling, add 1 ml. of 0.2% methylene blue solution.

9. Continue the addition of the standard inverted sucrose solution, and boil until the methylene blue is reduced to a colorless compound and the solution then becomes brick-red in color.

10. Record the volume used.

E. Determination of Sucrose Sugar in Egg Test Solution

Follow the procedures as outlined in steps 1 through 10 in **D Determination of Sucrose Standard** using filtrate of B6.

F. Calculation

$$\frac{\text{ml. of inverted sucrose standard solution} \times 10}{\text{ml. of test solution}} = \% \text{ total sugar}$$

% total sugar − 0.2% (correction factor) = % added sucrose

Notes:

(A) Do the first four steps of the test up to the cooling for both the sucrose standard and egg sample simultaneously. This provides equal time in the water bath.

(B) The heating of the sample to boiling may be with either a gas burner or an electric hot plate. The cold mixture must be brought to boiling within 2 min. Use a wire gauge as a shield between the flask and the source of the heat. This will reduce excessive bumping of the solution during boiling.

(C) Once boiling starts, the erlenmeyer flask must not be removed from the heat or the boiling interrupted until the test is completed.

A steam atmosphere in the flask is necessary until test is completed.

(D) It is not necessary to have the burette over the flask during titration. It should be adjacent to the burner or hot plate. An offset burette can be used.

(E) One milliliter of 0.2% methylene blue indicator is required for egg having approximately 10% sugar. If the approximate amount of added sugar is known, increasing or decreasing amounts of methylene blue are to be used, e.g., 5% added sugar, use 0.5 ml. of methylene blue.

(F) The total elapsed time for the initial heating, boiling, and completion of titration is to be about 3 min.

(G) The test as described above is within 1% accuracy. For more precise results, repeat titration adding almost all of the required sugar solution.

(H) A sugar standard needs to be run with each test. The alkaline tartrate solution will change in concentration with age.

(I) This test is for eggs containing added sucrose only. It is not applicable to eggs containing sucrose and added glucose.

SALT ADDED TO EGG PRODUCTS

Reference: *A.O.A.C.*, 11th Edition.

1. From a well-mixed egg sample, weigh accurately about 2 gm. of product into a 250-ml. Erlenmeyer flask.

2. Add 50 ml. of 0.1N silver nitrate solution ($AgNO_3$).

3. Swirl flask until egg sample and solution are in intimate contact.

4. Add 20 ml. nitric acid (HNO_3).

5. Mix.

6. Place flask on a steam bath for 15–30 min.

7. Add 15 ml. of 5% potassium permanganate solution ($KMnO_4$).

8. Let the flask remain on a steam bath for an additional 60–90 min., or until the solution becomes almost colorless. If not almost colorless, repeat addition of potassium permanganate and steam bath heating.

9. Cool to 25°C. (77°F.) or less.

10. Add 75 ml. of distilled water.

11. Add 1 ml. of nitrobenzene.

12. Stopper the flask with a rubber stopper and shake vigorously to coagulate the precipitate.

13. Add 5 ml. of saturated ferric alum indicator [$FeNH_4(SO_4)_2$ $12H_2O$].

14. Titrate excess silver nitrate with 0.1N potassium thiocyanate

solution (KCNS) at 25°C. (77°F.) or less, until yellow-orange end point appears. The solution is yellow-green before the end point.

15. At the first permanent color change, note burette reading of potassium thiocyanate solution and time. Stopper the flask, shake vigorously, and let it stand for 15 min. If the solution color changes back to milky-white, add potassium thiocyanate in 1-drop portions until the end point color of brick-orange reappears and remains.

16. Calculate the amount of salt (NaCl) after deducting a blank determination on the reagents using about 0.25 gm. of sucrose instead of the egg sample. This value is approximately 0.3.

Calculations:

$X = $ (ml. of $AgNO_3 \times N$ of $AgNO_3$) minus (ml. of KCNS $\times N$ of KCNS)

$$\% \text{ NaCl} = \frac{(X)(0.05845)(100)}{\text{weight of sample}} - 0.3$$

Notes (Rev. 6/29/73):

(A) Reagents

1. Ferric alum indicator.

Prepare a saturated aqueous solution by adding about 100 gm. of reagent grade ferric alum [$FeNH_4(SO_4)_2 12H_2O$] to 100 ml. distilled water. Hold 24 hr. at room temperature. Not all of the $FeNH_4$ $(SO_4)_2 12H_2O$ will dissolve.

2. Silver nitrate—0.1N.

Dissolve approximately 17.1 gm. of reagent grade silver nitrate ($AgNO_3$), previously dried at 110°C. overnight, in distilled water, and dilute to 1 liter. Mix.

3. Potassium thiocyanate—0.1N.

Dissolve 9.72 gm. of reagent grade KCNS in distilled water and dilute to 1 liter.

4. Potassium chloride.

Dry about 5 gm. of reagent grade potassium chloride (KCl) at 100°-110°C. for about 16 hr. Cool in a desiccator. Use immediately after cooling.

5. Five percent potassium dichromate solution.

Add 5 gm. of potassium dichromate.(K_2CrO_4) to 100 ml. of distilled water.

(B) Standardization of Reagents

1. Silver nitrate.

(A) Accurately weigh about 0.3000 gm. of dried KCl to a 250-ml. glass stoppered Erlenmeyer flask.

(B) Add about 40 ml. of distilled water.

(C) Add 1 ml. of 5% K_2CrO_4 solution. Mix.

(D) Titrate with the unstandardized silver nitrate solution to the first pale red-brown end point. Record volume used and mark as "A." (This should require about 40 ml. of silver nitrate solution.)

(E) To another 250-ml. glass stoppered Erlenmeyer flask, add 1 ml. of K_2CrO_4 solution.

(F) Add 75 ml. of distilled water.

(G) Titrate with the unstandardized silver nitrate solution to the first pale red-brown end point. Record volume used and mark as "B." (This should require about 0.5 ml. of silver nitrate solution.)

(H) Calculation for the normality of the silver nitrate solution:

$$N \text{ of AgNO}_3 = \frac{\text{grams KCl} \times 100}{(A-B) \text{ ml. AgNO}_3 \times 74.555}$$

Standardized silver nitrate solution is to be stored in an amber glass stoppered bottle away from the light.

2. Potassium thiocyanate.

(A) Add exactly 25 ml. of the standardized $AgNO_3$ into a 250-ml. glass stoppered Erlenmeyer flask.

(B) Add 80 ml. of distilled water. Mix.

(C) Add 5 ml. of a 1 to 1 dilution of concentrated nitric acid. Mix.

(D) Add 2 ml. of the ferric alum indicator. Mix.

(E) Titrate with the unstandardized potassium thiocyanate solution to a pale rose or tinge of light brown end point. Record the amount used.

(F) Calculation for the normality of the potassium thiocyanate solution:

$$N \text{ of KCNS} = \frac{(N \text{ of AgNO}_3)(\text{ml. of AgNO}_3 \text{ used})}{\text{ml. of KCNS}}$$

TOTAL SOLIDS OR MOISTURE—DETERMINATION OF EGG SOLIDS WHEN SALT AND/OR SUGAR IS PRESENT

Reference: *A.O.A.C.*, 11th Edition.

Aluminum dishes, 2 in. in diameter, $7/8$-in. deep, with covers, are recommended. Condition the empty dishes and lids by heating at

98°-100°C. (208.4-212°F.) approximately 1 hr. Then cool, and store in a desiccator.

I. Liquid Eggs

A. Vacuum method.

1. Accurately weigh 5.0000 ± 0.5000 gm. of a completely thawed well-mixed egg sample into a conditioned, tared, covered dish. Prepare at least duplicate samples.

2. Remove the covers, and evaporate most of the water by heating the dishes with the egg sample on a steam bath or in a thermostatically controlled air oven at 98-100°C. (208.4-212°F.). Approximately 2 hr. will be required.

3. Replace the cover loosely and dry in a vacuum oven. The vacuum oven is to be at 98-100°C. (208.4-212°F.) and at 25 mm. (1-in.) of mercury pressure, or less. Dry for approximately 5 hr. or until a constant weight.

4. Tighten lids and transfer dishes to a desiccator.

5. Cool, weigh, calculate, and report as percentage of total solids.

B. Air oven method.

1. Weigh sample as in I.A.1.

2. Place dish, with cover partly removed, in a thermostatically controlled forced air oven at 98-100°C. (208.4-212°F.) for 16 hr.

3. Continue as in I.A.4 and 5.

II. Dried Eggs

A. Vacuum method.

1. Accurately weigh 2.0000 ± 0.2500 gm. of a well-mixed dried egg sample into a tared, covered, conditioned dish. Prepare at least duplicate samples.

2. Loosen the covers and continue as in I.A.3., 4, and 5 except report as percentage of moisture.

B. Air oven method.

1. Weigh sample as described in II.A.1.

2. Evaporate moisture as described in I.B.2, and 3 except report as percentage of moisture.

III. Determination of Egg Solids When Salt and/or Sugar is Present

1. Determine the percent total solids (TS).

2. Determine the percent of salt and/or sugar (A).

3. Percent egg solids $= \dfrac{(\% \text{ TS} - \% \text{ A})(100)}{100 - \% \text{ A}}$

Notes:

(A) Sample dishes, during any weighing, cooling, and conditioning, are to be handled with clean tongs or forceps. Fingerprints will contribute added weight because of moisture and oil.

(B) All weighings are to be done as quickly as possible. This will reduce the chance of weighing errors because of a gain or loss of moisture during the weighing. The 5- or 2-gm. size of the sample required are approximate values but must be weighed to the fourth decimal point. Do not purposely attempt to weigh an exact 5- or 2-gm. amount. This will introduce a noticeable weighing error because of a loss or gain of moisture during the weighing.

(C) When sample dishes are removed from the oven to the desiccator, they are then to be weighed as soon as they have cooled to room temperature. However, conditioned dishes prior to weighing may be stored in a desiccator.

(D) Liquid eggs must be coagulated before starting the vacuum. Otherwise, the sample will boil in the vacuum oven.

(E) The vacuum must be released gradually. Any sudden release will explode the contents of either dried eggs or liquid eggs out of the dish.

(F) Connect a gas drying bottle containing a suitable desiccant to the vacuum oven for admitting dry air to release the vacuum.

(G) Dried flake egg albumen is to be crushed using a mortar and pestle. Then, sift through a No. 60 National Bureau of Standards sieve, or equivalent.

(H) As all moisture or solid determinations are to be at least duplicate tests, report the average of acceptable determinations.

(I) Acceptable moisture or solid determinations for egg products other than flake egg albumen should be within 0.2000% of each other, e.g., 48.7125% and 48.9065%, 2.4495% and 2.6185%.

(J) As each duplicate moisture or solids determination is to be calculated to four decimals, the duplicate results are to be averaged and the average reported to the first decimal. Any number at the second decimal place which is 4, or lower, will be dropped. (2.4499 is reported as 2.4.) Any number at the second decimal place which is 5 or larger will raise the first decimal one number higher (43.4542 is to be reported as 43.5).

(K) Acceptable moisture determinations for flake dried egg albumen should be within 0.4000%, e.g., 11.6124% and 11.9415%.

(L) If only duplicate samples have been prepared and the moisture or solid determinations are not acceptable, the test must be repeated. This problem may be avoided by using triplicate samples.

(M) The oven is to be at temperature prior to putting in the samples. After the samples are in, the temperature should drop and later be returned to normal. Do not make any readjustments because of a temperature drop.

(N) Constant weight can be determined by redrying approximately 1 hr. under vacuum or 3 hr. in a forced air oven.

LEAKAGE OF METAL CANS

Reference: None.

Equipment Needed:

1. Glass desiccator with a tubulated cover.
2. Vacuum pump.
3. Pressure gauge, range 0 to 30 in. of mercury.
4. Heavy duty vacuum tubing.
5. One two-hole rubber stopper for lid of desiccator.
6. One stopcock, metal or glass.
7. One metal or glass "T."
8. Metal or glass tubing, as needed.
9. Expanded hardware cloth for a shield for the desiccator.

Suggested Design of Equipment:

1. To "T," insert section of vacuum tubing.
2. Connect other end of the tubing to the vacuum pump.
3. Connect the stopcock to one end of "T." This will be the air vent to release the vacuum.
4. Insert remaining end of "T" in rubber stopper.
5. Connect vacuum gauge to remaining hole in rubber stopper.
6. All connections are to be completely through the rubber stopper.

Operations:

1. Half fill the desiccator with tapwater.
2. Place can to be tested in water. The can must be covered with at least 2 in. of water.
3. Replace desiccator cover.
4. Close the stopcock that is the air vent.
5. Place the hardware cloth in position.
6. Start the vacuum pump and prepare to draw a vacuum of 10 in. for 30 sec. It may be necessary to either open the stopcock slightly to hold the vacuum at 10 in. or else to stop the vacuum pump when 10 in. are reached.
7. Note any stream of air bubbles escaping from the seams of the

container or from the seal of either the lid or bottom covers.

A leak consists of a steady progression of bubbles. Isolated bubbles that can be caused by the release of air entrapped in the double seams of the lid or bottom covers are not considered as signs of a leak.

8. If a leak is noticed at less than 10 in., record the vacuum reading when it occurs. This will be a rejection. If a leak occurs during the 30-sec. hold at 10 in., record holding time when the leak occurred. This will be a rejection.

If no leak occurs at 10 in. of vacuum for 30 sec., this will be an acceptance.

9. Stop the vacuum pump.

10. Slowly release the vacuum in the desiccator by opening the air vent stopcock.

11. Report results as follows:

Leak test satisfactory. No leak in container at 10 in. of vacuum when held 30 sec.

Leak test unsatisfactory. Container leaks at _____ in. of vacuum.

Leak test unsatisfactory. Container leaks at 10 in. of vacuum after _____ sec. of hold.

PALATABILITY OF DRIED WHOLE EGGS

Reference: *Regulations Governing the Voluntary Inspection and Grading of Egg Products, July 1, 1971—(7CFR Part 55)*

1. Mix 33 gm. of dried whole eggs with 90 ml. of distilled water in a clean dry glass or stainless steel beaker.

2. Have prepared a water bath with boiling water. The bath is to be so constructed that the beaker will not rest directly on the bottom of the bath.

3. Place the beaker in the bath, and adjust the water level to the level of the reconstituted dried whole eggs in the beaker.

4. Cook, with occasional stirring as eggs begin to coagulate, and continue cooking until the eggs are firm and are completely coagulated. The cooked eggs will retain a slightly moist appearance.

5. Remove beaker.

6. Serve eggs while warm to a taste panel to determine palatability score.

7. Scoring:

    8   No detectable off-flavor, comparable to high quality fresh shell egg

    7½ Very slight off-flavor

7   Slight but no unpleasant off-flavor
6½   Definite but not unpleasant off-flavor
6   Pronounced off-flavor (slightly unpleasant)
5   Unpleasant off-flavor
4   Definite unpleasant off-flavor
3   Pronounced unpleasant off-flavor
2   Repulsive flavor
1   Definite repulsive flavor
0   Pronounced repulsive flavor

8. Score and record results. Report as Palatability. Palatability scores are to be reported individually.

Notes:

(A) A dried whole egg that is rancid, sour, fermented, musty, putrid, fishy, moldy or has other equally objectionable off-odors and -flavors is considered below grade, and is not to be reconstituted for a palatability test.

(B) It is recommended that three or more people be on the taste panel.

(C) Fresh shelled eggs are to be occasionally prepared as described above and served as a control. Such fresh shelled eggs should score an 8.

pH

Reference: None

A. Dried Eggs

1. Reconstitute 12 gm. of dried egg albumen with 88 ml. of distilled water, 25 gm. of dried whole eggs with 75 ml. of distilled water, or 45 gm. of dried yolks with 55 ml. of distilled water in a clean, dry 250-ml. beaker.

2. Mix until product is smooth and free of lumps.

3. Immediately determine the pH by use of a pH meter with glass electrodes.

4. Record reading.

B. Liquid Eggs

1. Place 100 gm. of the liquid egg in a clean, 250-ml. beaker.

2. Determine pH by use of a pH meter.

3. Record.

Notes:

(A) Distilled water, not ion exchange water, is to be used.

(B) When the pH determination is made, the temperature of the reconstituted dried egg or the liquid egg is to be 25°C. (77°F.).

WHIP TEST:
VOLUME MEASUREMENT
BLEED TEST

Reference:　None

I. Volume Measurement

A.　Liquid Egg Whites.

1. Pour 450 gm. of egg whites tempered to 21.1°C. (70°F.) into the bowl of a Hobart mixer, Model C-100, with a D-wire loop whip.

2. The egg whites are to be whipped for 90 sec. at speed 2 (middle speed), and then for 90 sec. in speed 3 (high speed).

3. Stop mixer, and remove the whip.

4. Remove any whipped egg whites adhering to or inside the whip, and add to the whipped foam in the bowl.

5. Gently level the foam to eliminate large air pockets without crushing the whipped foam.   Use a ladle or plastic petri dish cover.

6. Measure the depth of foam with a ruler held vertically into the lower bottom ring of the bowl.

7. Report height of foam in inches.

B.　Dried Egg Whites.

1. Dissolve 43 gm. of dried egg whites in 430 ml. of distilled water. Note: It may require overnight holding to dissolve pan-dried egg whites. Do not use warm water.

2. Stir.

3. With the mixture tempered to 21.1°C. (70°F.), continue, beginning with step A.2.

II. Bleed test

A.　Allow the foam from I.A. or I.B. to set undisturbed at 21.1°C. (70°F.) for 30 min. in the mixing bowl.

B.　Pour the separated liquid into a graduated cylinder.

C.　Report the volume of liquid to the nearest 1.0 ml.

BIBLIOGRAPHY

The following are required references for *USDA Laboratory Methods for Egg Products:*

1. *Official Methods of Analysis of the Association of Official Analytical Chemists (AOAC),* 11th Edition. Association of Official Analytical Chemists,

P. O. Box 540, Benjamin Franklin Station, Washington, D.C. 20044.

2. *Standard Methods for the Examination of Dairy Products*, 13th Edition. American Public Health Association, 1015 Eighteenth Street, NW., Washington, D.C. 20036.

3. *Recommended Methods for the Microbiological Examinations of Foods*, 2nd Edition. American Public Health Association, 1015 Eighteenth Street, NW., Washington, D.C. 20036.

4. *Bacteriological Analytical Manual for Foods*, 3d Edition. Division of Microbiology, Bureau of Foods, Food & Drug Administration; Superintendent of Documents Stock No. 1712-00162, U.S. Government Printing Office, Washington, D.C. 20402.

5. *Microbiology Laboratory Guidebook*, December 1969 Edition. U.S. Department of Agriculture, Animal and Plant Health Inspection, Scientific Services, Washington, D.C. 20250.

6. *Chemistry Laboratory Guidebook*, U.S. Department of Agriculture, Animal and Plant Health Inspection, Scientific Services, Washington, D.C. 20250.

7. *Regulations Governing the Voluntary Inspection and Grading of Egg Products* (7CFR Part 55) effective July 1, 1971. U.S. Department of Agriculture, Agriculture Marketing Service, Poultry Division, Washington, D.C. 20250.

Index